100 Campeones

Other books by Richard Lapchick

*100 Trailblazers: Great Women Athletes Who
Opened Doors for Future Generations*

*100 Pioneers: African-Americans Who
Broke Color Barriers in Sport*

*100 Heroes: People in Sport Who Make
This a Better World*

New Game Plan for College Sport

*Smashing Barriers: Race and Sport
in the New Millennium*

*Never Before, Never Again: The Stirring
Autobiography of Eddie Robinson, the Winningest
Coach in the History of College Football*

*Sport in Society:
Equal Opportunity or Business as Usual?*

*Five Minutes to Midnight:
Race and Sport in the 1990s*

Rules of the Game: Ethics in College Sport

*On the Mark: Putting the Student Back
in Student-athlete*

*Fractured Focus: Sport
as a Reflection of Society*

Broken Promises: Racism in American Sports

*Oppression and Resistance:
The Struggle of Women in Southern Africa*

*Politics of Race and International Sport:
The Case of South Africa*

100 Campeones

LATINO GROUNDBREAKERS
Who Paved the Way in Sport

Richard Lapchick

with

Jared Bovinet
Charlie Harless
Chris Kamke
Cara-Lynn Lopresti
Horacio Ruiz

FiT

FITNESS INFORMATION TECHNOLOGY
A Division of the International Center
for Performance Excellence
West Virginia University
262 Coliseum, WVU-CPASS
PO Box 6116
Morgantown, WV 26506-6116

Library of Congress Card Catalog Number: 2010933012

ISBN: 978-1-935412-18-2

Cover photographs (wrapping around from back cover): Lisa Fernández, Courtesy of UCLA Sports Information; Pablo Morales, courtesy of Stanford University Media Relations; Ayrton Senna, courtesy of Stuart Seeger; María Bueno, courtesy of the International Tennis Hall of Fame & Museum, Newport, RI; José Méndez, courtesy of the National Baseball Hall of Fame Library, Cooperstown, NY; Nancy López, courtesy of Tulsa Athletic Media Relations; Jim Plunkett, courtesy of Stanford University Media Relations; film strip, © Nicola Gavin, bigstockphoto.com; first base © Jim Mills, istockphoto.com.

Cover Design: Bellerophon Productions
Typesetter: Bellerophon Productions
Production Editor: Aaron Geiger
Copyeditors: Aaron Geiger, Danielle Bergamo
Proofreader: Mark Slider
Printed by Data Reproductions Corporation

10 9 8 7 6 5 4 3 2 1

Fitness Information Technology
A Division of the International Center for Performance Excellence
West Virginia University
262 Coliseum, WVU-CPASS
PO Box 6116
Morgantown, WV 26506-6116
800.477.4348 (toll free)
304.293.6888 (phone)
304.293.6658 (fax)
Email: fitcustomerservice@mail.wvu.edu
Website: www.fitinfotech.com

We dedicate *100 Campeones* to three of the people who inspired the book.

Roberto Clemente is perhaps the best known and most inspirational Latino athlete of my generation. His baseball skills were only surpassed by his devotion to humanity.

In the world's most popular sport, Pelé redefined how the game could be played while expanding the global impact of soccer.

We went to press just as Lorena Ochoa retired at the age of 28. While there were so many incredible Latina athletes, the best golfer of her generation left an indelible impact on women in sport.

Contents

Foreword by Dan Guerrero xvii

CHAPTER 1 • An Introduction:
Latino Groundbreakers Who Paved the Way in Sport   1
by Richard Lapchick

Part One: Professional Sport

CHAPTER 2 • Latinos in Major League Baseball   13
Introduction, by Richard Lapchick
Hall of Famers
José Méndez 23
Star of the National Baseball Hall of Fame, by Horacio Ruiz
Cristóbal Torriente 27
Star of the National Baseball Hall of Fame, by Horacio Ruiz
Martín Dihigo 30
Star of the National Baseball Hall of Fame, by Horacio Ruiz
Vernon "Lefty" Gómez 34
Star of the National Baseball Hall of Fame, by Chris Kamke
Roberto Clemente 37
Star of the National Baseball Hall of Fame, by Horacio Ruiz
Luis Aparicio 44
Star of the National Baseball Hall of Fame, by Chris Kamke
Orlando Cepeda 47
Star of the National Baseball Hall of Fame, by Chris Kamke
Juan Marichal 51
Star of the National Baseball Hall of Fame, by Chris Kamke

Atanasio "Tony" Pérez 54
Star of the National Baseball Hall of Fame, by Horacio Ruiz
Rodney "Rod" Carew. 57
Star of the National Baseball Hall of Fame, by Chris Kamke

Baseball Pioneers
Esteban Bellán. 63
First Latino to Play Professional Baseball in the United States,
    by Jared Bovinet
Hiram Bithorn 65
Puerto Rican Baseball Pioneer, by Richard Lapchick
Roberto "Bobby" Ávila. 67
Mexican Baseball Pioneer, by Jared Bovinet
Luis Tiant. 69
Cuban Baseball Pioneer, by Jared Bovinet
Saturnino "Minnie" Miñoso 72
First Black Latino Player in MLB, by Horacio Ruiz
Albert Pujols. 77
MLB Superstar and Future Hall of Famer, by Horacio Ruiz

Managers
Miguel "Mike" González 81
First Latino Manager in MLB, by Jared Bovinet
Alfonso "Al" López. 83
First Full-Time Latino Manager in MLB and Hall of Fame
    Manager, by Horacio Ruiz
Oswaldo "Ozzie" Guillén. 87
First Latino Manager to Win World Series, by Jared Bovinet
Alejandro "Alex" Pompez. 90
National Baseball Hall of Fame Executive and Pioneer,
    by Horacio Ruiz
Omar Minaya 94
First Latino General Manager in MLB, by Jared Bovinet

Administrators
Arturo "Arte" Moreno. 98
First Latino Majority Owner in MLB, by Horacio Ruiz

CHAPTER 3 • Latinos in the NBA   **103**

Introduction, by Richard Lapchick
Alfonso "Al" Cueto 107
First Latino to be Drafted by NBA Team, by Chris Kamke

Alfred "Butch" Lee 109
First Latino Player in the NBA, by Chris Kamke

Rolando Blackman 113
First Latino to Have Jersey Number Retired by NBA Team,
    by Chris Kamke

Mark Aguirre. 117
First Latino to be NBAs First Overall Draft Pick, by Chris Kamke

Emanuel "Manu" Ginóbili 120
Superstar of the NBA, by Chris Kamke

CHAPTER 4 • Latinos in the NFL   125

Introduction, by Richard Lapchick

Ignacio "Lou" Molinet. 131
First Latino to Play in the NFL, by Chris Kamke

Steve Van Buren 133
Star of the Pro Football Hall of Fame, by Horacio Ruiz

Thomas "Tom" Fears 137
Star of the Pro Football Hall of Fame and First Latino Head Coach
    in the NFL, by Chris Kamke

Theodore "Ted" Hendricks 140
Star of the Pro Football Hall of Fame, by Horacio Ruiz

Anthony Muñoz 144
Star of the Pro Football Hall of Fame, by Chris Kamke

Thomas "Tom" Flores. 147
First Latino Head Coach to Win a Super Bowl, by Chris Kamke

Jim Plunkett. 150
First Latino Quarterback to Win a Super Bowl, by Cara-Lynn
    Lopresti

Tony González 153
Superstar of the NFL and Future Hall of Famer, by Chris Kamke

CHAPTER 5 • Latinos in Golf   157

Introduction, by Richard Lapchick

Roberto De Vicenzo. 160
Star of the World Golf Hall of Fame, by Charlie Harless

Juan "Chi Chi" Rodríguez. 163
Star of the World Golf Hall of Fame, by Jared Bovinet

Lee Treviño 166
Star of the World Golf Hall of Fame, by Charlie Harless

Nancy López. 170
Star of the World Golf Hall of Fame, by Charlie Harless
Lorena Ochoa. 174
Future Star of the World Golf Hall of Fame, by Charlie Harless

CHAPTER 6 • Latinos in Tennis   179

Introduction, by Richard Lapchick

Francisco "Pancho" Segura. 184
Star of the International Tennis Hall of Fame, by Jared Bovinet
Ricardo "Pancho" González. 187
Star of the International Tennis Hall of Fame, by Jared Bovinet
María Bueno 190
Star of the International Tennis Hall of Fame, by Jared Bovinet
Alejandro "Alex" Olmedo 193
Star of the International Tennis Hall of Fame, by Jared Bovinet
Rafael Osuna. 195
Star of the International Tennis Hall of Fame, by Jared Bovinet
Rosemary "Rosy" Casals 197
Star of the International Tennis Hall of Fame, by Cara-Lynn
    Lopresti
Guillermo Vilas 201
Star of the International Tennis Hall of Fame, by Charlie Harless
Gabriela Sabatini. 204
Star of the International Tennis Hall of Fame, by Jared Bovinet
Beatriz "Gigi" Fernández 207
Grand Slam Women's Doubles Champion and Olympic Gold
    Medalist, by Charlie Harless
Mary Joe Fernández 211
Grand Slam Women's Doubles Champion and Olympic Gold
    Medalist, by Charlie Harless
Marcelo Ríos. 215
First Latino to be Ranked Number One in the ATP Tour,
    by Charlie Harless

CHAPTER 7 • Latinos in Boxing   219

Introduction, by Richard Lapchick

"Panama" Alfonso "Al" Brown 223
First Latino World Boxing Champion and Star of the International
    Boxing Hall of Fame, by Horacio Ruiz
Gerardo "Kid Gavilán" González. 228
Star of the International Boxing Hall of Fame, by Horacio Ruiz

Éder Jofre 232
Star of the International Boxing Hall of Fame, by Chris Kamke
José "Mantequilla" Nápoles 235
Star of the International Boxing Hall of Fame, by Horacio Ruiz
Rubén Olivares. 238
Star of the International Boxing Hall of Fame, by Chris Kamke
Roberto Durán. 242
Star of the International Boxing Hall of Fame, by Chris Kamke
Alexis Argüello 246
Star of the International Boxing Hall of Fame, by Chris Kamke
Salvador Sánchez 251
Star of the International Boxing Hall of Fame, by Horacio Ruiz
Julio César Chávez. 255
Star of the International Boxing Hall of Fame, by Charlie Harless
Oscar De La Hoya 259
Future Hall of Famer, by Chris Kamke

CHAPTER 8 ◦ Latinos in Major League Soccer and Professional American Soccer   263

Introduction, by Richard Lapchick
Hugo Pérez. 267
Star of the National Soccer Hall of Fame, by Jared Bovinet
Tabaré "Tab" Ramos. 270
Star of the National Soccer Hall of Fame, by Jared Bovinet
Marcelo Balboa. 273
Star of the National Soccer Hall of Fame, by Jared Bovinet
Claudio Reyna. 276
Future Star of the National Soccer Hall of Fame, by Jared Bovinet
Douglas "Doug" Logan. 279
First Latino Commissioner of Any Major American Sports League,
    by Jared Bovinet

CHAPTER 9 ◦ Latinos and Horse Racing   283

Introduction, by Richard Lapchick
Manuel Ycaza. 287
Star of the National Museum of Racing and Hall of Fame,
    by Horacio Ruiz
Avelino Gómez. 292
Star of the National Museum of Racing and Hall of Fame,
    by Horacio Ruiz

Braulio Baeza 296
Star of the National Museum of Racing and Hall of Fame,
  by Horacio Ruiz
Ángel Cordero, Jr.. 301
Star of the National Museum of Racing and Hall of Fame,
  by Horacio Ruiz
Laffit Pincay, Jr.. 304
Star of the National Museum of Racing and Hall of Fame,
  by Horacio Ruiz

CHAPTER 10 • Latinos in the NHL and NASCAR   309

Latino Players in the NHL, by Richard Lapchick   309
Latinos in NASCAR, by Richard Lapchick   312

Part Two: College Sport

Introduction, by Richard Lapchick   327

CHAPTER 11 • Latino Student-Athletes   327

Tony Casillas 327
Star of the College Football Hall of Fame, by Cara-Lynn Lopresti
Brenda Villa 331
Water Polo All-American and U.S. National Team Captain,
  by Cara-Lynn Lopresti
Lisa Fernández 335
College Softball and U.S. National Team Legend, by Cara-Lynn
  Lopresti
Eduardo Nájera 338
Chip Hilton Player of the Year Presented by the Naismith Memorial
  Basketball Hall of Fame, by Cara-Lynn Lopresti
Jessica Mendoza 342
College Softball All-American and U.S. National Team Member,
  by Cara-Lynn Lopresti
Stephanie Cox, formerly Stephanie López. 345
College Soccer All-American and First Latina to Play on United
  States Women's Soccer National Team, by Cara-Lynn Lopresti
Amy Rodríguez. 349
College Soccer All-American and U.S. National Team Member,
  by Cara-Lynn Lopresti

CHAPTER 12 • Latino Coaches in College Sport 353

August "Augie" Garrido 353
College Baseball Groundbreaker, by Jared Bovinet
Joseph "Joe" Kapp. 357
First Latino Football Coach at Division I-A Program,
　by Cara-Lynn Lopresti
Barry Álvarez 362
College Football Groundbreaker, by Cara-Lynn Lopresti
Leticia Pineda-Boutté 366
College Softball Groundbreaker, by Cara-Lynn Lopresti
Mario Cristóbal 370
First Cuban-American Football Coach at Division I-A Program,
　by Cara-Lynn Lopresti

CHAPTER 13 • Latino Administrators in College Sport 375

Dan Guerrero. 375
Groundbreaking Athletic Director, by Charlie Harless
Rudy Dávalos 380
Groundbreaking Athletic Director, by Cara-Lynn Lopresti
Irma García. 385
First Latina Athletic Director at Division I School,
　by Cara-Lynn Lopresti
Rick Villarreal 389
Groundbreaking Athletic Director, by Cara-Lynn Lopresti
Pete García. 393
Groundbreaking Athletic Director, by Cara-Lynn Lopresti

Part Three: International Sport

**The Olympics and Latino Superstars
on the International Stage**   399

by Richard Lapchick

CHAPTER 14 • Summer Olympics 411

Ramón Fonst 411
First Latino to Win Gold Medal at Summer Olympics,
　by Charlie Harless

Joseph "Joe" Salas 413
First Latino-American to Compete in Summer Olympics,
    by Cara-Lynn Lopresti
Joaquín Capilla 416
Summer Olympic Gold Medalist, by Charlie Harless
Teófilo Stevenson 419
Summer Olympic Gold Medalist, by Charlie Harless
Alberto Juantorena. 423
Summer Olympic Gold Medalist, by Charlie Harless
María Colón 426
First Latina To Win Gold Medal in Summer Olympics,
    by Jared Bovinet
Tracie Ruiz-Conforto 428
Summer Olympic Gold Medalist, by Cara-Lynn Lopresti
Pablo Morales. 431
Summer Olympic Gold Medalist, by Cara-Lynn Lopresti
Félix Savón 435
Summer Olympic Gold Medalist, by Charlie Harless
Trent Dimas 439
Summer Olympic Gold Medalist, by Charlie Harless
Claudia Poll. 443
First Central American Woman to Win an Olympic Gold Medal,
    by Jared Bovinet
Steven López 445
Summer Olympic Gold Medalist, by Cara-Lynn Lopresti
Irving Saladino. 448
First Central American Man to Win Olympic Gold Medal,
    by Jared Bovinet
2004 Argentina Men's National Basketball Team 450
First Latin American Country to Win Olympic Gold Medal
    in Basketball
Alberto Salazar. 453
American Marathon Star, by Charlie Harless

CHAPTER 15 • Winter Olympics   457

Jennifer Rodríguez 457
First Latina-American to Win Winter Olympics Medal,
    by Cara-Lynn Lopresti
Derek Parra 460
First Latino-American to Win Winter Olympics Gold Medal,
    by Jared Bovinet

CHAPTER 16 • **Latino International Superstars**
in Sports 465

Edson Arantes "Pelé" do Nascimento 465
International Soccer Superstar, by Chris Kamke
Alfredo di Stéfano 470
International Soccer Superstar, by Charlie Harless
Manuel "Garrincha" dos Santos 474
International Soccer Superstar, by Charlie Harless
Hugo Sánchez 478
International Soccer Superstar, by Charlie Harless
Diego Maradona 482
International Soccer Superstar, by Charlie Harless
José Chilavert 486
International Soccer Superstar, by Charlie Harless
Ana Fidelia Quirot 490
International Track Superstar, by Horacio Ruiz
Ana Guevara 494
International Track Superstar, by Horacio Ruiz
Juan Manuel Fangio 498
International Formula One Superstar, by Horacio Ruiz
Ayrton Senna 502
International Formula One Superstar, by Horacio Ruiz

CHAPTER 17 • **Conclusion/Epilogue**
Future of Latinos in Sport 509

by Richard Lapchick

About the National Consortium
for Academics and Sports 517

About the Authors 523

Foreword

Located on the border between Nepal and Tibet is the highest peak in the world, Mt. Everest. Part of the Himalayan mountain range and rising to 29,035 feet, it is one of the "Seven Summits"—the highest point on each continent—and remains a major undertaking for the most experienced of climbers and one of the most coveted of all high-altitude accomplishments. After numerous attempts, many with tragic outcomes, it was first successfully ascended in 1953. Do you recall by whom?

If you responded with Sir Edmund Hillary, you'd be only partially correct. Hillary's Sherpa climbing partner achieved the summit at virtually the same instant, yet the name Tenzing Norgay is rarely credited or even mentioned in most accounts. Yet another example is the famed "midnight ride" during the colonial period. Paul Revere is a household name but William Dawes remains anonymous in spite of equal participation in their 1775 effort to notify fellow patriots of British troop movements.

These historical inaccuracies and omissions, among others, whether intended or not, are intrinsic to the written word. History is interpreted and ultimately recorded through the eyes and works of writers who are every bit as human as you and I. Influenced by social trends, personal inclination, cultural loyalty, geographic location, era, marketability, and myriad other personal factors, no one account can be completely unbiased or wholly comprehensive. As time goes by, we continue to discover more notable people, events, and trends who may have been historically overlooked and examine their impact and influence on today's world. One of these very people leading the charge to unveil the full history is my friend Richard Lapchick, who has taken it upon himself to illuminate our knowledge of select historical gaps, if you will.

An acknowledged expert in the field of sport history, this book is the fourth in his series, and targets significant contributions made by Latinos. As you would expect, it is well-researched, entertaining, and written with Richard's trademark penchant for candor and insight. I would not have expected less. I've called Richard a "compadre" for nearly 20 years and as our friendship grew, I've come to know an educator and writer who is part crusader, part activist, and 100% in possession of a social conscience. I may not have expressed this to Richard out loud, but after he completed previous works, on female and African-American sports legends, I was hoping he would produce exactly this chronicle.

Richard and I first met in March of 1990. As the Director of Athletics at California State University, Dominguez Hills (CSUDH) in Carson, California, I was asked to serve as a panelist at a symposium conducted as part of a Young, Gifted and Black Residency Program, held as part of the university's celebration of Black History Month. The esteemed Dr. Lapchick, the Founder and Director of Northeastern University's Center for the Study of Sport and Society and the National Consortium for Academic and Sport, was included in the slate of featured speakers for the program. He, along with another individual who I admired greatly, the noble Arthur Ashe, who had just earlier released his landmark three-volume body of work, *The Hard Road to Glory*, the definitive documentation of African-American sporting history, were the keynote speakers. Not only was I captivated by Richard's well-chronicled personal story, but I was deeply moved by his conviction and touched by his lifelong commitment to "fight the good fight" against racism and social injustice. Our alignment of vision was apparent and an enduring relationship was established. However, my passion for social and racial equality was founded much before this as a young Latino growing up in Los Angeles.

As I reflect on my youth, a list of my heroes always begins with my father, Gene Guerrero, the most influential person in my life. My work ethic, competitive spirit, and love for music and sports were all fashioned by my dad. Growing up in Wilmington, California, a blue-collar community in the heart of the Los Angeles Harbor area, my dad and I were huge fans of the Dodgers, Lakers, and Rams. It was not surprising, therefore, that my sports heroes included such names as Sandy Koufax, Don Drysdale, Elgin Baylor, Jerry West, and Deacon Jones. They were icons, larger than life, and real to me primarily through television, newspapers, and trading cards.

Perhaps my biggest hero, though, was Jackie Robinson. His accomplishments, both on and off the field, were one of the main determinants when it came time for me to choose a college. Though I was recruited and offered a scholarship to play baseball by many universities during my high school senior year, as soon as UCLA made the offer, the decision was easy. The Guerrero family had always supported UCLA, largely because Jackie Robinson was a Bruin. My dad would say that because of Jackie, UCLA was a "university for the people." What he meant was that a person who looked like me, a minority, would not only be accepted at UCLA, they could thrive and excel. When I put the UCLA baseball uniform on for the very first time in the fall of 1969, the same uniform that Jackie wore, it was reverential.

There was a whole other set of sports heroes that I held in esteem for a much different reason than their celebrity or their stats; they were men with whom I could actually relate because they were Latino. They looked like me, they were from my neighborhood, and they dreamed big, like me. These guys made their impression with their fists, both in and out of the ring, not uncharacteristic of Wilmington and Harbor area boys of that era. Armando "Mando" Ramos and Raul Rojas were not only world-class boxers, they were local legends from my own backyard. Mando was one of the most popular and exciting fighters in the 1960s and became the youngest lightweight champion in history when he beat Carlos "Teo" Cruz in 1969 at the Los Angeles Memorial Coliseum. Raul Rojas was also a dynamic boxer and one year prior to Ramos's title victory, defeated Colombian Enrique Higgins in a tough fight at the landmark Olympic Auditorium in Los Angeles to win the WBA Featherweight title. During those years, Mando and Raul were the rage and a sense of pride to all Latinos in Southern California.

My biggest Latino sports hero, however, was irrefutable. My dear friend and mentor Joe Orbillo was also a boxer, a terrific young heavyweight, headliner, and fan favorite at the Olympic Auditorium in the 1960s. At 190 pounds, Joe always fought boxers much heavier than he, but was viewed by his peers and those who saw him in the ring during those years as one of the toughest to put on a pair of gloves. In matches against such standouts as Eddie Machen, Jerry Quarry, and Manuel Ramos, Joe fought with the heart of a champion and the ferocity of a lion. I exulted in his victories and felt his pain with the losses. We were extremely close, and as such, he graced me with the opportunity to accompany him to the gym as he trained for his fights and to many of his bouts at the Olympic Auditorium. From my perspective, there was nothing glamorous about life in the gym—the sweat, the blood, and the stench. There was something magical, however, about fight night; it was intoxicating to be sure and had one begging for more. In the bowels of the Olympic Auditorium prior to his fights, I witnessed the wrapping of his hands and the placement of the gloves by his irrepressible trainer, Jake Shugrue. I observed his mental preparation for the combat that was to ensue, and, whether he won or lost, I saw him stand toe to toe with his foe, never giving an inch or anything but his best effort. I learned a great deal from Joe and his experiences. Among other things, he taught me to be tough-minded and self-confident, to be a proud Latino, and to always set my goals beyond my grasp. Joe was my hero because he took the time to take me under his wing, challenge me on several levels, and teach me what he knew about life.

My point here is to illustrate that sports heroes come in various packages. They can be the legendary figures that are adored by many—the quarterback that throws the touchdown pass to win the Super Bowl, the pitcher on the mound that gets the final out in the World Series, or the player that hits the game winning shot at the buzzer to win the NBA Championship. They can also be the local high school coach, the parents that drive their son or daughter to practice religiously, or simply just that special person from the neighborhood that somehow finds a way to raise one's game.

To have Richard Lapchick feature a number of my other boyhood heroes—Lee Trevino and Roberto Clemente to name two—in *100 Campeones* was further satisfying. To be included myself in such a work is profoundly humbling.

Finally, there is, of course, a concern to be avoided, for it would be truly lamentable if this book's primary readership were limited to Latinos. I work at an institution, UCLA, that has been on the forefront of opportunity and diversity, whose athletes, particularly female and African-American, are on the rolls of sport's greatest pioneers and legends—Jackie Robinson, Arthur Ashe, Rafer Johnson, Kareem Abdul Jabbar, and Jackie Joyner Kersee, to name but a few. As both a student of and contributor to the positive social change that reverberates from such a foundation, I can express to you with conviction that the potential of both mind and spirit are amplified by knowledge and awareness of those few who went over, around, and through societal barriers. This holds true for any chosen endeavor, but particularly the arena of sport, given its popularity and following.

I hope you enjoy this book and wish to thank Richard for producing yet another compilation that reveals the story and character of those Latino sports figures whose contributions, both on the field and off, transcend wins and losses.

—Dan Guerrero
UCLA Director of Athletics

I

AN INTRODUCTION

LATINO GROUNDBREAKERS WHO PAVED THE WAY IN SPORT

Richard Lapchick

I have been doing diversity management training for almost 40 years. Most of the work has been with professional sports leagues, pro teams, and college athletic departments. In the mid-1990s I developed an Atheletic Quotient (AQ) test. As part of it, I would ask participants to write down the names of 20 male athletes, 20 female athletes, 20 African-American athletes, and 20 Latino athletes. In the five years I used the AQ almost everyone got the male names. Many women got 20 women while men averaged between 10 and 12 names. Women were only able to name a handful of African-Americans or Latinos. African-Americans also got the African-Americans but had less than 10 women and five Latinos. Latinos mostly also got 20 Latinos, ten African-Americans and only five women.

The exercise made me want to write about athletes by race and gender. After publishing a book on 100 African-American athletes and 100 women athletes in 2008 and 2009, respectively, this volume on 100 Latino athletes was the natural next book to write.

As a college professor and a speaker who talks on approximately 25 campuses each year, I recognize that young people today, even college educated ones, have little sense of history. I have to explain what apartheid was in South Africa and who Arthur Ashe was to American sport. Nelson Mandela's name is recognized but without a deep knowledge of the details of his life. Entertainment and popular cultural usually help. Thus, Clint Eastwood's *Invictus* brought immediate attention to Mandela among moviegoers.

Even with an African-American president, the people we know best too frequently are white men. People ask me who my heroes are. I tell them that among them are Martin Luther King, Nelson Mandela, Robert Kennedy, Malcolm X, and César Chávez. Chávez's name evokes blank stares. Others ask me who my sports heroes are. I respond with my father, Joe Lapchick, Jackie Robinson, Muhammad Ali, Arthur Ashe, Billie Jean King, and Roberto Clemente. Unless the person asking the question is Latino, few have heard of Clemente. Historical racism and sexism have obscured the stories of too many people of color and women.

For several decades when I wrote about and spoke about race and racism in sports, the discussions were about African-Americans and whites. While there was a vague awareness of Latinos, Asians, and Native Americans, they were rarely part of the mainstream discussion on race.

These were among the reasons why, along with Horacio Ruiz, Jared Bovinet, Chris Kamke, Cara-Lynn Lopresti, and Charlie Harless, I had to write this book about 100 Latino Groundbreakers Who Paved the Way in Sport.

It is the fourth book in a series devoted to shed light on the lives of people in sport whose life stories are important but are not well known enough.

First I should clarify how we are using the term "Latino." It includes people from Cuba, Mexico, Puerto Rico, Central or South America, or of other Spanish descent. We recognize that among people who fit this category, some identify themselves as Hispanic, Mexican-American, Chicano, or simply as American. Racially, Latinos can be white or Black and are not religiously homogeneous.

The fact that there have been a relatively small number of Latino athletes in sports in the United States will surely change rapidly now that Latinos, who make up about 15 percent of the total U.S. population, constitute the largest ethnic minority group in the country and are the nation's fastest-growing minority population. The number of Latinos is expected to rise even more dramatically in the United States from 46.7 million to 132.8 million between 2008 and 2050.

As athletes, the percentage of professional players who are Latino varies widely for a high of 27 percent in Major League Baseball to no Latina players in the 2008 WNBA season. There are three percent in the NBA, one percent in the NFL, and 16 percent in Major League Soccer. At the college level, 3.9 percent of male college student-athletes and 3.6 percent of female college student-athletes across NCAA Divisions I, II, and III were Latino according to the figures released by the NCAA for the 2006–07 year.

And, of course, Latinos will emerge not just as athletes but as decision-makers at all levels of sport. Latinos have gradually emerged as professional staff in pro sports league offices. Latinos hold 13, 7, 3, 5, and 22 percent of the professional positions in the league offices of Major League Baseball, the NBA, the WNBA, the NFL, and Major League Soccer, respectively. MLS is way ahead at the team level with 30 percent of professional positions, compared to 5, 8, 10, and 4 percent in MLB, the NBA, the WNBA, and NFL, respectively. Unlike the case of African-Americans, there are higher percentages of Latinos holding league and front office professional positions in the NBA and MLS than there are Latinos playing in those leagues.

At the highest level in pro sport is Arturo Moreno who became the first Latino majority owner of a major U.S. sports team when he purchased the Anaheim (now Los Angeles) Angels.

At the college level, only 2, 3, and 0 percent of the athletics directors in Division I, II, and III, respectively, are Latino. In the pipeline position of associate and assistant athletics directors, only 2, 2, and 0.4 percent in Division I, II, and III, respectively, are Latino. Irma García at St. Francis College in New York was the only Latina AD among the 300 Division I schools in 2009.

So, with all the population growth in the Latino community, we can expect the number of fans, athletes, and administrators to have a major expansion in the next decade. A key to how that growth takes shape will be how the sports are marketed and who sees and hears them on television and radio.

Soccer has been the number one sport for Latinos for many years, but baseball has grown rapidly with so many Latino stars in MLB. Marketers are using the star athletes to reach Latino consumers. Broadcasters have increased their targets to include the NFL, NBA, and NASCAR. Franchises use their Latino athletes in advertisements.

Now the networks showcase Latinos in every major sport. According to the *Hispanic Marketing Weekly*, "marketers use a variety of sports as advertising vehicles to increase ongoing efforts and launch new campaigns. In an interview, Ralph Paniagua, president of R. Paniagua, a New York-based sports event and online publishing company, said, "There is a lot of interest from corporations. They are looking at doing grassroots things that bring them closer to the community."

The creation of more multimedia packages by TV networks is making marketing to Latinos easier to sell to advertisers. The traditional forms advertising on TV, game signage, and billboards have expanded rapidly with websites, wireless devices, and grassroots events. Tom Maney, senior vice president of advertising sales for Fox Sports en Español, told the *Hispanic Marketing Weekly*, "It's the ability to do new things with programming in a multiplatform environment and reach consumers in new ways that counts."

The same is true at other networks such as Telemundo, Univision, and ESPN Deportes which are also significantly expanding their offerings of multiplatform advertising. The leagues and individual teams are doing the same, especially in cities and regions with large Latino populations.

Leagues, teams, and networks are also going for the masses with grassroots campaigns geared up for Latino audiences. Jorge Hidalgo, senior executive vice president of news and sports at Telemundo, told the *Hispanic Marketing Weekly*, "Advertisers aren't satisfied with eyeballs on television and online. They want to touch viewers and engage them through grassroots promotions."

All of this stems from the recognition that diversity is a business imperative. With the enormity of the Latino population and its growth, leagues, teams, networks, marketers, and advertisers are clearly targeting Latinos. As they do, the people written about in *100 Campeones* will become even better known.

The History of the Book Series

In 2009, we published *100 Trailblazers*. It tracked the revolution for women in sport that started in the 1970s when Title IX of the Education Amendment Act was signed by President Nixon on June 23, 1972 and tennis great Billie Jean King defeated Bobby Riggs in September 1973. The world of sports was never the same. But there was a rich history of great individual women athletes before Title IX and their stories are also featured in *100 Trailblazers*.

In 1971, girls competing in high school sport accounted for seven percent of all high school varsity athletes. In 2007–08, girls comprised 41.5 percent of all high school varsity athletes, a 900 percent increase. In 1970, one in 27 high school girls played a varsity sport vs. two out of five in 2008.

At the college level, in 1971 there were less than 30,000 women competing while there were 170,384 men. In 2006–07, there were 172,534 women and 233,830 men competing. Women had 42 percent of the college team slots in 2006–07. In 2008, we published *100 Pioneers: African-American Who Broke Color Barriers in Sport*. We recognized that almost everyone knew the story of Jackie Robinson and how his joining the Brooklyn Dodgers in 1947 began to change the face of American sports. We celebrate Jackie Robinson in every ballpark, his number has been retired and there are regular ceremonies in his honor. When Americans are asked who the greatest racial pioneer in sport is, Jackie Robinson's name will most often be mentioned.

Yet, few knew names of the people who broke the barriers in the American League just a few months later, in the NFL, NBA, NHL, and who were the first African-American athletes to break down the barriers of segregation at the Southeastern, Atlantic Coast, Big Ten, Big 8/Big 12, and Ivy League conference schools.

Some knew about Arthur Ashe and Althea Gibson in tennis but few knew the names of those who led the way in other sports. Many who know Muhammad Ali did not know Jack Johnson.

100 Pioneers was designed as the second book in a series to tell readers just that. The series began at the National Consortium for Academics and Sports (NCAS). Because of the work that we do in the NCAS and the DeVos Sport Business Management Program, we become all too aware of the problems that exist in sport. Each day we seem to read about a rule being violated, an athlete getting in trouble with drugs, an athlete arrested for sexual assault, steroid use in baseball, the NFL, or track and field, the threat that gambling poses to college sports, and agents recruiting young athletes with illegal monetary inducements. The list goes on and on. That is why it was so joyous for me when Dr. Taylor Ellis, the Dean of Undergraduate Education in the College of Business Administration at the University of Central Florida, came to my office February of 2005.

I had just put to bed a book called *New Game Plan for College Sport* and was frankly tired of writing. I vowed that I would not take up another book project for several years. Taylor changed all of that on the morning after the 2005 Consortium banquet. He came in, sat down, and said, "When I was a boy, I wasn't focused and wasn't living up to my potential." He said, "Then someone gave me this book." Taylor placed a well-worn copy of Barlow Meyers' *Real Life Stories: Champions All the Way*, published 45 years earlier, on my desk. He said, "Somebody gave me this book about seven athletes and the obstacles they overcame to do great things in life. This book transformed my life and gave me a sense of direction and hope." Taylor said, "Every year you honor five or six such athletes at the Consortium's award banquet. You have to write a book about them." So came the idea for *100 Heroes: People in Sport Who Make This a Better World*.

I had to undertake the project in spite of my vow to the contrary. This book could be, I thought, a real celebration of sport. It could portray the power of sport to transform not only individuals, but their impact on the broader society. I ran through my head the names of all the award winners I could recall and knew that their stories would inspire people collectively who could not be in the presence of these people in the halls when we honored them.

With the 20th anniversary of the Consortium exactly a year away, I knew that we would have to work hard to get this project done. I enlisted the support of Jessica Bartter, who is Assistant Director for Communications and Marketing of the National Consortium. We began to draw all of the names and addresses together and contact the previous award winners who were still alive. Their support for the project was overwhelmingly positive. We began to collect the biographical materials and stories that were the basis for the awards. We also asked Drew Tyler, Stacy Martin, Jennifer Brenden, Brian Wright, all graduate students in the DeVos Sport Business Management Program, to help write the individual stories. *100 Heroes* was published in February 2006. I knew there was more to do.

We divided ***100 Campeones*** into three parts.

Part One deals with professional sports including the largest chapter from Major League Baseball where we selected Latino Hall of Famers, baseball pioneers, and barrier breaking Latino MLB executives. Those covered include Hall of Famers José Méndez, Cristóbal Torriente, Martín Dihigo, Vernon "Lefty" Gómez, Roberto Clemente, Luis Aparicio, Orlando Cepeda, Juan Marichal, Tony Pérez, and Rod Carew.

Baseball pioneers included are Esteban Bellán, the first Latino to play professional baseball in the United States; Hiram Bithorn, the first Puerto Rican to play in MLB, Roberto "Bobby" Ávila; a Mexican pioneer in MLB; and Saturnino "Minnie" Miñoso, the first Black Latino player in MLB. The final player in the pioneer section is Albert Pujols, perhaps the greatest current superstar.

Barrier breaking Latino MLB executives include Miguel "Mike" González, the first Latino Manager in MLB; Alfonso "Al" López, the first full-time Latino Manager in MLB and a Hall of Fame Manager; Oswaldo "Ozzie" Guillén, the first Latino Manager to win the World Series; Alejandro "Alex" Pompez, who helped the New York Giants integrate Latino players into MLB; Omar Minaya, the first Latino General Manager in MLB; and finally, Arturo Moreno, the first Latino majority owner in MLB.

There are five Latinos covered in Chapter 3 on the NBA including Alfonso "Al" Cueto, the first Latino to be drafted by an NBA team; Alfred "Butch" Lee, the first Latino player in the NBA; Rolando Blackman, the first Latino to have his jersey number retired; Mark Aguirre, the first Latino to be the NBA's first overall draft pick; and Manu Ginóbili, perhaps the biggest current Latino superstar in the NBA.

There are eight Latinos covered in Chapter 4 on the NFL including Ignacio "Lou" Molinet, the first Latino to play in the NFL; and Pro Football Hall of Famers Steve Van Buren, "Tom" Fears (also the first Latino Head Coach in the NFL), Ted Hendricks, and Anthony Muñoz.

Also included are Jim Plunkett, the first Latino quarterback in the NFL to win a Super Bowl; Tom Flores, the first Latino Head Coach in the NFL to win a Super Bowl; and current NFL star Tony González.

Chapter 5 is on golf and includes four current and one future Hall of Famers: Roberto De Vicenzo, Juan "Chi Chi" Rodríguez, Lee Treviño, and Nancy López are all currently in the Hall. Recently retired Lorena Ochoa is a lock for future inclusion.

Chapter 6 on tennis includes eight International Tennis Hall of Famers: Francisco "Pancho" Segura, Ricardo "Pancho" Gonzáles, Maria Bueno, Alejandro "Alex" Olmedo, Rafael Osuna, Rosemary Casals, Guillermo Vilas, and Gabriela Sabatini.

Also featured are Grand Slam Women's Doubles Champions and Olympic Gold Medalists Beatriz "Gigi" Fernández and Mary

Joe Fernández, and Marcelo Ríos, the first Latino to be ranked Number One in the ATP.

Chapter 7 on boxing champions features International Boxing Hall of Famers "Panama" Alfonso "Al" Brown, who was also the first Latino World Boxing Champion, Gerardo "Kid Gavilán" González, Éder Jofre, José "Mantequilla" Nápoles, Rubén Olivares, Roberto Durán, Alexis Argüello, Salvador Sánchez, and Julio César Chávez. The chapter concludes with future hall of famer Oscar De La Hoya.

Soccer is, of course, one of the most popular sports for Latinos. Chapter 8 looks at professional soccer and Major League Soccer. Other soccer stars are profiled in Chapter 16 on international stars. This chapter includes both athletes and administrators. The athletes are National Soccer Hall of Famers from the United States Hugo Pérez, Tabaré "Tab" Ramos, Marcelo Balboa, and future Hall of Famer Claudio Reyna. Doug Logan is included as the first Latino Commissioner of any major American sports league.

Five Latinos who rode their way into the National Museum of Racing and Hall of Fame make up Chapter 9. The five are Manuel Ycaza, Avelino Gómez, Braulio Baeza, Ángel Cordero, Jr., and Laffit Pincay, Jr.

Chapter 10 focuses on Latinos in the NHL and NASCAR and is based on two articles I wrote for Hispanic Heritage Month for ESPN.com.

Part Two of *100 Campeones* is on college sport and includes student-athletes, coaches, and administrators.

Chapter 11 introduces seven student-athletes. Tony Casillas made the College Football Hall of Fame. Brenda Villa was a water polo star and National Team Captain. Lisa Fernández is a college, national team, and Olympic softball legend. Eduardo Nájera won the Chip Hilton Player of the Year Award presented by the Basketball Hall of Fame. Jessica Mendoza was another college and national softball team legend.

Amy Rodríguez and Stephanie Cox (formerly Stephanie López) were both soccer All-Americans and national team members. Cox was the first Latina to play on the U.S. Women's national team.

Chapter 12 focuses on coaches in college sport and includes baseball coach Augie Garrido, Joe Kapp, the first Latino Division IA head football coach; Barry Álvarez, one of the most successfull college football coaches ever; Leticia Pineda-Boutté: who broke ground as a college softball coach; and Mario Cristóbal, the first Cuban-American head football Coach at a Division I-A Program.

In Chapter 13 we focus on five college athletics directors including Dan Guerrero, Rudy Dávalos, Rick Villareal, Pete García, and Irma García, the first Latina Athletic Director at Division I school.

Part Three is on the Olympics and Latino Superstars on the International Stage.

Chapter 14 looks at Latino impact players in the Summer Olympics. Cuban Rámon Fonst was the first Latino to win a Gold Medal in the Summer Olympics. Joe Salas was the first Latino-American to compete in the Summer Olympics. Joaquín Capilla from Mexico was a gold medalist diver. Cuba's Teófilo Stevenson was perhaps the world's greatest Olympic boxer while Cuba's Alberto Juantorena was a track and field superstar in the Olympics. Another Cuban, María Colón, was the first Latina to win a gold medal, taking the javelin in 1980.

Americans Tracie Ruiz-Conforto, Pablo Morales, Trent Dimas, and Steven López won the gold in synchronized swimming, swimming, gymnastics, and taekwondo, respectively. Alberto Salazar never won the Olympic gold but was a great marathon runner. If anyone could be compared to Stevenson, it was Cuban boxer Félix Savón who also won three gold medals. Costa Rican swimmer Claudia Poll was the first Central American woman to win gold. Panamanian long jumper Irving Saladino was the first Central American man to win the Gold. Argentina was the first Latin American team to win the gold medal in basketball.

Chapter 15 includes speed skater Jennifer Rodríguez, who was the first Latina-American to win a Winter Olympics medal, while speed skater Derek Parra was the first Latino-American to win a Winter Olympics Gold medal.

There is a pantheon of superstars in Chapter 16 on International Stars including all-time great soccer star Edson Arantes "Pelé" do Nascimento. Other soccer stars here are Alfredo di Stéfano, Manuel "Garrincha" dos Santos, Hugo Sánchez, Diego Maradona, and José Chilavert from Argentina, Brazil, Mexico, Argentina, and Paraguay, respectively. Two women track stars in this chapter are Ana Quirot and Ana Guevara. Finally, there are two Formula One

Superstars: Juan Manuel Fangio and Ayrton Senna from Argentina and Brazil, respectively.

The conclusion in Chapter 17 looks at the future for Latinos in Sport through action sports and the X Games.

As I wrote in *100 Heroes*, I recognized that sport reaches all kinds of people for all different reasons. Sport can be played competitively or recreationally or sport can be watched and enjoyed as entertainment. We watch sports we never play and we play sports we never watch. Sport can help build friendships, families, respect, confidence, and character. Sport provides health benefits some medical professionals can only begin to understand.

Most importantly, sport smashes the barriers that too frequently divide us like nothing else can. The athletes in *100 Heroes*, *100 Pioneers*, *100 Trailblazers*, and *100 Campeones* represent that better than anyone because of their own life experiences.

Young people today have little or no sense of history and today's athletes often do not realize how different it was even a decade ago, let alone 100 years ago. While incidents in the history of race and gender may be studied by young Americans, for too many it is just history and they cannot relate. But young people do relate to sport. *100 Campeones* tells stories about people who will hopefully open the eyes of young people and make it a living history.

Like the other books in this series, *100 Campeones* will help young people who look up to athletes like Albert Pujols, Manu Ginóbili, Lorena Ochoa, Oscar De La Hoya, and Lisa Fernández know those who came before them to pave the way. For without these *Campeones*, today's stars might never have gotten through the gate.

PROFESSIONAL
SPORT

2

LATINOS IN MAJOR LEAGUE BASEBALL

by Richard Lapchick

A few years ago, Jayson Stark wrote, "Baseball isn't just America's sport anymore" for ESPN.com. He concluded that, "What is actually being invaded here is America and its hold on its theoretical national pastime. We're not sure exactly when this happened—possibly while you were busy watching a Yankees-Red Sox game—but this isn't just America's sport anymore.

It is Latin America's sport."

While it may not have gone that far yet, the presence of Latino players in baseball, especially in Major League Baseball, has grown enormously. In 1990, the *Racial and Gender Report Card* recorded that 13 percent of MLB players were Latino. In the *2009 MLB Racial and Gender Report Card*, 27 percent of the players were Latino. The all-time high was 29.4 percent in 2006.

Teams from South America, Mexico, and the Caribbean enter the World Baseball Classic with superstar MLB players on their rosters. Stark wrote, "The term, 'baseball game,' won't be adequate to describe it. These games will be practically a cultural symposium—where we provide the greatest Latino players of our time a monstrous stage to demonstrate what baseball means to them, versus what baseball now means to us."

American youth have an array of sports to play besides baseball, including soccer, basketball, football, and hockey. Now more and more play tennis, golf, and X-Game sports.

Some Latinos think baseball is the only sport and in many countries that is true. This is especially the case in Venezuela and the Dominican Republic. Nearly four out of every five international players in the minor leagues are from those two countries. And more than 40 percent of minor league players are from outside the US.

It is also not lost on corporate America that Latinos now comprise the second-largest population group in the United States, only surpassed by whites. They provide a huge marketplace and fan bases. Endorsement deals have made Latino athletes even richer. When the athlete is bilingual, his potential to reach Latinos in the US and in his or her home country is even broader.

Lots of MLB clubs market heavily to the Latino community but perhaps none more than the Los Angeles Angels of Anaheim. This approach soared after Arte Moreno bought the club in 2003 as pro sports' first Latino owner. They market their Latino stars in a bilingual blitz, putting the faces of the stars on billboards across L.A. Spanish language broadcasts are given on many teams. However, the influence of Latinos in professional baseball is hardly new. That is a fact that sportswriters, league and team administrators, fans, and even players are just starting to embrace.

It is our intent in this section on baseball to illuminate not only the greatest Latino names in baseball but also those that played historical roles in the game.

Before MLB was integrated by Jackie Robinson in 1947, Latinos played ball on both sides of the color line. Some light-skinned Latinos passed in MLB while others of all skin colors played in the Negro Leagues. In one of the ironies of racism, African-American players in the Negro Leagues were able to play winter ball in Mexico, the Caribbean, and South America but could not play in their own country's MLB.

It was no cakewalk for Latinos in baseball. *Viva Baseball*, directed by Dan Klores, allowed some of the silent voices of the early days after integration to be heard.

Luis Tiant, one of the greatest pitchers of his time, said in the film, "I used to go to my room and cry." He faced a double barrier because of his skin color and the fact that he had no English language skills when he entered pro baseball in the minors and MLB. Tiant became a dear friend and worked with me at Northeastern University's Center for the Study of Sport in Society in the 1990s. He would share with Boston-area youth the battles he faced from fans making racist assumptions. Tiant came from Cuba and by the time he joined us at NU, he was beloved in Boston.

The San Francisco Giants had great Latino talent including Felipe, Matty, and Jesús Alou, Orlando Cepeda, and Juan Marichal. They were actually ordered not to speak in their own language so they would not be suspected of talking about teammates in negative terms. Some Latino players anglicized their names. Vic Pellot became Vic Power. Some Latinos with darker complexions faced racism because people thought they were Black. When he was denied entrance to a movie theater, Cepeda tried to explain that he was Puerto Rican. He said the owner only saw him as being Black. Stereotypes went both ways. Felipe Alou said, "I thought all Americans were white . . . The first time I heard a black man speaking English, I was confused."

Players were criticized or stereotyped. Alvin Dark was the Giants manager in that era and admitted in the film that he did not understand Latinos. When he was manager, Dark suggested that Latino players were less intelligent and were not clutch hitters. Forty years later, he admitted, "I really did not know enough about their culture." Roberto Clemente was one of the greatest players of all-time yet at points in his Hall of Fame career he was criticized for not being a clutch hitter. There were so many stories like this.

Tony Menéndez compiled a list of the top 20 Latinos in MLB by country in the "Bleacher Report." Each country including Cuba, Mexico, Puerto Rico, the Dominican Republic, and Venezuela could have fielded its own MLB All-Star team. Menéndez noted to not forget "the greats from Central America, such as Nicaragua's Dennis Martínez and Panama's Rod Carew, Ben Oglivie, Carlos Lee, and Mariano Rivera; and the great shortstops from Colombia, Orlando Cabrera and Edgar Rentería."

So you can see how hard it was to choose those Latinos profiled in this chapter on baseball. To some degree we were guided by those who made the Hall of Fame. But there were others included for their special roles who are not in the Hall. And Albert Pujols, the only modern day player, was chosen because of his unique greatness as a player and as a humanitarian.

The Players

Historians credit Esteban Bellán with introducing Cubans to their national pastime. He was the first Latino and Cuban baseball player in the American Major Leagues. Bellán played baseball for the

Fordham Rose Hill Baseball Club while attending Fordham University in New York and participated in the first ever nine-man team college baseball game in 1859. In 1871, he joined the Troy Haymakers, which later became the New York Giants. Bellán returned to Cuba, where he participated in the country's first organized baseball game in December of 1874 and helped create the Habana Baseball Club, the country's first club dedicated to the sport.

In the early 1900s, José Méndez became the first baseball legend from Cuba. He was called "El Diamante Negro," or the "Black Diamond," and because the nickname was a giveaway for the color of his skin, there was no hope that Méndez would ever play in the major leagues. Méndez was 8-7 in exhibition games against major league competition and finished his Cuban League career with a 76-28 record. His .731 winning percentage is the highest among players with a minimum of 40 wins in Cuban League history.

Cristóbal Torriente earned the nickname "The Cuban Babe Ruth" for his tremendous power displayed in a 1921 showdown vs. the Major League's New York Giants who were touring with Ruth. For the series, Torriente batted .378 to Ruth's .345, and he hit three home runs to Ruth's two and his team won the series. In 1918, Torriente signed with the Negro League's Chicago American Giants. He would lead the American Giants to three consecutive championships by hitting .411, .338, and .342 during the three-year championship run. For his career, Torriente ranks 11th on the Negro League all-time list in RBI's with 309, 12th in slugging percentage with a .517 mark, and 16th in total bases with 1,055. He was inducted into the National Baseball Hall of Fame in 2006.

Hall of Famer and Negro League legend Buck Leonard said the best player of all time was Cuba's Martín Dihigo. Dihigo was legendary for being able to play all nine positions at an All-Star level. Dihigo played 22 seasons in Cuba (1922–29, 1931–46) and finished with a lifetime .291 batting average. As a pitcher he went 119–57 and in his career, spanning across several leagues in different countries, Dihigo is credited with more than 260 wins. In 1977, he was the first Cuban elected into the Baseball Hall of Fame in Cooperstown, NY.

In 1972, Lefty Gómez was inducted into the Baseball Hall of Fame, decades after his career as one of the 1930's most dominant pitchers ended. A six-time World Series champion with the Yankees,

Gómez's 6-0 win-loss World Series record made him the most winning World Series pitcher without a loss in major league history. Gómez made seven consecutive All-Star teams (1933–39), making five starts and recording three wins. In 1962, the American Baseball Coaches Association started presenting the annual Lefty Gómez Award. Considered one of the most prestigious awards in amateur baseball, it is awarded to an individual who has distinguished themselves amongst their peers and has contributed significantly to amateur baseball in America.

Many think of Roberto Clemente when they think of pioneers from Puerto Rico. Far less known, but every bit the pioneer, was Hiram Bithorn. On April 15, 1942—13 years before Clemente would play in the majors. Bithorn made his debut. He was light-skinned, had a name that did not sound Latino, and joined a field of Major League players that had been seriously depleted by World War II. Bithorn posted a 34-31 career record with a 3.16 ERA. He completed 30 of the 53 games he started and finished with eight shutouts. The national stadium that sits across the way from the Coliseum in San Juan was named Hiram Bithorn Stadium. Opened in 1962, it honors the island's first citizen to play in Major League Baseball.

Roberto Clemente was undoubtedly one of the most beloved MLB players of all time. He died when his plane crashed as he was trying to help the people of Nicaragua who suffered a terrible earthquake in December of 1972. His 12 Gold Gloves are tied with Willie Mays for the most ever by an outfielder. He was named to 12 All-Star teams and he hit .317 for his career with 3,000 hits. With every accolade Clemente earned, he went back to Puerto Rico a hero. It was a scene that repeated itself for many years in his career. On March 20, 1973 Clemente became the first Latino elected into the Hall of Fame, and the only player in history who had the five-year waiting period waived. In 1973, the Major League Baseball's Commissioner's Award was renamed the Roberto Clemente Award, which is awarded annually to a player that represents the game of baseball with dignity and serves as an ambassador to the community.

Luis Aparicio is considered one of baseball's all-time best shortstops. He led the American League in stolen bases in 1956, winning the MLB Rookie of the Year award. He led the American League in stolen bases for a record nine consecutive seasons

(1956–64), a record that still stands today. Even with his great skills on the base path, it was Aparicio's ability in the field that was his most valuable service. Aparicio was inducted to the Baseball Hall of Fame in 1984, becoming the first Venezuelan player to achieve this honor. He was given the honor of throwing out the ceremonial first pitch at Game One of the 2005 World Series, the first World Series home game to be played by the White Sox since the 1959 World Series, when Aparicio was the starting shortstop.

Orlando Cepeda's brilliant career, which began in 1958, included nine seasons batting .300 or better and eight seasons of 25 or more home runs. He won Rookie of the Year honors for the San Francisco Giants. Cepeda was named MVP and helped lead the Cardinals to a World Championship in 1967.

After his retirement in 1975, Cepeda was recognized for his humanitarian efforts as an ambassador for baseball. However, in 1978 he was arrested on charges of trying to pick up 160 pounds of marijuana. He was sentenced to five years in prison and served 10 months. This haunted Cepeda for years and affected his Hall of Fame balloting until 1999 when he was elected into the Hall by the Veterans Committee.

Juan Marichal was unquestionably one of the greatest pitchers the game as ever seen. In 1963 he had a breakout year, going 25-8 and leading the league in victories while totaling 248 strikeouts and a 2.41 ERA. Marichal was a dominant pitcher during the 1960s in which he won 191 games, more than any other major league pitcher.

For his career, Marichal started 457 games and worked more than 300 innings three times. Commanding excellent control, he had 2,303 strikeouts with only 709 walks, a strikeout-to-walk ratio of about 3.25 to 1. This ranks among the top 20 pitchers of all time. Marichal amassed 243 wins, including 52 shutouts and was named to nine All-Star teams.

I sat with Tony Pérez on a panel during MLB's Civil Rights Weekend in 2009 in Cincinnati. The audience of 500 showed the adulation that he had earned during his career there. He played 23 seasons of Major League Baseball, debuting with the Cincinnati Reds in 1964 becoming a key cog in Cincinnati's "Big Red Machine," the nickname given to the Reds for their dominance in the National League from 1970–1976 in which they won four National

League pennants and two World Series titles. By the end of his career, Pérez finished with a lifetime .279 batting average, 379 home runs, 1,652 RBI, and 2,732 hits. Pérez ranks first all-time among players from Latin America in career RBIs.

Born in the Panama Canal Zone in 1945, Rod Carew moved to New York in 1961. Six years later, he made the majors and was named American League Rookie of the Year. He was an amazingly consistent hitter with a .300 or better batting average for 15 straight years. He got his 3,000th hit in 1985. He was elected to the Hall of Fame on the first ballot in 1991 and became a coach in 1992.

Roberto "Bobby" Ávila introduced baseball to millions of Mexicans during his career. As a member of the Cleveland Indians, Ávila became only the fourth Mexican native to play in Major League Baseball and the first to have great success in the league. He was an excellent second baseman and clutch hitter. He had a .978 fielding percentage during his time with the Indians. Ávila helped the Indians win the American League pennant in 1954 when he became the first Latino to earn the American League batting crown with a .341 average. He batted over .300 three times in his 11-year career.

Saturnino "Minnie" Miñoso was the first black player in White Sox history and the first black Latino in Major League Baseball. In 1948 Miñoso was signed by Cleveland Indians owner Bill Veeck. Miñoso made his brief MLB debut with the Indians in 1949. He was one of the best players of the 1950s. He also made his mark by being the only player to compete in pro baseball in seven decades. Miñoso hit over .300 in eight seasons and made seven All-Star Game appearances. He also collected three Gold Gloves for his play in left field. He finished his major league career with 1,963 hits, 205 stolen bases, a .298 batting average, a .389 on-base percentage, and a .459 slugging percentage.

Miñoso was not done yet and played in the Mexican League for more than a decade. In 1973, he had a .265 average, 12 home runs, and 83 RBIs in 120 games in the league. In 2003, at the age of 77, Miñoso made an appearance with the St. Paul Saints, becoming the first player ever to play in seven different decades.

Albert Pujols is the only baseball player in history to hit 30-plus home runs in each of his first nine seasons. He is an eight-time

All-Star, has been named the National League MVP three times, and has claimed one World Series title. In May 2009, the *Sporting News* named Pujols the No. 1 player in baseball. In 2004 he led the Cardinals to the World Series, before being swept by the Boston Red Sox. In 2006, Pujols would lead the Cardinals back to the World Series, this time winning the Championship in five games versus the Detroit Tigers. By the accounts of many writers and historians, Pujols may go down as the greatest baseball player ever.

Latino Managers in MLB

Mike González's career as the first Latino manager in Major League Baseball lasted only 21 games over two seasons. Even so, he is undoubtedly a pioneering figure in the history of minority participation in the sport. He managed the Cardinals for the last 16 games of the 1938 season and for nine games during the 1940 season. More important than the number of games he managed was the symbolism behind his position as González proved that Latinos could move off the field and into positions of leadership in the league.

Al López became the first full-time Latino manager in Major League baseball history after the Cleveland Indians hired the former player in 1951. The 111 wins by the 1954 Indians was an American League record that stood for more than four decades until 1998. López became the Chicago White Sox manager in 1957, winning the pennant in 1959 with the "Go-Go" White Sox. López managed the White Sox for another six seasons before retiring after the 1965 season.

López finished his career with a 1410-1004 record, which as of the beginning of the 2009 season ranked him 22nd all-time in victories and his .584 winning percentage ranks eighth all-time. In 1977, López was inducted into the National Baseball Hall of Fame in Cooperstown, NY.

First Latino Manager to Win a World Series

Ozzie Guillén grew up in Venezuela, had a good career in MLB, and became the first Latino manager to win a World Series after his 2005 White Sox won their first American League pennant in 37 years and their first World Series title since 1917. The Sox won 11 of 12 postseason games and swept the Houston Astros in Guillén's second year at the helm. The Baseball Writers Association of American voted Guillén the 2005 American League Manager of the Year. After his first year with the White Sox in 1985, he was named American League Rookie of the Year. In 16 seasons, he was considered as one of the best shortstops of his generation.

Executive and Pioneer

Alex Pompez is credited for much of the Latino presence in baseball beginning early in the 20th century and running through the 1960's. The son of Cuban immigrants, his first team was the New York Cubans, which he formed in 1916 for a tour of the United States and the Caribbean. Among the players Pompez is credited with signing either directly or through his network are Orlando Cepeda, Willie McCovey, Monte Irvin, Juan Marichal, Minnie Miñoso, Tony Oliva, Camilo Pascual, and the Alou brothers. He is also noted for getting Stoneham interested in signing Willie Mays. All of this earned him induction in the Baseball Hall of Fame in 2006.

First Latino General Manager in Major League Baseball

Omar Minaya, of Dominican descent, but who was mostly raised in Queens, NY, became MLB's first Latino General Manager at the helm of the Montreal Expos. As the general manager of the Expos, Minaya was able to recruit star players who helped the 2002 team finish second in the National League East with a record of 83-79. In 2004, Minaya began serving as the New York Mets' general manager. He added stars like Pedro Martínez and Carlos Beltrán, among others. The Mets finished the 2005 seasons with 83 wins. The next season, Minaya's decisions continued to pay dividends as the Mets won the National League East and finished with 97 wins, tied for the best record in Major League baseball.

First Latino Majority Owner in MLB

In 2003, Arturo Moreno, a fourth-generation Mexican-American, purchased the Anaheim Angels to become the first Latino majority owner in Major League Baseball history and the first Latino to own a major sports team in the United States. A master marketer, Moreno challenged the L.A. Dodgers' local supremacy and put up the money to build a fine team. The Angels won the American League West for the first time since 1986 and the team drew 3.4 million fans to Angels Stadium, behind only the New York Yankees and Dodgers. The Angels have since won the AL West in 2005 and from 2007–2009.

As you can see, these key figures exclude virtually the entire country-by-country list compiled by Menéndez. An entire other book could be written about them. Latinos may not have taken over baseball in America but they surely have made it a richer game.

José Méndez

Star of the National Baseball Hall of Fame

by Horacio Ruiz

There were all sorts of comparisons for Cuban pitcher José Méndez. In the early 1900s, Méndez became the first baseball legend from Cuba, bringing comparisons to the greatest major league players including Grover Alexander and Walter Johnson. He was called "The Black Mathewson," a reference to all-time pitching great Christy Mathewson, one of the first five players inducted into the National Baseball Hall of Fame. Nicknames served to do nothing more than fill the imaginations of baseball fans that would never get to see Méndez play. Méndez was also called "El Diamante Negro," or the

Courtesy of the National Baseball Hall of Fame Library, Cooperstown, NY.

"Black Diamond," and because the nickname was a giveaway for the color of his skin, there was no hope that Méndez would ever play in the major leagues. It still didn't stop Méndez from leaving a lasting impression on the game.

In his professional debut in the Cuban League in 1908, Méndez went 9-0, helping lead his Almendares Blues team to the Cuban League pennant. In the summer of the same year, he made his debut in the United States with the Brooklyn Royal Giants, an independent baseball team composed of dark-skinned players. Mendéz finished his first season in the Cuban Winter League with a 15-6 record. Méndez's lore was cemented in the fall of 1908 in a series against the majors' Cincinnati Reds.

The Reds traveled to Cuba for an exhibition tour against teams that included Méndez's Blues. The Cincinnati Reds would easily take the series against the Habana Reds, but against the Blues, the

Cincinnati squad could only win one game out of five. Méndez was the biggest reason for frustrating Cincinnati, holding them scoreless for all 25 innings he pitched against them. By the end of the series he had allowed Reds batters eight hits and three walks while striking out 24 Reds batters.

Hall of Fame manager Miller Huggins, at the time the second baseman for the Reds, proclaimed that Méndez was "something marvelous"[1] and third baseman Hans Lobert said that Méndez threw pitches that he "really never could see."[2] In 1910 and again in 1911, Méndez would beat Mathewson in a ten-inning duel. The New York Giants traveled to Cuba under the guidance of manager John McGraw. By the end of their exhibition series, McGraw said he would have signed Méndez for $50,000 if he were white. Mary McGraw, McGraw's wife, called Méndez the "black Mathewson."

"He always pitched against the Giants," Mary wrote of Méndez in her memoirs, *The Real McGraw.* "Without mincing words, John bemoaned the failure of baseball, himself included, to cast aside custom or unwritten law, or whatever it was, and sign a player on ability alone, regardless of race or color."[3]

Méndez would go on to beat Hall of Famers Eddie Plank, Charles Bender, and Smokey Joe Williams later in his career. In 1913, he pitched a no-hitter against the Birmingham Barons. He played all of 1910 in Cuba, pitching in the summer and winter leagues, and compiling an 18-2 record. Through 1914 Méndez had a 62-17 career record in Cuba, but early in the 1914–15 season he injured his arm and would never again pitch regularly. Méndez finished 8-7 against major league competition. Unable to pitch regularly, Méndez made the switch to shortstop, while also playing every position on the field except catcher.

From 1912 to 1916, Méndez played for the All-Nations of Kansas City, a racially mixed roster composed of African-Americans, Caucasians, Native-Americans, Latinos, and Japanese players. The All-Nations would play around the country, mostly against semi-pro teams and the top Negro League teams of the time.

At the same time, one of Méndez's contemporaries, the light-skinned Cuban pitching great Dolf Luque, was traveling around the United States playing in major league venues. Luque, who dealt with discrimination on and off the field had his finest year in 1923 with the Cincinnati Reds when he led the league with 27 wins and a 1.93 ERA. Upon his return home to Havana, they held a celebration for Luque, who spotted Méndez in the grandstands. Luque approached Méndez and told him, "This parade should have been for you. Certainly, you're a far better pitcher than I am."[4]

Some of Méndez's greatest success came as a player-manager with the Negro League's Kansas City Monarchs from 1920–26. No longer able to pitch more than in a few spot starts and relief appearances, he stepped to the field as a shortstop, where he was one of the finest defenders in the Negro Leagues. As the player-manager, he led the Monarchs to three consecutive Negro National League pennants from 1923–25. In the 1924 Negro Leagues World Series against Hilldale, Méndez pitched in four games and went 2-0 record with a miniscule 1.42 ERA. In the last and deciding game of the series, the only game he started, Méndez threw a shutout. Before the game he was warned by doctors not to pitch because of recent surgical procedures performed on his arm, but Méndez replied, "I don't care. I want to win today."[5] Baseball writer Carl Beckwith would write about Méndez's clutch performance:

> The temperature had dropped oodles of degrees between Sunday evening and Monday noon and fur coats predominated in the stands. . . . Murmurs of discontent and surprise created a hum when Méndez was announced as pitcher for the Westerners. It was not hot enough for Joe so they thought. But they changed their minds. For inning after inning Jose kept the Easterners popping up or grounding out. Not a man reached second, and only four reached first. It is improbable that Méndez will ever pitch another such game. He wasn't there for a strike out record; just 'cut' any kind of way was what he wanted. He kept the Easterners popping up, hitting long flies, or grounding out all afternoon. And therein lies the answer to the win. He kept the ball, as cold as it was, under his control always.[6]

Méndez would finish his Cuban League career with a 76-28 record. His .731 winning percentage is the highest among players with a minimum of 40 wins in Cuban League history. He died in Havana on October 31, 1928.

In 1939, he was in the first group of players elected to the Cuban Baseball Hall of Fame. In 2006, Méndez was elected into the National Baseball Hall of Fame in Cooperstown, NY, where admirers can also see the Hall of Fame plaque of Mathewson, the white Méndez.

Notes

1. David Skinner, "Havana and Key West: Jose Mendez And The Great Scoreless Streak Of 1908," *The National Pastime*. January 1, 2004.

2. Ibid.

3. John B. Holway, "Cuba's Black Diamond," *The Baseball Research Journal* Archive, http://research.sabr.org/brj/index.php/cubas-black-diamond.

4. Thomas Harding,. "Mendez Dominated As Pitcher, Manager," February 9, 2006. Accessed May 11, 2009. MLB.com http://mlb.mlb.com/news/article.jsp?ymd=20060208&content_id=1308711&vkey=news_mlb&fext=.jsp&c_id=mlb

5. Lawrence D. Hogan, *Shades of Glory: The Negro Leagues and the Story of African-American Baseball*, (Washington, DC: National Geographic, 2006).

6. Ibid.

Cristóbal Torriente

Star of the National Baseball Hall of Fame

by Horacio Ruiz

Cristóbal Torriente earned the nickname "The Cuban Strongman" for his tremendous power. In the winter of 1921, Torriente would display his strength in front of Babe Ruth and the Major League's New York Giants. The Giants, touring Cuba for a nine-game exhibition series, added Ruth to their roster on a loan from the New York Yankees. During a game in the series, Torriente hit two home runs in his first two at-bats. On his third at-bat, with two men on base, the mighty Ruth came out of right field to pitch to Torriente. Ruth had been a very good pitcher for the Boston Red Sox, finishing with 94 career wins and a 2.28 earned run average. Torriente would hit a double off the "Babe" to drive in both runners on base. Ruth would then strike out the next three batters.

For the series, Torriente batted .378 to Ruth's .345, and he hit three homeruns to Ruth's two. Torriente's team, the Almendares Blues, also won the exhibition series versus the Giants. After the series, he would earn another moniker as "The Cuban Babe Ruth."

"Tell Torriente and Méndez that if they could play with me in the Major Leagues, we would win the pennant by July and go fishing for the rest of the season,"[1] said Ruth following the exhibition, also noting the pitching of José Méndez.

Frankie Frisch, another Hall of Famer on the tour, also took notice. "[Torriente] hit a ground ball by me, and you know, it's one of those things—look in the glove, it might be there," Frisch said. "It dug a hole about a foot deep on its way to left field. And I'm glad I wasn't in front of it! . . . I'd like to whitewash him and bring him up."[2]

Of course, there was no way that Torriente could be whitewashed. It was Frisch's way of saying that as good as the Cuban left fielder was, he could never play in the Major Leagues. Giants manager John McGraw considered luring the light-brown Torriente into the big leagues, but he could not have signed him because the rough texture of his hair gave away his racial composition.

Torriente didn't need the Major Leagues to showcase his skills. He started his professional baseball career with the Cuban Stars in

1913, a team of Cuban baseball players that played in the United States' Negro Leagues. Born in Cienfuegos, Cuba in 1893, Torriente built himself up by carrying heavy artillery while serving in the army. He would soon become one of the most powerful and dangerous Negro League players ever. In 1916, at the age of 20, Torriente had one of his finest seasons, leading the Cuban league in home runs, triples, and stolen bases while batting above .400.

In 1918, Torriente signed with the Negro League's Chicago American Giants, for whom Torriente would play from 1918–1925. Starting in 1920, the first year of the newly formed Negro National League, Torriente would lead the American Giants to three consecutive championships. He hit for averages of .411, .338, and .342 during the three-year championship run. He won the league batting title in 1920 and again in 1923 with a .412 average. Torriente was renowned for his ability to hit any pitch, his stellar defense in the outfield, and his speed. His power was Ruth-esque.

"I've seen a lot of home runs," said Jelly Gardner, a Negro League great. "But I think Torriente hit the longest one I ever saw. The American Giants had a fence there over 400 feet, and the ball went out of there on a line. The fence was about 20 feet tall. It didn't just get out, it went way out; center field, dead center."[3]

But Torriente's taste for the nightlife would doom him. Rube Foster, a Hall of Fame owner and pioneer of the Negro Leagues, would keep money from Torriente when he lingered at the bars. In 1926, Torriente was traded to the Kansas City Monarchs, in large part because of his excessive drinking. Torriente would play one year with the Monarchs and then was traded to the Detroit Stars where he played for two seasons from 1927–1928. After his stint with the Stars, Torriente was relegated to playing for semi-pro teams. He signed with Gilkerson's Union Giants in 1930, an independent all-black baseball team. He would play another year in 1932, for the Atlanta Black Crackers and the Cleveland Cubs.

For his career, Torriente ranks 11th on the Negro League all-time list in RBI's with 309, 12th in slugging percentage with a .517 mark, and 16th in total bases with 1,055. He finished his career with a .338 batting average versus black pitching, and a .311 average versus Major League pitchers. In 1952, Torriente was named to the all-black team by the editors of the *Pittsburgh Courier*. In describing him, the paper said he was "a prodigious hitter, a rifle-armed thrower, and a tower of strength on the defense." They also described him as having "deceptive speed and the ability to cover worlds of territory, from the right field foul line to deep right center. He was one of the best bad ball hitters in baseball and could hit equally well to all fields."

In 1938, an impoverished Torriente died in New York City at the age of 44. His struggles with alcoholism finally withered the baseball great, who died of tuberculosis. His body was sent to Cuba in a coffin draped with the Cuban flag. In 1939, he was elected posthumously to the Cuban Baseball Hall of Fame. How could Torriente have known, dying alone in New York City, that he would be inducted into the National Baseball Hall of Fame in 2006. Torriente's impact on the game can best be summed up by a quote from Negro League player and manager Dave Malarcher relaying what the great Negro League manager C.I. Taylor once told him.

"He was a powerful man," said Marlacher of Torriente. "C.I. Taylor said if he was standing on the street and saw Torriente go by, he would say, 'There goes a ball club.' And he was, too."[4]

Notes

1. Brian Wilson, "Good Enough For the Majors: Torriente Admired By Major Leaguers," http://mlb.mlb.com/mlb/history/mlb_negro_leagues_profile.jsp?player=torriente_cristobal (accessed April, 7, 2009).

2. John Holway, "The One-Man Team—Cristóbal Torriente," *The Baseball Research Journal* Archive, http://research.sabr.org/brj/index.php/cristobal-torriente

3. Ibid.

4. Ibid.

Martín Dihigo

Star of the National Baseball Hall of Fame

by Horacio Ruiz

Who is the greatest baseball player of all-time? If you ask Hall of Famer and Negro League legend Buck Leonard, it was not a player from the major leagues or from the United States. The best player of all-time—anywhere—according to Leonard, was Martín Dihigo of Cuba.

"I'd say he was the best ball-player of all time, black or white," Leonard said. "He could do it all. He is my ideal ball player, makes no difference what race either. If he's not the greatest, I don't know who is. You take your Ruths, Cobbs, and DiMaggios. Give me Dihigo and I bet I'd beat you almost every time."[1]

Dihigo was legendary for being able to play all nine positions at an All-Star level. He was called "The Immortal" and "El Maestro," and even to this day, baseball fans travel to Dihigo's grave in Cruces, Cuba to pay their respects. Dihigo was as dangerous with his bat as he was with his arm, and though he would make his appearances in the United States with several Negro League teams, he would also add to his lore by playing in the Cuban and Mexican Leagues where he was adored as much as he was revered. The 6'3" Dihigo was known for his terrific strength and speed, as well as for his exceptionally strong pitching arm.

Dihigo made his professional debut as a 16-year-old in the 1922–23 Cuban winter league as a substitute infielder. He made his debut in the United States in 1923 with the Negro League's Cuban Stars East as a first baseman. He struggled initially as a hitter, but he was already excelling as a pitcher. In a 1923 Cuban League game,

Dihigo outpitched another Cuban great, Dolf Luque, in a 1-0 ball-game. Luque was coming off a career season with the major leagues' Cincinnati Reds where he led the league in wins and earned run average. During the next two years, Dihigo would develop into one of the most versatile players in the history of the game, and he would refine his swing to also become one of the most feared hitters.

From 1923 through 1936, and then for one season in 1945 as a player-manager, Dihigo would play in the Negro Leagues for the Cuban Stars and then with the Homestead Grays, Hilldale Daisies, Baltimore Black Sox, and the New York Cubans. Dihigo would lead the Negro Leagues in home runs in 1926 and 1927, and finish his career in the Negro Leagues with a .307 batting average and a .511 slugging percentage. As a pitcher, he finished his Negro League career with a 2.92 earned run average and a 26-19 record in 55 games that he appeared in.

Dihigo's talent created a demand for him to play across all of Latin America. In 1938, Dihigo had perhaps his finest season. Playing in the Mexican League, Dihigo compiled an 18-2 record and led the league with a 0.90 ERA, while also winning the batting title with a .387 mark. In that same year in the Mexican League, Dihigo participated in a highly-anticipated pitching match-up against Satchel Paige. Paige, who was playing with a sore arm, pitched six scoreless innings before losing his control in the seventh inning to give Dihigo's team a 1-0 lead. Paige was removed for a pinch-hitter and his team later tied up the game against Dihigo to make it 1-1. In the bottom of the ninth, Dihigo ended the game by hitting a home run and giving his team a 2-1 victory.

Dihigo played 24 seasons in Cuba (1922–29, 1931–46). For the years that are documented in his Cuban League career, he had nine seasons batting above .300, to finish with a career .291 batting average. His pitching record is 93-48 from 1935–46. Dihigo's Mexican League totals include a career .317 batting average over 10 seasons and a 119-57 record as a pitcher. Dihigo is also credited with pitching the first no-hitter in Mexican League history. He would also later throw no-hitters in Puerto Rico and in Venezuela. For his career, spanning across several leagues in different countries, Dihigo is credited with more than 260 wins as a pitcher.

Throughout his playing career, Dihigo inspired a new wave of Cuban players, including Orestes "Minnie" Miñoso. He also earned the admiration of major leaguers that played in Latin America during the winter. As Miñoso recounts:

"Martín used to be my favorite, my idol before I played baseball professionally. I remember when I was a kid, I used to go buy a newspaper for three cents to see what happened in Havana, because I'm not from Havana. I used to live 80 miles from Havana, so I used to buy this newspaper to see what Martín Dihigo did the day before. I used to spend one penny to buy a sweet coconut, one penny for salt crackers and that used to be my lunch and the other pennies to buy the newspaper to see what happened with Martín. When I was a rookie, I remember one time I got a hit off him when he was manager and still pitching. I'll never forget it, with the bases loaded I hit one between right and center, a three-base hit. We scored about seven or eight runs off him and I said to myself, 'That was my idol.' But what could I do? He was one of the best ballplayers Cuba made. Some people try to include me in that group, I said, 'No way, you will never hear me put myself together with this guy.'"[2]

Hall of Famer Johnny Mize, who starred for the St. Louis Cardinals and New York Giants, before finishing his career with the New York Yankees, also echoed the sentiments of Miñoso and Leonard, saying: "The greatest player I ever saw was a black man. He's in the Hall of Fame, although not a lot of people have heard of him. His name is Martín Dihigo. I played with him in Santo Domingo in winter ball in 1943. He was the manager. He was the only guy I ever saw who could play all nine positions, run, and was a switch hitter. I thought I was having a pretty good year myself down there and they were walking him to get to me."[3]

After retiring from baseball, Dihigo became the Minister of Sports in Cuba until his death in 1965. At the time of his death, Fidel Castro's Cuba mourned Dihigo as a fallen hero of the Cuban Revolution and they gave him a hero's funeral. The government tried to distance itself of Cuba's sporting accomplishments prior to the Castro regime; ironic as it was that Dihigo was Minister of Sports for 12 years.

In 1977, he was the first Cuban elected into the National Baseball Hall of Fame in Cooperstown, NY. He is also the only person to have been elected to baseball halls of fame in five different countries: Cuba, the United States, Mexico, Venezuela, and the Dominican Republic.

In a poll taken in the early 1980s by former Negro League players and Negro League historians, Dihigo was elected to the first team all-time black All-Star team as a second baseman. Yet, Dihigo's greatness and versatility on the baseball field is such that former Negro League player and manager of the Kansas City Monarchs, Buck O'Neill, said if he could put Dihigo at any position, he would put him at pitcher. Dihigo's son, speaking for "El Maestro" said his father preferred playing center field best of all.

Notes

1. Peter C. Bjarkman, *A History of Cuban Baseball, 1864–2006*, (McFarland & Company, Inc., Publishers: Jefferson, North Carolina. 2007) p.30.

2. Robert Cassidy, "Cuba's Martin Dihigo: The Immortal. April 7, 2008," www.News day.com. http://www.newsday.com/sports/ny-spcuba-dihigo0407,0,6189096.story

3. "Martin 'El Maestro' Dihigo," http://www.theforgottenleagues.com/martin.htm.

Vernon "Lefty" Gómez

Star of the National Baseball Hall of Fame

by Chris Kamke

> "I want to thank all my teammates who scored so many runs and Joe DiMaggio, who ran down so many of my mistakes." [1]
>
> —Lefty

Lefty Gómez was a pitcher and a little bit of a screwball. Gómez was born on November 26, 1908, in Rodeo, CA. On the mound he stood 6'2" but weighed only 173 pounds. A highly skilled pitcher, he was known not only for his pitch velocity, nasty curveball, and high leg kick, but also for his wackiness. However, his propensity for practical jokes and self-deprecating wit never overshadowed his ability as a pitcher. The left hander was undoubtedly one of the best pitchers in the 1930s.

Gómez earned the nickname "El Goofy" for his zany behavior that differentiated him from the decorous rosters of the Yankees in the 1930s. Gómez once held up a game to watch a plane flying overhead. When he came to the bench at the end of the inning, Yankee manager Joe McCarthy howled, "Whaddaya tryin' to do out there, ya nut! Are ya tryin' to lose the game for us?"[2] To which Gómez replied, "Listen, Joe, I've never seen a pitcher lose a game by not throwing the ball."[3] For the record, the Yankees won the game by the score of 18 to 4.

Gómez's career as a pitcher was slightly the result of an accident. His father, Francisco Gómez, was a rodeo performer who settled in Rodeo, CA. At a young age Gómez hoped to be a rodeo performer as well. Luckily for the Yankees, Gómez fell off a horse while training and broke his right arm. It was then that Gómez took to throwing baseballs with his left.

A six-time World Series champion with the Yankees (1932, 1936, 1937, 1938, 1939, 1941), Gómez's 6-0 win-loss record in the World Series makes him the winningest World Series pitcher without a loss in Major League history. Included in those six wins were four complete games. Gómez made seven consecutive All-Star teams (1933–39), making five starts and recording three wins. He was the starting pitcher for the American League in the first ever All-Star game held in 1933. Never known for his talents with a bat, he made history during that game when he singled and drove in the first run in All-Star Game history. Gómez won the pitching Triple Crown in 1934 and 1937 by leading the majors in wins, strikeouts, and earned run average. His best season was possibly in 1934 when he posted a 26-5 win-loss record, 158 strikeouts, a 2.33 ERA, six shutouts, and 25 complete games.

Having suffered multiple arm injuries during his career Gómez's fastball lost its effectiveness and he was forced to retool his pitching style from power to finesse. Even though the transition wasn't smooth, the always colorful pitcher inserted humor into the situation. "I'm throwing as hard as I ever did, but the ball is just not getting there as fast,"[4] he said. Having spent basically his entire career with the Yankees, Gómez can call Lou Gehrig, Babe Ruth, and Joe DiMaggio teammates. During his 14-year career, he was a four-time 20 game winner, amassed a career record of 189-102, 28 shutouts, and 173 complete games.

In 1962 the American Baseball Coaches Association started presenting the annual Lefty Gómez Award. Considered one of the most prestigious awards in amateur baseball, it is awarded to an individual who has distinguished themselves amongst their peers and has contributed significantly to amateur baseball in America.

Gómez's World Series record proved that he was undoubtedly a big game pitcher. Missing games as a result of his multiple injuries, he failed to reach 200 wins in his career. This is probably what kept him out of the Hall for so long. However in 1972, Gómez was elected into the Major League Baseball Hall of Fame by the Veterans Committee.

At the age of 80, the Hall of Fame pitcher who starred with the grand New York Yankee teams of the 1930s and gained a reputation as one of baseball's great personalities, died of congestive heart failure. Famous not only for his ability as a pitcher, but also as a fun-loving, lighthearted ballplayer, Gómez loved the game and life. Known for his great wit, Gómez often remarked, "I'd rather be lucky than good."[5] He was both.

Notes

1. "Lefty Gomez," 2008 Cooperstown Chronicles, Lester's Legends. http://lesters legends.com/?p=2009 (accessed April 6, 2009).

2. C. Paul Rogers III, (2001). "Lefty Gomez: the Life of the Party," Elysian Fields Quarterly. http://www.efqreview.com/NewFiles/v18n1/onhistoricalground.html (accessed April 6, 2009).

3. Ibid.

4. "Lefty Gomez," 2008 Cooperstown Chronicles,Lester's Legends. http://lesters legends.com/?p=2009 (accessed April 6, 2009).

5. "Lefty Gomez," CMG Worldwide. http://www.cmgww.com/baseball/gomez/fact .html (accessed April 6, 2009).

Roberto Clemente

Star of the National Baseball Hall of Fame

by Horacio Ruiz

On December 23, 1972, the Nicaraguan capital of Managua experienced a 6.2 magnitude earthquake that killed an estimated 5,000 people. Managua was in utter ruin and chaos—the smell of burning and rotting flesh permeated the capital. People, countries, and charitable agencies from across the globe sent relief supplies. But it was reported that the government was hoarding the supplies and keeping it out of the hands and mouths of those in need. Roberto Clemente, who had already sent plane loads of supplies from his native Puerto Rico, caught word of the corruption and determined that he had to personally hand out the supplies to the Nicaraguans in need. Clemente's friends and family pleaded with him to wait, to at least spend the New Year at home. But Clemente insisted that the need in Nicaragua was greater than his own. On New Year's Eve in 1972, Clemente took off on an outdated and worn-down plane that plunged into the ocean within minutes. The plane shattered upon impact and his body was never found. In an instant, the most celebrated and beloved Latino in baseball history was gone. It was an incomprehensible moment, because the world lost one of its most electrifying athletes and one of its most compassionate human beings.

Only one month before, Nicaraguans had fallen in love with Clemente, and in return, Clemente had fallen in love with the Nicaraguans. In November of 1972 Clemente was in Managua managing the Puerto Rican baseball team for the twentieth amateur world championships. It was hoped that his presence would be able to lift the young Puerto Rican players over the favored American and Cuban teams. In the mornings, Clemente would exchange dollar bills at the Intercontinental Hotel, a pyramid-like structure in the middle of downtown Managua, for a bag full of coins. He would make his way through the streets, handing out fistfuls of coins to the poor men, women, and children who lived on the streets.

The Puerto Rican team did not play up to Clemente's standards, but he vowed to manage the team in the following year's tournament. During road trips in the major league season, Clemente made a habit of making unannounced visits to children in hospitals. He would organize a stack of fan mail by every city he visited and would see to it that when he had the time, he'd visit his youngest fans. Before leaving Managua, he befriended a twelve-year-old boy named Julio Parrales who had lost one leg and badly injured another while playing on a railroad track. Clemente raised the 700 dollars needed to buy Parrales a prosthetic leg and to teach him to learn to walk again by having every Puerto Rican player donate 10 dollars, securing a 50 dollar donation from the Cuban team, and Clemente making up the rest. Clemente left Nicaragua by telling Parrales that the next time he saw him, Parrales would be the Puerto Rican team's bat boy. But Clemente would never make it back to Nicaragua.

Clemente was born in the San Anton neighborhood of Carolina, Puerto Rico. Clemente's father, Melchor, was the supervisor at a sugarcane processing company and his mother, Luisa, made money by sewing and making food for Melchor's workers in the factory. The Clementes were not poor—they had all their basic needs and a roof over their heads—but they were a part of the Puerto Rican working-class, relying on family and their extended resources.

As a teenager, Clemente showed promise in track and field but it was on the baseball field that his talents shone through. When he was 14-years old, Clemente was playing on a softball team being sponsored by a rice-packing company. The next year, he would be playing with an amateur baseball team in Carolina named the Juncos Mules. In 1952, Clemente caught the eye of Pedrin Zorrilla, the owner of the Santurce Cangrejeros (Crabbers), one of Puerto Rico's professional baseball teams. Zorrilla was impressed by Clemente's cracking hits, his tremendous fielding ability, and famously strong throwing arm. Just barely eighteen-years old, Clemente signed with Santurce in 1952 to become the youngest team member. A little more than a year later, Clemente had caught the eyes of Brooklyn Dodgers scout Al Campanis. The Dodgers offered Clemente a $5,000 salary for one year that included a $10,000 signing bonus.

While Clemente had been offered a higher salary from other teams, he wanted to play for the Dodgers out of loyalty to Zorrilla, who had a strong relationship with the Dodgers. The Dodgers understood they had signed a great talent in Clemente, but their biggest motive in the signing was to keep him away from the New York Giants to break up the possibility of a Giants outfield tandem of Clemente and Willie Mays. Clemente would become frustrated for the entire 1954 season that he spent with the Dodgers' top farm club, the Montreal Royals. The Royals rarely played him, instead choosing to follow the orders of the Dodgers front office to keep him on the bench, hidden from other scouts so that Clemente would not be taken after his one season with the Dodgers in the next year's supplemental draft. But Clemente's greatness was evident in his pregame batting and fielding routines. Scouts knew all about Clemente, and while the Dodgers could keep him from playing regularly for one season, they could not hide him forever. The Pittsburgh Pirates took Clemente with the first overall pick in the supplemental draft of unprotected minor leaguers on November 22, 1954. The Pirates general manager at the time was Branch Rickey, who had signed Jackie Robinson to the Dodgers more than nine years earlier to break baseball's color barrier.

Clemente reported for the Pirates' spring training on February 28, 1955 in Fort Myers, FL. In Fort Myers, Clemente, who was dark-skinned, went through the same indignities as his African-American teammates when he could not eat in the same restaurants or stay in the same hotels as his white counterparts. Clemente, a very proud man, could not tolerate being treated any differently, especially since racism was not at the social fabric of his native Puerto Rico or as openly displayed as it was in the United States with its *Whites Only* or *Colored* signs. Even so, Clemente endured it because he had to, but he did not keep quiet.

"They say, 'Roberto, you better keep your mouth shut because they will ship you back,'" Clemente said. "This is something that from the first day, I said to myself: 'I am the minority group. I am from the poor people. I represent the poor people. I represent the common people of America. So I am going to be treated as a human being. I don't want to be treated like a Puerto Rican, or a black, or nothing like that. I want to be treated like any person that comes for a job.' Every person who comes for a job, no matter what type of race or color he is, if he does the job he should be treated like whites."[1]

At 20 years of age, Clemente made the Pittsburgh Pirates roster for the 1955 season, and spent the rest of his career with the club. Clemente would struggle in his first season with the Pirates, playing in 124 games and finishing with five home runs, 47 runs batted in, a .255 batting average, and .284 on-base percentage. The next year, Clemente appeared in 147 games and finished third in National League with a .311 batting average, sixth in doubles with 30, and seventh in singles with 125. But Clemente had a largely mediocre statistical major league career through his first five seasons. It wasn't until 1960 that a 25-year-old Clemente would play like the ballplayer that the world would come to know him by. That season, Clemente finished with 179 hits, 16 home runs, 94 RBI, a .314 batting average, and a .357 OBP. In 1960, Clemente made the first of 12 All-Star Game appearances and finished the season eighth in MVP voting. Perhaps Clemente's greatest contribution was his play in the 1960 World Series in which he batted .310 as the Pirates faced a powerful New York Yankee lineup. The Pirates would win the World Series for the first time since 1925 in seven games against the Yankees with a walk-off home run by Bill Mazeroski. In 1961, Clemente came back with a vengeance, leading the league with a .351 batting average and the first of 12 consecutive Gold Glove awards for his play and his unmatched throwing ability from the outfield. Throughout the 1960s, Clemente became one of the most feared hitters and one of the most feared defenders for his ability to throw a base runner out from any part of his outfield position.

Clemente would find that success did not lead to an adoring press. Clemente was often engaged in bitter fights with the media for the way they quoted him in newspapers. It was true that he spoke with a heavy accent, as is the case for anyone learning a new language and adjusting to a new country. Clemente felt the press was purposely ridiculing him because he was Puerto Rican and a native Spanish speaker. In a 1961 *Sports Illustrated* article that highlighted

Clemente's approach to hitting, Clemente was quoted with the exaggerated diction of his accent, "Sometimes I seet on the bench, the fellows are sayeeng, 'He's gonna peetch curve now, now he's gonna throw fast ball,'" Clemente was quoted. "I move away down the bench because I don' want to know eet. I rather heet whatever he throw up there."[2] It was an insult to quote him that way. Catcher Don Leppert, a teammate of Clemente's for two seasons could see the way some members of the media treated him. "They tried to make a buffoon out of him," Leppert said. "I was sitting there one night when [Les Biederman of the *Pittsburgh Press*] was asking Clemente something, and Biederman had a little smirk on his face. I went off on Biederman: 'Why the hell don't you ask him questions in Spanish?' I didn't endear myself to Biederman, but didn't give a rat's ass, either. They tried to take advantage of every malaprop."[3]

There was obvious tension between the press and Clemente. Sometimes pride would get the best of Clemente, and he remained suspicious that despite his stellar play, he rarely received any attention in the end-of-season MVP voting. For years, Clemente put up some of the best numbers in baseball, but other than a fourth-place showing in the MVP voting in 1961, Clemente did not finish in the Top 5 when he thought he should have. Part of it was some of Clemente's insecurities, for there were some very deserving MVP award winners voted ahead of Clemente. In 1966, he finished with a .317 batting average, .360 on-base percentage, 29 home runs, and 119 RBI to win the National League's MVP. For Clemente, the award was a validation of his stature in the game and a welcome recognition from the press. With every accolade Clemente earned, he went back to Puerto Rico a hero. It was a scene that repeated itself for many years in his career.

In 1970, the Pirates lost to the Cincinnati Reds in three games in the National League Championship Series. In 1971, however, the Pirates swept the San Francisco Giants in four games to win the NL pennant and face the Baltimore Orioles in the World Series. The Orioles were the overwhelming favorites to win the championship, and it seemed all but likely after taking the first two games in the best-of-seven series. The Pirates battled back to take the series to a seventh and deciding game. The Pirates would win the Series with a 2-1 Game 7 victory. Clemente scored the Pirates' first run when he hit a solo home run in the top of the 4th inning to give the Pirates the early lead. For the series, Clemente had a .414 batting average, two home runs, and four RBI. He was named World Series MVP.

His legacy as one of the greatest players ever was sealed on a national stage, now the entire country knew about Clemente. *Sports Illustrated* writer William Leggett said that Clemente, ". . . proved again, as if he needed to, that on certain days he belongs in a higher league than anyone else. In a classic Series, he was the classic player."[4] In the joyous locker room, Clemente spoke to Pirates announcer Bob Prince and delivered a message to his parents, family, and millions of Spanish-speaking listeners across the globe, "En el día más grande de mi vida, para los nenes la bendición mía y que mis padres me echen la bendición. [In the most important day of my life, I give blessings to my boys and ask that my parents give their blessing] . . ."[5] In 1972, the Pirates would again make it to the NLCS but fell short to the Reds in five games. In the last regular season game of 1972, Clemente hit a double in his final at-bat to become the 11th player in the history of baseball to have 3,000 career hits. It would be the final regular-season at-bat of Clemente's career.

When Clemente and his wife, Vera, heard about the earthquake in Managua on December 23, 1972, they felt a sense of shock and sadness. "As soon as we heard about the earthquake early that morning we were very upset because we met some very nice people down there and felt like we lost someone—you know, a relative or someone. We felt very involved with this," said Vera Clemente. Immediately after the disaster, Clemente and his wife were busy raising funds and receiving donations so that they could send to Nicaragua. Clemente had leased a cargo plane for three-round trips from San Juan to Managua. Word reached Clemente that the Somoza regime in Nicaragua was hoarding supplies from all over the world, compelling him to personally tend to the victims. Clemente hastily leased another plane for his trip that was doomed to take his life.

Only two minutes after becoming airborne, the overloaded, ill-equipped, and ill-piloted plane crashed off of Punta Maldonado. Clemente's remains were never found. In the subsequent years, Clemente and his legacy would be remembered. The Baseball Writers Association of America held a special election and agreed to waive the mandatory five-year waiting period for Clemente. On March 20, 1973 Clemente was voted in to become the first Latino elected into the Hall of Fame, and the only player in history who had the five-year waiting period waived. In 1973, Major League Baseball's Commissioner's Award was renamed the Roberto Clemente Award, which is awarded annually to a player that represents the game of baseball with dignity and who is an ambassador in the community. In 1998, Pittsburgh renamed its Sixth Street Bridge, which spans from the city's north bank over the Allegheny River into Downtown Pittsburgh, the Roberto Clemente Bridge. When Ozzie Guillen of the White Sox became the first Latino manager to win a World Series, he revealed that he had a shrine in his home dedicated to Clemente. In 1974, the Roberto Clemente Sports City in the outskirts of San Juan, Puerto Rico, was established and today is a multi-sport athletic complex that spans 304 acres. Vera is the Chairperson of the Sports City, which is a realization of the dream Clemente had for serving the youth in Puerto Rico.

Clemente finished his career with a .317 batting average, 3,000 hits, 1,416 runs, and 1,305 RBI. His 12 Gold Gloves are tied with Willie Mays for the most ever by an outfielder. He was named to 12 All-Star teams.

The center of Managua was never fully rebuilt. Nicaragua saw too many deaths and too much destruction to ever be the same. Great people, even those helping, became victims of the earthquake that took away too many lives. Clemente did not have to go to Nicaragua, but was guided by what he once said, "Any time you have an opportunity to make a difference in this world and you don't, then you are wasting your time on Earth."[6]

Notes

1. David Maraniss, *Clemente: The Passion And Grace Of Baseball's Last Hero* (New York: Simon & Schuster Paperbacks, 2006), 70–71.

2. Tex Maule, "The Thinking Hitter," *Sports Illustrated*, June 5, 1961.

3. David Maraniss, *Clemente: The Passion And Grace Of Baseball's Last Hero*. (New York: Simon & Schuster Paperbacks, 2006), 173–174.

4. William Leggett, "Some Kind Of A Comeback," *Sports Illustrated*, October 25, 1971.

5. David Maraniss, *Clemente: The Passion And Grace Of Baseball's Last Hero* (New York: Simon & Schuster Paperbacks, 2006), 264.

6. Citifieldofdreams.com, "Santana Gets Nod For Roberto Clemente Award. "http://citifieldofdreams.com/2009/09/02/santana-gets-nod-for-roberto-clemente-award/ (accessed September 29, 2009).

Luis Aparicio

Star of the National Baseball Hall of Fame

by Chris Kamke

Courtesy of the National Baseball Hall of Fame Library, Cooperstown, NY.

"The prettiest sight in baseball to a manager," says White Sox manager Al López, "is the double play. It means two outs instead of one. It's as simple as that. You seldom win a pennant without good strength up the middle."[1]

When most people think of the game of baseball, the long ball is the first thing that comes to mind. In a game where power is king, Luis Aparicio never fit this mold. Regardless of his lack of power, Aparicio's incendiary speed, and dexterity in the field and on the base path allowed him to soar to stardom. Over his career which spanned from 1956 to 1973, he spent time with three major league teams. Aparicio played for the Chicago White Sox (1956–62, 1968–70), the Baltimore Orioles (1963–67) and the Boston Red Sox (1971–73). Playing the position of shortstop, like his father before him, Aparicio is considered one of baseball's all-time best players at that position.

Aparicio was born into a baseball family. His father, Luis Aparicio Sr. was a prominent shortstop in Venezuela as well as a co-owner of a Winter League team with his brother. Aparicio was born April 29, 1934 in Maracaibo, Venezuela. Attending public schools in Maracaibo, the 5'9" and 160 pound Aparicio finished growing while in high school. After completing only two years of high school, Aparicio started playing with an amateur baseball team in Caracas, Venezuela. Finding success right away, Aparicio and his team competed in the Latin American World Series. Playing shortstop, Aparicio had progressed enough to take his father's place as shortstop for the Maracaibo Gavilanes by the age of 19. That same year, he was discovered by the Chicago White Sox and moved to the United States to play in their farm system. He impressed in the minors and went on to lead the American League in stolen bases in 1956 on his way to winning Rookie of the Year honors. Over the next decade, Aparicio defined the ideal model of a shortstop through spray-hitting, slick fielding, and all-around speedy play. "Aparicio is so quick," said White Sox manager Al López, "getting the ball, throwing it, pivoting. He makes all of the moves and he makes them so quickly."[2] Aparicio's play left its mark in the record books. His speed made him one of the most feared base runners in the league. He led the American League in stolen bases for a record nine consecutive seasons (1956–64). This record still stands today.

Even with his great skills on the base path, it was Aparicio's ability in the field that was his most valuable service. An acrobatic, graceful shortstop with exceptional range and hands, Aparicio was a key player for the White Sox during the 1959 pennant race. The White Sox were a team that didn't have a lot of offensive power and so relied heavily on their ability to limit the opposing team offensively. "The double play is doing the job for Chicago," said George Kell, broadcaster for the Detroit Tigers. "Here is a club trying to win on pitching and defense and little power. Their double-play combination of Fox and Aparicio is the most important factor in Chicago's strength. They are the best in baseball. Chicago could hardly win without them."[3]

Despite not being stellar with his bat, Aparicio managed to be on base all the time. Once on base, as in the field, Aparicio's speed was unequal. Yankees manager Casey Stengel said, "Give him a walk and you might as well figure it's a double. He's gonna be on second on the next pitch."[4]

Aparicio had a down year in 1962 and was traded to the Baltimore Orioles the following season. Aparicio bounced back in Baltimore; finishing ninth in the MVP balloting in 1966 as he helped the Orioles reach and win the World Series. He returned to the White Sox for the 1968 season after being traded for Don Buford and had his best overall offensive season in 1970, batting .312 and scoring 86 runs. He put in three more seasons with the Boston Red Sox before retiring for good in 1973.

At the time of his retirement, Aparicio was the all-time leader for most games played, assists, and double plays by a MLB shortstop. Aparicio held the major league record of 2,581 games played at shortstop for 25 years when he was surpassed by fellow Venezuelan Omar Vizquel, in May 2008. Incredibly, Aparicio never played in a position other than shortstop.

Aparicio was inducted into the National Baseball Hall of Fame in 1984, becoming the first Venezuelan player to achieve this honor. That same year, the White Sox honored him by retiring his number 11. He was given the honor of throwing out the ceremonial first pitch at Game One of the 2005 World Series, the first World Series home game to be played at the White Sox stadium since the 1959 World Series, when Aparicio was the starting shortstop. He has also been inducted into the Hispanic Heritage Baseball Museum Hall of Fame.

Aparicio's career totaled 506 stolen bases, including 50 or more in four seasons. Aparicio was a 10-time All-Star (1958–64, 1970–72) as well as a nine-time Gold Glove Award winner (1958–62, 1964, 1966, and 1970). As a player, though, Aparicio's ultimate achievement came in 1966, by winning a World Series championship with the Orioles.

Aparicio offered a dynamic baseball package; brilliant fielding skills, incredible base running abilities, and strong batting numbers. His base stealing and fielding skills created a level of fan excitement that rivaled home run hitters. Aparicio proved that size is not the only measure of sports excellence.

Notes

1. Les Woodcock,1(959). "Two For The Pennant," *Sports Illustrated* Vault. http://vault.sportsillustrated.cnn.com/vault/article/magazine/MAG1070879/index.htm (accessed April 18, 2009)

2. Ibid.
3. Ibid.
4. Ibid.

Orlando Cepeda

Star of the National Baseball Hall of Fame

by Chris Kamke

Orlando Cepeda is a former Major League Baseball first baseman whose 17-year professional career was comprised of time spent with the San Francisco Giants, St. Louis Cardinals, Atlanta Braves, Oakland Athletics, Boston Red Sox, and Kansas City Royals. The 6-foot-2 right-handed ball player was born in Ponce, Puerto Rico on September 17, 1937. Throughout his life, Cepeda has experienced both the highs and lows of life. Idolized by thousands before spending time in prison, Cepeda was cast out from a once loving society and has slowly worked his way back in. "Yes, yes, you can certainly say I've known both sides," said Cepeda. "No matter what happens to you, you have to overcome it."[1]

Orlando's father, Pedro Cepeda, was a professional baseball player in Puerto Rico while Cepeda was growing up. Being surrounded by baseball from an early age, Cepeda's interest in the sport was cultivated from an early age. Cepeda was discovered by an amateur baseball player and was recruited to join a local amateur team. His new team would go on to win Puerto Rico's amateur championship and would have an opportunity to play against an All-Star team from the Dominican Republic. It was during that game that Pedro Zorilla, the owner of the Santurce Crabbers, a professional team in Puerto Rico, noticed Cepeda. Zorilla offered Cepeda his first professional baseball experience—batboy for the Crabbers.

After Cepeda's father retired from baseball, he worked for the government checking the quality of river water. After taking this job he contracted and eventually died from malaria. The loss of Cepeda's father worsened the family's living condition, causing them to move multiple times, eventually settling in San Juan. Cepeda got his big break when Zorilla convinced Cepeda's family to let him attend a New York Giants tryout. Cepeda performed well at the tryout and went on to play for several minor league teams before being called up to the majors after the Giants moved to San Francisco.

In 1958, a 20-year-old Cepeda made his presence known in his major league debut by sending a solo shot off Don Drysdale over the fence to help the Giants beat the Dodgers. The game served as a perfect beginning to his brilliant career that included nine seasons batting .300 or better and eight seasons of 25 or more home runs. Cepeda went on to finish his rookie year with 25 homers, a National League-leading 38 doubles, 96 runs batted in, and a .312 batting average. Cepeda's efforts won him Rookie of the Year honors and praise from Giants manager Bill Rigney who called him, "The best young right-handed power hitter I've ever seen."[2]

His best season with the Giants came in 1961 when he led the NL with 46 home runs and 142 RBI. Despite being a great player and fan favorite in San Francisco, Cepeda did not mesh with team management. Conflict stemming from this inability to foster good relations bounced him to the St. Louis Cardinals during the 1966 season after eight productive seasons with the Giants.

With the Cardinals, Cepeda continued his strong play and became a leader in the clubhouse. In 1967, during his first full season with the Cardinals, Cepeda's leadership was heavily relied upon, both on and off the field. "Without Cepeda, we are down with the Pirates, and look where they are," said teammate Mike Shannon. "It's not just his statistics. It's also what happens in the clubhouse. It's intangible. I can't really explain. Orlando is a prestige player, and we have him—the other clubs don't."[3] The Cardinals went on to become world champions that season by beating the Boston Red Sox in a seven-game World Series. After hitting .325 and driving in a league-leading 111 runs during the season, Cepeda was named the 1967 MVP.

Cepeda's productivity decreased after leaving the Cardinals at the conclusion of the 1968 season. The decrease was in large part due to reoccurring injuries that would persist for the rest of his career. Even with injury problems, Cepeda was selected to play in seven All-Star games over the course of his career and became the first player from Puerto Rico to start in one. Cepeda played in three World Series, winning one. In his career, Cepeda amassed 379 home runs, 1,365 RBI, and a career batting average of .297.

After his retirement in 1975, all his good deeds were overshadowed. In 1978 he was arrested at an airport on charges of trying to pick up 160 pounds of marijuana. This single mistake haunted Cepeda for years to follow and affected his National Baseball Hall of Fame balloting in Cooperstown.

The effects of this crime would prove to extend past his potential Hall of Fame induction. Cepeda's television commercials were yanked from the air in Puerto Rico and businesses would turn him away saying that his money was no good there. Furthermore, his name was removed from the fields on which his children grew up playing. Perhaps even more devastating to Cepeda was the reaction by the Puerto Rican youth. "Little kids were telling me they didn't want to be like me anymore,"[4] Cepeda says.

It seemed as if baseball would never let Cepeda escape his drug-related conviction. The Giants, who Cepeda was working for as a goodwill ambassador, spent time and money to make sure everyone knew he was a good guy. They sent him on a promotional tour that took him across the country, providing opportunities for Cepeda to appear on *Larry King Live* and *The Today Show*, all in an effort to make his mistake fade away.

By the early 1990s, when his eligibility for the Hall of Fame was beginning to run out, many Puerto Ricans, celebrities and ordinary citizens alike, began campaigning for his induction. "I've been ready for this for 17 years," Cepeda said. "I've been through good things, bad things, but I was blessed to be born with the talent to play baseball."[5] His main desire to be elected into the Hall of Fame was so that kids would be more likely to listen when he was talking to them about staying away from drugs. In 1993, Cepeda was inducted into the Puerto Rico Sports Hall of Fame. In 1994, his last year of eligibility by voting, he came within seven votes of being elected into Cooperstown. In 1999, he was elected in the Hall of Fame by the Hall's Veterans Committee who took a long look at Cepeda's service since leaving baseball. "You can't give up on somebody because they made a mistake," Cepeda said. "I just wept and wept. I couldn't talk for a long time. I just cried every time I tried to speak."[6]

Cepeda's efforts in the community did not cease after being inducted into the Hall of Fame. In 2001, he won the Ernie Banks Positive Image Lifetime Achievement Award for his lifelong service to the community. The Giants decided to honor Cepeda by retiring his number 30. In September of the 2008 season, the Giants dedicated a statue of Cepeda beside his retired number.

Cepeda has continued to spread the game of baseball in the Latin community. Cepeda recently partnered with StarMedia Network, Inc., a leading Internet media company for Spanish and Portuguese speakers. The partnership announced the launching of an Internet multimedia program entitled, "La Voz Gigante de Orlando Cepeda," or "The Giant Voice of Orlando Cepeda." The program enables fans from around the world to access their favorite Spanish-speaking players.

Notes

1. Buzz Gray, (1999). "Cepeda Takes Long Road Back," *Albany Times Union*, July25, Sports.

2. "Orlando Manuel Cepeda. Latino Legends in Sports," http://www.latinosportsle gends.com/cepeda.htm (accessed May 11, 2009).

3. Mark Mulvoy, (1967). "Cha Cha Goes Boom, Boom, Boom," *Sports Illustrated*, July 24.

4. Dan Le Batard, (1994). "Orlando Cepeda Has a New Perspective," *Knight Ridder Newspaper*, January 14.

5. "Orlando Manuel Cepeda. Latino Legends in Sports," http://www.latinosportsle gends.com/cepeda.htm (accessed May 11, 2009).

6. Buzz Gray, (1999). "Cepeda Takes Long Road Back," *Albany Times Union*, July25, Sports.

Juan Marichal

Star of the National Baseball Hall of Fame

by Chris Kamke

The mention of the name Juan Marichal to a baseball fan during the 1960s and 70s will undoubtedly call to mind a distinctive pitching style. With a left leg raised high in the air, the grace of Marichal's pitch delivery hypnotized batters and concealed the nature of the pitch until the last moment. But beyond his form, Marichal was unquestionably one the greatest pitchers the game has ever seen.

In a small home just outside of Laguna Verde in the Dominican Republic, Marichal and his family scratched out a living. When Marichal wasn't helping his mother in the fields, he spent his time playing baseball. Equipment was rare to come by so Marichal would take matters into his own hands. As a young boy, he would unravel thread from old stockings and then carefully wind the thread around a scrap of rubber until he had a ball about 9 inches in circumference. At times lopsided, the simple object served its purpose and allowed a young Marichal to develop into a tremendous baseball talent.

Signed as an amateur free agent in 1957 by the New York Giants, Marichal wouldn't make his professional debut until a few years later when he took the mound against the Philadelphia Phillies in 1960 for the Giants, who had since relocated to San Francisco. In his debut, Marichal threw a complete game one-hit shutout, walking one and striking

Courtesy of the National Baseball Hall of Fame Library, Cooperstown, NY.

out 12. Marichal went on to start 10 more games that year, finishing with a 6-2 record and a 2.66 ERA. His win total climbed to 13 and 18 over the following two seasons. In 1963, he had a breakout year going 25-8, leading the league in victories, posting a 2.41 ERA, and totaling 248 strikeouts.

Marichal was a dominant pitcher in the 1960s. He won more games during that decade—191—than any other major league pitcher, but failed to receive any votes for the Cy Young Award. After the 1973 season, Marichal was sent to the Boston Red Sox. He had an average season in 1974, going 5-1 in 11 starts, and was released at season's end. He would go on to sign with the Dodgers in 1975, Marichal's last in the majors. After just two poor starts, Marichal retired.

Two games stick out in Marichal's career. The first notable game came on July 2, 1963, when the Giants faced the Milwaukee Braves. The pitching matchup was between the veteran and Hall of Famer Warren Spahn and Marichal. When two pitchers are at the top of their game, every play has extra meaning. The pitchers controlled this game and after eight innings of play the two teams remained scoreless. The tie was almost broken in the bottom of the ninth when a line drive shot by the Giants' Willie McCovey sailed over the outfield wall just foul.

Giants manager Alvin Dark wanted to pull his pitcher from the game in favor of a fresh arm but Marichal pleaded his case. "I begged Mr. Dark to let me stay a few more innings, and he did." Despite Marichal maintaining his shutout, Dark's thoughts didn't waver. "In the 12th or 13th, he wanted to take me out, and I said, 'Please, please, let me stay,'" Marichal said. "Then in the 14th, he said, 'No more for you,' and I said, 'Do you see that man on the mound?' and I was pointing at Warren. 'That man is 42, and I'm 25. I'm not ready for you to take me out.'"[1] Catcher Ed Bailey supported Marichal, telling him, "Don't let him take you out. Win or lose, this is great."[2]

After Marichal retired in the top of 16th inning, Willie Mays hit a walk off solo home run over the left field wall with one out, giving the Giants the 1-0 win. In 16 innings of work, Marichal allowed eight hits, zero runs, four walks, and ten strikeouts. During the 1960s, complete games were fairly common but the Marichal-Spahn showdown was epic.

The other game that stands out in Marichal´s career lives in infamy, a game against the Los Angeles Dodgers in 1965. Marichal was known for not being afraid to go after batters. In the first inning of the game, Dodger Maury Wills reached on a bunt and then Ron Fairly doubled him home, putting the Dodgers up by one. Marichal responded by knocking down Wills and Fairly, these actions set off a series of events. The Dodgers' Sandy Koufax retaliated by knocking down Willie Mays. Blood was boiling in both dugouts. When Marichal came to bat, he took the first two pitches and then objected to how closely to his head Dodgers catcher John Roseboro was throwing the ball back to the pitcher. Marichal proceeded to bash Roseboro over the head with his bat, inciting a bench clearing brawl. Roseboro was forced to leave the game with a bloody head and Marichal was suspended nine games and fined $1,750, then the largest in National League history. Marichal regretted his actions. "I did good things for the game, but wish I could take back that one incident," he says. "I regret it."[3]

Marichal started 457 career games. With a reputation for his durability and competitive nature, Marichal had 244 career complete games and worked more than 300 innings in a season three times. Commanding excellent control, he had 2,303 strikeouts to 709 walks, which amounted to a strikeout-to-walk ratio of about 3.25 to 1. That ratio ranks among the top 20 pitchers of all time in that category. Marichal amassed 243 wins, including 52 shutouts. He was named to nine All-Star teams and was the MVP of the 1965 All-Star Game.

Having gone down as one of the most renowned pitchers in Major League Baseball history, Marichal pitched for 16 successful seasons. In 1983, he was elected into the National Baseball Hall of Fame. Known for his delivery and brilliant ball control, Marichal's number 27 has been retired by the Giants. In 2005, Marichal was honored by the Giants before a game against the Oakland Athletics with a statue residing outside AT&T Park.

Notes

1. Richard Sandomir, (2008). "When Marichal and Spahn Dueled for a Game and a Half," *New York Times*, July 2, sec. Sports.

2. Ibid.

3. Paul Gutierrez, (1997). "Giants Pitcher Juan Marichal," *Sports Illustrated*, September 15.

Atanasio "Tony" Pérez

Star of the National Baseball Hall of Fame

by Horacio Ruiz

It had been a long time when the doors to the National Baseball Hall of Fame had finally opened for Tony Pérez. Since becoming eligible for induction into the Hall, Pérez had waited nine years to be elected into baseball immortality. Every year the seven-time All-Star seemed to come up just short. In what had become an annual ritual, Pérez was sitting by the phone in his Santurce, Puerto Rico, home when the call came in. His wife, Pituka, handed him the phone. When he received the news that he had been voted in, he was in a state of disbelief. "Are you sure?" he asked. "Are you sure?"[1]

Yes, they were sure. Pérez had received 77.2 percent of the votes from the Baseball Writers' Association of America, meeting the 75 percent requirement. The first person he called was his mother, Teodora, in Cuba to let her know that he had been elected. Teodora cried and Pérez said he "got emotional, too." There were people from across the baseball world rooting for the man nicknamed "Big Dawg." Years before, Teodora didn't want Pérez to leave Cuba in order to pursue a baseball career in the United States because she loved him so much.

Despite his mother's love, Pérez left his job in a Havana sugar-cane factory as a sixteen-year-old to pursue his baseball dreams in the United States. He didn't like working in the factory and he knew more than anything that he wanted to be a baseball player. When Pérez signed his first contract, his father told him, "Tony, go to America and do the best you can. If you help us, great, but do your best and always keep a positive attitude."[2] When he arrived in the United

States, he quickly needed to adjust to a higher level of competition and overcome the language barrier. Early in his career, he would order his food by pointing to a menu item, not yet able to read in English. Sometimes he was lucky and would be served a meal, and other times he would find out that he pointed to an apple pie for lunch. Pérez kept his father's advice in mind. "I never doubted myself and stayed positive through it all," Pérez said. "I believe this was a key to my long career."[3]

Pérez would play 23 seasons of Major League Baseball, debuting with the Cincinnati Reds in 1964. He would break out in the 1967 season when he made his first All-Star team, garnering All-Star Game MVP honors when he hit the game-winning home run in the bottom of the 15th inning. In 1969, after Pérez stole home plate on the front end of a double steal, Reds manager Dave Bristol said for the first time, "If a game lasts long enough, Tony will win it for you."[4] He became a key cog in Cincinnati's "Big Red Machine," the nickname given to the Reds for their dominance in the National League from 1970–1976 in which they won five National League Western Division titles, four National League pennants, and two World Series titles. Some would say that Pérez was the heart and soul of those Cincinnati teams. The "Big Red Machine" included Pete Rose, the all-time leader in hits, three future Hall of Fame players in Pérez, Johnny Bench, and Joe Morgan, and future Hall of Fame manager Sparky Anderson. They were supported by the likes of George Foster, César Gerónimo, Ken Griffey, Sr., and Dave Concepción. Together, the Reds dynasty compiled six National League MVP selections; four National League home run leading seasons; three National League batting champions; 25 Gold Glove winning seasons, and 63 collective All-Star Game appearances.

The 1970 season would prove to be Pérez's finest when he finished the season with a .317 batting average, 40 home runs, and 129 RBI. From 1967–1977 he drove in 90 or more runs every season, and from 1967–76, he led all major-league players with 1,028 RBI. Throughout his career, Pérez earned respect for his clutch hitting. In the 1975 World Series he hit three home runs, including a two-run home run in Game 7 which the Reds clinched with a 4-3 victory for the championship. The Reds would again win the World Series in 1976, but after the season, Pérez was traded to the Montreal Expos because of financial reasons. The "Big Red Machine" would stay competitive but would not get into the World Series again and made only one more playoff appearance.

Pérez played three seasons for the Expos, compiling a .281 batting average, 46 home runs, and 242 RBI. Nearing the end of his career after his tour with the Expos, the 38-year-old Pérez signed a free-agent contract with the Boston Red Sox where he would spend three seasons. In his first season with the Red Sox, Pérez experienced a rebirth by compiling a .275 batting average, 25 home runs, and 105 RBI. At the end of the season, Pérez was awarded the Lou Gehrig Memorial Award, which is given to the player who best exemplifies Gehrig's "character and integrity both on and off the field." After his stop in Boston, Pérez would spend one season with the Philadelphia Phillies as a role player, and then joined the Reds once again where he played three seasons until his retirement in 1986 at the age of 44.

By the end of his career, Pérez finished with a lifetime .279 batting average, 379 home runs, 1,652 RBI, and 2,732 hits. Pérez's 1,652 RBI ranks first all-time among players from Latin America. He also appeared in five World Series and six League Championship Series. In 1993, Pérez was hired to manage the Reds, but lasted only 44 games before being abruptly fired. In 2001, he was an interim manager for the Florida Marlins, replacing John Boles in mid-May, where he managed the team to a 54-60 record.

In 2000, after being elected to the Hall of Fame, the Reds retired Pérez's number 24, where he joined teammates Bench and Morgan with the honor. Baseball fans and writers saw it as a fitting tribute for Pérez, even though he was traded in his prime and fired as the Reds' manager after only 44 games. Pérez waited many years to receive the phone call that he had been elected into the Hall of Fame—when many thought he was a lock. But just like in his career, he stayed in the game just long enough, and came through in the end. Pérez is currently a Special Assistant to the General Manager with the Florida Marlins.

Notes

1. Richard Sandomir, (2008). "When Marichal and Spahn Dueled for a Game and a Half," *New York Times*, July 2, sec. Sports.

2. Ibid.

3. Paul Gutierrez, (1997). "Giants Pitcher Juan Marichal," *Sports Illustrated*, September 15.

4. Tony Perez Timeline. *The Cincinnati Post*. January 12, 2000.

Rodney "Rod" Carew

Star of the National Baseball Hall of Fame

by Chris Kamke

> "He has an uncanny ability to move the ball around as if the bat were some kind of magic wand."[1]
>
> —Ken Holtzman

Rod Carew spent most of his career as the best kept secret in American sport. His ascent to greatness was long and slow, but fate had decided that nothing would prevent Rod from becoming one of baseball's greatest hitters. An opposing player once said that "trying to sneak a pitch past him is like trying to sneak the sunrise past a rooster."[2] Enduring racism from birth through his playing days, Carew faced challenges his entire life. Ultimately, he prevailed to secure a spot in baseball history. Despite living in America for most of his life, Rod has never sought American citizenship. This is due to a profound attachment to his Latin background. By maintaining his Panamanian citizenship, he believes Panamanian kids can look to him and find hope to fuel their dreams of becoming a big league ballplayer.

Carew was born on October 1, 1945 aboard a moving train near the town of Gatún, in the Panama Canal Zone. Olga Carew, Rod's mother, knowing her baby was due, boarded a train for her journey to the clinic. The train was racially segregated, so Olga, a Panamanian woman, took a seat in the last car with other non-white passengers even though she was nine months pregnant. When her baby refused to wait any longer, Rodney Cline, a doctor seated in the "whites only" section, came to the rescue and helped deliver the new baby. The baby boy was named Rodney Cline Carew in the doctor's honor.

As a child, Carew was frequently ill. At age 12, he contracted a rheumatic fever and his resulting weakness alienated him from his father. Despite his illness, his uncle encouraged Carew to get involved with baseball. As he grew stronger, Carew's athletic talents bloomed. He joined older boys in pickup games of baseball using a broom handle as a bat. Eventually he won what would become his prized possession, a Ted Williams bat for his excellent play in Little League. From then on, it was hard to find him without a bat in his hands.

At the age of 15, Carew and his family immigrated to New York City. He lived in the impoverished Washington Heights section of Manhattan. Although he attended George Washington High School, he never played baseball for the high school team. His time after school was occupied by a part-time job in a grocery store to help support his family. Eventually, he began playing ball on the weekends for a sandlot team next to Yankee Stadium. It was there that a scout from the Minnesota Twins discovered Carew. When the Twins came to town for a series with the Yankees, Carew was invited to Yankee Stadium for a tryout. During that tryout, the 18-year-old showcased surprising power for his skinny frame, and it was obvious to all onlookers that he was exceptionally gifted. The day after his high school graduation, he signed a contract with the Twins. He played only three seasons in the Twins minor league system before jumping to the majors in 1967.

Playing second base for the Twins, Carew debuted against Baltimore on April 11, 1967. He batted left-handed and threw right-handed, finishing the game with two hits. He finished his first season batting .292 and was named American League Rookie of the Year. He hit .273 in 1968, but followed that season with 15 consecutive seasons batting over .300 (1969–83). Only Ty Cobb, Stan Musial, and Honus Wagner have exceeded that achievement. In 1969, Carew's .332 batting average won him his first of seven American League batting titles. Baseball is famous for its superstitions and Carew was no exception. He attributed some of his success to his bats. So he made sure to take care of them. He was known to keep bats near the sauna because he believed the heat of the sauna "bakes out the bad wood,"[3] as he phrased it. He also kept a supply of bats in his locker, safely away from the communal bin where other teammates would casually toss bats around. He believed a bruised bat was weaker.

In his first few years in the majors Carew was known as a loner who made friends slowly. Much of this would change after one night in 1968. Carew went out to a local nightspot with friends for drinks. That same evening, Marilynn Levy, a Jewish girl, had gone out to celebrate her birthday. They met that night and started seeing each other. However, they separated after Marilynn thought their relationship would upset her parents. This separation would not last, and after two years of dating and numerous death threats stemming from the interracial relationship, they were married in October 1970. Carew and Marilynn celebrated their love and did not let the racism of the fans, Twins officials, and teammates inhibit their lives.

In 1975, Carew achieved something only previously accomplished by Ty Cobb by leading both the American and National Leagues in batting average for three consecutive seasons. In 1976, Carew made a position shift from second to first base and emerged as a mature team leader. He fell short of winning his fourth consecutive batting title by the mere margin of .002 points. This must have motivated Carew as he came out sizzling the following season. In 1977, he bounced back by making a serious run at a .400 season, finishing with a .388 average. This marked his sixth batting title. The next best batting average in 1977 was .338, achieved by National League batting champ Dave Parker. This was the largest margin to date between the best and second best batting average in history. Combining his top batting average with his league-leading 16 triples, 239 hits, 100 RBIs, and 128 runs scored, Carew was the clear choice for the American League's Most Valuable Player in 1977. That same year, Carew was the Roberto Clemente Award winner, an honor given by Major League Baseball to the player who best exemplifies the game of baseball, sportsmanship, and community involvement. The honor is bestowed for a player's public acts, but unpublicized deeds most distinguish Carew's style. He made regular trips to clinics to visit patients. One time he had a run-in with a traffic cop who pointedly called him "boy" as he wrote Carew a ticket. The policeman later contacted Carew and asked him to visit his father, who was dying of cancer. When Carew returned from the visit he told his wife, "I guess this is how you change people, one at a time."[4]

Carew completed the 1978 season with the Twins, his twelfth with the organization. However, a few weeks later team owner Cal Griffith made some offensive racial comments. Griffith said, "I'll tell you why we came to Minnesota. It was when we found out you only had 15,000 blacks here. Black people don't go to ballgames, but they'll fill up a rassling ring and put up such a chant it'll scare you to death. We came here because you've got good, hardworking white people here."[5] The comments infuriated Carew. He had experienced racism throughout his life and Griffith's comments erased his desire to be a part of the Twins. Carew commented that he wanted off the team because he "didn't want to be another nigger on Griffith's plantation."[6] He announced that after the 1979 season he would seek free agency. This statement prompted the Twins to take action, trading the MVP to the California Angels in February of 1979. During his first season in California, Carew batted .318 and played a large role in California's first division title. Perhaps the largest achievement in Carew's career came on August 4, 1985, when he connected on his 3,000th career hit. The hit, ironically, came off Twins starting pitcher Frank Viola. Carew was the second foreign-born player and 16th overall to reach this milestone.

The 1985 season was Carew's last. After that season, Carew was not offered a contract by any team. He suspected that baseball owners were colluding to keep him out of the league. His suspicion was confirmed in Januray of 1995. Carew was awarded damages of $782,036, an amount he would have likely earned in 1986.

In his nineteen seasons, Carew totaled 3,053 career hits, still the most ever by a foreign born player and 21st most all-time. His .328 lifetime batting average still ranks 34th all-time. His career included five seasons in which he batted .350 or better. He is still the Twins' all-time leading hitter at .334 and the Angels' second all-time leading hitter at .314. He was such a feared hitter that he led the American League in intentional walks in three different seasons. This is an amazing feat considering he reached double digits in home runs just twice in his nineteen-year career and finished with just 92 overall. In addition to his success with the bat, Carew was an exceptional base runner. He perfected the art of stealing home thanks to instruction from former Yankee pitcher Billy Martin, who was also his manager with the Twins. According to Martin, "I taught him how to steal home. That's all I ever taught him. As for hitting, he knew how to do that all by himself."[7] In one game Carew stole second, third, and home in a single inning.

Considered a national hero in Panama, Carew was one of the most talented players of all time. During his memorable nineteen-year career, he was selected to eighteen All-Star teams (1967–84). He collected seven batting titles, fourth most all-time. Carew and Willie Mays are the only players to receive the distinctions of Rookie of the Year, Most Valuable Player, 3,000 hits, and Hall of Fame member. Carew was the third player to have his number, 29, retired by two teams. It was clear then why on January 8, 1991, Carew became the 22nd player in history to be a first-ballot inductee into baseball's Hall of Fame.

Carew once said, "I get a kick out of watching a team defense me. A player moves two steps in one direction and I hit it two steps in the other direction. It goes right by his glove and I laugh."[8] After his retirement from baseball, the man who could create art with his bat desired to pass his expertise to others. Carew opened a hitting school in Placentia, California in the spring of 1987. The facility has been a remarkable success ever since its doors opened. The school serves as a precious resource to major league teams as many have turned to Carew for his proven techniques.

In 1995, tragedy struck Carew's family as his daughter Michelle was diagnosed with leukemia. Michelle ultimately lost her fight against leukemia in 1996. Since then, Carew has been promoting awareness of bone marrow, quietly dedicating a great portion of his life to raising funds for pediatric cancer research. The 14th Annual Rod Carew Children's Cancer Golf Classic will be held in 2009. This cause has raised more than $2 million for cancer research.

Carew visited his native Panama as an ambassador for baseball. Armed with his mission to help make baseball a more international game, he conducted baseball clinics for Panamanian youth. In a wonderful gesture, he was invited to take a special ride on the train where he was born. At the conclusion of the ride, a ceremony was held and the formerly segregated train was renamed in his honor. He said, "To have the train that I was born on named after me is just another tremendous honor."[9] Carew's passion for baseball is confirmed through his continual efforts at both the grass roots and major league levels.

As former Twins Manager Gene Mauch stated, "As impressed as I am with Rod Carew the hitter, Rod Carew the baseball player, I am more impressed with Rod Carew the man."[10]

Notes

1. Rod Carew Quotes. Baseball Almanac. http://www.baseball-almanac.com/quotes/quocarew.shtml (accessed January 18, 2009).

2. Paul Witteman and B. J. Phillips, (1997). "Baseball's Best Hitter Tries for Glory," *Time*, July 18.

3. Ibid.

4. Rod Carew Quotes. Baseball Almanac. http://www.baseball-almanac.com/quotes/quocarew.shtml (accessed January 18, 2009).

5. James Ray, (2008). "Hall of Famer Rod Carew. Career Biography and Statistics of the Seven Time Batting Champion," Suite101.com. http://baseball.suite101.com/article.cfm/hall_of_famer_rod_carew (accessed January 18, 2009).

6. Ibid.

7. Paul Witteman and B. J. Phillips, (1997). "Baseball's Best Hitter Tries for Glory," *Time*, July 18.

8. Ibid.

9. Nate Bloom, (2008). "Interfaith Celebrities: A Surprising Dancer, A Head of State, and a Baseball Great," InterfaithFamily.com. http://www.interfaithfamily.com/arts_and_entertainment/popular_culture/Interfaith_Celebrities_A_Surprising_Dancer_A_Head_of_State_and_a_Baseball_Great.shtml?rd=2 (accessed January 18, 2009).

10. Paul Witteman and B. J. Phillips, (1997). "Baseball's Best Hitter Tries for Glory," *Time*, July 18.

Esteban Bellán

First Latino to Play Professional Baseball in the United States

by Jared Bovinet

The International Baseball Federation ranks the Cuban national baseball team number one in the world as of March 2009. In its participation in the Summer Olympic Games, starting in 1992, the team has won three gold and two silver medals, the best showing of any country across the globe. The country's obsession with the sport permeates its culture, and its baseball history is one rich in awards, championships, and gifted players.

Historians credit Esteban Bellán with introducing Cubans to their national pastime and later becoming the first Latino baseball player in the American major leagues. Born in Cuba in 1849, he grew up in an affluent family and attended high school and university in the United States, as was customary of children from wealthy Catholic backgrounds in Cuba.

Bellán played baseball for the Fordham Rose Hill Baseball Club while attending Fordham University in New York. He received praise from local media for his solid skills. The *New York Clipper* wrote that he was a "faithful guardian" of third base and "one of the pluckiest of base players."[1]

At graduation, Bellán played for the Union Club of Morrisania, a team in the National Association of Baseball Players. He helped the team win its only national championship that year. In 1871, Bellán joined the Troy Haymakers, which later became the New York Giants and then the San Francisco Giants, as the franchise is known today. The team became a charter member of the National Association, the forerunner of today's National League.

Bellán played with the Haymakers for two years, the New York Mutuals for an additional year and then returned to Cuba, where he participated in the first organized baseball game in December of 1874, (a game which his team handily won, 51-9). Bellán then helped create the Habana Baseball Club, the country's first club dedicated to the sport. He worked as both a player and a manager of the club, and helped lead it to three Cuban baseball championships.

While Bellán opened a prodigious door for Latinos, it took several decades for a significant Latino presence in baseball to develop in the United States. In fact, only one more Latino, Louis Castro from Colombia, entered the major leagues between 1871 and 1911. And between 1911 and 1947, only 54 players from Latin America entered the league. They were, however, classified as white due to their light skin.

The 1950s marked the first decade to experience a large wave of Spanish-speaking players, a wave which has steadily grown since. This brings up a point often forgotten in baseball history; Robinson's monumental step toward integration benefited not only African Americans, but Latinos and other races as well. "Jackie Robinson's breakthrough offered hope for [Latin Americans] greater opportunities in the United States. The fences of big league baseball now appeared within reach for all Latinos."[2]

Although his professional career in America spanned only 59 games, Esteban Bellán was a true pioneer in the world of baseball, opening his native Cuba and Latin America to the game. As historians put it, Bellán "performed the marriage between baseball and the Cuban people."[3] He died in 1932 and Fordham University inducted him into its Hall of Fame in 1989.

Notes

1. Adrian Burgos, Jr., *Baseball, Latinos, and the Color Line*. (Berkeley: University of California Press, 2009), 65.

2. Samuel Octavio Regalado, *Viva Baseball! Latin Major Leaguers and Their Special Hunger* (Champaign; University of Illinois Press, 1998), 36.

3. Peter C. Bjarkman, *Baseball with a Latin Beat* (McFarland, 1994), 239.

Hiram Bithorn

Puerto Rican Baseball Pioneer

by Richard Lapchick

Courtesy of the National Baseball Hall of Fame Library, Cooperstown, NY.

The real pioneer for Puerto Rican players was Hiram Bithorn, a man that few know today. There are many great current Major League Baseball players who come from Puerto Rico such as Carlos Beltrán, Carlos Delgado, Javier Vázquez, and Geovany Soto among many others. They have followed generations of baseball legends from Puerto Rico in what has become a rich tradition on the island, which has produced more than 250 MLB players. Like most people who know something about the role Jackie Robinson played in integrating MLB for African-Americans, many think of Roberto Clemente when they think of pioneers from the island. The Roberto Clemente Coliseum stands as a testimonial to Clemente's life as well as his death as a hero in 1972.

Far less known, but every bit the pioneer, was Bithorn. The national stadium that sits across the way from the Coliseum in San Juan was named Hiram Bithorn Stadium. Opened in 1962, it honors the island's first citizen to play in Major League Baseball. I hope that today's Puerto Rican baseball players get to know the history of Hiram Bithorn.

Bithorn played for the San Juan Senators. He was a fine pitcher but was not the best player on the island, where winter ball was king. It seemed unlikely he would be chosen to break the barrier in the majors. However, a combination of his personal background and the onset of World War II helped pave the way to Bithorn's ascension with the Chicago Cubs.

On April 15, 1942—13 years before Clemente would play in the majors—Bithorn made his debut. Bithorn was light-skinned, had a name that did not sound Latino, and joined a field of Major League players that had been seriously depleted by World War II. The United States entered the war after Japan attacked Pearl Harbor in December 1941, and more than 70 MLB players had joined the U.S. Armed Forces before the 1942 season. They were joined by almost 140 more before the 1943 season started. That was more than half of the players in the 16-team leagues.

Bithorn's family was of Dutch and Spanish origin, making him look more European than stars like Pedro "Perucho" Cepeda, whose son, Orlando, would become one of baseball's best once the racial barriers fell. Perucho Cepeda had hit .377 in the 1941–42 winter season. Francisco "Pancho" Coimbre hit .438 with the New York Cubans of the Negro Leagues in 1942. But it was Bithorn who got the call.

Bithorn went 9-14 in his first season. In 1943, he went 18-12 with 19 complete games and led the league with seven shutouts. No one from Puerto Rico has broken that record. But Bithorn joined the Army and, as others who had done so, lost his career momentum when he returned. He went 6-5 with the Cubs in 1946 and ended his career with the White Soxs. A sore arm hastened the end of what was once a promising career. Bithorn posted a 34-31 career record with a 3.16 ERA. He completed 30 of the 53 games he started, and finished with eight shutouts. He pitched in the Mexican winter leagues but never regained the touch that would have allowed him back into the majors.

Tragedy struck when a Mexican policeman shot and killed Bithorn, then 35, on December 31, 1951. The circumstances were cloudy at first; the officer said Bithorn identified himself as a member of a communist cell and acted violently. In the end, the police officer went to prison for the murder of Bithorn.

He was still such a source of pride for Puerto Rico that the stadium was named after him in 1962. Now it is no surprise to see great Puerto Rican players in Major League Baseball. But when you look at the careers of today's stars, remember they are all walking on the road paved by Bithorn.

Roberto "Bobby" Ávila

Mexican Baseball Pioneer

by Jared Bovinet

Not many people outslugged baseball great Ted Williams during his playing days. Not many people could hit home runs with broken thumbs, either. Roberto "Bobby" Ávila did both. Ávila's impressive hitting abilities led to his winning the 1954 American League batting crown, (the first Latino to do so), among many other awards, and introduced the sport to millions of Mexicans along the way.

Ávila was one of the first prominent Latino players in Major League Baseball. Born in Veracruz, Mexico, in April, 1954, he played soccer and dreamed of being a bullfighter before he discovered baseball. He started as a pitcher but then switched to the infield because he wanted more playing time. Ávila turned professional with the Puebla Parrots in the Mexican League when he was 18-years-old with the intention of going to college if he did not have success as a baseball player. He never ended up in college. Ávila experienced great success in these first two years and made enough money to support himself without a formal education.

U.S. scouts saw Ávila playing one day and immediately began trying to bring him to the major leagues in America. Ávila was an astute business man, too, and refused to consider leaving Mexico without a signing bonus, which was rare at the time. The Boston Braves, Brooklyn Dodgers, and Washington Senators all tried to sign him but did not offer a bonus so he refused. Finally, the Cleveland Indians offered a $20,000 bonus and Ávila agreed to sign.

As a member of the Indians, Ávila became only the fourth Mexican native to play in Major League Baseball and the first to have great success in the league. He quickly made his mark as an excellent second baseman and clutch hitter. Ávila led the American League in fielding percentage in 1953, and compiled a .978 fielding percentage during his time with the Indians.

1954 proved to be the best year in Ávila's career. That year he helped the Indians win the American League pennant and he won the batting title with a .341 hitting average. *The Sporting News* named him the Outstanding Player in the American League and the major league All-Star second baseman at the end of the season. He finished his 11-season-career with more than 80 home runs and batted over .300 three seasons.

Ávila's business acumen led him from the Indians to the Baltimore Orioles where he earned more money. "I would have liked to have stayed in Cleveland," Ávila said. "But I'm a professional. I would have played in China if they'd paid me."[1] In his career, he played with the Indians, the Baltimore Orioles, and the Boston Red Sox, but he had the most success with the Indians.

Ávila returned to Mexico and briefly played for the Mexico City Tigers, after which he started a career in politics. He served two terms as a member of the Congress in Mexico and as mayor of the city of Veracruz. Ávila later served as supervisor of the city's tax collection. He attributed much of his success in politics to the lessons he learned on the baseball field. "Baseball helped me in a lot of ways with politics," Ávila said. "When you live with people so closely like you do in baseball, you learn how to deal with people. You learn what they're thinking about. You're always learning something."[2]

His participation in Major League Baseball had a huge impact on the league's popularity in Mexico. Mexicans continued to follow his career in America and took interest in other players and teams as a result of Ávila's introduction to the major leagues. Undoubtedly, Avila's career fostered the love of baseball for many of his countrymen. Ávila also helped to bring a permanent Mexican League baseball team to the city of Veracruz. This was especially important because Veracruz had never had a baseball team for more than a decade at a time. Ávila became president of the team and eventually president of the league before he returned to politics.

At the age of 78, Ávila died from complications of diabetes. He successfully balanced his careers in baseball and government with his large family, which includes four children and 10 grandchildren. He is remembered for being one of the first Latinos to play in the major leagues, and considering the magnitude of the Latino presence in baseball today, this is quite an accomplishment.

Notes

1. Rich Westcott, *Splendor on the Diamond* (Gainesville: University Press ofFlorida, 2000), 123.

2. Ibid., p. 118.

Luis Tiant

Cuban Baseball Pioneer

by Jared Bovinet

Few families were as affected by Jackie Robinson and his integration into Major League Baseball in 1947 than the Tiant family. Luis Tiant Sr., a great baseball player and one of Cuba's most celebrated athletes during his time, never had the opportunity to play professional ball in the United States because he played before the historic day when Robinson stepped on the field as a Brooklyn Dodger. Instead, Tiant Sr. played in the Cuban League and for the New York Cubans of the Negro League.

Tiant Sr.'s son, Luis Jr., had a much different experience. Born on November 23, 1940 in Marianao, Cuba, Tiant would enter Major League Baseball 18 years after integration and because of it had the opportunity to play in a more diverse league. Throughout his career, he worked to change the culture of baseball and made an especially lasting impression on Bostonians.

Tiant spent his childhood playing baseball and participated in Little League in Havana, Cuba, where he was born and his family lived. It did not take long for him to show his knack for pitching. He excelled on the Havana Juvenile League team and earned a spot on

the league all-star team. Bobby Ávila, the famous Indians player, was a talent scout in Havana at the time and saw the young Tiant play. Ávila told the manager of the Mexico City Tigers baseball team about Tiant and the manager soon offered Tiant $150 per month to play with the team. Tiant accepted and played for both the Tigers and the Sugar Kings in Havana.

The Major League noticed Tiant and offered a contract in 1961 when the Cleveland Indians bought Tiant's playing rights from the Cuban leagues for $35,000. In moving to the United States, Tiant knew that he would not have the opportunity to see his family anytime soon; the new communist regime led by Castro would make it nearly impossible for Tiant to return. It would be 14 years before he saw his father again.

Tiant performed well in the Indians' farm system, which included playing for teams in West Virginia and North Carolina in Single-A leagues and then in Oregon with a Triple-A league. His major league debut occurred with the Indians in Yankee Stadium in 1962. He played brilliantly as he limited the Yankees to four singles and struck out 11 batters. In 1968, Tiant had an earned run average of 1.60—the American League's lowest since 1919. After peaking that year, he experienced nagging injuries that prevented him from pitching at his best for the next three seasons. Tiant was subsequently traded to the Minnesota Twins but could not finish the season because of a sore shoulder. He signed with the Red Sox Triple A affiliate in Louisville, where he played well enough to earn a spot with the Sox.

No one knew how well Tiant would do with the Red Sox when he joined in 1972; he had spent a few seasons off the field and was 30 at the time. He struggled through his first season and won only one game. The crowd quickly turned on him, yelling racial slurs and telling him to go back to Cuba. Fortunately, Eddie Kasko, the team manager, had faith in Tiant and encouraged him to stay in Boston. During his second year with the Red Sox, Tiant turned things around and went 15-6 with an American League-best 1.91 ERA. During the next four years, he won at least twenty games per season for the Sox.

Howard Bryant, a Boston Red Sox historian and author of *Shut Out, A Story of Race and Baseball in Boston*, described Tiant as the foundation of the team in the 1970s. "Tiant was valiant, and there was a sizzle to his steak . . . Tiant was the backbone of those exciting, perilously flawed teams."[1] His status as a team leader grew simultaneously with his number of wins. His teammates "loved him because he kept them laughing, largely by making fun of everyone, including himself."[2] One teammate said about Tiant, "Unless you've played with him, you can't understand what Luis means to a team." [3]

He left Boston after the 1978 season and went to the Yankees, where he played for two seasons and had a record of 21-17. He finished with the Pittsburgh Pirates and California Angels. Tiant retired in 1982 with a career total of 229 wins, 172 losses and 49 shutouts. He was inducted into the Boston Red Sox Hall of Fame in 1997 and named the 1972 American League Comeback Player of the Year for his brilliant second season with the Red Sox. In addition, he won the Babe Ruth Award for being the best player in the 1975 World Series and was named an All-Star three times throughout his career. He lives in Boston with his wife María del Refugio and has three children: Luis Tiant Jr., Isabel, and Daniel.

While Tiant brought many things to baseball, including an impressive curving windup and numerous clutch performances, he is perhaps most respected for changing the racial landscape of baseball in Boston. Team management had passed up the opportunity to draft legends like Jackie Robinson and Willie Mays and as a result was accused of racism by many. Tiant's time in Boston helped to change these perceptions. Later in his book, Howard examines the effect Tiant had in Boston. "Luis Tiant was the first player of color in the city's history to be so totally embraced that he would enter a space usually reserved for white stars." His easygoing, affable personality helped fans see beyond the color of his skin and see him for who he was—a man who loved baseball and played it well. Tiant was a pioneer for Latino athletes in a city with a deep history of racial tensions and, like Jackie Robinson, helped to forever change the culture of baseball in America.

Notes

1. Howard Bryant, *Shut Out: A Story of Race and Baseball in Boston.* (Routledge, 2002).

2. Mark Armour, "El Tiante: Loo-Eee, Loo-ee," *The Baseball Research Journal,* January 1, 2001.

3. Ibid.

Saturnino "Minnie" Miñoso

First Black Latino in Major League Baseball

by Horacio Ruiz

Minnie Miñoso is frozen in time—in September 2004, the Chicago White Sox unveiled a statue of Miñoso in section 164 of U.S. Cellular Field. For the man also known as "The Cuban Comet" and "Mr. White Sox," the sculpture is a snapshot of Miñoso in his prime, taking his right-handed batting stance while crowding an imaginary home plate. To Miñoso, the first black player in White Sox history, and the first black Latino in Major League Baseball, it was an honor he would always remember. "I'm so happy they would do something like this for me," said Miñoso at the unveiling of his statue. "It will make me happy forever."[1]

Miñoso is a pioneer, revered as much for his ability on the field and easy-going demeanor, as for the barriers he broke for Latino ballplayers. "Believe me when I say that Minnie Miñoso is to Latin ballplayers what Jackie Robinson is to black ballplayers," Hall of Famer Orlando Cepeda wrote in his autobiography. "As much as I loved Roberto Clemente and cherish his memory, Minnie is the one who made it possible for all us Latins. Before Roberto Clemente, before Vic Power, before Orlando Cepeda, there was Minnie Miñoso. Younger players should know this and offer their thanks. He was the first Latin player to become a superstar."[2]

Miñoso was an electric player, who as a boy growing up 100 miles outside of Havana, Cuba, wanted nothing more than to be a baseball player. His youth consisted of going to school, doing his homework, playing baseball, and at night dreaming about becoming a professional ballplayer. When he was nine-years old, Miñoso created a team with his friends that challenged an older team from a cigar factory. His older brother played for the other team. Miñoso, pitching for his team, knocked down his older brother twice with inside pitches. "Don't be afraid, get up there," Miñoso told his brother. "We're not brothers here on the field. We're enemies."[3]

When he was 16, Miñoso moved to Havana to pursue his dream of playing professionally in Cuba. There, he caught the eye of scouts, and soon he realized he was good enough to play in the

United States. According to Miñoso, he turned down a $30,000 contract to play for four months in the Mexican League and accepted a contract paying him $600–650 per month to play for the New York Cubans of the Negro Leagues. This way, he could fulfill his goal of playing professionally in the United States. Despite earning less money, his decision to play in the United States allowed him to play with the best, and Miñoso was one of them. He was one of the most dangerous hitters and base runners on a New York Cuban squad that won back-to-back Negro League Championships in 1947 and 1948, respectively. He also endured the prejudices of the time—with some good humor.

"While we were traveling on the bus, we slept a lot and played cards," Miñoso said of playing in the Negro Leagues. "Some places where players could not get out (of the bus), they would send me in to get food because I was Cuban. I would take it back out on the bus for everyone. Finally, I told them if I was going to be the one going in and taking the chance of getting killed while they sit on the bus, they would have to pay for my lunch. We had a good time. They were tough, but good times. We enjoyed it."[4]

In 1948, Miñoso was signed by the Cleveland Indians and Hall of Fame owner Bill Veeck. He made his brief MLB debut with the Indians in 1949. But it would be in 1951, his first season with the White Sox after being traded from Cleveland, that Miñoso broke out as one of the best players of the 1950s. He was elected to the All-Star game in 1951 and was voted the American League Rookie of the Year by *The Sporting News*.

The Baseball Writers Association of America, though, did not recognize Miñoso as the rookie of the year, instead giving the award to the New York Yankees' Gil McDougald. The snub was conspicuous because Miñoso was statistically better in hits, stolen bases, runs, runs batted in, doubles, triples, batting average, on-base percentage, and slugging percentage. McDougald did hit 14 home runs to Miñoso's 10. Oddly enough, those same writers voted Miñoso fourth for the Most Valuable Player Award, while McDougald finished a distant ninth. Some claimed Miñoso's race and ethnicity influenced the voters. If it wasn't the writers that snubbed him, Miñoso had to be careful with those he played against.

"I hit a home run off Hal Newhouser, and in my next at-bat, he threw a fastball right at me," Miñoso said. "The pitch broke sunglasses I had in my pocket, and he says, 'You nigger, you're not sup-posed to hit a homer.' What can I say? I'm black."[5] As a form of self-defense, when Miñoso thought pitchers were aiming for his head, he would lighten the grip on the bat, and fling it at opposing pitchers in mid-swing.

Miñoso wouldn't let those experiences keep him from becom-ing the most popular White Sox player, including being the inspira-tion for the "Go, Go White Sox" chants of the 1950s. His speed and fielding were ideally suited for the large, pitcher-friendly Comiskey Park the White Sox played in. Miñoso would hit over .300 in eight seasons, and made seven All-Star Game appearances. He also col-lected three Gold Gloves for his play in left field. He was the league leader in stolen bases and triples on three occasions and he led the league in hits once. He finished his major league career with 1,963 hits, 205 stolen bases, a .298 batting average, .389 on-base percent-age, and .459 slugging percentage. He was in the top 10 of American League MVP voting in five seasons.

But he extended his career beyond the majors. After leaving Major League Baseball following the 1964 season, Miñoso took up play in the Mexican League. Even as he was past his prime in the United States, he flourished in Mexico. In 1965, he batted .360 in his first season with Jalisco and led the league with 106 runs and 35 dou-bles. In 1973, a 50-year-old Miñoso had a .265 average, 12 home runs, and 83 RBIs in 120 games in the Mexican League.

In 1976, Veeck, then the owner of the White Sox, signed Miñoso as a coach. Veeck convinced Miñoso to insert himself as a player, which he did, and was able to get one hit in eight plate appearances. In 1980, at the age of 54, Miñoso made two plate appearances with the White Sox, making him the second-oldest player to ever bat in the majors and the third-oldest to ever play. In 1993, he appeared with the independent St. Paul Saints, grounding out in the only at-bat of the appearance. The ball and the bat were sent to the National Baseball Hall of Fame as the game had its first six-decade player. Then, in 2003 at the age of 77, Miñoso made another appearance with the St. Paul Saints, becoming the first player ever to play in seven different decades.

In 1983, the White Sox retired Miñoso's number nine. He was elected into the Chicago Sports Hall of Fame in 1984 and the World Baseball Hall of Fame in 1990. In 2002, he was elected into the Hispanic Heritage Baseball Museum Hall of Fame. But the one omission has been Miñoso's election in the National Baseball Hall of Fame in Cooperstown, NY. While his stats compare favorably to a number of Hall of Fame inductees, his omission from Cooperstown is seen by many as an injustice and a disappointment.

Since his retirement from baseball, Miñoso has been an ambassador for baseball and for the White Sox. He has been a community relations representative for the White Sox, giving speeches and making appearances in the Chicago area. In the meantime, the case for his induction into Cooperstown continues to be made by those who feel his exclusion is unfair. In 2006, when a panel of experts were set to vote on a number of great Negro League players into the Hall of Fame, Miñoso, who was up for induction, was not voted in. To many, it rang of the 1951 Rookie of the Year voting.

"Americans at the time didn't seem to pay that much attention to the Latino breakthrough, perhaps because many light-skinned Cubans had preceded Miñoso," said baseball historian Jules Tygiel. "More likely it is because Americans have a binary perception of race—black and white, making no distinction for Latinos. At the time, it did not seem that what Miñoso was doing was comparable to Robinson and [Larry] Doby. In retrospect, however, Miñoso's breakthrough looms large."[6]

For his part, Miñoso is just happy for the experience. "If it's meant to be, it's meant to be," Miñoso said about being inducted in Cooperstown. "I am truly honored to be considered. I've given my life to baseball, and the game has given me so much. That's what matters most to me."[7]

Notes

1. John Kuenster, (2005). "Minnie Miñoso Added An Unforgettable Touch To The Game," *Baseball Digest.* http://findarticles.com/p/articles/mi_m0FCI/is_1_64/ai_n85 65513/ (accessed April 15, 2009).

2. Alex Belth, (2006). "Nothing Minor About Minnie," *CNNSI.com.* http://sportsil lustrated.cnn.com/2006/writers/alex_belth/02/22/minnie.minoso/index.html (accessed April 15, 2009).

3. Minnie Miñoso, (2003). "Miñoso Made His Dream Come True," *MLB.com.* http://chicago.whitesox.mlb.com/news/article.jsp?ymd=20030124&content_id=1935 68&vkey=news_cws&fext=.jsp&c_id=cws (accessed April 15, 2009).

4. Ibid.

5. John Kuenster, (2005). "Minnie Miñoso Added An Unforgettable Touch To The

Game," *Baseball Digest.* http://findarticles.com/p/articles/mi_m0FCI/is_1_64/ai_n85 65513/ (accessed April 15, 2009).

6. Alex Belth,, (2006). "Nothing Minor About Minnie," *CNNSI.com.* http://sportsil lustrated.cnn.com/2006/writers/alex_belth/02/22/minnie.minoso/index.html (accessed April 15, 2009).

7. Mark Stewart, "Minnie Miñoso," http://bioproj.sabr.org/bioproj.cfm?a=v&v= l&bid=1437&pid=9763 (accessed April 15, 2009).

Albert Pujols

MLB Superstar and Future Hall of Famer

by Horacio Ruiz

There is an ESPN commercial depicting Albert Pujols as a Terminator-style robot standing at a copy machine. In the commercial, two news anchors greet Pujols and say, "Hey, there he is—the machine." Pujols denies that he is a machine, even as he looks at them with a Terminator "point-of-view," quickly placing a target on the anchors' faces to capture their vitals, and then deciding not to destroy them. The anchors keep telling Pujols he is a machine, but Pujols, in an electronic voice that only he and the TV viewers can hear, insists, "Guys, I'm not a machine, ok? I'm just Albert." The two news anchors walk away convinced that somehow, some way, Pujols is not human. In the end, the copy machine speaks to Pujols and asks, "Albert, why didn't you eliminate them?"

The obvious truth is that Pujols is human. It's what he's done on the baseball field that seems superhuman. Pujols is the only baseball player in history to hit 30-plus home runs in each of his first nine seasons. He is an eight-time All-Star, three times been named the National League (NL) MVP, and has claimed one World Series title. It's off the baseball field that Pujols has asserted himself to the rest of humanity, because as Pujols says, even though he is one of the best in the game, he would prefer to be remembered for his works off the field.

On a trip just prior to the beginning of the 2009 baseball season, Pujols traveled to the Dominican Republic, his home country, to bring doctors, medical supplies, and new mattresses to families that slept on little more than wooden boards held up by cinder blocks. The charitable trip to the Dominican Republic is an annual occurrence that Pujols and his wife, Deidre, make through the Pujols Family Foundation. Through the Foundation, started in 2005, Pujols has been able to provide medical service and supplies to hundreds of impoverished children. Pujols continues to be changed by his giving, such as when he was delivering a new mattress to a poor mother. "His heart gets tender," says his wife, Deidre. The "woman is so happy, she's crying on his shoulder. It completes him."[1]

Born in the Dominican capital city of Santo Domingo, Pujols grew up the only child of Bienvenido and America Pujols in what was considered the country's middle class. He lived in several homes, including some with dirt floors and others that were without plumbing. Sometimes he would haul gallons of water so that his grandmother could cook and clean. His family, though, would always have lunch and dinner on the table and because of that, Pujols did not consider himself to be poor. It was one of the lessons that made Pujols grow up faster. His father, Bienvenido, was a great softball pitcher. After games, his father would drink with friends. When Pujols' father finished drinking, Pujols would help walk him home when had too much to drink. "God made me older,"[2] Pujols said.

Baseball always seemed to come easy to Pujols. He grew up playing catch with limes and using gloves made out of milk cartons. As a 13-year-old, Pujols played against players that were four to five years older, and hitting the radar gun in the 90s. But when he moved from the Dominican Republic to Kansas City at the age of 16, things became more difficult. Pujols remembers not being able to understand a word of English. His English tutor would sit across him trying to teach him, but he couldn't understand her, and she couldn't understand him. He wanted to be anywhere but in front of that awkward silence. But there was always baseball.

As an 18-year-old, Pujols dominated the high school baseball scene in Kansas City. All the opposing coaches believed Pujols was much older. He was physically imposing, but more than anything, it was the way he carried himself that distinguished him. Out of his 88 plate appearances, teams walked Pujols 55 times, both out of respect and out of protest. Coaches did not want their teenage pitchers throwing to who they thought was a grown man. In the 33 plate appearances he was pitched to, Pujols hit eight home runs. Despite putting up fantastic numbers, Pujols was not named to the local newspaper's first-team baseball squad. In the 1999 season, he played baseball in Maple Woods Community College in Kansas City, highlighted by a .421 batting average and 22 home runs. Still, he was not regarded as one of the top prospects for that year's draft.

"We all saw Albert about the same way," said Allard Baird, the former general manager of the Kansas City Royals. "We weren't sure he had a position. He didn't have a great baseball body. We all saw him the same way, and we were all wrong."[3]

Pujols was drafted in the 13th round by the St. Louis Cardinals. He would spend the 2000 season in the minor leagues, his only season in the minors. By the end of 2000, Pujols was jumped from Single A to Triple A baseball where he hit .367 in the Pacific Coast League playoffs and was named postseason Most Valuable Player. The following year, he was invited as a non-roster invitee to Cardinals training camp where Pujols impressed so much that manager Tony Larussa said, "I've never seen anyone quite like him."[4]

In May 2001, Pujols was named the National League Rookie of the Month, and the next month was named to the NL All-Star Team. He was the first Cardinals rookie since 1955 to be selected. At the end of his rookie season, Pujols finished with a .329 batting average, 37 home runs, and 130 RBIs. He was the unanimous pick as NL Rookie of the Year, and his 37 home runs was one shy of tying the NL rookie record. His 130 RBIs is still the NL rookie record. Since then, Pujols has not looked back.

In May 2009, *The Sporting News* named Pujols the No. 1 player in baseball. In 2004 he led the Cardinals to the World Series, before being swept by the Boston Red Sox. In 2006, Pujols would lead the Cardinals back to the World Series, this time winning the championship in five games versus the Detroit Tigers.

Many years before, though, Pujols's life had been changed when he met his wife, Deidre. On the way to superstardom and still years away from making his baseball dreams a reality, Pujols met Deidre at a 21 and over dance club when later that night, he told her he was only 18 and a high school senior. She told him that she had a baby girl named Isabella who had Down Syndrome. Instead of backing away, Pujols would babysit Isabella while Deidre worked one of her three jobs. And in return, Deidre would find Pujols, the baseball prodigy with a shot at the big leagues, a job at a pizzeria. Pujols gave every cent he earned to Deidre so she could take care of Isabella. After his first minor league season, the same one in which he was named Pacific Coast League postseason MVP, Pujols took on a part-time catering job at a Kansas City country club. In that off-season, Pujols and Deidre were married with little money, spending $150 on their wedding.

Deidre took Pujols to church when they first met, changing his spiritual path. Soon, it seemed all that mattered to Pujols was playing baseball and going to church. With the creation of the Pujols

Family Foundation, Albert has continued to change the lives of the poor while also creating awareness and raising money for children with Down Syndrome.

"As he gets older, he realizes how important that is," Deidre says. "He hungers to utilize his resources to empower others. He believes that if God is going to promise salvation as a free gift, he's going to do what God requires. It is that simple. That's the kind of person he is. That's what makes him special."[5]

In his nine-year career, Pujols has been compared to such baseball greats as Joe DiMaggio, Jimmie Foxx, Ted Williams, Frank Robinson, and Hank Aaron. By the accounts of many writers and historians, Pujols may go down as the greatest baseball player ever. If he does, he has done so while earning the respect of the fans and his teammates.

"He's a 10 in every department," said Larussa, his longtime manager. "Albert is competitive and smart. He has a tremendous amount of preparation and a strong religious faith. He doesn't want to dishonor any of those qualities."[6] Just like another Cardinal great, Stan "The Man" Musial, they call Pujols *"El Hombre,"* for his fantastic baseball skills, his demeanor, and the way he treats others. In 2008, Pujols was awarded the Roberto Clemente Award as the player who "best exemplifies the game of baseball, sportsmanship, community involvement and the individual's contribution to his team." He became the fifth Latino player to win the award in its 38-year history. As for what Pujols would talk about with Clemente, who died in a plane crash on a mission trip to Nicaragua, he would first ask, "Why did you go? I think I know the answer," Pujols says. "He felt a responsibility. I feel that responsibility too."[7]

Notes

1. Mel Antonen, (2009). "Focus Of Cardinals First Baseman Pujols: Higher Power," *USAToday*, April 1.

2. Joe Posnanski, (2009). "The Power To Believe," *Sports Illustrated*, March 16.

3. Ibid.

4. Ibid.

5. Mel Antonen, (2009). "Focus Of Cardinals First Baseman Pujols: Higher Power," *USAToday*, April 1.

6. Ibid.

7. Joe Posnanski, (2009). "The Power To Believe," *Sports Illustrated*, March 16.
Miguel "Mike" González

Miguel "Mike" González

First Latino Manager in MLB

by Jared Bovinet

In Ernest Hemingway's *The Old Man and the Sea*, the boy asks the old man which Cuban baseball manager was the best at the time, Adolfo Luque or Mike González. The man responds that they are equal, which might surprise some baseball fans because González's career as the first Latino manager in Major League Baseball lasted only 21 games. Even so, he is undoubtedly a pioneering figure in the history of minority participation in the sport.

González was born on September 24, 1890 in Havana, Cuba. He made his professional debut as a catcher with the Fe baseball club in the Cuban Winter League when he was 19 and then joined the Cuban Stars of the Negro League one year later. He played with the Boston Braves for one game and then spent 16 seasons with the Reds, St. Louis Cardinals, New York Giants, and Chicago Cubs. He reached the pinnacle of baseball when he played in the 1929 World Series with the Cubs. He had a .290 career batting average, and peaked in 1924, with a .296 average and 53 RBIs.

His coaching career started with the Columbus Red Birds, the Cardinals' American Association farm club, and then joined the Cardinals as an assistant coach in 1934, helping that year's team win the National League pennant. He coached with the Cardinals through 1946.

González is well known for having a central role in "Slaughter's Mad Dash" in the 1946 World Series. In the bottom of the eighth inning during the seventh game of the series, (and the final game he coached), González was at third base when Henry Walker hit what looked like would be a double, but Enos Slaughter, who was on first base, sprinted past third to home plate. Slaughter made it home and in doing so won the World Series for the Cardinals. Fans and historians are not sure if González tried to get Slaughter to stay on third or score the run, but in the end, the decision to run toward home plate paid off and the Cardinals won their sixth World Series.

The phrase, "Good field, no hit" is attributed to González. He created it after the Cardinals asked him to scout a player, who

González determined had excellent defensive skills, but was a poor batter. The phrase remains in the baseball lexicon to this day. His managerial career lasted for only a few games over two seasons. He managed the Cardinals for the last 16 games of the 1938 season and for nine games during the 1940 season. More important than the number of games he managed was the symbolism behind his position; in managing a team, González proved that Latinos could move off the field and into positions of leadership in the league. When he retired from baseball, González returned to Cuba. He remained there during the Cuban Revolution and died in 1977 at the age of 86.

Major League Baseball has come a long way from having its first Latino manager, Mike González, to today, when one third of team managers are people of color.[1] Individuals like González played critical roles in the transformation of professional teams into organizations whose leadership reflects the diversity of their players and fans.

Notes

1. Richard Lapchick, Alejandra Diaz-Calderon, and Derek McMechan. *The 2009 Racial and Gender Report Card: Major League Baseball*, (The Institute for Diversity and Ethics in Sport), 3.

Alfonso "Al" López

First Full-Time Latino Manager in MLB and Hall of Fame Manager

by Horacio Ruiz

At the time of his death, the gentle Hall of Fame baseball manager had become a hero to the Latino community in his hometown of Tampa. Al López had grown up the son of a cigar factory worker in the Spanish-speaking neighborhood of Ybor City. In 1954, the Al López Field in Tampa was named in his honor. The Field was torn down in 1989 to make room for a parking lot for Legends Field, the New York Yankees' spring training home, but the city presented him with a commemorative bronze plaque that read "Al López Field." Years later after the Field had been torn down and its grounds now part of the south end zone of Raymond James Stadium, the plaque was still one of López's prized possessions. He would show his plaque to journalists that would occasionally drop by his doorstep to talk baseball.

"He was someone we could be proud of, a Hall of Fame inductee who grew up on the streets of Ybor City and did good," said Patrick Manteiga, the editor of *La Gaceta* and the board chairman of the Tampa Sports Authority. "This was someone who didn't have any advantage over others because of wealth. Whatever advantage he had was because of his skills."[1] Mark Beiro, a sports announcer in Tampa and whose father was a López fan said, "Al López was God almost in my house. For anyone who took Al López's legacy seriously, you aspired to be like him. You always wanted to be his kind of man."[2]

López was born August 20, 1908, in Tampa, a son of immigrants from Spain who went to Cuba, then settled in Tampa's Ybor City neighborhood. López could not stand the smoke that permeated the cigar factory that his father worked in. From an early age he vowed never to work in a cigar factory and as a 16-year-old he dropped out of high school to play baseball for the Tampa Smokers of the Florida State League. López caught the attention of legendary pitcher Walter Johnson during a barnstorming tour. Soon he developed a reputation for being a savvy handler of pitchers. On August

26, 1927, he was signed by the Brooklyn Robins, later known as the Brooklyn Dodgers, of the National League. During the 1928 season, as a 19-year-old, López made his big league debut and appeared in three games. He would become a regular by the beginning of the 1930 season, spending seven seasons with Brooklyn, five seasons with the Boston Braves, seven seasons with the Pittsburgh Pirates, and one final season in 1947 with the Cleveland Indians.

At the end of his career, López held the major league record for the most games played as a catcher. His record would last for more than 40 years, having appeared in 1,918 games in that position. His 19-season playing career produced a solid, if not spectacular, career stat line that included two All-Star game appearances, a .261 batting average, 1,547 hits, and 652 RBI. López had two full seasons where he hit over .300 and six times he finished in the top 25 in MVP voting. Upon his retirement at the end of the 1947 season, López began his managerial career with the Indianapolis Indians of the American Association, the minor league at the Triple-A level of baseball.

In 1951, López became manager of the Cleveland Indians, becoming the first full-time Latino manager in Major League baseball history. López posted 93 victories in his inaugural managerial season, but the team would finish second to the Yankees. From 1951–53 the Indians finished in second place behind the Yankees, but in 1954, the Indians finished the regular season with a 111-43 record and won the American League pennant. The 111 wins by the 1954 Indians was an American League record that would not be broken until 1998. But nothing went right for Cleveland during the 1954 World Series, as they were swept by the New York Giants. "We just went cold in the World Series," López said. "Nothing went right for us."[3]

López would manage the Indians to two more second-place finishes before joining the Chicago White Sox as manager in 1957. He would lead the White Sox to two straight second-place finishes in the American League from 1957–58, until capturing the American League pennant in 1959 with the "Go-Go" White Sox, the team's first league championship since the infamous 1919 Black Sox Scandal. López's White Sox, however, would go on to lose the World Series to the Brooklyn Dodgers in six games. After the 1959 World Series, López would manage the White Sox for six seasons, including three second-place finishes and a 1964 season in which the White Sox posted 98 victories and finished just one game behind the Yankees for the American League pennant. After the 1965 season with the White Sox, López retired to take an advisory post within the team. He returned briefly to manage the White Sox in 1968 for 47 games and then managed 17 games in 1969 before retiring again because of a stomach illness.

From 1951–1965, in every one of his 15 full seasons as manager of the Indians and White Sox, López's teams finished with a winning record, at least 85 victories each season. From 1947–1964 the Yankees won the American League championship in all but three seasons. They were interrupted in 1948 by the Cleveland Indians, and then twice more in 1954 by López's Indians and again in 1959 by López's White Sox. López finished his career with a 1410-1004 record, which as of the beginning of the 2009 season ranked him 22nd all-time in victories and his .584 winning percentage ranks eighth all-time.

Throughout his career, López gained the respect of his teammates and those he managed through his calm demeanor and fairness to the players. He earned the nickname "El Señor" for handling his baseball team with respect and with standards.

"He was very fair," said Jim Rivera, an outfielder for the 1959 White Sox. "If you did something good, he would compliment you. If you struck out or made an error, he wouldn't say a word as long as you hustled and worked hard."[4]

In 1977, López was inducted into the National Baseball Hall of Fame in Cooperstown, NY. On the Hall of Fame website with López's profile is a quote from Hall of Fame pitcher Hal Newhouser, who López managed while with the Indians.

"Probably the finest manager I ever played for, baseball-wise, running a ball club and just being the gentleman that he is," Newhouser said. "He wasn't all that easy, he was the manager and no one ran all over him."[5] López told baseball historian Donald Honig what Bill Veeck, then the owner of the 1959 White Sox, thought about López's style, saying, "Veeck once said that if I had a weakness as a manager, it was that I was too decent. Well, I never took that as a negative comment. I'd like to think I'm a decent guy. Nothing wrong with that, is there?"[6]

López died at the age of 97 on October 30, 2005 in his Tampa home. At the time of his death he was the oldest living Hall of Fame member, and the last living major leaguer to play in the 1920s. In the wake of the razed Al López Field, López's Tampa community, the one with so many admirers, would go on to honor their native son again in 1992, renaming a 132-acre park Al López Park. A statue of López during his playing days was erected in the park, allowing Tampa a chance to show anybody who passes by a depiction of the man who for so long was one of the city's prized possessions.

Notes

1. Justin George, "He Was 'Pride Of Tampa Latinos,'" *St. Petersburg Times*, November 1, 2005.

2. Ibid.

3. John Kuenster, "Oldest Hall of Fame Member Revives Baseball Memories," *Baseball Digest*, July 1, 2003.

4. Richard Goldstein, "Al Lopez, A Hall Of Fame Manager, Is Dead At 97," *The New York Times*, October 31, 2005.

5. The National Baseball Hall of Fame and Mueum. Al Lopez. http://www.baseball halloffame.org/hofers/detail.jsp?playerId=117914 (accessed May 27, 2009.)

6. Richard Goldstein, "Al Lopez, AHall Of Fame Manager, Is Dead At 97," *The New York Times*, October 31, 2005.

Oswaldo "Ozzie" Guillén

First Latino Manager to Win a World Series

by Jared Bovinet

To think that a volleyball player from Venezuela would one day become a professional baseball player in the United States and go on to win the American League Rookie of the Year is interesting enough. To know that this same man would become the first Latino Manager of a Major League Baseball team to win a World Series is even more remarkable. Ozzie Guillén did just this.

Born in Ocumare, Venezuela on January 20, 1964, Guillén grew up the oldest of five children in a close family. He began playing volleyball at a young age and was good enough to make the national youth team. His friends thought he was too skinny to be a baseball player, but when Guillén was given the opportunity to play the sport that he would make a career of, he quickly showed his potential. He joined the Venezuelan Winter League and became known for his speed and defensive skills. In the league, he played with fellow baseball legends Luis Aparicio and Omar Vizquel.

One month before his 17th birthday, Guillén signed a professional contract with the San Diego Padres and later made his debut with the White Sox in 1985. He had an immediate impact through his fielding and strong work ethic. At the end of his first season he was named American League Rookie of the Year and *The Sporting News* Rookie of the Year and was already being called one of the best shortstops of his generation. He played with the White Sox until 1997, then with the Baltimore Orioles, the Atlanta Braves and retired as a member of the Tampa Bay Devil Rays. He played 16 seasons in total, earning All-Star honors three times, the Gold Glove in 1999 and the National League Pennant with the Braves that same year.

After he ended his playing career, Guillén served as the third base coach for the Montreal Expos in 2001 and as the third base coach for the Florida Marlins in the 2002 and 2003 seasons, winning his first World Series during the latter.

Guillén took his current job as the Manager of the White Sox in 2004. Some questioned his qualifications for the job because he had never managed a team before. Others, like columnist Jay Mariotti, praised the choice. Mariotti wrote, "Guillén is the right man for the right job at the right time, emotion in motion, a motivator and a salesman all in the same package."[1] White Sox leadership agreed and extended Guillén's contract one year later.

In October of 2005, Guillén led the White Sox to their first American League pennant in 37 years and their first World Series title since 1917. In doing so, he became the first Latino Manager to win a World Series. The fact that his team won 11 of 12 postseason games and swept the Houston Astros is a true testament to Guillén's leadership and preparation. One month after the championship, the Baseball Writers Association of American voted Guillén the 2005 American League Manager of the Year.

After winning the World Series with the White Sox, Guillén planned to retire. Amid the cheers of fans celebrating the team's championship at the victory parade, however, he decided to continue. Following this World Series win, the White Sox struggled for a few seasons but rebounded to set a new home record of 54-28 and winning the American League Central title during the 2008 season.

Throughout his career, Guillén has become legendary for his colorful personality both on and off the field. In his 2008 ESPN.com article titled "Rating Ozzie's most memorable blowups," Jerry Crasnick described Guillén as a "beat writer's best friend and social provocateur" and that "sorting through Guillén's run-ins is like picking your favorite Bruce Springsteen CD."[2] Crasnick listed Guillén's 2005 altercation with his former White Sox teammate Magglio Ordóñez, which occurred after Ordoñez left the White Sox and signed with Detroit, as the number one blowup.

After the altercation, Guillén said, "[Ordóñez] played with the wrong guy. He was bad-mouthing my team. He was bad-mouthing my trainer . . . But when he said Ozzie—uh-oh. As soon as he named me, it was on."[3] *Chicago Tribune* White Sox beat reporter Mark González said this about the exchange between Ordóñez and Guillén, "If they would have met face-to-face, there's a chance somebody wouldn't have come out alive."[4] The former teammates would make amends, but not before creating some amusing headlines.

Guillén has come a long way from volleyball courts in his native Venezuela to becoming the first Latino Manager to win a World Series. While his fearless personality often puts him at the center of the media's attention, it is his knowledge of baseball and proven leadership ability that has established him as a timeless and pioneering figure in professional baseball.

Notes

1. Jay Mariotti, "Oz Could be Just the Wizard Sox Need," *Chicago Sun-Times*, November 3, 2003.

2. Jerry Crasnick, "Rating Ozzie's Most Memorable Blowups," *ESPN.com*, July 23, 2008.

3. Ibid.

4. Ibid.

Alejandro "Alex" Pompez

National Baseball Hall of Fame Executive and Pioneer

by Horacio Ruiz

Before Arturo Moreno of the Anaheim Angels became the first Latino majority owner in Major League Baseball, there was Alex Pompez. He was a team owner in the Negro Leagues who opened and developed a pipeline of great Latino players, creating an influence being felt to this day. Pompez is credited for much of the Latino presence in baseball beginning in the teen years of the 20th century and through the 1960s that has endured into the beginning of the 21st century.

"His work as a team owner, Negro League executive, and talent scout places him alongside Rube Foster, Gus Greenlee, J.L. Wilkerson, Effa Manley, and Cum Posey as one of black baseball's most significant executives," said professor and Pompez biographer, Adrian Burgos. "Considered within baseball's transnational circuit, his longevity and contribution stand alone. He was present at the creation of Negro League baseball and was there at its end, and as a major-league scout, he helped shape its historical legacy."[1]

Pompez was born in 1890 in Key West, FL., a son of Cuban immigrants who lived most of his life in New York City. Pompez became hooked on baseball after returning to Tampa, FL., from a trip to Havana, Cuba in 1910. By the end of the year, he moved to New York and found employment as a cigar maker for 20 dollars a week. By 1911, he was able to open a cigar store which he maintained until his death. Out of the cigar store, Pompez became wealthy by illegally "running numbers" for the local lottery. For as little as one cent, a gambler picked any three-digit number. The winning number would usually be picked out from the total amount wagered at a local racetrack or the next day's volume at the stock exchange. With the money from the "numbers game," Pompez was able to finance his baseball teams and bring Latinos into the United States to play in the Negro Leagues. Pompez's first team was the New York Cubans, which he formed in 1916 for a tour of the United States and the Caribbean.

The formation of the Cubans infuriated another baseball owner and pioneer, Abel Linares. In 1899, Linares brought the first Cuban team to the United States, at the time called the All Cubans, and later renamed the Cuban Stars. When Linares caught word that Pompez was creating a second Cubans team, he protested to the officials that had organized Pompez's 1916 tour. The officials extended an invitation to both teams to play in a one-game playoff for the rights to the name. If Linares' team won, he would be the sole owner of the franchise name, but if Pompez's team won, he would be able to use the Cubans name.

Linares' club, armed with Hall of Famers José Méndez and Cristóbal Torriente, still fell short 3-2 to Pompez's squad. Pompez was able to keep the Cuban Stars name for his squad, which was about to begin its year-round tour. In 1917, the team changed its name to the Havana Cuban Stars, and the following year became known as the New York Cuban Stars. The Cuban Stars remained independent until joining the Eastern Colored League in 1927. It was composed strictly of Latino players until 1935, when they joined the Negro National League. Through the Cuban Stars, Pompez traveled Latin America, scouting and signing new talent to play in the United States through the Cubans.

Pompez helped broker the deal for the first-ever Negro League World Series in 1924, showcasing the champions of the Eastern Colored League and the National Negro League. In 1935, with his numbers business, Pompez was able to remodel Dyckman Oval stadium in the Innwood neighborhood of Manhattan Island to give the Cuban Stars a permanent home. A home park was a rarity for Negro League teams who most of the time had to lease different playing grounds from booking agents. He spent a reported $60,000 to increase the stadium's capacity to 10,000, modernize the amenities, and install lights. Pompez installed lights for the Cuban Stars before many of the major-league teams ever did.

Pompez became one of the biggest numbers kings in New York, and the biggest in Harlem. It was reported that he was making $2,000,000 annually by 1931. But a gangster named Dutch Schultz took over all the numbers kings in New York. In 1932, after being threatened with his life by Schultz, Pompez gave up his numbers business and signed an agreement to receive $250 monthly payments from Schultz to become his agent.

Schultz was killed in 1935 by rival gangs, and Pompez soon reclaimed his business with a partner. In no time, Pompez was grossing $5,000,000 annually on the numbers game. Pompez's activity caught the attention of New York City special prosecutor Thomas Dewey, who was looking to put an end to Pompez's illegal business. Dewey obtained an indictment against Pompez. Pompez fled to Mexico in 1936, but was extradited in October 1937. He reached a plea deal with prosecutors to testify and turn in evidence in the trial of an elected judge who protected Schultz's interests and used bribes for political gain. By 1939, Pompez pledged to stay clean, and he did. The Cubans rejoined the Negro National Leagues and Pompez was welcome back into the Harlem community as a benefactor, rather than as a criminal. Through his business dealings, Pompez had created desperately needed jobs, spent lavishly, gave loans to individuals, and donated to charity at the time of the Great Depression. The numbers game, or lottery, was absorbed by state governments and currently thrive to this day.

In the 1940s, Pompez served as vice president of the National Negro Leagues, and in 1942 the Cubans won three games out of four against the Brooklyn Dodgers in a series played in Havana. The Negro Leagues were running at a loss, both because of financial issues that plagued the league and because of integration of the majors. By the late 1940s, Pompez began selling his players to other Negro League teams and to the majors. In 1948, he reached an agreement with New York Giants owner Horace Stoneham to make the Cubans a farm team for the Giants. In effect, Pompez created the only known partnership between a Negro League team and a Major League team. In 1950, the Cubans folded along with most every Negro League team. Stoneham, who relied on Pompez for advice on the signing and scouting of African-American and Latino players, hired Pompez as a scout. The Giants would become one of the first teams in the Major Leagues to rely on African-American and Latino talent as a result of Pompez's scouting networks.

Pompez was bilingual and unique in that he could traverse the Major League infrastructure as easily as he could traverse the African-American and the Latino baseball worlds. Pompez would eventually be named Director of International Scouting. He was a regular at Giants spring training games, acting as a mentor for the Latin players he scouted and signed.

"He saved my career in '55," said Hall of Famer Orlando Cepeda of Pompez. "The Giants wanted to release me when I was in spring training. I was ready to go home. He talked to (farm director) Jack Schwarz, and the next thing I knew I was on a train to Salem, Virginia, where I started my pro career."[2]

Among the players Pompez is credited with signing either directly or through his network are Cepeda, Willie McCovey, Monte Irvin, Juan Marichal, Minnie Miñoso, Tony Oliva, Camilo Pascual, and the Alou brothers. He is also noted for getting Stoneham interested in signing Willie Mays.

"Pompez was one of the first guys to tell Stoneham to take a look at Mays," Burgos said. "Many people don't realize how much Pompez was in Stoneham's ear. He recommended the Giants sign other Negro League players, including Monte Irvin and Hank Thompson. Although others may have been credited for the actual signing of these players, Pompez directed the Giants to them."[3] Pompez was so well respected for his involvement in baseball and scouting that he was asked to serve on the Hall of Fame committee responsible for the induction of Negro League players in 1971. Pompez helped elect the first four classes of Negro Leauge players into the Hall of Fame, and he himself was enshrined in 2006. He died in New York City in 1974 at the age of 83.

"He was quite a man," said Felipe Alou, a long-time baseball manager and one of the players Pompez signed. "What a giant of the game he was. He helped a lot of Latin players make the transition to baseball in America. I know he helped me."[4]

Notes

1. Brian McKenna, "Alex Pompez," http://www.baseball-fever.com/showthread.php?t=85128 (accessed April 21, 2009).

2. John Shea, (2006). "A Giant In His Field, And Now A Hall Of Famer," *SFGate*. http://www.sfgate.com/cgi-bin/article.cgi?f=/chronicle/archive/2006/07/30/SPGHHK7 T981.DTL&type=printable (accessed April 21, 2009).

3. Ibid.

4. Ibid.

Omar Minaya

First Latino General Manager in MLB

by Jared Bovinet

Omar Minaya and his family lived during a time of great political turbulence in the Dominican Republic during the 1950s and 1960s. Rafael Trujillo, the country's military dictator, was infamous for his suppression of civil rights and freedoms and quickly stifled political dissidents. He was assassinated in 1965, but the country continued to experience political strife as a result of several attempts to overthrow his successors. After Minaya's father, Lolo, rescued two of his cousins from political fights, he and his wife Antonia decided it was finally time to bring their family to the United States.

The family arrived in Queens, New York and settled near Shea Stadium when Minaya was eight years old. A friend introduced him to baseball that same year, and he fell in love with the sport that united so many children of so many backgrounds and ethnicities throughout the neighborhood. Minaya always embraced the patchwork of nationalities he found in New York, and at 16, moved to Elmhurst, the most ethnically diverse zip code in the United States. He grew up surrounded by many friends and showed his leadership abilities at a young age. In fact, his peers voted him sophomore class president but he decided not to run because he wanted to devote his time to baseball, his real passion.

Minaya had so much baseball talent he was offered a scholarship to play baseball at Mississippi State. He decided against attending and instead signed with the Oakland A's as a 14th round draft choice in 1978. He gave half the $13,500 he received from his first contract to his parents, which enabled them to move back to the Dominican Republic, which had recently become a full democracy.

He was released by the A's after one season in Class A and his tenure with the Seattle Mariners, his next team, was even shorter. Minaya then played in Italy, where he enjoyed learning Italian and the intricacies of its culture. He returned to the States after two seasons when he was offered a part-time scouting job for the Texas Rangers in 1984.

Minaya became a successful scouting director, concentrating on talent in Latin America. He worked to establish a strong connection between talent in this region and the Rangers team and used his fluency in English and Spanish to his advantage when talking to potential players like the then 16-year-old Sammy Sosa. He soon established a Rangers baseball academy where 15 prospective players learned the game and lived together. In a few years, he went on to become the director of professional and international scouting for the team.

Minaya moved to New York to become the assistant general manager of the Mets in 1996, helping them to reach the National League Championship Series in 1999 and the World Series in 2000. While becoming assistant general manager of an MLB team is an accomplishment in itself, Minaya had always dreamed of becoming a general manager. His friends reminded him of the fact that there had never been a Latino general manager, but he continued to believe that he would someday reach his goal.

The goal seemed as distant as ever after he interviewed for the position of general manager with the Los Angeles Dodgers, Milwaukee Brewers, and Colorado Rockies but was not chosen. When the Seattle Mariners, Anaheim Angels, Pittsburgh Pirates, and Boston Red Sox continued the streak, Minaya still did not give up and believed that he was not the best fit for what these teams were looking for. Teams wanted Ivy League-educated lawyers and businessmen to run their teams. Minaya responded, "I'm not your guy. I see the job in bigger terms. Paperwork, that's false hustle. It takes away creativity. The more paperwork the opposition does, the better my chances are."[1]

Minaya finally got his opportunity to be a general manager with the Montreal Expos. One day, MLB Commissioner Bud Selig called and offered him the job. Minaya hesitated at first because he knew the position would not last long due to the team's impending relocation to Washington. He decided to take it anyway. He said, "I know that I'd be the first Hispanic general manager in Major League Baseball history, and that if I showed my management skills, it would not only help me in the future, but show others what Hispanics can do in the front office and thereby open the door."[2] Despite having one of the lowest salary budgets in the league, Minaya was able to recruit star players Bartolo Colón and Cliff Floyd, which helped the 2002 Expos finish second in the National League East with a record of 83-79.

In 2004, Mets owner Fred Wilpon asked Minaya to return to New York to serve as the Mets' general manager. Minaya agreed, excited by the opportunity to realize his long-held dream. He quickly made personnel changes after he arrived, adding stars like Pedro Martínez and Carlos Beltran, among others. The Mets finished the 2005 seasons with 83 wins. The next season, Minaya's decisions continued to pay dividends as the Mets won the National League East and finished with 97 wins, tied for the best record in Major League baseball. The following two seasons were not as successful, however.

Minaya came under fire in the summer of 2009 for the poor performance of the Mets during the 2008–2009 season. The team had slipped to fourth place in the NL East because of injuries and had missed the playoffs the previous season. Top management remains committed to keeping Minaya as general manager. Fred Wilpon declared, "Am I going to bring Omar back next year? Absolutely. That's a fact."[3]

Wilpon has good reason to have faith in Minaya. Minaya has proven himself both as a talented player, scout, assistant general manager, and general manager. And even with all his success in the world of baseball, Minaya has not forgotten about his native country and giving back to the people of the Dominican Republic. Minaya has worked to help establish Esperanza International, a community organization in his native country that helps poor families generate income to support their education and health needs.

In addition, Minaya has worked with the Baseball Tomorrow Fund, a community investment initiative of Major League Baseball, to renovate baseball fields in the Dominican Republic. At the ceremony to unveil the restored fields, Minaya encouraged hundreds of young baseball players to work hard to follow their dreams, even if the path presents challenges. Minaya certainly could relate to what he was preaching; in becoming the first Latino general manager in Major League Baseball, he realized a dream that at times seemed a million miles away, but through tenacity and dedication, his dream became a reality.

Notes

1. Gary Smith, "The Story of O," *Sports Illustrated*. June 23, 2007.

2. Ira Berkow, "Amid Some Uncertainty, The Expos Play to Win," *The New York Times*, July 18, 2002.

3. "Mets General Manager Omar Minaya is Expected Back Next Season," AP, August 23, 2009.

Arturo "Arte" Moreno

First Latino Majority Owner in MLB

by Horacio Ruiz

On May 22, 2003 Arturo Moreno was introduced as the new owner of the Anaheim Angels to become the first Latino majority owner in Major League Baseball history and the first Latino to own a major sports team in the United States. One of the very first actions that Moreno took was a lowering of beer and concession prices. With a drop in beer prices Angels fans were quickly won over by Moreno, and they would swoon over their new owner when he aggressively approached the free-agency market to make the Angels a perennial contender in the American League. The Angels, owned by the Walt Disney Company for seven years prior to Moreno's arrival, were considered to be an afterthought in the Disney conglomerate despite a 2002 World Series Championship. In stepped Moreno, a savvy businessman ever aware of a good deal, he purchased the defending World Series champions for $183.5 million with the franchise value estimated at $225–$250 million.

Moreno, a fourth-generation Mexican-American made his fortune in the billboard and outdoor advertising industry. After graduating from Tucson High School, Moreno briefly attended the University of Arizona before being drafted into the United States army to serve in the Vietnam War. He served a tour of duty in Indochina before returning to the University of Arizona where he graduated with a marketing degree. Moreno's first job out of college was selling billboard advertising space for Eller Outdoor. Moreno's start was less-than-auspicious; his first commission check was for $2.25. He said he would have liked to have framed the check, but he needed the money so he cashed it in.

Despite the rocky start, Moreno loved the business and began working his way up the executive ladder. "It's a fun business, a people business. Lots of entertaining, going to ballgames or the theater,"[1] Moreno told *Fortune*. In 1983, Moreno left Eller for Outdoor Systems, at the time a small Phoenix-based billboard firm. Moreno would become the company's president and CEO, and in 10 years annual sales for the firm would grow from $500,000 to $90 million. In 1996, Moreno spearheaded a move to take Outdoor Systems public on Wall Street. The initial public offering soared, and within three years Outdoor Systems' stock had increased in value by 1,460 percent.

Months before the bottom fell out of the market in 1998, Moreno and business partner Bill Levine sold the company to Infinity Broadcasting / CBS for $8.3 billion in stock and assumed debt. With that sale, Moreno became one of the richest men in the United States. A long-time sports fan who as a boy listened to the Dodgers' Vin Scully on the radio, Moreno had wanted to own a major league baseball team for some time. In 2001, Moreno attempted to become the managing partner of the Arizona Diamondbacks but was bought out by majority owner Jerry Colangelo. He also owned minority shares of the Phoenix Suns until 2003.

Moreno had forayed into ownership many years before attempting to become the Diamondbacks owner. From 1986 to 1992, Moreno and 17 other investors bought the minor league Salt Lake City Trappers of the Class A Pioneer League. The ownership bought the team for $150,000 and sold the Trappers for $1.75 million—a 1,006 percent profit in a span of six years. Minor league baseball ownership held a special place in Moreno's heart where he would sometimes answer sales calls or take tickets at the gate. The owners would smoke cigars and drink beer in the stands while sitting behind the dugout cheering the team and talking to fans. As fun as owning a team was for Moreno, he also took the business side of it seriously. "From the get-go, [Moreno] understood it was a business deal," said Steve Pearson, a former general manager of the Trappers. "For some of the other guys, it was a toy. But for Arte, he always saw it as a business." The day Pearson was hired, Moreno took him out to dinner and explained to him that the more fans Pearson could bring to the games, the more he would get paid.

When Moreno became owner of the Angels, he brought back some of the Single A excitement from the Trappers. "The most important thing is to focus in on the fans," Moreno said. "People in the minor leagues really work hard to market to their fans and there is a lot of sizzle and excitement."[2] Moreno sits in the bleachers with the fans, walks around the concession areas to make sure they are running smoothly, and aggressively marketed his team beyond the Anaheim area into parts considered Los Angeles Dodgers territories that include Malibu and Pasadena, and at Los Angeles International Airport. Buses in Los Angeles had advertisements of Vladimir Guerrero, the Angels' newest acquisition of the 2003 off-season and the biggest free agency signing in that year's off-season. In 2004, Moreno's first full-year as owner, Guerrero won the AL MVP Award, and the team payroll went up from $73 million in 2003 to $110 million in 2004. The Angels also signed pitcher Bartolo Colón who would win 18 games in 2004 and in 2005 became the first Angels pitcher to win the Cy Young Award since 1964. In 2004, The Angels won the American League West for the first time since 1986 and the team drew 3.4 million fans to Angels Stadium, behind only to the New York Yankees and Dodgers. The Angels have since won the AL West in 2005 and from 2007–2009.

At the beginning of the 2006 season, the Angels signed a lucrative 10-year deal with Fox Sports Net for the broadcasting rights to their games. At the beginning of the 2009 season, the Angels were valued at $509 million, a 277 percent increase in value since 2003. Moreno is considered one of the best owners in baseball and his goal has been the same since day one, which is to win a World Series. In 2003, the very same year that Moreno purchased the Angels, he was listed as the fifth most influential minority in American sports by *Sports Illustrated*, just below Charlotte Bobcats owner Robert Johnson, Tiger Woods, Serena Williams, and Michael Jordan. "It's one thing to have the means to buy a baseball team," Moreno told *Time Magazine*, "but more important, do you really respect the opportunity?"[3] Moreno is reported to be intensely private, even as he is one of the biggest supporters of the University of Arizona's athletics department and is a season ticket holder in basketball and football, he shuns the prime seats for more private locations.

"I'm fourth-generation Mexican-American and I've always called myself Mexican," Moreno said. "But I am an American, and I love my heritage. I think with everyone, you get an opportunity to represent your people and you try to show people that there are plenty of opportunities in America for anyone who is willing to work. I am living proof that the system works."[4]

Notes

1. Jjonathan J. Higuera,, Craig Harris, Jjoseph A. Reeves, "Baseball More Than A "Business For Moreno," *The Arizona Republic*, April 23, 2003.

2. Darrell Satzman, "Ballpark Frank: Arturo Moreno, New Owner Of the Anaheim Angels, Moved Quickly To Make Changes At The Ballpark To Make The Outing More Appealing," *Los Angeles Business Journal*, August 11, 2003.

3. Sean Gregory, "Arturo Moreno," *Time Magazine*, August 13, 2005.

4. Darrell Satzman, "Ballpark Frank: Arturo Moreno, New Owner of the Anaheim Angels, Moved Quickly to Make Changes at the Ballpark to Make the Outing More Appealing, "(People)(Interview)." *Los Angeles Business Journal*. 2003. *HighBeam Research* .(September 15, 2009). http://www.highbeam.com/doc/1G1-106982407.html

3

LATINOS IN THE NBA

by Richard Lapchick

The National Basketball Association has helped make basketball the international giant that it is. While the NBA started as an all white league and then became the league with more African-American players than any other, it is now far from just black and white. Latinos have been making their mark on the league and the NBA is counting on that to increase its own market.

In October 2009, the NBA unveiled its biggest-ever Latino marketing effort that included the placement of commercials on English and Spanish language television, radio, Websites, and at community-based events. The NBA will also now have a Latino portal for fans who want the game in Spanish. The NBA recognized the potential of the Latino market years ago and started Latino outreach efforts in 2000. The NBA Finals in 1999 and 2000 were broadcast in Spanish along with the 2000 NBA All-Star Game.

The San Antonio Spurs and Miami Heat have been marketing and reaching out to the Latino community for more than a decade according to Saskia Sorrosa, senior director of U.S. Hispanic Marketing at the NBA. The results have been dramatic.

The early efforts by the Spurs and the Heat have delivered strong results for the NBA franchises with 58 percent of all adult attendees at a Spurs home game being Latino while 45 percent of those attending Heat games are Latino. The Lakers are third with 32 percent. Other markets with high Latino concentrations include Phoenix (28 percent), Sacramento (25 percent), New York (24 percent), and Dallas (20 percent).

The new initiative will put Latino stars in all their promotional campaigns. According to *Hispanic Sports Business* published in the

Hispanic Market Weekly, NBA Commissioner David Stern said, "This is a great moment for me, because this is a subject that is near and dear to my heart . . . We have looked at our assets to see how we can utilize them in attracting the Hispanic market. . . . We've discovered that there is no monolithic Hispanic market . . . Yet there is one unifying factor—the use of the same language, no matter where they come from."

The campaign, called "Éne•bé•a" (which is how the NBA is pronounced in Spanish), will have spots featuring Laker Paul Gasol from Spain, Heat guard Carlos Arroyo from Puerto Rico, Brazilian point guard Leandro Barbosa of the Phoenix Suns, and Mexican Eduardo Nájera of the New Jersey Nets.

It is estimated that overall, 15 percent of today's NBA fans are Latino. The NBA plans to grow that rapidly with "Éne•bé•a." Latino youth are playing the game. According to the Simmons teen/adult combined study conducted in 2007, some 2.2 million Latino teens play basketball, followed by soccer at 1.9 million.

As the 2009–10 season started, there were six Latino players born in the United States in the NBA and19 Latino players from outside of the U.S. The NBA counts players from Brazil in the mix. Starting this season, the Chicago Bulls will air 21 home games in Spanish. The New York Knicks offer limited game-day broadcasts in Spanish. There will be Spanish language TV broadcasts on ESPN Deportes. The NBA originally had a three-year contract with Telemundo starting in 2002. This season ESPN Deportes will broadcast 18 games in Spanish as well as the Eastern Conference Finals.

So now that the growth of both Latino players and fans seems assured, it is time to meet the Latino Campeones in the NBA. Al Cueto was the first Latino selected in the NBA Draft. Born in Havana, Cuba in 1946, his family moved to Miami in 1960 short after Fidel Castro was sworn in as Prime Minister of Cuba. Standing 6'8", Cueto was drafted by the Seattle SuperSonics with the third pick in the 10th round of the 1969 NBA draft. He was also selected by the Denver Rockets in the 1969 ABA Draft. When Denver realized that Cueto was Cuban they traded his rights to the Miami Floridians.

Cueto joined Miami. Cueto made the Floridians and played a solid roll in his first season in the ABA. After his second season, the newly married Cueto decided his playing days were over because of a need to find something more certain to start a family. Cueto averaged 5.3 points and 4.3 rebounds during his professional career.

Alfred "Butch" Lee was the first Latino to play in the NBA. Butch became the first Puerto Rican-born player to play in the National Basketball Association. He was selected with the 10th pick of the first round by the Atlanta Hawks. He played for the Hawks, Cleveland Cavaliers, and the Los Angeles Lakers while in the NBA. In his injury-shortened NBA career, he played in 96 games averaging 8.1 points per game and 3.2 assists per game.

Lee had a great college career at Marquette where he enrolled in 1974 after Marquette had a runner-up finish at the NCAA Tournament. In 1977, Marquette made it to the championship of the Final Four. Matched against North Carolina in the finals, Butch led the way, scoring 19 points as the Warriors came from behind to win the national championship. Lee was the MVP for the tournament. In 1978 he was awarded the Naismith Award for Men's College Player of the Year.

Rolando Blackman was the ninth player selected in the 1981 NBA Draft by the Dallas Mavericks. Dallas came away with three talented rookies in the 1981 NBA Draft, including first overall pick Mark Aguirre. Blackman became the first Latino to have his jersey retired.

In 1983, Blackman was named team captain. From 1984 to 1990, the Mavericks reached the playoffs six times and Blackman steadily increased his scoring average to 20 points per game over that span. At the time Blackman left the Mavericks he was their all-time leading scorer with 16,643 points. For his career Blackman tallied 17,623 points, 3,278 rebounds and 2,981 assists in his 980 games. He ended his career with the New York Knicks and contributed to the team's run to the 1994 NBA Finals.

Mark Aguirre was the first Latino picked number one in the NBA Draft. He earned the distinction with a fantastic college career at DePaul University. As a freshman, he averaged 24 points and 7.6 rebounds a game while leading the team to the Final Four where they lost 74-76 to the Larry Bird led Indiana State Sycamores in the national semi-finals. In three years as a starter, Aguirre averaged 24.5 a game. He was a two-time All-American, was named the 1980 Player of the Year by the Associated Press and was the 1980 Naismith Award winner. He was also named a member of the 1980 U. S. Olympic team that didn't play because of the country's boycott of the Moscow Games. Mark skipped his senior year to enter the NBA. The Dallas Mavericks selected Aguirre with the first pick overall. His greatest statistical season came in the 1983–1984 season, when he averaged 29.5 points per game, making him the second leading scorer in the league. He later helped the Detroit Pistons win two championships in 1989 and 1990. Over his 13-year career Mark amassed 18,458 points. As of the start of the 2008 NBA season, Mark ranked 45th in all-time scoring.

Born in Argentina, Manu Ginóbili is considered the first Latino NBA superstar. Ginóbili made his professional debut in Argentina in 1995 with Andino. In 1998, he joined the Argentina National Team and then moved to Italy to face tougher competition. In 1999, Ginóbili entered the NBA Draft and the San Antonio Spurs selected him with the 57th overall pick. He continued to play in Ginóbili and joined the Spurs in 2002.

In 2005, he was just the second Latin American born player to play in an NBA All-Star game. Ginóbili has steadily increased his points per game throughout his career, averaging 19.8 for the 2007–08 season which was his career high. To date, Ginóbili has been a member of three NBA championship teams and one All-Star team.

Alfonso "Al" Cueto

First Latino to be Drafted by NBA Team

by Chris Kamke

The first Latino to be selected in a NBA draft was Al Cueto. Standing 6'8", Cueto was drafted by the Seattle SuperSonics with the third pick in the 10th round of the 1969 NBA Draft. He was also selected by the Denver Rockets in the 1969 ABA Draft.

AL CUETO
PROS' FORWARD

Courtesy of Al Cueto.

Cueto picked up a basketball for the first time around age 10. Born on August 2, 1946 in Havana, Cuba, Cueto and his family moved to Miami in 1960 shortly after Fidel Castro was sworn in as Prime Minister of Cuba. Cueto continued to play basketball in junior high and at Coral Gables High School. During his sophomore year at Coral Gables, a 5'10" version of Cueto played point guard. By his senior year Cueto had sprouted to 6'8" but his weight failed to increase at the same rate and he graduated high school weighing less than 150 pounds. Due in part to his frail frame and lower-than-desired grades, Cueto attended St. Gregory Junior College in Shawnee, Oklahoma. There he quickly put on 80 pounds and transferred to the University of Tulsa.

During his senior year at Tulsa, Cueto and Bobby "Bingo" Smith led the Hurricanes to a top ten AP ranking and a spot in the 1969 NIT Tournament. Tulsa suffered a surprising first round loss to St. Peter's in Madison Square Garden. To Cueto, the unexpected loss meant the end of his playing days. Then he received a call informing him that he had been drafted in both the NBA and ABA drafts. "It was a surprise to be drafted. I knew I was good but I didn't realize I was that good,"[1] recalls Cueto. Seattle of the NBA and Denver of the ABA were both interested in the power forward. When Denver realized that Cueto was Cuban they traded his rights to the Miami Floridians.

Cueto decided to pursue the opportunity in Miami. "I figured if I couldn't make it in Miami, I had no shot in Seattle,"[2] Cueto said. Cueto would make the Floridians and played an effective roll in his first season in the ABA. At 23 years old, Cueto had developed a solid frame but still possessed the ball handling skills he had built back in high school while he ran the point guard position. In his first ABA season, Cueto appeared in 78 games, averaging 6.0 points and 5.8 rebounds. The 1969 season was tough for the Floridians. They finished in sixth place in the Eastern Conference with a 23-61 record—36 games out of first place.

The next season Cueto joined the Memphis Pros. A much stronger team than the Floridians had been in the previous season, the Pros finished the season in third place in the Western Conference. Cueto's numbers dropped slightly from his first season but were still an important part to his team. The Pros faced the top-seeded Indiana Pacers in the first round of the ABA playoffs. Just like with his collegiate postseason, Cueto's team suffered another first round exit as the Pacers swept the Pros in four games.

After that season the newly married Cueto decided his playing days were over. "The worst part about playing professionally was that you always had to defend your position on the team,"[3] Cueto said. Needing to find something more certain to start a family, Cueto ended his playing days despite opportunities in Europe and Mexico. Still, Cueto has fond memories from the ABA. "The best part of playing basketball was visiting all the cities and meeting players with different backgrounds. At the time I was the only foreign player in the league and it was great experiencing the different backgrounds."[4] Cueto averaged 5.3 points and 4.3 rebounds during his professional career.

Recently, Cueto has worked with the Orange Bowl Committee in Miami, Florida. In 2003 he served as President for the bowl game that featured the University of Southern California Trojans and the Iowa Hawkeyes.

Notes

1. Alfonso Cueto, (2009). Interviewed by Chris Kamke. September 6.
2. Ibid.
3. Ibid.
4. Ibid.

Alfred "Butch" Lee

First Latino Player in the NBA

by Chris Kamke

Butch Lee was quite a basketball player. As a star guard for the Marquette Warriors during the late 1970s, Lee helped to solidify Marquette basketball's location on the national map. "There wasn't one thing that made Butch great," says Al McGuire, Lee's coach at Marquette, "He was a silent assassin, gentle, lovable, a competitor from within."[1] Born in San Juan, Puerto Rico on December 5, 1956, the Lee family moved to New York when Lee was a child. It was in New York that the future NBA player developed his game and earned national recruiting interest. While attending De Witt Clinton High School in the Bronx, Lee became a first team all city player and honor student.

Lee's play impressed many college scouts and in 1974 he decided to accept an offer to play for Al McGuire at Marquette University. He joined a Marquette team in the fall of 1974 that was fresh off a runner-up finish at the NCAA Tournament. As a starting guard from the moment he stepped onto campus, Lee was an impact player. Marquette was impressive during Lee's first few years, making deep runs in the NCAA Tournament, but failing to reach the Final Four. During his sophomore season Lee asked McGuire for permission to play for Team USA in the 1976 Games in Montreal, but his coach said no, having already sent players to the tryout. With his request denied, Lee turned to his home country for an opportunity to compete. At the age of 19, Lee made the Puerto Rican national team. During round play, Lee got the opportunity to face the team that he never got a chance to be a part of. Team USA possessed the greatest players in the world and was coached by Dean Smith. They were the team to beat. In a game that should have been no contest, Puerto Rico, thanks in large part to Lee's shooting, was able to close out the first half tied against Team USA at 51. As the second half got underway, Lee, the youngest player on the Puerto Rican team, kept knocking down shots, keeping Puerto Rico within striking distance. With only seconds remaining in the game and Team USA leading by one point, Puerto Rico had the ball and a chance to win. Everyone in the arena knew who the ball was going to. Puerto Rico's upset bid was interrupted when Lee was called for a charge as he drove to the basket. In a heroic effort, Lee's 35 points weren't enough as Puerto Rico fell to Team USA 95-94. "I would have liked to come out on top, but I'm glad I was a part of it," Butch said. "It was a big game on a big stage. We lost, but made Puerto Rico proud."[2]

Lee would use the momentum and experience he gained from the Olympics to fuel the remainder of his collegiate basketball career. In 1977, after an outstanding season, Lee starred on the Warrior team that made it to the Final Four. In the semifinal round of the tournament, the Warriors faced UNC—Charlotte. The game featured great back and forth play and required an epic last-second effort by Marquette to surpass UNC—Charlotte. In the closing moments of the game, Lee heaved a pass the length of the court to Jerome Whitehead for a buzzer-beating shot to give Marquette a two-point victory. Marquette then moved on to face North Carolina in the Finals. Lee led the way again, scoring 19 points as the Warriors came from behind to win the national championship and the right to cut down the nets. For his efforts the star guard was named the tournament's most outstanding player.

Lee won numerous other honors while at Marquette. For his outstanding play during both his junior and senior seasons, he earned All-American honors, second-team and first-team, respectively. In 1978 he was awarded the Naismith Award for Men's College Player of the Year. Butch was also named the Adolph Rupp Trophy winner and won the Associated Press College Basketball Player of the Year

Award in 1978. As a four-year starter at Marquette, Lee totaled 1,735 points and his number 15 jersey is now retired.

After an impressive collegiate career, Lee became the first Latino and Puerto Rican player in the National Basketball Association. He was selected with the 10th pick of the first round by the Atlanta Hawks. During his first season in the NBA he averaged 7.7 points for the Hawks before being traded to the Cleveland Cavaliers 49 games into the season. With the Cavaliers, Lee's offensive productivity increased. Over the final 33 games of the regular season he averaged 11.5 points which brought his season average scoring to just over nine points per game for his rookie season.

During his second season he was traded to the Los Angeles Lakers where he played a very limited role alongside Kareem Abdul-Jabbar and Magic Johnson. Lee suffered a right knee injury that would ultimately prove too large an obstacle to overcome. The injury he sustained forced him to the bench for most of his second season, but he was still part of the Lakers' 1979–80 championship team. After that season, Lee decided to retire. A few years later he would return to Puerto Rico.

Lee traveled back to Marquette for a halftime ceremony to honor the 1977 National Champions. "We all went to a pub that night and played pool. When it was over, I felt like it was time to go back to the dorms," Lee said. "Over the years, I've come to appreciate how difficult it is to do what we did. My career wasn't as long as

Courtesy of Marquette University Athletics.

I wanted it to be, but I was able to be on a championship team. I don't envy anyone."[3] When he is asked about his favorite memory one would instantly think of the 1977 NCAA Championship, but that isn't the case. "The championship was big," Lee said. "I made the cover of *Sports Illustrated* after that, so that was really something, but my best game was in the Olympics."[4]

McGuire taught Lee a lot about basketball while playing at Marquette, but more importantly, McGuire taught Lee how unimportant the game really is. "Al told us that basketball was a big thing to us, but it was just a small part of life," Lee said. "I paid attention to that. I always thought of myself as more than just a basketball player."[5]

Notes

1. Seth Davis, (1997). "Marquette Guard Butch Lee," *Sports Illustrated*, April 7.
2. *Marquette Tribune*, (2007). "Finally Coming Out On Top," February 1, Sec. Sports.
3. Seth Davis, (1997). "Marquette Guard Butch Lee," *Sports Illustrated*, April 7.
4. *Marquette Tribune*, (2007). "Finally Coming Out On Top," February 1, Sec. Sports.
5. Seth Davis, (1997). "Marquette Guard Butch Lee," *Sports Illustrated*, April 7.

Rolando Blackman

First Latino to Have Jersey Number
Retired by NBA Team

by Chris Kamke

Rolando Blackman was born on February 26, 1959 in Panama City. After spending the first eight years of his life in Panama, Blackman moved to Brooklyn with his sister to live with his grandmother. His parents, John and Gloria, followed their children a few years later. Blackman grew up playing soccer but eventually picked up the game of basketball. The transition to basketball wasn't easy. He was cut from his 7th, 8th, and 9th grade teams at Meyer Levin Junior High School. These early setbacks did not dissuade Blackman from the game. Determined to succeed, he spent his summers going through early morning workouts with playground coach Teddy Gustus, instead of hanging around with friends. Blackman then enrolled in William E. Grady Vocational School on Coney Island, New York. It was there, under Coach Fred Moscowitz, that Blackman developed his game to collegiate level potential.

Blackman was heavily recruited but the 6'6", 200-pound guard chose to play for a lesser known school at the time, Kansas State University, then of the Big Eight Conference (BEC). At Kansas State, Coach Jack Hartman served as a second father to Blackman. As a sophomore, Blackman became a team leader, earning First Team All-BEC honors. Although Blackman was classified as a Panamanian citizen, he won a spot on the 1980 U.S. Olympic team. However, President Carter barred American teams from competition in the Moscow Games. Blackman later became a US citizen in 1986.

One of Blackman's greatest moments at Kansas State happened in 1981 against Oregon State in the second round of the NCAA Tournament's Western Regionals. With the game tied with just two seconds remaining, Blackman sunk a 16-foot jump shot from the right baseline securing the victory over the second-ranked Beavers. Three times Blackman was selected as the BEC Defensive Player of the Year. In 1981 he was named a First Team All-American.

In his 121 collegiate games, Blackman scored 1,844 points, an average of 15.1 points per game. Kansas State retired Blackman's number 25 in 2007.

Blackman was the ninth player selected in the 1981 NBA Draft by the Dallas Mavericks and it didn't take long for him to provide significant contributions. Dallas came away with three talented rookies in the 1981 NBA Draft, including first overall pick Mark Aguirre. Blackman proved to be a fierce defender and a great outside scorer. This trio of stars formed the foundation of the Mavericks. In their first season, the trio led the Mavericks to a 28-54 record, nearly double the team's win total from their expansion year.

By 1983, Blackman was named team captain. In 1984 the Mavericks had their first winning record and made their first playoff appearance. From 1984 to 1990, the Mavericks reached the playoffs six times and Blackman steadily increased his scoring average, settling around the 20 points per game mark over that span. Blackman and fellow backcourt teammate Derek Harper were considered to be one of the best backcourt combinations in the league during the 1980s. By the mid 1980s, the Maverick fans had become accustomed to winning in the regular season but yearned for success in the playoffs. In 1986, two player moves were made, Roy Tarpley was drafted and disgruntled Dale Ellis was traded. Blackman provided a lot of the scoring, averaging 21.5 points, as the Mavericks secured the second seed in the Western Conference. However, they suffered a disappointing first round exit at the hands of Dale Ellis' new team, the Seattle Supersonics. In the 1988 playoffs, the Mavericks, led by Blackman's nine consecutive points in the fourth quarter against the Denver Nuggets, opened an insurmountable lead and clinched their first Western Conference Finals appearance. "He's just a clutch player," teammate Derek Harper said of Blackman. "He's been doing it since he was in the league. You can see it in his eyes. He loves those situations."[1]

However, like several of the Mavericks playoff appearance in their short history, they were eliminated by the Los Angeles Lakers, this time in the Conference Finals. That was the closest Blackman would get to an NBA Championship with the Mavericks. Known for his ability to make a clutch shot and play suffocating defense, Blackman was selected to four NBA All-Star Games (1985–87, 1990) while playing for the Mavericks. Blackman provided a lot of thrills in Dallas but in June of 1992 Blackman was traded to the New York Knicks for a first round draft pick.

Blackman joined Patrick Ewing and the title contending Knicks for the 1992–1993 season. There were high expectations for the guard who had averaged 18 points per game for most of his career and Blackman was motivated by a realistic shot at a championship. "I don't think I'm the only missing piece to a championship, but I'm one of them,"[2] said Blackman. However, much of Blackman's two seasons with the Knicks were filled with injuries, which along with the emergence of John Starks, often kept him out of the starting lineup. "I've played for 13 years and 11 of those were great years," said Blackman. "Not good years, they were great years. For me, I'm just trying to get the rust off, trying to find my place on this basketball team and gain acceptance again from the guys I'm playing with."[3] Still the Knicks were an extremely strong team during the early 90s and Blackman supplied a nice spark off the bench.

In 1994, at the age of 35 Blackman was introduced back into the starting lineup while Starks was recovering from a knee injury. Some fans were skeptical of the Knicks' decision but Blackman's coach was not. "I've said this 100 times about Rolando: he's a pro's pro," said Pat Riley, the Knicks coach. "I've always believed in him. I don't care how old he is, he can play the game of basketball."[4] They reached the NBA Finals but lost to Hakeem Olajuwon and the Houston Rockets in a seven game series. The Knicks released Blackman after the NBA Finals, ending Blackman's 13-year NBA career. At the time Blackman left the Mavericks he was their All-Time leading scorer (16,643 points). For his career, Blackman tallied 17,623 points, 3,278 rebounds and 2,981 assists in his 980 games. Blackman's number 22 jersey is only one of two retired numbers by the Dallas Mavericks. After his time in the NBA, Blackman played two years in Europe. He spent one year each with AEK Athens BC (1994–1995) and Stefanel Milano (1995–1996), winning Italian Cup MVP in 1996.

Throughout his career, Blackman gave back to the community. He has been involved with Big Brothers, Big Sisters, the Special Olympics, the Muscular Dystrophy Association, and the American Cancer Society. He has also put forth efforts in renovating the playground on which he grew up. He and his wife, Tamara, have four children, Valerie, Brittany, Briana, and Vernell.

Notes

1. *New York Times*, (1988). "Mavericks Gain Final; Jazz Ties Series; Mavericks 108, Nuggets 95," May 20, New York edition, Sec. D.

2. Clifton Brown, (1992). Blackman Rates Knicks From Perimeter," *New York Times*, August 14. sec. B.

3. Clifton Brown, (1994). "Blackman Is Fitting In, So Forget the Early Jitters," *New York Times*, March 21. Sec. C.

4. Ibid.

Mark Aguirre

First Latino To Be NBA's First Overall Draft Pick

by Chris Kamke

Considered one of the greatest athletes to ever come out of the Windy City, Mark Aguirre was known for his ability to score the basketball. Born on December 10, 1959, Aguirre, a Mexican-American, was not always the most popular player on the court, but he was regularly the best.

Aguirre was a stellar high school player. In 1978 he was named a McDonald's All-American and participated in the inaugural Mc-Donald's All-American game held at The Spectrum in Philadelphia, PA. As a Chicago native, he chose to stay close to his roots and signed with DePaul University. There, he quickly found himself in the national spotlight.

From the moment he stepped on the DePaul University campus, Aguirre infused life into the basketball program. As a freshman, Aguirre average 24 points and 7.6 rebounds and led the Blue Demons to an upset win over number one seed UCLA to reach the Final Four. When the team arrived back home they were greeted by thousands of fans at the airport. "We didn't know," Aguirre said. "There were no cell phones. Nobody could call us to say the entire city of Chicago was at the airport. Nobody on the plane knew what was waiting for us. We got off the plane, and the gate was filled with people. It was shocking, crazy."[1] DePaul then lost 74-76 to the Larry Bird-led Indiana State Sycamores in the national semifinals.

As a three-year starter for DePaul, Aguirre contributed 2,182 points, an average of 24.5 points per game. As a two-time All-American, he was named the 1980 Player of the Year by the Associated Press as well as the 1980 Naismith Award winner. Aguirre was also a member of the U.S. Olympic team for the 1980 Games that ultimately didn't participate because of the United State's boycott of the Moscow Games. Mark sacrificed his senior year to enter the NBA.

The Dallas Mavericks, who had three first round picks in the 1981 NBA draft, selected Mark with the first overall pick. The draft class that also included Rolando Blackman (9th) and Jay Vincent (24th) transformed the team in a few short years from league doormat to potential title contender. The trio finished their rookie season as the team's top three scorers in points per game.

Known in his college days for having a tough and clever post game, Aguirre also possessed a solid shot from the perimeter. He was a career 32.1 percent shooter from behind the three point arc. Individually, his greatest season in the NBA was from 1983–1984, when he averaged 29.5 points per game, making him the second leading scorer in the league. He finished the season with 2,330 total points.

According to John MacLeod, Dallas' coach at that time, "He (Aguirre) had a complete offensive game. He was a passer, he was a power player inside—he played against bigger people—and then he had the ability to drive the ball to the basket. So, he was a complete player."[2]

While in Dallas, he gained a reputation for becoming irritable, hampering him at times as a professional. This was one reason that cultivated a swap on February 15, 1989 between the Mavericks and Detroit Pistons, sending Aguirre to Detroit for Adrian Dantley.

With the Pistons, Aguirre came off the bench. This was a role unbeknownst to him. The Pistons were a strong defensive team, featuring a lineup that included Bill Laimbeer, Dennis Rodman, Rick Mahorn, Joe Dumars, and Isiah Thomas. Carrying with them the reputation as the NBA's "Bad Boys," the Pistons were in need of an offensive spark and Mark provided that off the bench. Mark was instrumental in igniting the Pistons to back-to-back championships in 1989 and 1990.

The 1980s were the golden age of the NBA small forward. A group led by three-time MVP Larry Bird and one-time MVP Julius Erving. Aguirre falls right in line with Adrian Dantley, Alex English, Dominique Wilkins, and James Worthy to make up the rest of the elite class at the small forward position.

The 6'6" forward had a catalog of offensive tricks. A talented one-on-one player, Aguirre used his offensive catalog to score on both weaker small forwards and slower power forwards. Over his 13-year career Aguirre amassed 18,458 points, as of the start of the 2008 NBA season, Aguirre ranked 45th all-time in scoring. Aguirre appeared in the playoffs nine times, was a member of three All-Star teams, and won two NBA championships.

Aguirre started his post-playing career as director of player development for the Dallas Mavericks. Since then, he has spent time with both the Indiana Pacers and New York Knicks as an assistant coach. Aguirre and his wife Angela have four children and make their home in Dallas.

Notes

1. Neil Hayes, (2008). "No.11 Mark Aquirre: Warrior in High School, Blue Demon in College, 'Hard-core Chicago' Always," *Chicago Sun-Times*, October 12, sec. Sports.

2. David Friedman, (2007). "Dropping Knowledge: Hoops Hype," http://hoopshype .com/articles/aguirre_friedman.htm (accessed April 10, 2009).

Emanuel "Manu" Ginóbili

Superstar of the NBA

by Chris Kamke

In a country where soccer reigns supreme and children's dream are filled with winning the World Cup, one wouldn't be surprised to see a three-year-old boy working on his ball handling, at least not until they realized he was using his hands rather than his feet. It isn't everyday that a child is born who will go on to inspire an entire nation to pick up a ball and dribble with their hands rather than their feet. That is precisely the effect Manu Ginóbili has had in Argentina.

Ginóbili grew up in a family with basketball roots, something extremely rare in Latin America, during the 1970s and 80s. He was born on July 28, 1977 in Bahia Blanca, Argentina to Jorge and Raquel Ginóbili. Ginóbili's father was very involved with basketball in Argentina. Growing up with his two older brothers, Sebastian and Leandro, Ginóbili idolized Michael Jordan. A poster of Jordan hung on his bedroom wall and he watched Jordan and the Bulls play on television, attempting to imitate the great player's moves.

The Ginóbili boys received their basketball education just a block from their home at the Bahiense del Norte basketball club. Ginóbili, stood out from other players because of his enormous desire to win. Another aspect that benefited Ginóbili on the court was his ability to integrate the game of soccer. Ginóbili played both sports as a child and he was successful bringing creative aspects of soccer to the basketball court. The moves he developed were unusual on the hardwood and often left defenders puzzled. Fearless in his approach to the game despite his frail frame, 6'3" and 160 pounds, Ginóbili became a standout player as a teenager.

Ginóbili made his professional debut in Argentina in 1995 with Andino. In 1998, as he grew stronger and taller, standing 6'6", Ginóbili joined the Argentina National Team and moved to Italy to play professionally against tougher opponents. In 1999, Ginóbili entered the NBA Draft, not expecting to be selected. The San Antonio Spurs, however, selected him with the 57th overall pick. Ginóbili did not join the Spurs that year, instead he returned to Italy to play for

Kinder Bologna. In 2001, Kinder Bologna was the Champion of the Italian League, Coppa Italia, and the Euroleague. Ginóbili received several individual honors as well, including the 2001 Euroleague Finals MVP and the Italian League MVP, an honor he would win again the following year.

It was not until 2002 that Ginóbili joined the Spurs. In his first season in the NBA, Ginóbili got off to a slow start, in part due to mild injuries. Serving as a back up to veteran guard Steve Smith, Ginóbili transitioned to the NBA as the season progressed and won the Rookie of the Month in March. The Spurs experienced great success during Ginóbili's first year, securing the top seed in the Western Conference. During the second round of the playoffs, the Spurs faced the three-time defending NBA Champion Los Angeles Lakers. Ginóbili's play proved to be critical in this series. He averaged just under 12 points per game, more than four points more than he did during the regular season. The Spurs ended the Lakers' shot at a fourth consecutive title by winning the series in Game 6. Ultimately, the Spurs went on to defeat the New Jersey Nets in the NBA Finals, earning Ginóbili his first NBA Championship.

Ginóbili's next big basketball accomplishment came in 2004 with the Argentina National Team. Argentina entered the 2004 Olympic Games in Athens having never medaled in basketball. Nonetheless, hopes were high for Argentina and Ginóbili as Argentina was entering the Games following a silver medal finish at the 2002 FIBA World Championships. Wearing number five, Ginóbili would lead Argentina to the gold medal game. The excitement started in Argentina's first game as Ginóbili sunk a buzzer-beating shot to give Argentina a one-point win over Serbia and Montenegro. Argentina later met Team USA in the semifinals where Argentina, led by Ginóbili, shocked Team USA with an 89-81 victory. In the gold medal game, Argentina handled Italy to win the gold and Ginóbili was named MVP of the tournament, having led Argentina in both scoring and assists.

Although Ginóbili was already considered a national celebrity in Argentina, bringing home Olympic gold cemented his standing. However, with fame and fortune, envy can follow and in Ginóbili's economically devastated home country, crime had become a major concern. Abductions for ransoms in Latin America were high and wealthy families were often targets. In the summer of 2004, police intercepted a call and learned that Ginóbili's father was on a list of targets. Ginóbili took steps to ensure his family's, the core of his life, safety.

After the triumphant Olympic Games, Ginóbili returned to the Spurs for the 2004–2005 NBA season commanding additional respect. Flagged as possibly the best European-based player to grace the NBA, Ginóbili's high-tempo and intense play made him one of the toughest players to guard in the league. Having developed into an effective one-on-one player, Ginóbili is respected as a great clutch player. Ginóbili's talents have given Spurs head coach Greg Popovich the luxury of putting the ball in the hands of three star players; Tim Duncan, Tony Parker, or Ginóbili.

Ginóbili fits in nicely in San Antonio. The Spurs' roster is filled with international players and Ginóbili has become a favorite with the city's large Latino community. According to Ginóbili, "I got attention when I was in Europe, but nothing like this."[1] Part of Ginóbili's appeal is that he isn't like most NBA players. He is not a typical superstar who wants to take all the shots. "He has a no-holds-barred mentality because all he thinks about is, 'What can I do to help us win?'"[2] says Popovich. Ginóbili wants to guard the opponent's best player in the fourth quarter. He wants to dive on the floor or take a charge.

His willingness to do the little things doesn't mean Ginóbili lacks the ability to score in bunches. In Game 1 of the 2005 NBA Finals, the Detroit Pistons learned that first hand. Ginóbili surprised the Pistons with 15 fourth-quarter points, leading the Spurs to an 84-69 victory in the opening game. The Spurs would go on to win the NBA Championship that year, Ginóbili's second NBA Championship. Recounting Ginóbili's play during the series, Pistons coach Larry Brown said, "He took the ball anywhere he wanted to. He made every hustle play. He got to the rim. His will was greater than ours."[3]

Ginóbili is one of only a few players to experience success in both the physical NBA as well as the more technical FIBA. In 2005, he was just the second Latin American born player to play in an NBA All-Star game. Ginóbili has steadily increased his points per game throughout his career, averaging 19.8 for the 2007–08 season. To date, Ginóbili has been a member of three NBA championship teams and one All-Star team while establishing himself as a dazzling player in the NBA.

Back in soccer-frenzied Argentina, Ginóbili has shown future generations of Argentineans that there are sport opportunities other than soccer. In Argentina, Ginóbili is basketball. He remains modest when he returns home, preferring to visit in his parent's kitchen with family and friends rather than venture out. "I want to enjoy my time here, which means spending time with my family and my friends, late-night dinners, talking to 4 a.m."[4]

Fearless on the court, there is nothing that seems impossible for Ginóbili, no situation too risky for inventiveness. His willingness to create on the court has had an effect on his coach, "Manu has changed me as a coach," says Popovich. "He's made me believe that you can do the strange and unpredictable and be out of position once in a while yet still make something positive happen. Whatever he does, he does only to win, because he has the exact competitive nature of a Michael Jordan."[5]

Notes

1. Bill Cormier, (2003). "Ginobili Spurs Manu Mania," *APWorldstream*, May 21.

2. Jack McCallum, (2005). "Off To The Races," *Sports Illustrated*, June 13.

3. Sam Smith, (2005). "Ginobili's Moves Are Right Out of Soccer," *Chicago Tribune*, June 11, sec. Sports.

4. Chris Ballard, (2005). "A Hero In Hiding," *Sports Illustrated*, June 29.

5. Jack McCallum, (2005). "Off To The Races," *Sports Illustrated*, June 13.

4

LATINOS IN THE NFL

by Richard Lapchick

Like the NBA, the NFL is trying to further cultivate Latino fans through expanded marketing efforts. They are off to a strong start. According to the *Hispanic Sports Business*, the following are some current statistics to show a snapshot of the NFL in the Latino community.

- The Super Bowl is the most watched sports program ever among Latinos. More than 2.5 million Latinos watched Super Bowl XLIII than the World Cup Final.
- 28.5 million Latinos watched the NFL during the 2008 season. The NFL was the leading English language TV program watched by Latinos.
- 73 percent of Latinos are NFL fans, including 80 percent of young Latino males.
- 26 percent of Latinos chose the NFL as their favorite spectator sport.
- 34 percent owned licensed apparel

The last three of these statistics are higher than numbers in MLB, NBA, MLS, and NHL.

The NFL is using the media to make these inroads. Television games are broadcast on ESPN Deportes, Fox Sports en Español, Telemundo, and Univision. There are weekly live Spanish-language radio broadcasts of NFL games on Univision Radio. There is weekly print coverage in ten of the top Spanish-language newspapers.

As a league, the NFL has been actively marketing to Latino fans since the end of the 2003 season. The NFL appointed an "Hispanic Task Force." There have been Latino community events across the United States to raise interest in the league and its teams. The NFL licensed special team T-shirts with Spanish phrases. The Dolphins shirts used the word *azúcar*, or "sugar." The Denver Broncos shirts had "*de todo corazón.*" The NFL celebrates Hispanic Heritage Month. During the month in 2008 Latino viewership of NFL games was up by 300,000 while traffic on NFLLatino.com was up 27 percent. They have even started NFL Flag football for Latino youth. They know that the future of Latinos and the NFL will include a crop of talented young Latino players.

The Dolphins have always had a presence in the huge Latino market in South Florida. They have aired their games on Spanish-language radio since 1981. René Giraldo and Roly Martín have called every regular-season game *en Español* for the Dolphins since 1984. The 2009 season is their 25th.

Twelve teams—the Dallas Cowboys, Oakland Raiders, San Diego Chargers, Arizona Cardinals, Denver Broncos, San Francisco 49ers, Houston Texans, New York Jets, Miami Dolphins, Minnesota Vikings, New Orleans Saints, and Washington Redskins—broadcast their games on local Spanish-language radio.

But the real key to success will be the presence of Latino stars on NFL teams. The New York Jets started the 2009 season with a 3-0 record and the media was in a frenzy over quarterback Mark Sánchez, especially after he outgunned superhero Tom Brady and the New England Patriots in Week 2 of the NFL season. Less noticed, though, was Sánchez's presence among the less than 1 percent of NFL players who are of Latino background. Their numbers are growing, but those players remain mainly off the radar screen. So does the history of Latinos in the NFL, despite the fact that many broke through with landmark achievements in the league well in advance of African-Americans. For example:

- Cuban born Ignacio Molinet became the first Latino to play professional football when he debuted in 1927 with the Frankford Yellow Jackets team. Molinet's contract guaranteed him 50 dollars per game.
- Joe Aguirre became the first Latino drafted by an NFL team when the Washington Redskins chose him in the 11th round in 1941, five years before Kenny Washington and Woody Strode became the first African-American players in the modern era of the NFL.

- Jim Plunkett was a Latino quarterback who won Super Bowl XV for the Oakland Raiders in January of 1981, seven years before Doug Williams became the first African-American quarterback to win one.

- Tom Fears became the first Latino head coach when the expansion New Orleans Saints hired him in 1967, more than two decades before Art Shell became the first African-American head coach with the Raiders in 1989.

- And with Plunkett calling the signals, Tom Flores coached the Raiders to their Super Bowl XV championship, 26 years before Tony Dungy became the first African-American head coach to win the big one.

While many can name those first African-Americans, few can cite the names of the first Latinos in each category. But when Sánchez was thrust into the spotlight as the starting quarterback for the University of Southern California in his junior year, he immediately became a role model for many Mexicans and Mexican-Americans in Southern California and around the country. He is proud of his heritage, and wore a mouthpiece with a small Mexican flag painted on the front in a game against Notre Dame. His fans reveled in the shared pride.

Nonetheless, Sánchez received a number of angry e-mails and letters after that Notre Dame game, telling him, among other things, to go back to Mexico, according to the *Los Angeles Times*. It had an echo in the African-American community, when so many athletes were told to "go back to Africa," even when generations had passed since anyone in their families had set foot in Africa. Sánchez was born in the United States and has two older brothers who played football at Yale and DePauw. Their heritage was never a topic of controversy at those places, but their public exposure never rose to the level that Mark's did. Nor did they flash their ethnic pride on a national stage.

Sánchez starred in the Los Angeles spotlight and finished at USC with a 2009 Rose Bowl victory over Penn State. He was picked fifth in the 2009 NFL draft by the Jets and ultimately was named the starting quarterback. It was a heady time for Sánchez, as he joined Latino quarterback Tony Romo of the Dallas Cowboys, also of Mexican descent, as a starting quarterback in the NFL.

Flores became the first Latino quarterback in pro football history two years after he finished playing in college, when he joined the Oakland Raiders of the American Football League in 1960. Flores immediately led the league by completing 54 percent of his passes, gaining 1,738 yards and throwing for 12 touchdowns. Flores' best season was in 1966 when he passed for 2,638 yards and 24 touchdowns in 14 games, earning him a Pro Bowl slot.

Oakland traded him to the Buffalo Bills in 1967, where he was primarily a backup. He ended his playing career with Kansas City in 1970, the year the Chiefs won Super Bowl IV behind starting quarterback Len Dawson.

When Flores retired as a player, he became an assistant coach, and finally succeeded John Madden as the Raiders' head coach in 1979, finishing his first season with a 9-7 record.

He made coaching history in his second year. After finishing the regular season at 11-5, Flores and the Raiders' Mexican-American quarterback Plunkett captured the franchise's third Super Bowl. By defeating the Philadelphia Eagles 27-10 in Super Bowl XV in 1981, Flores became the first minority head coach to win a Super Bowl and Plunkett became the first minority quarterback to win one.

That duo won a second championship in Super Bowl XVIII over the Washington Redskins. Flores went on to coach the Raiders for a total of nine seasons, amassing a regular-season record of 83-53 and winning two Super Bowl rings.

A linebacker that stood at 6-foot-7, Guatemalan Ted Hendricks was one of the most dominant defensive forces in the NFL history. He was a Pro Bowl selection eight times and played on four Super Bowl championship teams, three with Oakland and one with the Baltimore Colts. Hendricks is a member of the NFL's 1970s All-Decade Team and the NFL's 75th Anniversary All-Time Team. In 1990, he was inducted into the Pro Football Hall of Fame.

Joe Kapp made headlines on and off the field. By standing up to the NFL in an antitrust case, he helped future generations of players earn far more than they made during his career.

In 1969, following a very successful career in the Canadian Football League, Kapp led the Minnesota Vikings to Super Bowl IV to play the Chiefs. A headline in *Sports Illustrated* in 1970 called him "The Toughest Chicano." When he signed a four-year contract with the Boston Patriots, Kapp became the highest-paid player in the NFL.

Later, though, NFL commissioner Pete Rozelle demanded that he sign a standard player contract. Kapp refused based on the recommendations of his lawyer and the NFL Players Association. As a result, his 12-year career as a professional football player ended in 1971. However, his NFL journey continued with the antitrust lawsuit against the league, claiming its standard contract was unconstitutional and a restraint of trade.

In 1974, a federal judge agreed that the NFL had violated antitrust laws, in part because there was no collective bargaining agreement in place on the date in question. The NFL settled with the Players Association in a multimillion-dollar case. The old system died and was replaced, and NFL players were the big winners. While Kapp was not awarded any personal damages, he won the respect of a generation of players. Kapp broke more ground when he returned to Cal—Berkeley, his alma mater, in 1982, becoming the first Latino head coach in Division IA football. He was named Pac-10 Coach of the Year that season, 24 years after he led them to the league championship as a player in 1958.

Arguably the most well-known Latino football player is offensive lineman Anthony Muñoz. Muñoz played in two Super Bowls and was an 11-time Pro Bowl selection, as well as the offensive lineman of the year in 1981, '87, and '88. In 1994, he was one of three offensive tackles named to the NFL's 75th Anniversary All-Time Team. When Muñoz was elected into the Pro Football Hall of Fame in 1998, it was widely reported that he was the first Latino to be inducted into the Hall. In fact, Muñoz had joined three other Latino Hall of Fame members. That was a testament to the poor attention being paid to the heritage of Latino athletes at the time.

Among the greatest tight ends of all-time, the still active Tony González owns most of the notable football records at his position. Over the first 12 years of his career, González has already established himself as the all-time leader in receptions (916), receiving yards (10,940), and touchdowns (76) among tight ends.

The first Latino to be inducted into the Pro Football Hall of Fame was Honduran-born Steve Van Buren. Van Buren was orphaned when he was very young and was raised by his grandparents in New Orleans. He earned a scholarship to play at Louisiana State and was a first-round draft pick in 1944.

Van Buren twice rushed for more than 1,000 yards, won four

NFL rushing titles and a "triple crown" in 1945 when he led the league in rushing, scoring, and kickoff return average. He was a first-team All-NFL selection in each of his first six seasons. From 1947 through '49, Van Buren won three consecutive rushing titles, an accomplishment matched only by Jim Brown, Earl Campbell, and Emmitt Smith. At his retirement after the 1951 season, Van Buren held the all-time record for rushing yards and rushing touchdowns.

The second was Fears, who went into the Hall of Fame in 1970, nearly 30 years before Muñoz was elected. Fears was born in Guadalajara, Mexico, and moved to the United States at the age of 6. His college career was interrupted by a stint in the Air Force during World War II. Upon leaving the military, he finished his college career at UCLA. Originally drafted as a defensive back by the Los Angeles Rams, he was switched to the offense after he intercepted two passes and returned one for a touchdown in his first game.

Fears led the league in receptions in his first three NFL seasons, improving his total each year, setting a league record with 77 catches in 1949 and breaking that mark the following year with 84 receptions. In his nine NFL seasons, Fears totaled 400 career receptions for 5,397 yards and 38 touchdowns. Those were almost unheard-of numbers at the time. He had more than 1,000 receiving yards in two seasons and played in a Pro Bowl. Fears served as head coach of the Saints from 1967 to 1970, becoming the first Latino head coach in the NFL. He was fired after compiling a 13-34-2 overall record, but his mark had been made.

Hendricks, who was inducted in 1990, was the third Latino in the Hall of Fame. Now, as Sánchez is emerging as a leader for the next generation of Latinos in the NFL, he can look back on the legacy of those who came before him. Sánchez is among a talented group of current Latinos that includes, besides Tony González, punter Daniel Sepuveda, guards Roberto Garza and Louis Vasquez, defensive end Luis Castillo, wide receiver Greg Camarillo, and long snapper Ken Amato.

It is obviously too early to call it, but perhaps Sánchez was taking his first steps toward that sort of career in his rookie season. Maybe his journey in the NFL will help shed more light on those Latinos who broke barriers without the recognition of their heritage. It is a goal of this chapter to do just that.

Ignacio "Lou" Molinet

First Latino to Play in the NFL

by Chris Kamke

A typical football fan has never heard of Ignacio "Lou" Molinet. Most likely even a big football fan wouldn't think twice when hearing the name mentioned. It is quite possible that even some of the top football historians could be hazy on the meaning behind the name. The reason for this is because up until 1999 the significance of Molinet's involvement in the sport of American football was unknown. When the Cuban-born fullback debuted in 1927 with the Frankford Yellow Jackets team in Philadelphia he became the first Latino to play professional football.

Until 1999, Jesse Rodríguez was considered the first Latino player in professional football history. Rodríguez played with the 1929 Buffalo Bisons. It took the curiosity of a sports historian from Texas, a granddaughter in New Hampshire, and an archivist in Ohio to discover and verify the truth. The unearthing started in 1980 when Molinet's granddaughter, Heidi Cadwell, was looking through the late Molinet's belongings. It was then, 53 years later, that she came across Molinet's 1927 NFL contract and correspondence about the negotiations. She decided to save the documents in remembrance of her beloved grandfather. For two decades the proof of Molinet's accomplishments stayed tucked away as a simple memento rather than as a piece of football history.

It wasn't until 1999 that Cadwell contacted the Pro Football Hall of Fame about their interest in the contract. When the Hall learned that Molinet was Cuban they decided to research Molinet's ethnicity. Molinet's parents had moved to Cuba from Spain. The Molinets were a well-to-do family and Molinet was born in Chaparra, Cuba in 1904. The younger of two boys, Molinet was educated in America and attended prep school in New Jersey before entering Cornell. During his first two years at Cornell, Molinet displayed great athletic talent, lettering in both basketball and football for the Big Red. After his sophomore year both of his parents died. Drained by their loss, Molinet left Cornell to return home to Cuba. It was then that the Frankford Athletic Association of Philadelphia contacted him about joining the defending NFL champion Frankford Yellowjackets.

The contract that Molinet signed on July 20, 1927 guaranteed him 50 dollars per game that he played in and 10 dollars per day of practice. Lining up as a halfback, Molinet's single NFL season did not yield impressive numbers. In the nine games in which he played he totaled 74 rushing yards, 35 passing yards, and scored one touchdown. Despite being the defending champions, the Yellowjackets finished that season in seventh place out of eight teams. Although his numbers may not have been that significant, his participation in the sport and the position that he played were. "[His position] is important, because if you ask the average pro football fan nowadays about Latinos, they'll mention only kickers and linemen," says Mario Longoria, the football historian that helped verify Molinet's place in history. "But the initial history of the Latino presence in professional football is at the running back spot, and it starts with Molinet."[1]

After that season Molinet returned to Cornell and completed his mechanical engineering degree. Although he played in just one season, the 5'11", 195-pound Molinet, nicknamed "Molly," is still arguably the most significant person from Cornell to ever play in the NFL. After returning to Cornell, Molinet was never involved with football again. Although Terri Van De Carr Godshell, one of Molinet's children and Heidi Cadwell's mother, cannot remember Molinet ever discussing his pro football career, she does remember rooting for the Big Red. "I can still remember listening to Thanksgiving football—Cornell versus Penn," she says, "and hearing that wonderful announcer say, 'Molly could have made that play.'"[2]

On July 8, 1933, the NFL awarded the Frankford franchise to an association headed by Bert Bell and Lud Wray. Bell and Wray formed a new team, which they inaugurated as the Philadelphia Eagles.

Notes

1. Brad Herzog, (2003). "Pigskin Pioneer Remembered," Ivy League Sports. http://www.ivyleaguesports.com/article.asp?intID=2577 (accessed August 23, 2009).

2. Ibid.

Steve van Buren

Star of the Pro Football Hall of Fame

by Horacio Ruiz

The greatest running back of the 1940s was in a rage. His Philadelphia Eagles teammates were playing for a second consecutive NFL Championship at the Los Angeles Coliseum against the Los Angeles Rams on a rain-beaten turf. The Eagles' Steve van Buren, referred to by an endless stream of nicknames that included "Wham Bam," "Supersonic Steve," and "Blockbuster," led a group of players from both teams to implore then-NFL commissioner Bert Bell to suspend the game. The field resembled a soup of mud and the players worried that with their pay determined by ticket sales less than a third of the seats in the Coliseum had been sold. Bell ignored the players' pleas and the game was played on the rain-soaked field. An angry Van Buren, who Rams players tried to intimidate before kickoff, finished the day with a then NFL-record 196 rushing yards en route to a 14-0 victory to capture Philadelphia's second consecutive championship. Following one of the greatest performances in football history, Van Buren was modest telling the *Evening Bulletin*, "I got 196 yards? I thought I was doing pretty good, but figured it was only a little over 100 yards. Boy, that's what you can do with blocking."[1] The game against the Rams cemented Van Buren as the first great modern-day running back in NFL history.

Van Buren was born in La Ceiba, Honduras on December 28, 1920. He grew up in the town of Tela, a port on the northern Caribbean shore of Honduras that for many years was the Honduran headquarters for the United Fruit Company, a major United States corporation that traded in tropical fruit mostly grown in developing nations. The United Fruit Company is now known as Chiquita Brands International. Van Buren was orphaned when he was 10-years old and moved to New Orleans to live with his grandparents.

In his sophomore season at New Orleans' Warren Easton High, Van Buren did not make the football team as a 125-pounder, but as a senior he played well enough to earn a scholarship to play for Louisiana State. By the end of his LSU career, Van Buren had grown into a 6-0, 210-pound battering ram. His senior year, Van Buren led the country with 847 yards rushing on 150 carries. In his final game as a Tiger, Van Buren ran for a touchdown and passed for another in the second quarter of the 1944 Orange Bowl against Texas A&M. In the third quarter he would gash Texas A&M for a 63-yard touchdown run. It was his 16th touchdown of the season, a LSU single-season touchdown record that would stand until 1977. In the 1944 NFL Draft, Van Buren was taken by the Eagles with the fifth overall pick at the urging of LSU coach Bernie Moore.

From 1940–43 the Eagles posted a 10-31-2 record. In 1944, Van Buren's first year, the Eagles improved to 7-1-2 while Van Buren finished fifth in the league with 444 rushing yards in nine games and was second in the league in punt return yards. After a successful rookie season, Van Buren was named to the first of five Associated Press first-team All-NFL selections. In 1945 Van Buren won a "triple crown" when he led the league in rushing, scoring, and kickoff return average. Van Buren would go on to win four rushing titles in his career, including three straight from 1947–49, a feat since matched only by Jim Brown, Earl Campbell, and Emmitt Smith. In 1948, Van Buren scored the only touchdown in the Eagles' first-ever championship victory, a 7-0 triumph against the Chicago Cardinals on a snow-covered field.

During a scrimmage in Hershey, PA., prior to the 1952 season, Van Buren broke his leg and had to be taken off the field on a wheelbarrow. The injury was so severe that he was forced to retire. At the time of his retirement, Van Buren was the all-time leader in rushing yards with 5,860 and rushing touchdowns with 69. Twice Van Buren finished a season with more than 1,000 yards rushing. He finished his career with an average of 4.4 yards per carry in an era when the run was the primary offensive attack and when everyone knew Van Buren would be carrying the ball. At one point in time, Van Buren was the highest-paid player in the NFL, earning $15,000 per year. In the eight seasons that Van Buren spent with the Eagles from 1944–51, the franchise enjoyed a 58-30-3 record, and delivered two of the franchise's three NFL championships. Eagles Hall of Famer Chuck Bednarik, a rookie on the 1949 championship team said, "Steve Van Buren was my hero, I felt honored just to be his teammate. He was a great running back and an even better person. When we played the Rams for the 1949 Championship, they were the glamour boys of the NFL. They were a great team. But he just put us on his shoulders, and absolutely ran wild on that day."[2]

In 1965, Van Buren became the first Latino inducted into the Pro Football Hall of Fame. In his normally quiet and humble self, Van Buren's speech lasted no more than 20 seconds. "Thank you Clark Hinkle [the Hall of Famer who introduced him]," Van Buren said. "I'm certainly glad to have broken your record [career rushing yards]. Since you people can't hear too good and I'm not too good a speaker, I won't say much, but it's certainly an honor to be here. The two days I've spent in Canton will certainly bring me back every year from now on. Thank you very much."[3]

Van Buren was elected a member of the NFL's 1940s All-Decade Team and in 1994 was one of seven running backs elected to the NFL's 75th Anniversary All-Time Team. In 1999, *The Sporting News* ranked Van Buren 77th on its list of the 100 greatest football players. Van Buren, who is living with Alzheimer's disease, has been residing in Lancaster, PA., since September 2002.

Van Buren is one of the most respected elder statesmen of professional football, laying the groundwork for the multi-billion dollar enterprise it is today. "Steve is such a special person," said Pro Football Hall of Fame writer Ray Didinger in 2008. "I never met a superstar so humble and modest like Steve. A couple years ago, NFL Films was doing a story on the NFL's 75th Anniversary All-Time Team and they had a lunch-in at the Hall of Fame. And all the guys were mingling and the room got real loud. Then Steve walked in the room, and the place went silent. And all these great players like Jim Brown, Jim Taylor, every single person in that room wanted to shake

Van Buren's hand. That to me spoke volumes about the respect everyone had for Steve and his place in NFL history. I'll never forget that moment."[4]

Notes

1. Ashley Fox, "As The Team Prepares For A Milestone Season, A Group Of Experts Selects The Greatest Eagles Players," *Philadelphia Inquirer*, August 12, 2007.

2. Gary Kravitz, "Where are They Now: RB Steve Van Buren," Philadelphiaeagles .com, February 23, 2008, http://www.philadelphiaeagles.com/news/Story-WhereAre TheyNow.asp?story_id=15134 (accessed September 23, 2009).

3. Lee Feinswog, "Tales From The LSU Sidelines: A Captivating Collection Of Tiger Football Stories," Sports Publishing LLC, 2003. p. 163.

4. Gary Kravitz, "Where Are They Now: RB Steve Van Buren," Philadelphiaeagles .com, February 23, 2008, http://www.philadelphiaeagles.com/news/ Story-WhereAre TheyNow.asp?story_id=15134 (accessed September 23, 2009).

Thomas "Tom" Fears

Star of the Pro Football Hall of Fame and First Latino Head Coach in the NFL

by Chris Kamke

Originally drafted for the defensive backfield, the Los Angeles Rams coaching staff promptly realized Tom Fears' abilities in his first game when he intercepted two passes, returning one interception for a touchdown. From then on Fears' weapons were utilized on the offensive side of the ball. The move was a wise decision. Fears would lead the league in receptions in his first three seasons. He improved his total receptions each year, setting a league record with 77 receptions in 1949 and breaking it the next season with 84 receptions.

Fears was born in Guadalajara, Mexico and moved to America at the age of six. Fears was an excellent high school football player at Los Angeles' Manual Arts High School. He then went to play for Santa Clara University. His time at Santa Clara was cut short when he joined the Air Force during World War II. While in the military, Fears captained the Second Air Force Superbombers football team. Upon leaving the military he finished his college career at UCLA.

After being drafted by the Los Angeles Rams in 1948, Fears' pass catching abilities and work ethic boosted the Rams to the Western Division Championship for three consecutive seasons from 1949–51. The Rams' NFL championship quest came up short in both 1949 and 1950. In 1951, Fears' trio of touchdown receptions in the divisional playoff game against the Chicago Bears led the way for the Rams' third straight championship berth. After delivering big in the divisional championship, Fears continued his strong contributions by hauling in a short 13 yard pass from quarterback Norm Van Brocklin and then scrambling another 60 yards for the winning touchdown in the championship.

Standing 6-2 and 216 pounds, Fears lacked speed but made up for it by running precise patterns. A tremendous competitor, Fears was always determined to make something happen after he caught the ball. His professional playing career spanned from 1948–56. Known for his great hands and strong blocking abilities, he was respected by his peers. According to former Rams teammate Don Paul,

"He was never a guy to get by on ability. He intimidated defensive backs because he was a great blocker. The defensive guy knew if Tom didn't like the way he was tackled, he'd take his head off on the next play."[1]

In nine seasons, Fears finished with 400 career receptions, 5,397 receiving yards, and 38 touchdowns, setting a benchmark in career totals for future generations of receivers to follow. He led the NFL in receptions in three seasons, twice gained more than 1,000 receiving yards, and was named to one Pro Bowl.

After his playing career ended, Fears got into coaching, initially as an assistant during Vince Lombardi's reign with the Green Bay Packers. The next season Fears joined the Rams staff under former teammate Bob Waterfield. After two seasons with the Rams, Fears returned to the Packers as an assistant again and was part of two championship teams. In 1965, after being unsuccessful in landing the head coaching position with the St. Louis Cardinals, Fears moved to the expansion Atlanta Falcons where he would have more responsibilities. In 1967, Fears was named the first head coach in the history of the newly-formed New Orleans Saints. This move marked the first time a Latino held a head coaching position in the NFL.

His first task as head coach was to study the rosters of the other teams to try and guess which players would be available to the Saints. "We spent three weeks, day and night, studying rosters,"[2] Fears said. He decided to target athletes rather than fill specific positions. "We kept in mind a little balance, but first we wanted good, young athletes,"[3] he said. Fears' strategy of drafting athletic ability first and position second resulted in New Orleans getting a solid group of linebackers. New Orleans took a linebacker with their first choice in the expansion draft from Baltimore. After that, Baltimore felt like the rest of their linebackers were safe and left them unprotected. Fears snatched them up to establish his anchor on defense. With the addition of linebackers Jack Burkett, Ted Davis, and Steve Stonebreaker, the Saints had a defensive foundation.

Fears coached the Saints from 1967 to 1970. After a 1-5-1 start to the 1970 season, Fears was fired after coaching the Saints to a 13-34-2 overall record. Things quickly turned around for Fears as he was inducted into the Professional Football Hall of Fame in 1970.

Four years later, Fears got another chance as head coach, this time in the World Football League for the Southern California Sun. The entire league was in a fragile state financially and folded within two years of Fears' arrival. Again, his disappointment was relieved, this time with his 1976 induction into the College Football Hall of Fame.

Fears' final coaching position in football would come in 1990. He was named head coach of the Milan franchise in the International League of American Football. In 1994, Fears was diagnosed with Alzheimer's disease. Fears spent the final six years of his life battling his disease away from the field with the same vigor he displayed during playing days. He finally succumbed on January 4, 2000 at the age of 77.

Notes

1. Frank Litsky, (2000). "Tom Fears, NFL End and Coach, Dies at 77," *New York Times*, January 8, sec. Sports.

2. Tex Maule, (1967). "Some New Saints In The NFL Temple," *Sports Illustrated*. August 14.

3. Ibid.

Theodore "Ted" Hendricks

Star of the Pro Football Hall of Fame

by Horacio Ruiz

He wasn't too fond of the nickname his coach had given him as a player at the University of Miami. The 6-foot-7 Ted Hendricks was a three-time All-American as a linebacker and defensive end at Miami. He made his reputation and earned his moniker by the way he used to rush the quarterback with his arms and legs flailing in a series of furious movements like a menacing bird, hence how he came to be known as "The Mad Stork." Hendricks never liked the nickname, but it stuck throughout a decorated college career and a Hall of Fame professional career. By the time Hendricks moved to play for the Oakland Raiders in 1975 he had earned another nickname, "Kick 'Em in the Head Ted."

Hendricks was born in Guatemala City, Guatemala, where his father, a Texas-born Pan-Am mechanic, was stationed and met his mother. Hendricks moved to Miami and starred at Hialeah High School where he excelled as a multi-sport athlete in track, baseball, basketball, and football. At the University of Miami he made a total of 327 tackles from his sophomore to senior seasons. In 1968, Hendricks finished fifth in Heisman Trophy voting and to date is one of 22 defensive players to have ever placed in the Top 5 of Heisman balloting.

As a student, Hendricks studied physics and math, in one semester taking electromagnetic theory, statistics, differential equations, topology and mathematic analysis. Charlie Tate, then Miami's head coach heaped nothing but praise on Hendricks. "He could be a Rhodes scholar," Tate said. "He could be anything. Listen, he could be governor."[1] What he became instead was one of the greatest defensive players in NFL history.

Though he was projected to be a first-round pick in the 1969 AFL-NFL Draft, concerns about his thin frame dropped Hendricks to the second round with the 33rd overall pick when he was chosen by Don Shula's Baltimore Colts. Originally drafted as a defensive end, Shula converted Hendricks to the linebacker position where he would be the starter by mid-season of his rookie season in 1969.

During the 1970 season Hendricks helped anchor a defense at strong-side linebacker where he recorded 67 tackles, one and a half sacks, and an interception. The 1970 Colts defense yielded only two touchdowns all season on their way to winning Super Bowl V against the Dallas Cowboys. Hendricks would enjoy the first of eight Pro Bowl seasons in 1971 and would also earn the first of four First-Team All-Pro selections when he recorded 63 tackles, five interceptions, five sacks, and two blocked kicks. Hendricks' tall and thin frame—Hendricks topped out at 235 pounds during his playing career—made an effective combination in blocking passing lanes, blocking punts and field goals, and chasing down ball carriers. Hendricks was a Pro Bowler from 1971–1973 and in 1972 and 1973 he was a second-team All-Pro selection.

With the Colts in a downward spiral, Hendricks was traded after he signed a contract to play for Jacksonville of the World Football League in 1975. With one season left on his contract with the Colts, he was traded to the Green Bay Packers for what was supposed to be a lame duck season before jumping to the WFL. At Green Bay for the 1974 season, Hendricks enjoyed yet another Pro Bowl season and earned his second First-Team All-Pro selection. With the Packers Hendricks had 75 tackles, five interceptions, seven blocked kicks, and two sacks. The next season, Hendricks was supposed to jump ship to the WFL, but the league had gone bankrupt and he had not re-signed with the Packers. In stepped owner Al Davis of the Raiders who signed Hendricks as a limited free agent in 1975 and where Hendricks would retire after nine seasons.

The 1975 season would be a tough one for Hendricks who had to win the confidence of his new coach, John Madden, to use Hendricks in his defensive schemes. While Hendricks would ride the bench for most of the season, the Raiders would soon realize their mistake when an injury to starting defensive end Tony Cline in the final regular season game put Hendricks on the field in the Raiders' first playoff game against the Cincinnati Bengals. Hendricks sacked quarterback Ken Anderson four times in the game, leading Cincinnati coach Paul Brown to declare about Hendricks, "Today he earned his entire season's salary."[2] In 1976, Hendricks would again become a starting linebacker for Oakland's defense and he would not disappoint, as he would be a second-team All-Pro selection and lead the Raiders to the franchise's first Super Bowl victory. Hendricks continued to put up stellar numbers, earning second-team All-Pro honors in 1977 and 1978.

After the 1979 season and with his workload gradually diminishing, it seemed as if Hendricks' career with the Raiders was over. Though Raiders management disputed his claims, Hendricks claimed that the majority of coaches on the team wanted to waive him at season's end, but new defensive coordinator Charlie Sumner and Davis insisted on keeping Hendricks. It turned out that both Sumner and Davis made a wise decision. Hendricks was named the defensive captain in 1980. "The first thing I did as captain was to get them to cut out all that hand-holding crap," Hendricks said. "They'd started copying the Broncos. Can you imagine that, on a team like the Raiders? I told them, 'Do what you want, but don't anyone grab my hand.' To me, the idea of captain was what you see on the Raider emblem, the guy with the patch over one eye. Arrr, Matey, walk the plank!"³

Hendricks had an incredible season in 1980, making the Pro Bowl for the first time since 1975 and becoming a first-team All-Pro for the first time since 1974. He also led the Raiders to victory in Super Bowl XV, Hendricks' third Super Bowl title and the second in Raiders history. Hendricks made the Pro Bowl in his final three years. In June 1983, prior to the beginning of his final season, Hendricks was asked how much longer he would like to play. "Well, I'd like to retire in about a month," he said, "but the thing is, I'm having too much fun playing. I know there are things I can't do now that I once could. I can't run with a receiver all the way down the field, so the coaches have a system where I'll pass a receiver off to a safety-man. I can't recover from a game the way I used to. If you got up some Monday mornings feeling like I do, you'd understand that. But it's still fun—the game, my teammates, the fans. That's what it's all about."⁴ Hendricks' last game was in Super Bowl XVIII in which the Raiders defeated the Washington Redskins 38-9.

After coaching Hendricks for four seasons and being won over by his feats on the field, Madden had a particularly fond memory of his linebacker. "Once he missed bed check in camp," Madden says. "I called him in the next morning and told him I was going to fine him. He said he'd missed it because he'd gone out with Marv Hubbard. Hubbard had just been cut; it was his last day and he wanted someone to go out with him. So I didn't fine him. I would have done the same thing."

"I'll tell you how it is with Ted Hendricks. Whatever he has in him, he will give it to you on the field Sunday. You are going to get every last bit. There's no reason to mess with a guy like that. Hey, I've never even seen him limp."[5]

Hendricks retired a Super Bowl winner in 1983. He played in 215 straight regular-season games and was an eight-time Pro Bowler. He has a career record of 25 blocked field goals or point-after-touchdowns, 26 interceptions, 16 opponents' fumble recoveries, and four safeties. He finished a four-time Super Bowl champion, a four-time first team All-Pro, and a five-time second team All-Pro. Hendricks was named to the First Team NFL 1970s All-Decade Team and was one of seven linebackers on the NFL's 75th Anniversary All-Time Team. In 1990, Hendricks was inducted into the Pro Football Hall of Fame and in 1997 he was inducted into the College Football Hall of Fame.

"I want to be remembered as a nice guy," Hendricks said in his last professional season. "I know I can play the game. That's all I need now."[6]

Since his retirement, Hendricks has worked under the Ted Hendricks Foundation for the benefit of youth and seniors. In the past 10 years, Hendricks has helped raise more 1 million dollars for research and direct benefit to the Cystic Fibrosis Foundation, Alzheimer's and Dementia Research projects, and the Milwaukee and Miami Children's Hospital Birth Defect support programs. Hendricks has also recently lent his financial support to sports-related head trauma research.

Hendricks, a fluent Spanish speaker, has appeared as a Super Bowl commentator for ESPN Deportes and can be heard during the NFL regular season on the Raiders en Español network. In 2006, he was honored by his native Guatemala with the Presidential Medal of Honor for his athletic achievements and vast charitable work.

Notes

1. *Sports Illustrated*, "3 Miami," September 11, 1967.
2. Paul Zimmerman, "Who Is This Mad Hatter?," *Sports Illustrated*, October 17, 1983.
3. Ibid.
4. Ibid.
5. Ibid.
6. Ibid.

Anthony Muñoz

Star of the Pro Football Hall of Fame

by Chris Kamke

"He's one of the greatest football players I've ever been associated with at any position."[1]—John Robinson, University of Southern California (USC) Head Coach
Physically, Muñoz has always been distinguished by his size. During his playing days he stood 6'6" and weighed 287 pounds. But Muñoz has truly distinguished himself in life by caring for the less fortunate. Muñoz was born in 1958 and grew up as the middle child of five siblings. Growing up his family struggled financially. The children were brought up by their single mother, Esther. Muñoz recalls when growing up, "We were provided for, but we didn't have any extras."[2] Having experienced tight financial times as a child, Muñoz committed himself to providing for others when the opportunity presented itself. Some of the work he has done includes the Salvation Army, the Cystic Fibrosis Foundation, and mission trips to Mexico with his church.

While growing up in California, Muñoz was told he was too big to play Pop Warner football. So instead he focused on other sports and became an excellent baseball player. While attending Chaffey High School he turned into a terrific all-around athlete, playing baseball, basketball, and football. It was his size and skill on the football field that brought him national attention and a scholarship to play football with USC in 1976.

Muñoz was limited at USC due to multiple knee injuries that would force him to miss much of his junior and senior years. Going into his senior year Muñoz was ready to make a major impact after missing much of the previous year. Devastation set in when he suffered another knee injury during the first game of the season. The injury looked as if it would end Muñoz's college career and conceivably the remainder of his football playing days. But through hard work, faith, and a little bit of luck, the football door remained cracked open for him. A late season injury to another offensive lineman left the Trojans in need of a replacement, and Muñoz convinced the coaches to let him return for the bowl game. Muñoz played in the 1980 Rose Bowl against Ohio State and was part of the offensive line that opened holes for Charles White to score the winning touchdown. Due to his numerous knee injuries, some NFL teams considered Muñoz to be too much of a risk to select in the 1980 NFL Draft. However, his play during his first two years in college and his dominating size and agility on the offensive line caused the Cincinnati Bengals to select the offensive tackle with the third overall selection. Muñoz would spend the next 13 seasons playing for the Bengals, proving their gamble was a wise investment, possibly the best venture ever made by the franchise. Muñoz became a starter in his rookie season and never relinquished the position. He is considered one of the greatest offensive linemen in NFL history. For all the doubt that centered on Muñoz being injury prone, he missed only three games during his first 12 seasons.

Muñoz was an exceptional player who was agile, quick, and strong. He became the model for the next generation of offensive linemen. "He had tremendous God-given skills that he then developed,"[3] said Sam Wyche, former Bengals head coach. His quickness and agility made him extremely effective at blocking quick defensive ends. Known for his blocking abilities, Muñoz possessed other football weapons. Drawing on the athletic ability that he had displayed his entire life, Muñoz hauled in seven passes, including four touchdowns on tackle eligible plays during his career.

Known for his workout routine and holding himself to high standards, Muñoz worked tirelessly throughout his career. His determination elevated him to a leadership role with the Bengals. According to Wyche, "He'd be out there in bad weather at lunchtime, running so he could get himself loose for practice. Other guys were catching a little nap, but there was nothing but pride in the way Anthony prepared himself—and played."[4]

Muñoz appeared in Super Bowls XVI and XXIII with the Bengals, suffering defeats both games at the hands of the San Francisco 49ers. He was an 11-time Pro Bowl selection, and was named offensive lineman of the year three times. In 1994, Muñoz was further honored by being one of three offensive tackles selected to the NFL's 75th Anniversary All-Time Team.

The Pro Football Hall of Fame inducted Muñoz as a member in 1998. Having built a reputation during his career of helping others, Muñoz used his induction speech to thank those who helped him reach his pinnacle from a humble background in Ontario, California. "A lot of times when we strive to get to the pinnacle of our profession, it's like a triangle," Muñoz said in his hall of fame induction speech. "You reach the pinnacle, and you have a broad base of people . . . that make that possible. Well, I had those people. Lots of people."5

Throughout his playing career Muñoz made his presence known not only on the playing field but also in the community, taking the initiative to lead by example in both areas. After a notable and long NFL career, Muñoz resolved to bring his charitable efforts together to make a greater impact by establishing the Anthony Muñoz Foundation in 2002. Today, Muñoz and his family remain one of the most visible, devoted, community-minded families in the Cincinnati area and have stimulated others to follow their lead. Meanwhile, the Anthony Muñoz Foundation continues to prosper, impacting Cincinnati area youth mentally, physically, and spiritually.

Notes

1. David Porter, (2004). *Latino and African American Athletes Today*. (California: Greenwood Press).
2. Ibid.
3. Paul Zimmerman, (1994). "Don't Cross This Line," *Sports Illustrated*, September 5.
4. Ibid.
5. Chris Haft, (1998). Reaching the Pinnacle: Munoz Spreads Credit for success," *Cincinnati Enquirer*, August 2, sec. Sports.

Thomas "Tom" Flores

First Latino Head Coach to Win a Super Bowl

by Chris Kamke

"Here you are walking down the sidelines with less than a minute to play and you know that you're World Champions and that you and your team will be put down in history as one of the best of all times is a feeling that is hard to describe in words. You never really want that feeling or moment to end."[1]—Super Bowl Coach Tom Flores

As one of the original Raiders, Tom Flores has spent the majority of his football career as part of one of the most storied franchises in professional football history. Flores played his college ball at the University of Pacific before attempting to make a run at a professional career in the sport of football. Flores graduated 1958, but struggled to find a job in professional football. He was first cut by the Calgary Stampeders of the Candian Football League in 1958 and then cut by the Washington Redskins of the National Football League in 1959. It wasn't until two years after leaving college that Flores found his first real home when he landed a quarterback position with the American Football League's Oakland Raiders, a charter member of the league. This position was significant because it marked the first time a Latino played the position of quarterback in American professional football.

The Raiders had it rough that first year. Being late to be awarded a franchise in the new AFL, there was very little talent from which to select a team of players. To further complicate matters the Raiders had no home in Oakland and ended up playing games at Kezar Stadium and Candlestick Park in San Francisco. Flores moved into the starting quarterback role just a few games into the season and would go on to lead the league in completion percentage, 54.0, as he threw for 1,738 yards and 12 touchdowns.

In 1966, Flores had his most productive season, throwing for 2,638 yards and 24 touchdowns. His performance that season earned a Pro Bowl invitation. The following year Flores was traded to the Buffalo Bills. In the two years that followed in Buffalo and a third year in Kansas City, Flores served primarily as a backup. During his last year in the league and his lone year with Kansas City, the Chiefs won the Championship. He retired as a player after the 1970 season.

After retiring, Flores started as an assistant coach in Buffalo but soon found his way back to Oakland under head coach John Madden. "When I first came back (to the Raiders) they had an opening. I had an interview with John Madden and became an assistant coach and coached the wide receivers, tight ends, and quarterbacks. I mainly focused on the passing game for the team."[2] Flores was a part of the 1976 Super Bowl Champion team that defeated the Minnesota Vikings in Super Bowl XI.

Flores succeeded Madden, taking over the reins in 1979. Flores started his head coaching career off strong, producing a 9-7 record during his first season. However, it was Flores' second season where history was made. That season the Raiders finished the regular season at 11-5. Flores and quarterback Jim Plunkett fought their way through the post season and captured the Raiders third Super Bowl championship. The 27-10 victory over the Philadelphia Eagles in Super Bowl XV marked the first time a minority head coach won a Super Bowl title. Three seasons later, in Super Bowl XVIII, Flores would win his second Super Bowl as a head coach, this time over the Washington Redskins 38-9 and again with Plunkett behind center.

Flores coached the Raiders for four more years, nine in total. During his time with the silver and black, his regular season record was 83-53 and he led the Raiders to two Super Bowl championships. After retiring, Flores stayed with the Raiders for one more year as a consultant before leaving the franchise to take on President and General Manager responsibilities of the Seattle Seahawks.

The coaching bug had not left Flores completely and in 1992 he took over the head coaching position of the Seahawks when he was unsuccessful in luring Dennis Erickson away from the University of Miami. Flores' three seasons coaching the Seahawks produced diminutive results, especially when compared to the success he experienced with the Raiders. Following the 1994 season and a 6-10 record, Flores resigned.

Flores has spent the majority of his life involved with professional football. He played 10 seasons as a quarterback; with the Oakland Raiders (1960–61, 1963–66), the Buffalo Bills (1967–68), and the Kansas City Chiefs (1969–70). He roamed the sidelines for nine years as an assistant, both with the Bills (1971) and the Raiders

(1972–78). He served as head coach for 12 years for both the Raiders (1979–87) and the Seahawks (1992–94). Flores also spent time in the front office for both the Raiders and Seahawks.

Through his achievements, Flores helped to pave the way for minority head coaches in professional football. Flores compiled a career regular season coaching record of 97-87 and an impressive 8-3 playoff record. Flores is a true Raider at heart, "I was the very first quarterback for the Raiders. During our first year we played at Kezar Stadium in San Francisco back in 1960. I'm an original Raider and spent the first seven years of my playing career with the Raiders. I got traded to Buffalo and then ended up in Kansas City. I came back to the Raiders, started coaching for them back in 1972 as an assistant, and became the Head Coach in 1979 after Coach Madden retired. I have spent 23 years of my professional life with the Raiders,"[3] Flores said. Flores can currently be heard with Greg Papa during the radio broadcasts of Raiders games.

Notes

1. Larry Garcia, (2007). "Super Bowl XV, XVII Champ Tom Flores," Raiderdrive .com. http://www.raiderdrive.com/tom_flores.htm (accessed July 14, 2009).
2. Ibid.
3. Ibid.

Jim Plunkett

First Latino Quarterback to Win a Super Bowl

by Cara-Lynn Lopresti

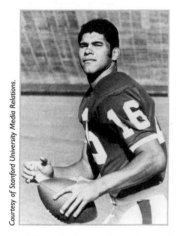

Courtesy of Stanford University Media Relations.

Jim Plunkett's life is a remarkable underdog story of how a poor Mexican-American child can overcome adversity, hardship, and injury and rise to stardom. Born in San Jose, California, Plunkett spent most of his childhood working long hours to help support his parents, both of whom were blind. His mother permanently lost her vision at the age of 19 after being afflicted with typhoid fever. Plunkett's father suffered from progressive blindness and worked hard to provide for the family, although they often depended on welfare to make ends meet. Plunkett was able to persevere through his poor financial conditions by achieving excellence on the football field. At James Lick High School, Plunkett played quarterback and defensive end and led the football team to an undefeated season in his senior year. His exceptional performance earned him a scholarship to Stanford University in 1967.

In the summer prior to starting at Stanford, a tumor was discovered on Plunkett's thyroid. The growth proved benign, but the operation slowed him physically and academically, causing his first year's performance to suffer as a result. In the spring, Stanford head coach John Ralston decided to move Plunkett to defensive end. Plunkett refused to let his hardships become an excuse for failure. He was determined to regain the starting quarterback position and "threw 500 to 1,000 passes per day" to make sure it happened. [1] He eventually earned the opportunity in his junior year, and in his first game, threw for 277 yards and four touchdowns. Plunkett finished the season throwing for 14 touchdowns and setting a Pac-8 record with 2,156 yards passing.

Following his junior year, Plunkett became eligible to enter the NFL draft and had the opportunity to receive a substantial signing bonus. However, Plunkett decided to forgo the paycheck and instead finish college out of loyalty to his school and team, and "to set a good example for the Chicano youngsters he tutored and urged to stay in school."[2] During the rest of his college career, Plunkett supported himself and his recently widowed mother by working a series of construction jobs in between class and practice.

After setting school, conference, and national records in nearly every passing category, Plunkett's sensational college career was cemented with the Heisman Trophy in 1971, an honor never before awarded to a Stanford or Latino player. His "first place title was unanimous across voting regions and his deservingness was confirmed less than a month later"[3] when Plunkett guided Stanford to a 27-17 triumph against Ohio State in the Cardinal's first trip to the Rose Bowl since 1941. Plunkett finished his college career with a NCAA record of 7,887 yards in total offense. In 1989, he was inducted to the Rose Bowl Hall of Fame and the following year was inducted in the College Football Hall of Fame.

Going into the draft, Plunkett was considered the best pro quarterback prospect. His excellent arm strength, precision, and speed along with his unique drop-back passing style made him attractive to NFL teams. The New England Patriots selected Plunkett as number one in the draft, making him the only Latino in history drafted first overall. Plunkett "compiled a brilliant freshman record as starting quarterback passing for 2,158 yards and winning Rookie of the Year honors."[4] However, he struggled with various injuries and a weak offensive line during the rest of his time with the Patriots and was eventually sidelined in 1975.

The following year, Plunkett was traded to the San Francisco 49ers and spent two seasons with the team before joining the Oakland Raiders, where he served as a reserve quarterback to Dan Pastorini. However, Plunkett's career was resurrected in 1980 when Pastorini suffered a knee injury. Even though he initially struggled off the bench, the 33-year-old Plunkett was able to persevere once again. He passionately led Oakland through the rest of the season, winning nine of the eleven games and earning a bid to the playoffs as a wild card. Plunkett quarterbacked his team past Houston,

Cleveland, and San Diego to face the highly-favored Eagles in Super Bowl XV. Passing for 261 yards and connecting on three touchdowns, Plunkett instrumented the first-ever wild card victory in the Super Bowl history by upsetting the Philadelphia Eagles 27-10. Plunkett was named the game's MVP and was the first minority quarterback to win a Super Bowl and the first Hispanic to be named Super Bowl MVP. Plunkett was recognized as the NFL Comeback Player of the Year for his incredible leadership and drive in directing the Raiders to Super Bowl glory.

Plunkett took over as Raiders quarterback to an injured starter in 1983, guiding the team to another Super Bowl appearance. The Raiders dominated the Washington Redskins, culminating in a 38-9 victory. Plunkett eventually retired after an outstanding 17-season pro football career, but his legacy as an exceptional quarterback, devoted, honorable, and resilient man will forever be remembered. Currently Plunkett owns a Coors Distributorship in Stockton, California and is involved in radio and television work covering his very own Oakland Raiders. Plunkett is also a motivational speaker and was named the First Recipient of the Leukemia Society of America's Ernie Davis Award.

Notes

1. David Pietrusza, "Jim Plunkett: Every Underdog Has His Day," http://www.davidpietrusza.com/Plunkett.html.

2. Ibid.

3. "Stanford Legends,"http://www.gostanford.com/halloffame/legends-plunkett.html.

4. "Heisman Winners,"http://www.heisman.com/winners/j-plunkett70.html.

Tony González

Superstar of the NFL and Future Hall of Famer

by Chris Kamke

Possibly the greatest tight end of all-time, the still active Tony González owns most of the notable football records at his position. Over
the first 12 years of his career, González has already established
himself as the all-time leader in receptions (916), receiving yards
(10,940), and touchdowns (76) among tight ends. González's numbers are so good that they stack up quite nicely against the greatest
receivers of all-time. As of the start of the 2009 season, González is
in the top 10 in receptions and will more likely be in the top twenty
in both receiving touchdowns and receiving yards after the season.
In 2008, he became the fifth player and first tight end in NFL history
to have 50 or more receptions in 11 straight seasons.

González was born on February 27, 1976 and attended Hunt-
ington Beach High School in California. Showcasing his athletic
abilities, he lettered in football and basketball. During his senior
year, González was a first-team All American selection at both tight
end and linebacker. He also received recognition in basketball, earn-

ing Orange County MVP honors by averaging 26 points per game. González went on to attend the University of California Berkeley where he played both football and basketball for the Golden Bears.

While playing for the Golden Bears, González lined up at tight end for future NFL coach Steve Mariucci. He had a standout year during his junior season; one of the best seasons to date for a Division I tight end. He caught 92 passes for 982 yards and 23 touchdowns. That season González earned All-Pac 10 and All-American honors. González also performed well on the basketball court. During his junior year he averaged 6.8 points and 5.4 rebounds per game as California advanced to the Sweet 16 of the NCAA Basketball Tournament. González gave up his final year of eligibility and declared for the 1997 NFL Draft. Possessing great speed and strength, he was rated as one of the top players available in the draft. Although the Chiefs knew González was a great talent, it is doubtful they expected González to deliver as wonderfully as he has during his NFL career. To ensure they got their man, the Chiefs decided to trade up to get González and drafted him with the 13th selection.

To be truly great, the tight end position requires a unique skill and mind set. Physically having to possess the power to block and drive defensive players off the line of scrimmage as well as the agility and coordination to get down the field and receive a pass, not all players are cutout for the job. A typical tight end doesn't receive a lot of attention. Historically the position was viewed as a blocker first, and then a third or fourth option in the passing game. As a result, a tight end doesn't find their name in the headlines often. Of course, González isn't a typical tight end, nor is he a typical football player for that matter.

He entered the league and his presence was almost immediately noted. He hauled in 33 passes his rookie season and 59 in his second season. It was in just his third year that González solidified his name among the top active tight ends. González caught 76 passes, including 11 touchdowns and was named to his first of 10 straight Pro Bowl teams. In 2004, González led the league in receptions with 102. This was the first time a tight end was the league leader since 1986.

Although he is naturally gifted, González still desires excellence and has committed himself to that endeavor. Carrying with him the reputation of never leaving the practice field without doing something extra, his sensational appetite to get better is never satisfied. When his progress became stagnate, González incorporated meditation and goal setting into his training. According to González, "When you talk about that zone you have to get in, where you're not even thinking about what you have to do, where you're so focused and your concentration is sharp, that's where I am right now. I go to the line each play and I feel like I know what's going to happen even before the ball is snapped. I'm totally in the moment. That's the feeling you want on the football field."[1]

One reason González is possibly the best tight end pro football has ever seen is because he is a threat on every play. "He's a cross between a wide receiver and a tight end,"[2] says former Chiefs coach Gunther Cunningham, which is a scary thought for defensives. With the size of a linebacker at 6'4" and 250 pounds, and speed, hands, and leaping ability of a wide receiver, there isn't an easy way to stop González with single coverage. As a result, it isn't uncommon to see González celebrating his latest touchdown by slam dunking the ball over the crossbar. Through his play, González has revolutionized the tight end position, like Lawrence Taylor did with the linebacker position.

In addition to his commitment on the field, González has demonstrated great commitment to his community. He is one of the leaders in NFL philanthropy. He founded the "Tony González Foundation" in 1998 to support the Boys & Girls Club, The Shadow Buddies Organization, and various other organizations throughout Kansas City and California. He hosts an annual "Shop with a Jock" for 75 children and also works with the United Way.

Along with giving back, family is an important part of González's life. One way he demonstrates this is by wearing a necklace that his mom gave him during every game he plays. Inscribed on the necklace are the Chinese characters for "Protection" and "Longevity." After spending his first 12 NFL seasons with the Chiefs, González will be terrorizing defenses as a member of the Atlanta Falcons starting with the 2009 season. González lives with his wife and two children.

Notes

1. Ivan Carter, (2005). "González Still Benchmark for NFL Tight Ends," Official Website of All Pro Tightend Tony González. http://tonyGonzález88.com/benchmark.htm (accessed August 14, 2009).

2. Steve Smyth, Jr.,(2000). "Tony González is a Unique Headache for Defenses," *Knight Ridder Tribune*, Nov 2.

5

LATINOS IN GOLF

by Richard Lapchick

Legendary Latino golfers like Roberto De Vicenzo, Lee Treviño, Nancy López, and Chi Chi Rodríguez paved the way for breaking the all-white color barrier within the sport that now welcomes the likes of Argentine-born Ángel Cabrera and Mexico's Lorena Ochoa, perhaps the most dominant female golfer in the early 21st century. Cabrera played mostly in Europe and was less well known in the United States until he won the 2007 US Open and the 2009 Masters. Ranked 69th on the PGA tour, he became the lowest ranked player to win the Masters. Now he has a large presence in the U.S. and European golf communities.

Born in 1969 into an impoverished family in Argentina, Cabrera had to quit school at age 10 to become a caddy to help support his family. He played during the early years as a caddy and became good enough that club members helped launch his career in Europe in 1996. Now Cabrera, seemingly at the peak of his game with the wins at the U.S. Open and Masters, is further paving the way for his son Federico who turned pro in 2008.

In 2009 Cabrera teamed up with Gary Player Design to build golf courses in Latin America. This seems like a perfect circle since golf was welcomed into the Olympics which will be played in Brazil in 2016. Just as Federico and other aspiring young Latino golfers will be in his father's debt, so is Cabrera in the debt of golf's legendary pioneers depicted in this chapter. Roberto De Vicenzo won the Bob Jones Award in 1970, which honored the golfer who displayed the best sportsmanship. Buoyed with a respect amongst his peers in the golfing world and an incredible 230 tournament victories worldwide, including six PGA titles and one major with the 1967

British Open, De Vicenzo was inducted to the World Golf Hall of Fame in 1989. Born in Buenos Aires, De Vicenzo learned the game at a young age before turning professional at the age of 15. He enjoyed the peak of his playing success in his forties when he recorded eight top ten finishes at the four majors, and claimed the 1977 British Open at 44 years of age to become the oldest man ever to win that tournament.

Juan "Chi Chi" Rodríguez was a great role model for Latino golfers. Throughout his career, he won eight PGA titles, 22 Champions titles and represented his native country on 12 World Cup teams. Rodríguez turned professional and went on to win eight PGA Tour Titles in the 1960s and '70s and played on the 1979 Ryder Cup Team. Rodríguez was even more dominant on the Senior PGA Tour in the 1980s, where he won an impressive 22 titles, including the Players Championship. He is tied for fifth most all-time on the Champions tour. His career winnings total almost $8 million.

In 1986, he won the Hispanic Achievement Recognition Award and in 1988 was recognized with Replica's Hispanic Man of the Year Award. He was the first Puerto Rican inducted into the World Golf Hall of Fame. For his humanitarian efforts, Rodríguez received the Bob Jones Award from the United States Golf Association and in 1994 was again honored by being elected to the World Humanitarian Sports Hall of Fame.

Mexican-American Lee Treviño won the tour's 1967 Rookie of the Year honors and finished an impressive fifth at the U.S. Open Championship. One year later, Treviño rewrote the record books by becoming the first player to ever record four rounds with a score in the 60s at the U.S. Open as he won his first major at the Oak Hill Country Club in New York. As a top player, he won the Vardon Trophy, awarded to the player with the lowest scoring average over the course of a season, four times between 1970–1974. He won 29 times on the PGA tour level, including two wins each at the U.S. Open (1968 & 1971), The British Open (1971 & 1972) and the PGA Championship (1974 & 1984). In the 1984 PGA Championship win he set the scoring record by shooting a 15-under-par for the weekend. He is, of course, in the World Golf Hall of Fame.

In 1978, Nancy López exploded onto the golf scene like no other female golfer had ever done before or has done since. After winning nine tournaments, including five in a row over a two-month stretch, López became the first player ever to win LPGA Rookie and Player of the Year during the same season. López, also a Mexican-American, accumulated 48 LPGA victories and more than $5 million in prize money. She was a four-time Player of the Year and is considered among the greatest female athletes of all-time. López was the people's champion, a golfer who flashed a championship smile to the galleries and would consistently sign countless autographs for all of her adoring fans.

After she became a mother, López changed many lives, opening new doors for female athletes while also becoming a public and cultural icon of the 1980s on how to successfully manage career and motherhood.

Mexico's Lorena Ochoa burst onto the golf scene in 2003 when she won the LPGA Rookie of the Year award. In 2008, Ochoa won a remarkable five of the first six events she entered, including an 11-stroke margin of victory at the HBSC Championships. She was number one for the third consecutive season. As of this writing, just six years removed from her professional debut, Ochoa has already claimed 26 tournament wins on the LPGA tour, including two major championships and nearly $14 million in prize money. She is already third on the all-time earnings list.

Ochoa's altruism makes her even more special. Founded in 2004, the Lorena Ochoa Foundation operates and issues financial support for lower-income students to attend an elementary school called La Barranca, near where she grew up in Guadalajara. It is here where nearly 300 children now receive the best education possible through the use of inspired teaching methods and an embrace of the arts. The Foundation has spread its mission by opening a high school in 2008 and providing funding to assist other programs for at-risk youth as well as a child cancer treatment center. Ochoa has also inspired a generation of young Mexicans to pick up the game of golf not just through her play, but by making the sport more accessible and popular in her home country.

Roberto De Vicenzo

Star of the World Golf Hall of Fame

by Charlie Harless

Argentinean poet Jorge Luis Borges once wrote that, "Any life, no matter how long and complex it may be, is made up of a single moment—the moment in which a man finds out, once and for all, who he is."[1] Without context, this observation can speak to any number of pivotal moments we collectively and individually encounter during the highs and lows of our lives. When applied to the story of fellow Argentinean Roberto De Vicenzo and his life-changing moment at the 1967 Masters Golf Tournament, Borges' words become more prescient than he could have imagined.

After shooting the round of his life at 7 strokes under par on the final Sunday of the Masters, De Vicenzo walked off the course toward the clubhouse to sign his scorecard and force a playoff with Bob Goalby and, unbeknownst to him at the time, write his name into the history books for the biggest gaffe in golf history. Despite shooting a birdie at the 17th hole, De Vicenzo's playing partner mistakenly recorded the score for the hole as a par. Declining to double-check the scorecard, De Vicenzo signed a scorecard that indicated he shot a six-under, 66 instead of the 7-under round of 65 he had shot. When informed by tournament officials that his incorrectly recorded, but signed, scorecard would be counted towards his final score, thus negating the chance at a playoff and giving the coveted Masters title to Bob Goalby by one stroke, De Vicenzo had the eyes of the sporting world upon him to see how he would react. In this single moment, in a prose perhaps not as polished as Borges but just as powerfully effective, De Vicenzo conceded to tournament officials that "what a stupid I am for being wrong here."[2]

A mistake of this magnitude was devastating and could have very easily derailed the career of many a golfer. Yet in this moment of infamy, De Vicenzo did not throw a tantrum or speak negatively about the officials or his opponent. Instead, keeping with the character of a man who was idolized by his country and affectionately nicknamed "maestro," De Vicenzo would leave the Masters with his trademark class intact and go on to rebound and win a PGA event in

Houston a mere two weeks later. De Vicenzo went on to win the Bob Jones Award in 1970, which honored the golfer who displayed the best sportsmanship. Buoyed with a respect amongst his peers in the golfing world and an incredible 230 tournament victories worldwide, including six PGA titles and one major with the 1967 British Open, De Vicenzo was inducted to the World Golf Hall of Fame in 1989. Although his mistake at the 1968 Masters will likely never be forgotten by the golfing world, how De Vicenzo moved past that moment spoke to the resiliency and class that more accurately define the golfer and man.

Born in Buenos Aires, De Vicenzo learned the game at a young age by working as a caddy's assistant before turning professional at the age of 15. Despite an early introduction to the game, De Vicenzo did not achieve overnight success. De Vicenzo would not reach the peak of his playing career until he was in his 40s, when he recorded eight Top-Ten finishes at the majors and claimed the 1977 British Open at 44 years of age, holding off golf legend Jack Nicklaus by two strokes to become the oldest man to ever win that tournament. After playing his last major round at the British Open in 1978, De Vicenzo continued to play strong into his 50s and 60s as he won the inaugural United States Senior Open in 1980 and several smaller tournaments on the Argentinean and South American circuits. Over the span of his career, De Vicenzo won titles across the globe, from Belgium to Jamaica to Venezuela and many countries in between, prompting essayist Jack Whitaker to quip that if golf were war, De Vicenzo would have conquered more countries than Alexander the Great.[3]

Although he achieved phenomenal success on the global stage, the size of De Vicenzo's trophy case is dwarfed by the size of his heart. Though some of the details of the story could have changed in its subsequent iterations in the press and Internet, there is a motivational yarn about De Vicenzo's giving spirit that has inspired countless readers, many of whom may not know or particularly care about De Vicenzo's playing prowess. The story goes that a young woman approached De Vicenzo in the parking lot after he won a tournament. After congratulating him on the win, the woman told De Vicenzo that she was distressed because her young child was gravely ill. Upon hearing this claim, De Vicenzo wrote the young woman a check in the amount of his tournament winnings to help give medical attention to the ill child and, as he was alleged to have said, to "make some good days to the baby."[4] The woman of course turned out to be a con artist and a golf official soon broke the news to De Vicenzo that the woman was a phony and that "she fleeced you, my friend." De Vicenzo responded to the official by replying, "You mean there is no sick baby?" When the official confirmed this statement, De Vicenzo showed his enormous heart by stating, "That's the best news I've heard all week."[5]

Borges once stated that "life itself is a quotation."[6] Roberto De Vicenzo's infamous quote at the Masters will forever be associated with the golfer, but De Vicenzo's words of relief when learning that there was no sick child speaks greater volumes about why he continues to be admired and respected from his legions of fans. Today, there are museums and gymnasiums in his hometown named in his honor and De Vicenzo can look back fondly at his life beyond that brief moment of infamy in 1968. "Every now and then I will drop a tear, but I've moved on," De Vicenzo recounted in a *Sports Illustrated* profile. "I got to see the world through golf. No one should feel sorry for me."[7] The world in turn saw De Vicenzo, both in victory and defeat, as a classy professional who proudly carried the flag for both Argentina and good guys everywhere.

Notes

1. Adriana Cavarero, *Relating Narratives: Storytelling and Selfhood.* (New York: Routledge, 2000).

2. Jason Sobel, "Forty Years Later, De Vicenzo's Gaffe Remains Unbelievable," *ESPN.com*, April 5, 2008.

3. World Golf Hall of Fame, "Roberto De Vicenzo." http://www.wgv.com/hof/member.php?member=1047 (accessed on June 3, 2009).

4. Alan Campbell, "A Gentleman and a Major Player," *The Sunday Herald*, July 16, 2006.

5. Ibid.

6. Laurence Chang, *Wisdom For the Soul: Five Millennia of Prescriptions For Spiritual Healing.* (Washington, DC: Gnosophia Publishers, 2006).

7. Farrell Evans, "Roberto De Vicenzo," *Sports Illustrated*, July 14, 2008.

Juan "Chi-Chi" Rodríguez

Star of the World Golf Hall of Fame

by Jared Bovinet

"How long does John Daly drive a golf ball? When I was a kid, I didn't go that far on vacation."[1] These are the words of Juan "Chi Chi" Rodríguez, one of golf's most accomplished (and comical) players. Throughout his career, he won eight PGA titles, 22 Champions titles, and represented his native country on 12 World Cup teams. While his list of winnings is impressive, it is his path to golf that proves all the more interesting.

Rodríguez was born in Rio Piedras, Puerto Rico in 1935. One of six children, he spent much of his childhood helping his father cut down sugar cane with a machete to supplement the 18 dollars a week his father earned. He was a gifted all-around athlete and a particularly strong baseball player. He even played baseball with the legendary Roberto Clemente when the two were children.

Rodríguez's interest in golf began when he started caddying at age six because he thought caddying could earn more money than working in the fields. While most golfers start with traditional clubs and golf balls, he fashioned his own clubs from guava trees and his own golf balls with metal cans.

He immediately developed an amazing ability to drive balls several hundred yards and hit up to 350 yards as a professional. In fact, many experts called Rodríguez the strongest golfer, pound for pound, in the history of the sport.[2] This fact is even more impressive given that he stands only 5'7" and weighed 117 pounds when he turned pro.

Rodríguez turned professional in 1960 and won the Denver Open three years later. He considers this his favorite victory. He went on to win eight PGA Tour Titles in the 1960s and 70s and played on the 1979 Ryder Cup Team. Rodríguez was even more dominant on the Senior PGA Tour in the 80s, where he won an impressive 22 titles, including the Players Championship. This is tied for fifth most all-time on the Champions Tour. His career winnings total almost $8 million.[3] Rodríguez is also known for his ability to improvise shots from any distance and for hitting unforgettable wedge shots from bunkers. Historians believe Rodríguez would have won many more tournaments had he been a better putter.

In his years on the course, Rodríguez became a fan favorite because of his colorful antics and personality. After making a challenging birdie putt, he would cover the hole with his straw hat and use his putter as a sword. He performed matador routines and made impersonations of his fellow golfers on the course. While many of his fellow players found this behavior irritating, the fans loved it, and the players eventually did too.

In retirement, Rodríguez formed his own eponymous management consulting group. It looks to bring humility, integrity, and enthusiasm to the sports marketing and management industry. Its ethics are based on those that Rodríguez embodies as a player.[4]

While Rodríguez enjoyed many incredible moments on the golf course, he considers the greatest moment of his life to be his encounter with Mother Teresa. This event led to him establishing the Chi Chi Rodríguez Youth Foundation, whose mission is to instill in troubled youth a strong sense of self-esteem and worth. Through the program, students work at the municipal golf course, where they learn about different aspects of the game.

Rodríguez has raised more than $4 million for the Foundation for the 600 children who use its resources every year. His mission can be summed up with this: "If I made it, anybody can do it. They look at me and say, 'Look, he's a small guy, he was poor and he worked and made it.' If I can help one kid become successful, that's all I ask for."[5]

Juan "Chi-Chi" Rodríguez has made great progress for Latinos in the world of golf. In 1986, he won the Hispanic Achievement Recognition Award and in 1988 was recognized with Replica's Hispanic Man of the Year Award. He was the first Puerto Rican inducted into the World Golf Hall of Fame. For his humanitarian efforts, Rodríguez received the Bob Jones Award from the United States Golf Association and in 1994 was again honored by being elected to the World Humanitarian Sports Hall of Fame.[6]

Notes

1. *The Gigantic Book of Golf Quotations*, Ed. Jim Afelbaum, 2007.
2. "Word Golf Hall of Fame—Juan "Chi Chi" Rodriguez,"—http://www.wgv.com/hof/member.php?member=1099.
3. "Chi Chi Rodriguez,"http://www.pgatour.com/players/00/20/15/.
4. "About Us—Our Philosphy,"http://www.chichigroup.com/about_us.htm
5. "Juan A. Chi Chi Rodriguez,"http://www.chichigroup.com/chichi_rodriguez.htm
6. Word Golf Hall of Fame—Juan "Chi Chi" Rodriguez,"http://www.wgv.com/hof/member.php?member=1099.

Lee Treviño

Star of the World Golf Hall of Fame

by Charlie Harless

> "If you are caught on a golf course during a storm and are afraid of lightning, hold up a 1-iron. Not even God can hit a 1-iron."[1]
>
> —Lee Treviño

Lee Treviño, a six-time major winner and tops in golf when it comes to comedic one-liners, found out the hard way that lightning is no joking manner when he was struck on the links of Chicago at the Western Open in 1975. Hit at the height of his career, the wave of electricity that ran from his golf club up through the left side of his body was a freak occurrence that threatened to not only derail his career, but could have claimed his life. When doctors told the elite golfer that the scars on his shoulder were usually only seen on patients in the morgue, Treviño recalled that "the pain in my left arm and shoulder was killing me but I kept fighting it," and he told himself "I knew I had to hang in there."[2] Treviño has been a fighter his whole life, beating insurmountable odds to rise from a poor childhood where he lived with no electricity in his Dallas house, to becoming the outsider that took the professional golf world by storm upon his debut in 1967. Thus, when Treviño beat death and overcame the physical toll the incident took on his back to again hoist a major championship trophy as a 44-year-old legend at the 1984 PGA Championship, it was keeping in character with a man who has shown time and again that he cannot be knocked down. As Treviño puts it, "When it comes to the game of life, I figure I've played the whole course."[3]

Treviño's tough resolve was formed at a young age, as his father Joseph Treviño was rarely in the picture. Treviño and his two sisters were raised by their mother, Juanita, and their maternal grandfather, Joe, a Mexican immigrant who worked as a grave digger. Money was hard to come by, leading Treviño to joke years later that, "my family was so poor, when somebody threw our dog a bone, he had to call for a fair catch."[4] Although Treviño lived in poor conditions and was sent to work in the cotton fields at the tender age of five, he developed a keen interest in the rich man's game of golf by watching members of the Glen Lake Country Club play on a course whose seventh hole fairway was a mere couple hundred yards away from where his family's house sat. An eight-year-old Treviño would first pick up a club when he began caddying and within a few years, he dropped out of the eighth grade to work on a nearby driving range. As a teenager, Treviño mostly taught himself how to play but received some coaching from Hardy Greenwood, the owner of the driving range where Treviño worked.

While Treviño proved to be a natural for the game, he did not find a place on a college team or the tour circuit, instead joining the Marine Corps at 17. While serving for four years, Treviño managed to continue developing his game by playing against some of the Marine officers and for the Third Marine Division golf club. After the Marines, Treviño made money in the early 1960s by hustling people on the golf course. However, by 1966 Treviño realized that after beating highly skilled players and professionals at the El Paso Country Club where he worked, he had to try his hand at playing alongside these professional players as an equal instead of as their caddie or clubhouse attendant.

Treviño wasted little time making a name for himself after he got his PGA tour playing card in 1967, winning the tour's Rookie of the Year honors and finishing an impressive fifth at the U.S. Open Championship. One year later, Treviño rewrote the record books by becoming the first player to ever record four rounds with a score in the 60s at the U.S. Open as he won his first major at the Oak Hill Country Club in New York. Looking back on his success years later, Treviño recalled that "I never dreamed I could play with those guys on tour. The longer I played, the easier it got. But I never dreamed I was going to be as good as I turned out to be."[5] Treviño became one of the top players on tour and would win the Vardon Trophy, awarded to the player with the lowest scoring average over the course of a season, four times in a five-year period from 1970–1974. Treviño would win 29 times on the PGA tour level, with two wins each at the U.S. Open (1968 & 1971), The British Open (1971 & 1972), and the PGA Championship (1974 & 1984). The 1984 PGA Championship win at Shoal Creek was particularly impressive because not only was it his first major win since the lightning strike, but in the victory he set the Championship scoring record by shooting a 15-under-par for the weekend. Even at a relatively advanced age for the game of golf, Treviño showed that he still had the skills to take the lead into a Championship Sunday and the resolve to win in the face of pressure that caused others to wilt. Fellow tour player and golf legend Tom Watson said of Treviño, "I'll tell you why he is so hard to beat when he's ahead. Because I think he is one of the best ever to play the game."[6]

A few years after the 1984 win, an aging Treviño quipped that "I'd play on the Senior Tour tomorrow if they'd let me. I'm getting tired of playing against these flat bellies. I want to get out there with the round bellies."[7] Playing competitively well into his 50s and 60s on the Senior PGA Tour beginning in 1990, Treviño was named that tour's "Player of the Year" three times as he won another 29 tournaments, enough for second most all-time on that tour, and four majors as well. Treviño never officially retired from the game, but basically called it quits from playing on a regular basis in the late 1990s so that he could spend more time with his family as a father of six children. Looking back on his career at age 57, Treviño remarked in 1997 that "golf has been very good to me. There's no way I could repay the game for what it's done for me."[8]

In all of his modesty, Treviño failed to mention that the game of golf and his legions of fans could never possibly find a way to properly repay the "Merry Mex" for all the joy he brought to the sport with his memorable play, engaging personality, and incredible life story. Treviño the golfer, Treviño the comedian, and Treviño the legend are all well loved, but history will most likely remember the Hall of Famer as Treviño the fighter. Reflecting upon his legacy, Treviño proudly stated that "I showed that a guy from across the tracks, a minority kid with no education from a very poor background, can make it."[9] In a life filled with rough patches and possible traps along his path, Treviño stayed the course and used all of his skills to become a champion in the game of golf as well as life.

Notes

1. George Fuller, *I Golf, Therefore I Am Nuts* (Champaign: Human Kinetics, 2009).

2. Barry McDermott, "Lee Trevino, Midnight Room 170, Holiday Inn, Pensacola, Florida," *Sports Illustrated*, June 15, 1981.

3. Bob Carter, "'Merry Mex' was Golf's Showman," *ESPN*, March 29, 2006.

4. Sally Jenkins, "Trevino the Enigma," *The Washington Post*, August 10, 1985.

5. Barry McDermott, "Lee Trevino, Midnight Room 170, Holiday Inn, Pensacola, Florida," *Sports Illustrated*, June 15, 1981.

6. Sally Jenkins, "Trevino the Enigma," *The Washington Post*, August 10, 1985.

7. Steve Hershey, "Trevino: On a Roll to PGA Seniors," *USAToday*, December 6, 1989.

8. Rick Fraser, "Trevino Planning Time Off, Children Take Top Priority," *The Toronto Star*, June 12, 1997.

9. Bob Carter, "'Merry Mex' was Golf's Showman," *ESPN*, March 29, 2006.

Nancy López

Star of the World Golf Hall of Fame

by Charlie Harless

Browsing through the career résumé of golfer Nancy López, there are plenty of titles (48 LPGA victories), rewards (more than $5 million in prize money), accolades (LPGA Rookie of the Year and four-time Player of the Year) and other accomplishments on the golf course that clearly position López to be considered among the greatest female athletes of all-time. Yet

a stat sheet alone does not explain López's greatness. In fact, some golf analysts and critics have felt López's Hall-of-Fame career was incomplete as she came up short several times in her quest to win the sport's biggest major, the U.S. Open. To be sure, failing to capture that elusive title was bothersome to the competitor within López, but playing golf was never about just majors and the spoils bestowed to the victor. "I don't play for the money, that's for sure. I play for the applause when you come up to the 18th green on the final round, and for the excitement of being in contention, for winning and feeling chilled and thrilled."[1] López was the people's champion, a golfer who flashed a championship smile to the galleries and would consistently sign countless autographs for all of her adoring fans. Golf fans around the world found someone they could relate to and could cheer for in this fighter, this mother of three girls and proud Mexican-American who exuded greatness on and off the course.

In 1978, López exploded onto the golf scene like no other female golfer had ever done before or has done since. After winning nine tournaments, including five in a row over a two-month stretch, López became the first player ever to win LPGA Rookie and Player of the Year during the same season. The then 21-year-old shared much of her winnings and gifts that came rolling in with her father

Domingo, a Mexican immigrant who first taught an eight-year-old López the game on the public courses of Roswell, New Mexico. As Domingo played the fairways, his daughter followed behind hitting balls with one of his wife's clubs, doing, as López later recalled, her very best to keep "hitting and hitting and hitting, struggling to stay ahead of the next group of grownups."[2] Pretty soon, López showed a natural talent that Domingo, an auto mechanic, helped cultivate by working extra hours so that his daughter could travel and play in youth amateur tournaments. López began winning title after title and brought much glory to her hometown, leading one of the town's high school golf teams (all-male except for López) to two state titles and finishing second as a high school senior with amateur status at the LPGA's 1975 U.S. Open.

The success at the junior level helped López become the first woman to ever earn a full scholarship to play golf at the University of Tulsa. López made good on Tulsa's belief in her, winning the AIAW National Championship as a freshman before she left school to turn professional after the 1977 college season. While Domingo was able to witness his daughter make good on the promise she showed as a kid trailing behind on the public links, López's mother, Marina, died suddenly from complications after an appendectomy in 1977. Marina did not get the chance to see her daughter have her spectacular professional debut. While the loss of her mother was undoubtedly devastating to López, there is no doubt that Marina would have been proud at the champion and person López would become as an adult.

López became a mother herself to three daughters, Ashley, Erinn, and Torri with second husband Ray Knight, a professional baseball player. During the 1980s, López was recognized as a public and cultural icon for how to successfully balance career and motherhood. After giving birth to her first child Ashley in 1983, Knight proclaimed that López worked hard to get back and compete at the elite level of women's golf because, "Nancy wanted to prove that she could win as a mother."[3] While still the ultimate competitor, Knight did go on to acknowledge that "motherhood is her No. 1 priority" and López added that "your priorities are so different after you've had a child. It changes your life."[4] While López was thrilled to become a mother, fans became even more enamored with López as she made good on her intention to prove she still belonged, as she won her second LPGA Championship trophy along with four other titles as the Associated Press Female Athlete of the Year in 1985. People who did not play golf or did not normally pay attention to the accolades bestowed upon a female golfer became aware of López for her magnetic personality and what she had accomplished as an athlete and a mother. López recalled that right from the start of her first professional season that, "I loved signing autographs, taking pictures, and shaking hands."[5] Some competitors, however, felt her trademark smile and sunny disposition obscured her true nature as a cutthroat competitor, lending her former caddie, Dee Darden, to jokingly nickname López the "smiling rattlesnake."[6] While intense about winning, nobody could argue that the genuinely caring and genial López truly was a first-class ambassador for the sport. Fellow tour member and Hall-of-Fame member JoAnne Carner said of López that "people who have never played golf in their life, they know her name. That's a rare thing. I've always enjoyed Nancy, and I think she's one of the finest champions to have been in any sport."[7]

López won her last LPGA tour title in 1997 and then soon began cutting back on tournament appearances to spend more time at her Georgia home with her family. Faced with the prospect of basically stepping off the course and away from the game that had brought so much success and opportunity, López surmised that "if I can't play my best golf, then I'm wasting my time not being with my family."[8] López never truly abandoned the sport, but rather embraced a new role as mentor to current and future LPGA stars such as Natalie Gulbis and Paula Creamer. Of her mentees, López said that "the girls are like my daughters. I'm all about contributing to the future of the LPGA and these girls are definitely the future."[9] While López is likely correct in her assessment of the amazing future that awaits these young stars, it should go without saying that the days ahead have been made brighter for the LPGA tour thanks to the trailblazing efforts of López. López has said of her legacy that "it's important to be modest, be grateful for what you have and be appreciative of the fans."[10] The fans, however, need not be modest in sharing their appreciation for the amazing accomplishments and winning attitude that have made López not only a Hall-of-Fame golfer, but a first class mother and vanguard for women in sport.

Notes

1. Ira Berkow, "The Open Feeds Lopez's Competitive Desire," *The New York Times*, June 30, 1998.

2. "A New Star Lights Women's Golf," *Time*, April 3, 1978.

3. Dave Anderson, "Sports of the Times: Sports family," *The New York Times*, April 6, 1984.

4. Ibid.

5. Rick Lipsey, "Nancy Lopez," *Sports Illustrated*, July 14, 2008.

6. Jerry Potter, "Lopez's Modesty Belies Career Full of Accomplishment," *USA Today*, November 13, 1996.

7. Ira Berkow, "The Open Feeds Lopez's Competitive Desire," *The New York Times*, June 30, 1998.

8. David Davies, "Aching Lopez Says Goodbye to All That," *The Guardian*, March 28, 2002.

9. Rick Lipsey, "Nancy Lopez," *Sports Illustrated*, July 14, 2008.

10. Jerry Potter, "Lopez's Modesty Belies Career Full of Accomplishment," *USAToday*, November 13, 1996.

Lorena Ochoa

Future Star of the World Golf Hall of Fame

by Charlie Harless

"Influence, like those other categories, is subjective, but you try to measure it in the effect people have on the world."[1] Lorena Ochoa, recognized the world over for her magnificent play after joining the LPGA tour in 2003, has rightly earned her way onto most lists ranking the best female golfers and athletes of all-time. Yet Ochoa's athletic achievements only scratch the surface of the person the Guadalajara native has become. Ochoa's

roles as humanitarian, entrepreneur, friend, and torchbearer for an entire nation make it easy to recognize why the editors of *Time Magazine* felt her influence was so great that she had to be included in their 2008 list of the 100 most influential people in the world. Ochoa is a woman of many talents and passions that through golf, has found a way to use her gifts to make the world around her a better place. "I play golf for a reason," Ochoa has said. "To be able to reach other people. I'm very fortunate to have an image that allows me to do that. The more tournaments I win, the more I can help. If you can change one person's life, it is worth it."[2]

The world's introduction to Ochoa came on the golf course, where in 2003 she won the LPGA Rookie of the Year award and quickly made a name for herself as one of the sport's bright young stars. In 2008, Ochoa went on a tear as she won five of the first six events she entered that year, including an astounding 11-stroke margin of victory at the HBSC Championships, on her way to achieving the year-end number one ranking for the third consecutive season. By the age of 28, just seven years removed from her professional debut, Ochoa racked up 27 tournament wins on the LPGA tour, including two major championships and nearly $15 million in prize money, a total that placed her third on the all-time earnings list. The consummate professional, Ochoa was well-liked on tour by her colleagues, who rather than displaying animosity at their sport's dominant player, instead recognized what her excellent play meant for women's golf. Young superstar Morgan Pressel has said of Ochoa's play that, "she's very calm out there, and she's very composed when she's out there playing. She's definitely somebody who I look up to, and that's where I want to be."[3] Fellow tour standout Angela Stanford added, "Lorena might be one of these legends that come around once in a lifetime."[4] Stanford also spoke of Ochoa as a person saying, "Obviously, she's a great player, but I've always said she's a better person. She has a big heart and is very sincere."[5]

While Ochoa's play was fantastic, there have been other greats on the LPGA tour, like Annika Sorenstam, Kathy Whitworth, Mickey Wright, or Patty Berg, that have similarly dominated the sport before her. What makes Ochoa a once-in-a-lifetime player is the all-around impact she has had in the world at such a young age. A fellow golfing legend of Mexican heritage, Nancy López, described the power of Ochoa's influence by saying, "as a professional golfer, Lorena will continue dominating and breaking records for years to come. As a humanitarian, she has already left an indelible mark."[6] Founded in 2004, the Lorena Ochoa Foundation operates and issues financial support for lower-income students to attend an elementary school called La Barranca, near where she grew up in Guadalajara. It is here where nearly 300 children now receive the best education possible through the use of inspired teaching methods and an embrace of the arts. The Foundation has spread its mission by opening a high school in 2008 and providing funding to assist other programs for at-risk youth as well as a child cancer treatment center. Taking a hands-on approach to her humanitarian work, Ochoa often dropped in at La Barranca when she was not on tour to personally encourage the students to do their best. Speaking about these visits, Ochoa confided that "the teachers say it is good for the students, but I think I am the one who gets inspired."[7]

Ochoa has also inspired an entire generation of young Mexicans to pick up the game of golf not just through her play, but by making the sport more accessible and popular in her home country. Ochoa's coach, Rafael Alarcón, has said that, "in Mexico, the masses don't even know what golf is, but if you ask any taxi driver in Mexico City, he'll know who Lorena Ochoa is."[8] Part of a family-run enterprise called Ochoa Sports Management, Mexico's top golfer has overseen the development and management of two tour stops in her home country, the LPGA Corona Championship and the Lorena Ochoa Invitational. Ochoa has also overseen the launch of the Lorena Ochoa Golf Academies to develop the sport in a country that did not have a single public course during Ochoa's childhood. Ochoa recalled that as a child, she knew of only two other girls in her area that played golf, but that as she rose to number one for the first time in 2006, "now there are more than 300 girls between 5 and 10 in Guadalajara playing."[9] While golf has given Ochoa so many accolades and made her a household name in Mexico, Ochoa never planned on staying on the tour for the long haul. Ochoa stated in a 2008 interview that "life is too short. It's not just about golf. I don't want to be too old when I get married, start a family, and do my work in Mexico."[10]

Ochoa proved to be a woman of her word, as the number one ranked golfer announced her retirement from the sport in April 2010. At a press conference to discuss her reasons for retirement, Ochoa indicated that "Today is the most special day in my career. Every career has a beginning and an end, and we are at an end."[11] Speaking before a crowded, standing room-only audience in Mexico City, Ochoa recounted that when she envisioned her retirement, she had specific goals for that moment. "First, I wanted to retire as number one. Second, I always dreamed of saying goodbye in Mexico. Now, I want to leave and enjoy everyday life. I want to give to my family the times I haven't been able to give them the last eight years. I am very satisfied with my achievements."[12] Ochoa said she would continue to play annually at her tournament in Guadalajara and would be devoting even more time to running her foundation. "The best present from God has been my foundation. My commitment to Mexican society is strong. Now, I am going to have more time with you."[13] Additionally, Ochoa enters retirement as a new wife, having married Aeroméxico executive Andrés Conesa the previous December, and as a step-mom to his three children, thus meeting her desire to start a family.

Whatever the future has in store for Ochoa, one can be certain that she will carry herself through life's new challenges with a purpose and grace that has won her legions of fans the world over. Ochoa the golf superstar was one of the world's most elite female athletes, yet Ochoa the person has not let fame and awards change the giving spirit and pleasant attitude that those who know her have said defines her. On tournament stops, one often found Ochoa off of the fairways and mixing in with the course maintenance crews and clubhouse support staff, engaging in friendly conversation and offering her thanks to many of these workers who were from her native Mexico. "They are good people, and they work hard to help their families," she says. "I want them to know I support them and that I play for them."[14]

As Ochoa plays for an entire nation, the rest of the world has been rewarded by becoming an audience to her extraordinary achievements on and off the links. Upon her retirement, Ochoa thanked "all the Mexican people and all the fans who have been following me throughout the world. My career will be something special for those who want to reach for their special skills. If I can do it, I am sure many Mexicans can do it."[15] Clearly, to borrow a familiar line from Shakespeare, "All the world's a stage," for Ochoa, but she was not merely a player on it; rather, she is the main attraction, rewriting the script for how much impact a female athlete can have on a sport, a country, and the world.

Notes

1. Richard Stengel, "The TIME 100 Team," *Time*, May 1, 2008.

2. Paul Forsyth, "People's Champion," *The Sunday Times*, July 27, 2008.

3. Damon Hack, "For Ochoa, Being a Role Model Comes With the Territory," The New York Times, May 17, 2007.

4. Steve DiMeglio, "Ochoa Takes Respite From LPGA Reign," *USAToday*, April 23, 2008.

5. George Tanber, "Ochoa's Lasting Legacy May Have Nothing to do With Golf," *ESPN.com*, October 13, 2008.

6. Nancy Lopez, "Heroes and Pioneers: Lorena Ochoa" *Time*, May 1, 2008.

7. Allan Shipnuck, "Simply the Best," *Sports Illustrated*, June 9, 2008.

8. Damon Hack, "Fairways, Greens and Flags in Her Gallery," *The New York Times*, December 7, 2006.

9. Ibid.

10. Paul Forsyth, "People's Champion," *The Sunday Times*, July 27, 2008.

11. Ron Sirak, "On Her Own Terms," *Golf Digest*, April 23, 2010.

12. Ibid.

13. Ibid.

14. Allan Shipnuck, "Simply the Best," *Sports Illustrated*, June 9, 2008.

15. Ron Sirak, "On Her Own Terms," *Golf Digest*, April 23, 2010.

6

LATINOS IN TENNIS

by Richard Lapchick

It is ironic that there are so many Spanish-speaking tennis stars yet so few are from the United States. In the 2009 U.S. Open there were a total of 18 players from South American nations including Argentina, Chile, Ecuador Colombia, Uruguay, and Paraguay. Superstar Rafa Nadal is from Spain. Yet there were no American-born Latinos on the WTA or ATP Tour in spite of the fact that there are nearly 47 million Latinos in the United States.

There is no doubt that tennis was historically a country club sport played mainly by wealthy white families. While it has been slow to happen, African-Americans and Asians have broken into the game. Role models like Althea Gibson, Arthur Ashe, and now the Williams sisters helped popularize the sport among African-Americans.

Including this chapter on Latinos in tennis is an attempt to put the more historic role models in front of Latino youth to inspire them to take up the game.

Francisco "Pancho" Segura's career in tennis helped him break the stereotype of tennis as an all-white sport only played by the rich. Raised in the impoverished Guayaquil, Ecuador, he became among the best tennis players in the world. At the University of Miami, he became the only man to earn three consecutive NCAA singles championships. As an amateur, he finished in the U.S Top Ten six times and then turned professional in 1947.

Segura's name is not in the record books of Wimbledon, the U.S. Open, or the French Open because he played at a time when those tournaments were only open to amateur players and Segura turned professional to support himself financially. He won the U.S.

Pro Championships three times in a row in the early 1950s and became the first Latino tennis player to reach the number one ranking in the world. The International Tennis Hall of Fame recognized his accomplishments when they inducted Segura in 1984.

Bud Collins called Ricardo "Pancho" González one of the top five male tennis players who ever lived. González won four major titles including two singles titles at the U.S. Open, one in doubles at the French Open, and one in doubles at Wimbledon. At the peak of his career, González dominated the field, winning the United States Professional Championship eight times and the Wembley tournament in London four times. He earned a total of 91 singles titles and was the world's number one ranked player for an astounding eight years in the late 1950s and early 1960s.

González died in 1995 at the age of 67 but left an even greater legacy than the victories he amassed by helping to open up tennis to thousands of players who might otherwise have never played the game. Serena Williams, who had won 11 Grand Slam singles titles as of this writing, has commented that Pancho was a pioneer for many inner-city kids.

Throughout her three decade career, Maria Bueno won 19 Grand Slam titles and opened tennis' door to countless Latinos and Latinas. She was a great juniors player in Brazil before turning pro.

Teaming with Althea Gibson to win the 1954 Wimbledon doubles title, she won her first Grand Slam tournament victory. She won the singles title there in 1959, and a few months later won the U.S. Open at Forest Hills. She was named World Champion at the end of that year and Athlete of the Year from the Associated Press.

After working through a serious illness in the early 1960s, Bueno finished second in the world for both 1962 and 1963. In 1964 she won both Wimbledon and the U.S. Open and was the runner-up at the French Open. She ended the year as the number one ranked player in the world. After ten operations in her career in an effort to remain one of the top players in the world, she finally retired.

Born in March, 1936 in Arequipa Peru, Alex Olmedo was just nine-years old when his father gave him a tennis racquet. At the University of Southern California, he earned four NCAA tennis titles—two in singles and two in doubles. In 1959, he won the singles and doubles titles at the U.S. Indoor Championships, Wimbledon, and the Australian Open. He was inducted into the International Tennis Hall of Fame in 1987.

Thought by many to be the greatest ever Mexican tennis player, Rafael Osuna had a brilliant collegiate career and won four Grand Slam events before his life ended tragically at the age of 30. He starred at the University of Southern California, where he earned one NCAA men's singles championship, three doubles championships, and two team championships. He was the world's number one player in the year he graduated.

Osuna is perhaps best known as the leader of the Mexican Davis Cup team. In 1969, he won his singles and doubles Davis Cup matches against heavily-favored Australia, which had won the Davis Cup 17 times. In addition, he won Mexico's only gold medal in tennis, in men's doubles with Vicent Zarazúa.

Known as a fighter both on and off the court, Rosemary "Rosie" Casals was a tennis champion and a women's rights activist. During a tennis career that spanned more than two decades, she won 11 singles and 112 doubles professional titles while spending 11 years in the U.S. top ten.

Her aggressive and determined playing style made her among the most powerful and the most acrobatic athletes in tennis. She and her doubles partner, Billie Jean King, dominated the doubles championships, including five Wimbledon titles. Like King, Casals was a pioneer for the sport of tennis and especially for women. Together they were a force behind many of the changes that shook the tennis world during the 1960s and 1970s, including adding prestige and more money for the women's game.

For Argentinean tennis legend Guillermo Vilas, the year of 1977 was like being in a rocket ship as he compiled an astonishing 145-14 win-loss record for the year. For four months after Wimbledon, Vilas compiled a record-setting 50 match winning streak while winning seven straight tournaments, including an upset of tennis icon Jimmy Connors at the U.S. Open. Vilas would never quite replicate the magic of 1977, but still went on to have a very successful career, winning a total of four Grand Slam titles out of his eight finals appearances.

Argentina's Gabriela Sabatini turned professional in 1985 and was named *Tennis* Magazine's Rookie of the Year. By 1988 she had worked her way up to fifth in the world and beat Steffi Graf in a thrilling three set match to win the 1988 Virginia Slims Championship. She won her first Grand Slam at the 1990 U.S. Open becoming the first Argentinean woman to win a Grand Slam. She soon reached the number one ranking in the world.

Citing a loss of interest the still young Sabatini retired from professional tennis in 1996. Sabatini was ranked in the top 10 for 10 consecutive years, from 1986–1995. Furthermore, she led the Argentine Fed Cup team three times and finished her career with a record of 632-189. In 2006, she received the Outstanding Woman of the Americas Award from the International Olympic Committee.

The Olympic women's doubles team of Mary Joe Fernández and Puerto Rican native Gigi Fernández won two gold medals for the United States in 1992 and 1996. Gigi was 28 years old in 1992 but her career was not reflective of her great potential. Then it all changed.

Between 1992–97, she would go on to win 12 more Grand Slam doubles titles. Gigi and doubles partner Natasha Zvereva of Belarus were virtually unstoppable. The partnership would end up becoming one of the most successful pairings in women's tennis history. They won 38 doubles titles, 14 of those major championships, between 1992 and 1997, holding the top doubles ranking for much of that time frame. After retiring in 1997, she created the Gigi Fernández Charitable Foundation to raise hundreds of thousands of dollars for Hispanic youth in the South Florida region.

As a junior player, tennis fans saw who they assumed would become a superstar in Mary Joe Fernández. By the age of 14, she had won the Orange Bowl, the preeminent event in the world of junior tennis, for four straight years. However, when her career ended in 2000, she had a solid but not spectacular record. She won seven singles titles, 19 doubles championships, reached a career-high ranking of number four in the world and won gold medals at the Barcelona and Atlanta Olympic Games.

She has had a great post-playing career. Fernández was a 2001 Hispanic Heritage Awards Honoree for Sports in recognition of her athletic talents and dedicated work in the community. Serving as the spokesperson for both "Will to Win" and "Breathe Easier," she has been a leading advocate in building awareness about asthma in the

Latino community, a demographic that has seen a high incidence of childhood asthma.

Mary Joe Fernández has served as an ambassador for the game of tennis, promoting several initiatives aimed at inspiring more American youth to pick up the sport. She is a top tennis television commentator for ESPN and CBS Sports. In 2009, she was named the United States Federation Cup Captain.

Marcelo Ríos is included in *100 Campeones* because he became the first Latino to attain the number one ranking in the ATP. In doing so, he knocked Pete Sampras from his throne that he had previously held for 102 straight weeks. The fast-rising 22-year-old lefty from Chile conquered Agassi on the court in a straight sets victory at the finals of a top tournament in Miami in March 1998. In Chile, people poured the streets of Santiago to welcome Ríos home shortly after the win.

Ríos achieved the number one ranking without winning a Grand Slam singles title, having only made one Grand Slam Final appearance. Analysts said he had outstanding instincts, likening his game to former world number one John McEnroe, a fellow lefty known for his ability to out-think his opponent. Ríos and McEnroe shared the same coach, Larry Stefkani. Ríos' attitude and fiery temperament became the thing fans largely remember about him. In Ríos, tennis had another interesting personality to shake up the sport and fuel some drama to the game.

So Segura, González, Bueno, Olmedo, Osuna, Casals, Villas, Sabatini, Gigi Fernández, Mary Joe Fernández, and Ríos all became part of our *100 Campeones*. They all broke barriers and changed the way Latinos thought about tennis. Hopefully they will inspire Latino youth to pick up the game and for some, become Campeones themselves.

Francisco "Pancho" Segura

Star of the International Tennis Hall of Fame

by Jared Bovinet

The first Latino tennis player to be ranked number one in the world barely survived his first day of life. Born prematurely on a bus in Guayaquil, Ecuador on June 20, 1921, Francisco "Pancho" Segura almost died soon after. The baby who would become the first Latin player to reach number one in the world pulled through the incredibly difficult first few months, but his childhood years presented him with many more daunting challenges.

Given Segura's childhood, most people would never have imagined the success that he would experience in tennis. His growth was stunted by deformed legs and he suffered such an intense hernia that he could barely walk for the first ten years of his life. Finally, he underwent surgery to correct the problems, but even after surgery he hardly enjoyed normal health. When he was nine, he contracted malaria, which he suffered with for the next 11 years.

Segura's escape from his sickly childhood was tennis. His grandfather saw the sport as a way to develop his grandson's strength and enrolled him as a ball boy at a nearby club. Soon, Segura began sneaking on its courts to hit a few balls and drew the attention of the city's tennis elite, who were looking for someone they could coach into representing Ecuador at the World Championships. He then began extensive training to become one of the best in the world. It was undeniable that Segura had found something at which he could excel and he continued to hone his skills in the coming years.

At the time, tennis was an all-white, upper-class, country-club sport that had seen few Latinos. Segura was in many ways an outsider; his poor family did not fit the mold of the typical tennis family in Ecuador at that time. This never stopped Segura from continuing to pursue his passion. Amazingly, Segura looks back at his childhood, with all its challenges, and is thankful for how it shaped him. In an interview with *Tennis Week* he said,

> I was lucky. I came up the hard way and when you grow up the hard way you learn a lot of strength of character. And no matter what you go through, if you love the game like I did and I still do, and you have the passion that I do then you overcome all the suffering that one has to go through.[1]

He soon reaped the rewards of dedication and perseverance when he won the Ecuadorian junior title at age 17, along with several other Latin American titles. He enrolled at the University of Miami on a tennis scholarship where he became the first and only man to earn three consecutive NCAA singles championships. During this period from 1943–1945, he won 107 of 122 matches. As an amateur, he finished in the U.S Top Ten six times, and then turned professional in 1947.

One will not find Pancho Segura's name in the record books at Wimbledon, the U.S. Open, or the French Open, not because he was not an outstanding player but because he played at a time when tournaments were only open to amateur players. Segura had to turn professional to support himself financially and therefore lost his amateur status.

He did, however, experience great success as a professional. He won the U.S. Pro Championships three times in a row in the early 1950s and became the first Latin tennis player to reach the number one ranking in the world. Years later, the International Tennis Hall of Fame recognized his accomplishments when they inducted Segura in 1984.

The professional circuit in this time was quite different than it is today. Only a handful of players traveled around the country, bringing actual tennis courts with them because the matches took place in school gyms, playgrounds, and theatres. This proved to be difficult because there was often little light and low ceilings prevented players from playing traditional points. Segura's years of success on the tour proved that he was a talented competitor capable of adjusting to the most challenging circumstances.

Segura earned the nickname "Little Pancho" because he stood only about 5'6", much shorter than the taller and more well-known Pancho González. Segura was also called "Sneaky" because of his ability to disguise his shots, catching his opponents off guard and forcing them to guess where his next shot would land.

Segura's two-handed forehand is still considered one of the best strokes in the history of tennis. But he claims that his mental strength and ability to break down an opponent is "probably 100 percent the reason [he] made it."[2] He viewed tennis as a game of chess, moving forward and back and taking advantage of his opponents' weaknesses. His ability to play pivotal points of a match and maintain an intense concentration better than anyone else helped make him a champion. "My concentration was so intense that when I played tennis I was in a trance . . . I could have been in Hoboken or Hong Kong, playing before the Queen or a bum on the street."[3]

Segura retired from tennis and settled in Southern California, where he served as a teaching professional. He coached Jimmy Connors who went on to become one of the best ever.

Pancho Segura's career in tennis helped him break the stereotype of tennis as an all-white sport only played by the rich. During his rise from poor surroundings in Guayaquil to the best tennis player in the world, he faced incredible physical challenges but worked through them to prove that anyone with a determined heart and fighting spirit can accomplish what most people never dreamed possible.

Notes

1. "The Tennis Week Interview: Pancho Segura," TennisWeek.com, http://blog.ten
nisweek.com/?p=487, April 15th, 2009.
2. Ibid.
3. Ibid.

Ricardo "Pancho" González

Star of the International Tennis Hall of Fame

by Jared Bovinet

Most people consider the epic 2008 Wimbledon final between Roger Federer and Rafael Nadal the best tennis match ever played. If Ricardo "Pancho" González were alive, he would probably beg to differ. González's 1969 third-round Wimbledon match against Charlie Pasarell was considered the best match ever played up until last year, and some say it still is. González won the match, 22-24, 1-6, 16-14, 6-3, 11-9, which helped him blazon his name in the record books as one of the best tennis players ever.

The famed sportscaster Howard Cosell once called González one of the most competitive athletes he knew, second only to Jackie Robinson. Bud Collins called González one of the top five male tennis players who ever lived, writing "If I had to choose someone to play for my life, it would be Pancho González."[1]

There is ample evidence to back these statements. In his career, González won four major titles including two singles titles at the U.S. Open, one in doubles at the French Open, and one in doubles at Wimbledon. At the peak of his career, González dominated the field, winning the United States Professional Championship eight times and the Wembley tournament in London four times. He earned a total of 91 singles titles and was the world's number one ranked player for an astounding eight years in the late 1950s and early 1960s.

González took a unique path to becoming one of the best tennis players of his generation. He was born on May 9, 1928 and grew up in South Central Los Angeles. His parents, who were from Mexico and arrived in the United States in the early 1900s, worked tirelessly to support González and his six siblings. González received his first racquet from his mother on his 12th birthday. He had asked for a bicycle, but his mother thought that would be too dangerous. He never took formal tennis lessons and learned the game by observing players at public courts in Exposition Park in Los Angeles.

González soon began pouring all of his energy into improving his tennis game. He eventually stopped going to school altogether so he could spend more time on the court. His truancy, combined with a few run-ins with the local police, helped get him banned from the Los Angeles tennis establishment. Many believe there were also racial motivations behind this banning; at the time, tennis in the area was full of wealthy Caucasians who preferred members who looked and acted like they did.

When González turned 18, the ban on his participation was lifted and he started entering tennis tournaments. By the end of 1947, he was ranked 17th in the country. The next year, he won his first clay tournament and his wife, Henrietta, gave birth to their first child.

González enjoyed years of tennis success. At 6'3", he had a large height advantage over most of his toughest competitors. He used his height to help him control points around the court and move beautifully around it. He was perhaps best known for his powerful serve and the way it dictated points. Tony Trabert, one of González's opponents, told the *Los Angeles Times* that González was "just like a big cat . . . Pancho's reflexes and reactions are God-given talents."[2] Gussie Moran, another opponent, said González controlled the court "like a god patrolling his personal heaven."[3] Interestingly, he used the serve-and-volley strategy so often that the tour temporarily changed the rules to prevent him from running to the net after serving. He continued to win even with this amendment, so the rule was eventually changed back.

While many of today's professional tennis players retire in their late 20s, and with the age of 30 considered elderly, González continued to play at a high level well into his 40s. At age 44, a championship win in Iowa made him the oldest man to win a pro circuit tournament. He initially retired in 1962 but that did not last long. He came back in 1963 and when the Open Era began in 1968, he returned to play in major championships. He continued to play on the circuit until he was 46, and played senior events until the mid-1980s.

Tennis fans often talk about González's competitiveness and charisma on the court. Historians say that it was often his passion for the game and desire to win that ultimately proved the most important factors in his career. This incredible spirit won González many fans but also some detractors. As one commentator noted, "Everybody either hated or loved González. If they hated him, they hated him with zeal. And if they loved him, he was their boy, their favorite."⁴ While not everyone loved him, it is undeniable that the way he competed and his fiery personality left an indelible impression on the world of sports. He gave everything to every match he played, and his results speak for themselves.

In 1995, Ricardo "Pancho" González died from stomach cancer at the age of 67. González's greatest legacy is opening up tennis to thousands of players who might otherwise have never played the game. Serena Williams, who has won 11 Grand Slam singles titles commented, "Pancho opened up a lot of doors for inner city kids. His legend will always live on."⁵

His legend continues to help inspire tennis players around the world. In 2007, the Latin American Youth Center created the Pancho González Youth Tennis Academy, which introduces low-income immigrant and minority youth in Washington, D.C. to tennis. The Academy offers camps for girls and boys, along with scholarships for students who want to pursue tennis further at academies. The Center, whose goal is to inspire and motivate youth who face significant challenges, is undoubtedly carrying on the legacy of the great González.

Notes

1. "Collins: Top Five Men's Stars of All Time," NBC Sports, http://nbcsports.msnbc.com/id/14489546/?pg=3#spt_0823_Greatestplyr.

2. Pancho Gonzalez and Cy Rice, *Man with a Racket, The Autobiography of Pancho Gonzalez, as Told to Cy Rice* (London: Thomas Yoseloff, 1959), 129.

3. S.L. Prince, "The Lone Wolf," *Sports Illustrated*, June 26, 2002. 18.

4. "Pancho Gonzalez: The Latino Legend of Tennis," Dir. Nick Athas and Danny Haro. 16 September 2005. http://www.youtube.com/watch?v=Nd0gJzm_EQY.

5. Ibid.

María Bueno

Star of the International Tennis Hall of Fame

by Jared Bovinet

Wearing all white is a time-honored tradition at Wimbledon. The tradition is not as old as one may think, however. It was started in 1962 after María Bueno, one of Latin America's most successful tennis players, showed up to the All-England Club in a white dress over hot pink undergarments. "Every time she would swing, the thing would fly up," Billie Jean King remembered. "Everyone at Centre Court would see pink and gasp."[1] Tournament organizers

were not pleased and swiftly created the rule requiring players to wear white. Fortunately, the memory of Bueno's tremendous tennis skills and career trump that of this comical incident. Throughout her three-decade career, Bueno won 19 Grand Slam titles and opened tennis's door to countless Latinos.

Born on October 11, 1939, Bueno grew up in São Paulo, Brazil. All it took to find a place to play tennis was to walk across the street where a tennis club awaited her. Her entire family, composed of her parents and her older brother, enjoyed the sport. They spent most of their free time honing their skills across the street. Bueno never took a formal lesson and taught herself by observing how the world's best players at the time struck the ball and moved around the court.

Bueno quickly developed an aggressive playing style, preferring to charge the net and finish off points quickly. She became the number one ranked junior player in Brazil and won the Brazilian Senior Nationals and the Under 14 competition. One year later, in 1955, she went on to compete in the Pan American Games in Mexico. She won the Orange Bowl two years later and then entered the Caribbean Circuit, where she won 14 of the possible 15 titles.

All her success as a junior helped Bueno decide to turn professional. She was soon traveling the world from tournament to tournament and the public's interest in her could not be contained. Thousands of fans lined up to see this young Brazilian with a penchant for graceful movement across the court, and Brazilians in particular were captivated by their new hero.

Bueno teamed with Althea Gibson to win her first Grand Slam tournament, the 1954 Wimbledon doubles title. She won the singles title there in 1959 and a few months later won the U.S. Open at Forest Hills. She was named World Champion at the end of that year and Athlete of the Year from the Associated Press. She continued her success the next year, winning the Ladies' Singles title at Wimbledon and the Grand Slam in doubles in Australia, France, Wimbledon, and Forest Hills with three different partners.

Just as it looked as if Bueno would dominate the women's game for many years to come, she was diagnosed with hepatitis and forced to return to Brazil, where she recovered for eight months. In the following months, she worked to gain back her strength and stamina. She fought her way to the semifinals at Wimbledon and the U.S. Open and won the U.S. Open the next year.

Bueno's illness proved to be a distant memory when she finished second in the world in 1962 and 1963. In 1964 she won Wimbledon and the U.S. Open and was the runner-up at the French Open. She ended the year as the number one ranked player in the world and earned the praise of many. In a *New York Times* article, Billie Jean King explained, "[Bueno] was the reigning queen of tennis in her day. She just projected well, and was so graceful with long, flowing strokes. She had all the things people liked in a champion."[2]

In the following years, Bueno dealt with an injury to her left knee that required surgery. She was so determined to get back on the tennis court after being sidelined for the second time that she checked herself out of the hospital early and created her own rehabilitation regimen. She returned to dominate Nancy Richey at the final in Forrest Hills. But in the end, her body simply could not keep up with her playing schedule. She had ten operations in her career in an effort to remain one of the top players in the world. She earned her final Grand Slam title by winning the doubles crown with Margaret Smith Court at the 1968 US Open.

Bueno continued to play tennis years after she retired. She played many senior events at Wimbledon, the US Open, and the Virginia Slims Championships in New York City before playing her last competitive match in Flushing Meadow, New York in 1993. She also served as a consultant to the South American womens' tennis development program in the 1980s and worked with the Women's Tennis Association to develop player education seminars.

The tennis culture in Brazil and in Latin America, has been forever changed because of Bueno. In her hometown stand two statues of her, and the Brazilian government issued an official stamp recognizing her achievement in becoming the world's top ranked female tennis player for several years. Not bad for a woman who showed up at the sacred grounds of Wimbledon wearing hot pink.

Notes

1. Roy S. Johnson, "Tennis; Bueno Brings History Onto the Court," *New York Times*, November 23, 1987. http://www.nytimes.com/1987/11/23/sports/tennis-bueno-brings-history-onto-the-court.html. (accessed July 29th, 2009).

2. Ibid.

Alejandro "Alex" Olmedo

Star of the International Tennis Hall of Fame

by Jared Bovinet

Tennis was not always at the center of Alejandro "Alex" Olmedo's life. As a student at Modesto Junior College and then the University of Southern California, he replaced a desire to improve his tennis skills with a desire to be anywhere but on the court. Olmedo once pondered, "'Here it is one hundred degrees in the shade and I run myself dizzy chasing a little white ball—and not a peso in it.' How stupid can I be?"[1] His coaches saw a lot of promise in him but found it challenging to keep him interested in the game, as evidenced by his thought.

When Olmedo did warm up to the idea of becoming one of the world's best tennis players, he proved his coaches were right in seeing so much promise in him. He made a career of winning tournaments, including the U.S. Open doubles championship, American Davis Cup matches, and the Wimbledon and Australian Open singles championships. In his Wimbledon finals victory, Olmedo took only 71 minutes to beat Rod Laver, considered the best player of his generation. In doing this, Olmedo became the first Latino player to win Wimbledon.

Born on March 24, 1936 in Arequipa, Peru, Olmedo's mother was Spanish and his father was one fourth Inca. He had six brothers and sisters, all of whom were introduced to tennis through their father, a caretaker at the local tennis club. Olmedo was just nine years old when his father gave him a tennis racquet and started coaching Olmedo and his brother.

When Olmedo was 14, he won a men's tournament at the club where his father worked. During the following year, he attracted the attention of the president of the Peruvian National Tennis Association, who arranged for Olmedo to go to school in Lima, where he would start intensive lessons. From Lima, he moved to Los Angeles to train with a coach who would prepare him for the American leagues. He and his coach communicated with signs until Olmedo started English classes at night and mastered the language.

Olmedo then enrolled at the University of Southern California, where he earned four NCAA tennis titles; two in singles and two in doubles. Perry Jones, the U.S. Davis Cup captain persuaded him to join his team in 1958. Jones noted, "On the court [Olmedo] is like poetry in motion . . . He just glides like water. His shots are like beautiful geometric designs."[2] Olmedo used this movement and shot selection to stun a crowd of 18,000 Australians by beating their country's team in a singles match and two doubles matches in what became known as the biggest upset at the Davis Cup in four decades.

Olmedo was able to represent the United States at the Davis Cup because he had been living in the country for five years and because Peru did not have a Davis Cup team. Many Americans, however, felt that he was not worthy to represent America. After Olmedo helped beat the Australians, *New York Times* sports columnist Arthur Dailey wrote, "This would seem to be the saddest day in the history of American tennis. A few more rousing victories and the prestige of this country in tennis will sink to a new low."[3] Many felt the Cup should have been sent to Peru and that the United States should have been ashamed of itself for having to borrow talent from a much smaller country. Olmedo responded with appreciation for the United States and for the opportunity to play, "The United States is my tennis home, my adopted country. I am merely paying back for all the help which has been given to me and my friends in America."[4]

In the coming year, he was able to put this controversy behind him. He won the singles and doubles titles at the U.S. indoor championships, Wimbledon and the Australian Open.

Olmedo retired in 1965 after wanting to spend more time with his wife, Ann, and their three children. He then served as the teaching pro at the Beverly Hills Hotel until 1992. There, he taught legends such as Katharine Hepburn, Chevy Chase, and Robert Duval how to master the game. Inducted into the International Tennis Hall of Fame in 1987, Olmedo continues to follow his passion for tennis by teaching others the sport and playing in senior tournaments.

Notes

1. Will Grimsley, "The Laziest Star in Tennis," *The Saturday Evening Post*, June 27, 1959.

2. Ibid.

3. "While Critics Cry, He Wins," *Lakeland Ledger*, August 23, 1959, 19.

4. Will Grimsley, "The Laziest Star in Tennis." *The Saturday Evening Post*. June 27, 1959.

Rafael Osuna

Star of the International Tennis Hall of Fame

by Jared Bovinet

Known as the greatest ever Mexican tennis player, Rafael Osuna had a storied collegiate career and won four Grand Slam events. He would have undoubtedly won many more titles but died on a plane crash at the age of 30. Even in a shortened career, Osuna put Mexico on the tennis world's map.

Born in Mexico City on September 15, 1938, Osuna excelled as a table tennis player and even beat the adult Mexico City Table Tennis Champion when Osuna was only ten years old. He also won the doubles championship at the tournament. For five years of his childhood, he was ranked in the top ten in Mexico's Open singles table tennis league.

Osuna traded his table tennis paddle for a tennis racquet quite successfully. So successfully, in fact, that he received a full tennis scholarship to the University of Southern California. He earned one NCAA men's singles championship, three doubles championships, and two team championships. He graduated in 1963 with a degree in business administration and ended that year with the title of the number one ranking in the world.

Even before he graduated from college, Osuna dominated Grand Slam events. He entered Wimbledon to play doubles with Dennis Ralston, his soon-to-be roommate at USC, and the two made history in becoming the first unseeded pair to win the men's doubles title at the All England Club. He went on to win his only Grand Slam singles title at the U.S. Open in 1963.

Osuna is perhaps best known as the leader of the Mexican Davis Cup teams of the 1960s. He led the team to its only Davis Cup final, and seven years later he won his singles and doubles Davis Cup matches against heavily-favored Australia, which had won the Davis Cup 17 times. This soon proved to be one of the great upsets in the tournament's history. In addition, he won Mexico's only gold medal in tennis in men's doubles with Vicente Zarazúa.

Osuna left an indelible mark on the tennis world. Fellow players admired him for his remarkable character off the court. Former Greek Davis Cup member Taki Theodoracopulus recalled,

> I was in the locker room at Roland Garros stadium, and *[Cliff]* Richey had just beaten me in the doubles in five sets during the French championships. He was totally in the wrong, and Osuna had been a witness. Just as we were about to square off, he jumped in and said, "Let me have him; if you fight him, they won't invite you again.' Richey and Osuna were stars, I was a nobody . . . I will never forget Osuna's kindness and sense of fair play.[1]

Osuna died in a Mexicana Airlines plane crash on June 4th, 1969. Seventy eight other people were killed. His many posthumous honors include the NCAA creating an award to recognize him—the Rafael Osuna Sportsmanship Award—which awards the collegiate men's tennis player who best displays a combination of competitive excellence, sportsmanship, and contribution to tennis. At the beginning of the century, he was named "Sportsman of the 20th Century" for tennis by the Mexican president. He was inducted into the USC Athletic Hall of Fame in 2007 and the International Tennis Hall of Fame in 1979. Lastly, the annual Osuna Cup was created as a contest between Mexican and American teams to strengthen the relationship between these two countries. These awards and honors reflect the fact that Osuna served as a pioneer for Mexican tennis players in the short amount of time he was given to do so.

Notes

1. Taki Theodoracopulos, "Back to Nature," *Spectator*, May 22, 2004. http://www.takistopdrawer.us/2004/may/article_2004-May-22.html.

Rosemary "Rosie" Casals

Star of the International Tennis Hall of Fame

by Cara-Lynn Lopresti

Although Rosemary Casals had sweet-sounding nicknames like Rosie and Rosebud, she was anything but nice when it came to the sport of tennis. As a championship tennis player and women's rights activist, Casals has garnered the reputation of "the classic rebel, the pugnacious outcast from the wrong side of the tracks, who carved out a life for herself in tennis battling the authorities, as well as her opponents, every step of the way."[1] During a tennis career that spanned more than two decades, Casals won eleven singles and 112 doubles professional titles. She spent eleven years in the U.S. top ten. Her aggressive and determined playing style made her "among the most powerful and the most acrobatic, with an overhead that could take the cover off a ball and a few flat-on-the-floor and behind-the-back shots that hadn't been named yet."[2]

Casals is also well known for her doubles play with partner Billie Jean King, with the two of them winning several grand-slam championships, including five Wimbledon titles. However, even more important than her athletic success is her role as a pioneer for the sport of tennis and especially for women. Casals served as "a motivating force behind many of the changes that shook the tennis world during the 1960s and 1970,"[3] including "attending prestige and money for the women's game."[4] Even today she continues to work at improving the game of tennis for people of all ages, genders, and races.

Casals was born on September 16, 1948 to poor immigrant in El Salvador. As an infant, Casals' parents struggled financially to care for her and older sister Victoria. The two were raised by their great-uncle, Manuel Casals Bordas, a former member of the El Salvador National soccer team, and great-aunt, María Casals. Casals was first introduced to tennis by Manuel, who encouraged her to watch him play doubles with his friends at the San Francisco Golden Gate Park. Once Casals grew older she was given the opportunity to play and when she did, she immediately fell in love with the sport.

She spent all her free time trying to find a game, and if no one would play she would hit tennis balls against the backboard. Her great-uncle eventually became the Casals' first and only coach. However, despite never taking a single professional lesson in her life, Casals quickly turned into an accomplished player. As a 16-year-old, she was the top player in northern California, and at 17, Casals was ranked eleventh in the country and earning admiration for her "intense, instinctive, and creative"[5] play.

As a teenager, Casals disliked the guidelines restricting her to play against only younger players on the junior circuit because junior competitions made her feel like "a little girl playing little girl games."[6] Determined to advance her game to the next level, Casals rebelled against the system and competed in tournaments with girls who were older than her. However, her issues with the juniors were just one of many obstacles that Casals encountered in tennis. At 5'2", she was one of the shortest players in tennis and experienced a decided disadvantage on the court. Casals was also confronted with the class distinction prevalent in tennis circles during that time. Tennis took on the image of a country club sport best suited for the white upper class. Casals' Central American heritage and poor background differentiated her from the traditional tennis players.

Casals' unfamiliarity with the country club etiquette also gave her difficulties in the tennis world. Audiences traditionally cheered politely during matches and players wore only white apparel during competition. However, "traditions such as polite applause from the crowd instead of noisy cheering, or wearing only white on the courts, were concepts that were nonsensical to the future tennis star."[7] She believed in hard work to become the best possible player and wanted the tennis audience to appreciate her hard work. For this reason, Casals "brought color and charisma, fire and fury to a sport that ladies and gentlemen were in the habit of applauding politely. You didn't applaud a Rosie Casals, you cheered her until your throat got hoarse, because that's what her game was all about."[8] More than any other player, Casals "brought gut-clutching excitement to the women's game, and excitement that was the natural extension of her personality."[9] Although Casals was nearly kept out of competition for ditching her white attire for a more colorful garb in one of her first appearances at Wimbledon, she stayed true to her convictions and is now known for her brightly colored outfits.

After graduating from high school, Casals continued to compete on the national and international levels. In 1966, Casals and King won the U.S. hard-court and indoor tournaments. The following year, they captured the doubles crown at Wimbledon, the U.S. championships, and the South African championships. Casals and King "continued to dominate women's doubles play for years, becoming one of the most successful duos in tennis history."[10] Among other accomplishments, they won four more Wimbledon titles in 1968, 1970, 1971, and 1973 and became the only tandem to win American titles on every playing surface. Most recently, the two won the U.S. Open Senior Women's Doubles Championship in 1990.

In addition to their influence on the court, Casals and King were also instrumental in opening the doors for women in sports. The two "were perfect role players, feisty but good-humored kids off the public courts who believed women had a destiny in professional sport."[11] Their major contributions included the development of the Virginia Slims Invitational and World Team Tennis, both of which increased the popularity and media attention of professional tennis in the 1970s. As a result of their influence, professional tennis also became open to both amateur and professional players, and the disparity in prize money between women's and men's events was notably reduced.

Casals remains dedicated to supporting women, tennis, and other important causes to this day. Casals has been president of Sportswomen, Inc. since 1981. The organization promotes women in business by developing leadership skills and encouring them to break down barriers. In addition, Casals is co-founder of the Women's International Tennis Association, which advocates for women tennis players. Casals has also provided an opportunity for older players to remain competitive with the Tennis Classic, the "Over-30" tournament circuit, which provides opportunities for high-needs youth, and supports the Endangered Species Project through her own celebrity tennis tournament.

Notes

1. Grace Lichtenstein, "A Long Way, Baby," (1974).. Morrow. http://tennis.quick found.net/history/rosie_casals.html

2. Ibid.

3. "Women's History: Rosemary Casals," *Gale Cencage Learning*. 1996.http://www .gale.cengage.com/free_resources/whm/bio/casals_r.htm

4. "Rosemary Casals," Marin Women's Hall of Fame, (2009). http://www.marin-womenshalloffame.org/honorees-by-year/1990-1999.html

5. "Women's History: Rosemary Casals." *Gale Cencage Learning*. 1996. http://www.gale.cengage.com/free_resources/whm/bio/casals_r.htm

6. "Notable Hispanic American Women," http://books.google.com/books?id=d CWqXOE5lmgC&pg=PA81&lpg=PA81&dq=Rosie+(Rosemary)+Casals+%22Rose-bud%22&source=bl&ots=ENdSvpvUWG&sig=YWj-iP9plv6rtmdaXVF37CrjaPw& hl=en&ei=6r22Sr6vJeeTtgfdmuyxDQ&sa=X&oi=book_result&ct=result&resnum=8 #v=onepage&q=Rosie%20(Ros&f=false

7. Ibid.

8. Grace lichtenstein, "ALong Way, Baby," (1974). Morrow. http://tennis.quickfound.net/history/rosie_casals.html

9. Ibid.

10. "Women's History: Rosemary Casals," *Gale Cencage Learning*.1996. http://www.gale.cengage.com/free_resources/whm/bio/casals_r.htm

11. "Rosie (Rosemary) Casals "Rosebud," *International Tennis Hall of Fame*. 2006. http://www.tennisfame.com/famer.aspx?pgID=867&hof_id=68

Guillermo Vilas

International Star of the International Tennis Hall of Fame

by Charlie Harless

There are few words that can justly depict the poetic beauty of the artful playmaking, mental resilience, and unrivaled dominance exhibited by Argentinean tennis legend Guillermo Vilas in the year of 1977. Whether it was on the hard, clay or grass courts of the world professional tennis tour, few opponents conquered Vilas as he compiled an astonishing 145-14 win-loss record for the year. For a period of four months after Wimbledon, Vilas was unbeatable, as he compiled a record-setting 50 match winning streak en route to winning seven straight tournaments, including an upset of tennis icon Jimmy Connors at the U.S. Open. Although at year's end the computers listed Vilas as the number two ranked player behind Connors, there is little doubt that history notes 1977 as the year of Vilas.

After a season of such transcendent success, many had to wonder what Vilas could do as a second act. Vilas would never quite replicate the magic of 1977, but still went on to have a very successful career, winning a total of four major titles out of his eight Grand Slam final appearances. The more than 60 total singles titles won by Vilas catapulted the Mar del Plata native to a frenetic level of celebrity in Argentina. Return trips to Argentina would cause a rush of fans to follow his every move, forming lines outside restaurants to take pictures, and shower adulation upon Vilas. Blessed with both an athletic frame and flowing locks of brown hair, men and women alike were impressed by the star power that Vilas exuded. Vilas focused his attention on creative outlets outside of tennis during his career, dabbling in writing and performing his own poetry and music. A *Sports Illustrated* profile of Guillermo Vilas painted the best picture of the man when saying that "You might not want your daughter to marry a tennis player, but Guillermo Vilas you'd approve of."[1]

For all of his excellence achieved on the court, Vilas was not born with a love of tennis. Attracted to soccer at a young age, he only picked up tennis at a young age after some prodding by his father. Recalling his memories of starting the sport, Vilas recollects that "I remember when I started tennis, it was considered a sissy game. We used to walk down the street and hide the rackets in our bags."[2] Vilas's love and talent for the sport would soon grow and he became a player who appreciated the nuances of the sport. "I liked the creativity of the game. A tennis player could create more than a painter. Create combinations of things. Nothing was secure. There were the variables of the racket, the surface, the weather, the opponent, the spin and speed of the ball. Where you were. Who you were. For me this was an unbelievable attraction. When someone said, 'come, go to the court,' it was like saying, 'come, paint.' Only better."[3] The same father that pushed him into the sport would attempt to turn his son's interests away from tennis to focus on a more stable career in law, but the effort proved to be futile after Vilas quickly dropped out of law school to rededicate himself to a tennis career. Vilas said that "The law was too square. Rules, more rules. You had to have the same opinions as the professors. Nothing ever was flexible enough."[4]

The celebrity that comes with the territory of being a successful professional athlete has afforded Vilas flexibility in his post-tennis career ventures. While the transition to life after tennis can often be difficult for players who have spent years meticulously perfecting their craft and striving to compete at the highest levels, Vilas and his array of interests have helped make for a smoother shift into his post-playing days. Vilas recounted to the *Boston Globe* that "one of the things I noticed about players when they finished playing was that they would go into depression. If somebody ever makes an article about a tennis player after they are finished, a lot of the time, the players are broke and have problems. There are players who are difficult to write about because they don't do much outside of tennis. And then when they finish playing tennis, they do nothing. They may turn to businesses and things that are just time-consuming activities to prove that they are doing something. But does it make them happy?"[5]

While Villas has lived the life most can only dream about, his creative work off the court indicates that he appreciates both the joys and hardships of life. Vilas has said that "I cannot write when I'm content. When something nice happens, I live it. When something sad happens, I write it."[6] Written in 1981 as his best playing days were beginning to appear in the rearview mirror, the following excerpt from Vilas' poem *Entretiempo*, meaning "in between times," is an example of both his willingness to explore dark topics and a fitting allegory to his inevitable transition into his post-tennis playing days, which would come after his retirement in 1989.

Entretiempo (In between times)

Estaba transpirando (I was sweating)
Esperaba sentado que todo terminase (I was sitting down
    hoping that it would all be over)
Mis ojos se cerraron fuertemente (My eyes closed shut)
Mi cuerpo se estremeció (My body trembled)
Miré a mi alrededor (I looked around me)
Aparentemente ya todo había pasado (Apparently every-
    thing had passed)
Un suspiro de satisfactión salió de mi boca sedienta (A sigh
    of satisfaction exited my thirsty mouth)
Me puse de pie, ya tranquilo (I stood up, and felt calm)
Tiré la cadena, y me fui a jugar el segundo tiempo (I threw
    the chain, and left to play the second half)[7]

Vilas's passion for life is felt in everything that he has done. Whether it is the memory of his spectacular play on the court or reverence for his artistic contributions off of it, Vilas has crafted himself a unique legacy that will not easily be replicated by the many singularly-focused athletes of today. While a new generation of Latin American players have or may soon supplant the record achievements of Vilas on the court, it will take a special individual to live up to the "Renaissance Man" ideals that makes Vilas a champion unlike any other.

Notes

1. Curry Kirkpatrick, "Guillermo Villas," *Sports Illustrated*, May 29, 1978.
2. Ibid.
3. Ibid.
4. Ibid.
5. Michael Holley, "Vilas, 45, Still an Artist On and Off the Court," *The Boston Globe*, August 5, 1998
6. Martha Smilgis, "Tennis gets a classy Sex Symbol," *People*, January 30, 1978.
7. Vilas, Guillermo. From the book *Cosecha de Cuatro*

Gabriela Sabatini

International Star of the International Tennis Hall of Fame

by Jared Bovinet

Courtesy of Michael Baz/International Tennis Hall of Fame & Museum, Newport, RI.

In a sport where so many young players fail to find success at the professional level, Gabriela Sabatini was an exception. Signed by an agent when she was 15, Sabatini became one of the highest profile Latina tennis players ever. During her 12-year professional career, she won the 1990 U.S. Open single's title and a silver medal in singles at the 1988 Olympic Games in Seoul, South Korea.

Sabatini was born on May 16, 1970 and grew up in Buenos Aires, Argentina. Her father and brother introduced her to tennis when she was six and she immediately began showing a natural talent for the sport. Said her brother Osvaldo, "She begged me to let her play . . . She was only six but right away I could see she could hit."[1] Soon after, her father enrolled her in a clay court program to help her develop her skills.

This natural talent along with her dedication created a gifted player on the court. In only four years, Sabatini became the number one ranked player in Argentina's 12-and-under division. She became number one in the junior world rankings in 1984. When she had conquered all the local competition, she signed with Patricio Apey, a coach who played in the Chilean Davis Cup, and moved to Florida to take her game to the next level.

The tennis world and Argentineans in particular soon noticed this great talent. Her compatriots saw in her a refreshing sense of hope. Apey commented, "Suddenly in the middle of all the depression and bad news, when everything seemed to be wrong in Argentina, there comes this little angel who makes only good news."[2] Her nickname, "The Great Sabatini," soon followed. She turned professional in 1985 and earned instant acclaim. She was named *Tennis* Magazine's Rookie of the Year and the WTA Tour named her most impressive newcomer. In one of her first professional tournaments at the Family Circle Cup, she beat two players ranked in the top ten in one morning. Only two months later, she fought all the way to the semifinals of the French Open and in doing so, became the youngest player to go that far at Roland Garros.

Sabatini continued to play well for the next few years but decided to switch coaches in an effort to compete at the highest level. She hired a former Spanish player named Ángel Giménez to help her increase her stamina and conditioning. The results instantly paid off. In only a year, she had worked her way up to fifth in the world and beat Steffi Graf in a thrilling three set match to win the 1988 Virginia Slims Championship.

By 1990, however, Sabatini felt like her career had stalled yet again. She was not improving and still had not realized her dream of winning a Grand Slam tournament. She lost both the U.S. Open and Summer Olympic finals to Graf and did not win any titles the next year. As a result, she decided to hire coach Carlos Kimayr, who placed a special emphasis on increasing her speed and connected her with a sports psychologist. This new coaching change proved fruitful when Sabatini finally won her first Grand Slam at the 1990 U.S. Open and soon reached the number one ranking in the world.

In winning her first Grand Slam, Sabatini beat Steffi Graf, considered by many to be the greatest female tennis player ever. Sabatini enjoyed a storied history with Graff. The two played each other in every Grand Slam final Sabatini reached, with Graf winning two of the three. They were also doubles partners in many tournaments and won the 1988 Wimbledon Ladies' Doubles Championship together.

Sabatini's 1990 U.S. Open Championship provided a compelling twist in the rivalry's history. In the preceding years, analysts doubted her ability to win a major and did not give her much of a chance to win. Graf had beaten her 18 of their previous 21 meetings and was dominating the sport, having won the only "Golden Grand Slam" (all four majors and the Olympic gold medal) in tennis history two years prior. However, Sabatini had other plans. Using a combination of clever topspin and strategically-placed shots, she controlled the pace of the match and Graf had 40 unforced errors.

The match created a buzz that Graf-Sabatini would be the next great rivalry in tennis, comparable to the one between Martina Navratilova and Chris Evert a few years before. The former rivalry never reached the intensity of the latter, however, but still provided some memorable matches. Sabatini's career peaked at that Open while Graf dominated the women's game until the mid-1990s.

Sabatini retired from professional tennis in 1996. A few years earlier, she began to lose her enthusiasm for the game. After a first round exit from the 1994 French Open, she began to realize she was losing her will to compete. She played her last match in October of 1996. In an interview with Charlie Rose at the end of that year, Sabatini reflected on her retirement. "I didn't feel the same desire I used to have . . . You just want to start seeing other things,"[3] she said.

Sabatini took advantage of the opportunity to pursue her other interest after she retired. She created her own line of specialty perfumes that has been successful for years. She also worked tirelessly to develop junior tennis in her native Argentina.

Sabatini's list of accolades is extensive. She was ranked in the top 10 for 10 consecutive years, from 1986–1995. Furthermore, she led the Argentine Fed Cup three times and finished her career with a record of 632-189. In 2006, she received the Outstanding Woman of the Americas Award from the International Olympic Committee. Sabatini was inducted into the International Tennis Hall of Fame in 2006. While all these accomplishments are impressive, Sabatini is perhaps best known for being the first Argentinean woman to win a Grand Slam, a feat that speaks volumes for her determination and will to succeed.

Notes

1. *People*, September 7, 1987, 127.
2. Bruce Newman, *Sports Illustrated*, May 2, 1988, 52.
3. Charlie Rose, "A Conversation with Gabriela Sabatini," http://www.charlierose.com/view/interview/5832 (accessed July 10th, 2009).

Beatríz "Gigi" Fernández

Grand Slam Women's Doubles Champion and Olympic Gold Medalist

by Charlie Harless

In the tennis world, beating one player named Fernández was tough; beating two proved nearly impossible. The Olympic women's doubles team of Mary Joe Fernández and "Gigi" Fernández went unbeaten in the 1992 and 1996 games, capturing two gold medals for the United States. Before the 1992 gold medal performance, it was Mary Joe who was the better known 'Fernández' in the tennis world, having already reached the semifinals or finals in singles for each Grand Slam tournament. Gigi Fernández had achieved success on the doubles court, having won five Grand Slams and reaching as high as number 17 in the rankings on the singles side. Yet, prior to 1992, Gigi was known more as a talented, yet somewhat underachieving journey woman. The 1992 Olym-

Courtesy of USF Athletics.

pic Games ended up marking a new beginning of sorts for the then 28-year-old Gigi, as after Barcelona she would go on to win 12 more Grand Slam doubles titles in the final five years of her career to secure her place as an all-time tennis great and truly make a name for herself.

Growing up in Puerto Rico, Fernández attracted attention from the media and her fellow Puerto Ricans after showing some promise as a tennis player in her teenage years. In a country not known for producing tennis talent, Fernández's acceptance of a scholarship offer to play collegiate tennis at Clemson University was big news.

Fernández would make her supporters even prouder when announcing her decision to turn professional a few months after making the finals of the 1983 NCAA Singles Championships. As Fernández navigated her way through the WTA tour, she had a rough start to her career as she produced mixed results. Fernández recalled that, "I wasted my first four or five years on the tour. I was floating around with no direction and really didn't know what I wanted to do."[1] Soon however, Fernández got her game on track and had her first major breakthrough by winning back-to-back U.S. Open women's doubles titles in 1989 and 1990, solidifying her reputation as a doubles specialist. Thus, when it came time to select the representatives for the 1992 United States Olympic team, there was little surprise that Fernández was chosen to play doubles.

After Fernández accepted the invitation to play for the United States team, her decision was met with some resentment in her native Puerto Rico. Fernández explained that she was not turning her back on her country, but instead stated that "all Puerto Ricans are U.S. citizens and that is what makes me eligible. And since Puerto Rico has only recently started competing as a team in women's tennis, the country will not qualify for the Olympics. So I am proud to represent the U.S."[2] The Puerto Rican would bring glory to her home nation, upsetting the number one doubles team and host country favorites of Spain's Arantxa Sánchez-Vicario and Conchita Martínez in a three-set thriller. Fernández spoke of her national pride in the post-match press conference, revealing that, "I'm happy to win for my country. When I chose to play for the US it was controversial, but perhaps people now will understand why I did it. If I'd played for Puerto Rico I'd be back home because there's no way I'd have had as good a partner as Mary Joe. I'm pleased for the people of America and Puerto Rico."[3]

One month after her first Olympic triumph, Fernández won her third doubles major title of the year at the 1992 U.S. Open with partner Natasha Zvereva of Belarus. The partnership between Fernández and Zvereva, which began with a victory earlier that year at the Australian Open, would end up becoming one of the most successful pairings in women's tennis history. According to Fernández, the pair got together after "our partners dumped us" in the summer of 1991 and a *Sports Illustrated* feature highlighting the duo described the two players as polar opposites in personalities, stating that "the only thing they have in common is a problem with authority."[4] While Zvereva was generally reserved in her expressions on the court, Fernández was fiery and unafraid to slam a racket or chastise herself for mistakes. Fernández once sent a check to the WTA in the amount of $250 to pay in advance for the fines she would accumulate for being unable to control her temper on the court. The prize money Fernández and Zvereva would earn together more than helped offset the cost of sportsmanship infringements. The duo won 38 doubles titles, 14 of those major championships, between 1992 and 1997, holding the top doubles ranking for much of that time frame and drawing comparisons to the doubles team of Martina Navratilova and Pam Shriver, widely believed to be the best women's pairing of all-time. The great Navratilova herself felt that Fernández-Zvereva was a duo to be reckoned with, saying "we were power. They are finesse," and that if the teams played a match, "it would have been close."[5] Hypothetical matchup aside, Fernández's doubles career is clearly seen as one of the best ever. Upon retiring at the end of the 1997 season, Fernández looked back proudly on what she had accomplished on the tennis court and with the knowledge that even in the late stages of her career she could still compete with the sport's young guns. A 33-year-old Fernández stated that, "I'm happy that I'm going out on a good year. I don't want to go out losing first and second rounds."[6]

Losses were few and far between for Fernández in her doubles career and she continued her winning ways off the court as well. After her final match at the 1997 Chase Championships, Fernández spoke of her post-playing plans, saying "I want to work with kids. I'm going to make myself available to different organizations, different clubs, to go play with juniors, talk to them about their aspirations."[7] Fernández has made good on these intentions, having spent a few seasons as the tennis coach at both the University of South Florida and for the Puerto Rican Fed Cup team while also creating the Gigi Fernández Charitable Foundation to raise hundreds of thousands of dollars for Hispanic youth in the South Florida region. Not only did Fernández make a name for herself on the court with her trademark passion and excellence, but she is using these same traits to gain even more fans off the court as well. Fernández is a common name in both tennis and Puerto Rico, but Gigi Fernández has made sure that hers is a name that will not be forgotten.

Notes

1. Jim Carson, "Gigi Fernandez is Focused on Winning Olympic Medal," *St. Petersburg Times*, April 8, 1992.

2. Ibid.

3. Guy Hodgson, "Spaniards Fall to Rising Stars," *The Independent*, August 9, 1992

4. Sally Jenkins, "Terrible Two," *Sports Illustrated*, February 20, 1995.

5. Ibid.

6. Robin Finn, "Fernandez Retires After Loss in Doubles," *The New York Times*, September 7, 1997.

7. Darrell Fry, "Fernandez to Retire, 'Have Fun,'" *St. Petersburg Times*, September 7, 1997.

Mary Joe Fernández

Grand Slam Women's Doubles Champion
and Olympic Gold Medalist

by Charlie Harless

Like Cinderella arriving to the ball well before nightfall, tennis experts often thrust the sport's young female talent into the international spotlight by proclaiming them to be the next superstar and royalty of the sport before they even reach high school. At the age of 14, Mary Joe Fernández had won the Orange Bowl, the preeminent event in the world of junior tennis, for four straight years. She also had the titles of "youngest ever" to have won matches against a professional and at the U.S. Open. Followers of the sport predicted the tennis kingdom could soon be hers to rule over. Mary Joe similarly dreamt of grand slam titles, the number one ranking, and all the successes that come with being the best.

When the clock struck midnight on Fernández's career in 2000, she had a solid, if not the wildly spectacular record of achievement that was once envisaged. She won seven singles titles, 19 doubles championships, reached a career-high ranking of number four in the world and won gold medals at the Barcelona and Atlanta Olympic Games. No fairy tale would be complete without a nemesis, as Fernández faced down her fair share of adversaries. Although the Dominican-born player achieved great successes for herself and her adopted home country of the United States, one might concur that her fairy tale rise to the top of the tennis world did not culminate with the requisite 'happily-ever-after' finale. Jumping to such a conclusion would be as uninformed a decision as judging a book by its cover. Fernández was not as physically imposing as a Martina, Steffi, or Venus, but her slight frame disguised a steely resolve and dedication that has helped her overcome so many obstacles in her life.

After grabbing the tennis world's attention with her stellar results in the junior ranks, there was an understandably elevated level of anticipation as to when Fernández would join the WTA Virginia Slims Tour. While greats like Tracy Austin had won a grand slam title in the earlier part of the decade at the age of 16, Fernández remained committed to graduating high school. Fernández's immigrant parents, José from Spain and Silvia from Cuba, taught their prodigy daughter the importance of an education and maintaining balance in her life. When *Sports Illustrated* profiled Fernández after her fourth win at the Orange Bowl, José Fernández was quoted as saying "If Mary Joe doesn't want to study, we make her study. If she doesn't want to play tennis, we don't make Mary Joe play."[1]

Upon graduating from Miami's Carrollton School of the Sacred Heart in 1989, Fernández became a full-time professional tennis player, quickly posting stellar results on the tour and in short time winning her first titles in Tokyo and Filderstadt. She reached the finals of the Australian Open in singles in both 1990 and 1992 and won a grand slam title in doubles when partnering with Patty Fendick to defeat Jana Novotna and Gigi Fernández in Melbourne at the 1991 Australian Open.

American compatriot Gigi Fernández (no relation), quickly changed roles from Fernández's adversary to becoming her doubles partner as the two represented the United States in the 1992 Olympic Games in Barcelona. The pair faced the toughest of matches in the gold medal round, when they took on the venerable home-country duo of Arantxa Sánchez-Vicario and Conchita Martínez in front of a wildly partisan crowd on the red clay. After the Americans claimed the first set, the Spanish team stormed back after being inspired by the crowd and the arrival of the King and Queen of Spain to the Royal Box. Facing a decisive third set, Fernández and Gigi overcame the tough conditions and prevailed 7-5, 2-6, 6-2 to win the gold. The pair would prove to be a winning partnership again four years later, when Fernández and Gigi beat the Czech Republic team in straight sets to win their second gold medal together. Mary Joe enjoyed great success in the doubles game during her career, going on to win 19 doubles titles in total, partnering with great players like Sánchez-Vicario, Novotna, Martina Hingis, and Lindsay Davenport.

In singles, Fernández never quite reached the pinnacle, yet it was not for lack of talent or effort, as seen in her memorable run at the 1993 French Open. Seemingly on the brink of packing her bags for home, she found herself staring at a 6-1, 5-1 hole to Gabriella Sabatini in a quarterfinal matchup. Finding a new resolve after saving a few match points against her, Fernández began to do the unimaginable when she came roaring back to win the second set in a tiebreaker to force a deciding third set. As the match moved well beyond three hours in length, the two engaged in a see-saw affair marked by tense drama. With little separating the two, Fernández came up bigger in the critical points and was able to secure a 1-6, 7-6, 10-8 victory that is viewed by many tennis experts as one of the greatest comebacks in the sport's history. Riding the momentum of the Sabatini match, the fifth-seeded Fernández knocked out the second-seeded Sánchez-Vicario on her best surface and advanced to take on top-seeded Steffi Graf in the final. Although she was able to take the first set off of the favored Graf, Fernández ultimately lost in three sets, 4-6, 6-2, 6-4, and was denied that elusive grand slam title.

While the 1993 French Open Final was a tough loss after playing so well throughout the tournament, the pain of losing was nothing compared to the intense pains Fernández began feeling in her stomach. She had breathing difficulties her entire childhood, which, led to her asthma diagnosis as a 20-year-old. She had also dealt with undiagnosed stomach cramps her entire professional career. When the pain had intensified to its most unbearable level during the 1993 season, Fernández knew something was wrong and sought to determine the source of the pain. She was diagnosed with endometriosis, a condition in which cysts form in the pelvic area and cause severe pain. After undergoing surgery to remove the growths, Fernández returned to the tour, but felt weaker than before. The medication used in the rehabilitation process left her immune system depleted and resulted in Fernández coming down with a host of illnesses during the mid-1990s. After coming down with the flu and pneumonia, and losing a great deal of weight and physical strength, Fernández finished 1994 outside the top ten for the first time in her career.

Fernández acknowledged in an interview near the end of her career that she had likely missed her opportunity to win a major. "I don't know that I'll ever win a Grand Slam. The French Open in '93 might have been my last opportunity . . . I had been playing really well, I was about to make a breakthrough. I was ready to challenge for No. 1 in the world. And then, boom, the endometriosis. I didn't know if I'd ever be able to play again."[2] Fernández did manage to rally her career and win a doubles title at the 1996 French Open, and make a surprise run in singles to the semifinals of the 1997 Australian Open. She won her last singles title in 1997. In that same interview, Fernández's words clearly showed the resolve and never-quit attitude that will define how history views Fernández as a tennis player. "I've still got some dreams and goals I want to pursue. What's the worst that can happen? I might fall short, but I'll do my best . . . It's not important whether or not you reach your dream. What is important is that you trust in God, try your hardest, and do your best."[3]

In her post-playing days, Fernández has continued to achieve great personal and professional milestones. In 2000, she married sports agent Tony Godsick and the couple has since had two children, Isabella María and Nicholas Cooper. Fernández was a 2001 Hispanic Heritage Awards Honoree for Sports in recognition of her athletic talents and dedicated work in the community. Serving as the spokesperson for both "Will to Win" and "Breathe Easier," she has been a leading advocate in building awareness about asthma in the Latino community, a demographic that has seen a high incidence of childhood asthma. She has served as an ambassador for the game of tennis, promoting several initiatives aimed at inspiring more American youth to pick up the sport. Fernández is most recognized today as a leading television commentator with her work as a tennis analyst for ESPN and CBS Sports. In this role, she is able to draw upon innumerable anecdotes of her playing days to provide insightful commentary. This year, she will take on a new challenge as the United States Fed Cup Captain.

Fernández did not let the weight of lofty expectations or medical setbacks deter her from constructing a winning life on and off the court. While her career may not have followed the expected narrative of a tennis princess, Fernández has shown that by consistently rewriting the record books, defying the odds, and serving the community, her story is as fascinating as any.

Notes

1. McDermott, Barry. "Young Mary Joe is on the go" *Sports Illustrated*, January 6, 1986.

2. Moring, Mark. "When dreams slip away" *Christianity Today*, November 1, 1998.

3. Ibid.

Marcelo Ríos

First Latino to Be Ranked Number One in the ATP Tour

by Charlie Harless

The names 'Sampras' and 'Agassi' will be forever recognized, both collectively and individually, as two of the giants of professional tennis. Throughout the 1990s, their Grand Slam successes and legendary face-offs showcased their starkly contrasting personalities and playing styles that simultaneously elevated the sport's popularity and made them the gold standard to which other players were measured. Marcelo Ríos, a fast-rising 22-year-old lefty from Chile, had never beaten Pete Sampras or Andre Agassi on the professional circuit, yet all that changed on March 30, 1998. With foot speed virtually unrivaled on tour, and utilizing his unique groundstroke mix of sublime angles and a pace to keep opponents unbalanced, Ríos conquered Agassi on the court in a straight sets victory at the finals of a marquee tournament in Miami. Additionally, the win meant that the 5'9" Ríos would measure up to the giants of the sport as no South American man had ever done before, by claiming the number one ranking in the world on the ATP Tour and knocking off Sampras from his throne that he had previously held for 102 straight weeks. The citizens of Chile took to the streets of Santiago and welcomed home Ríos shortly after the win, heralding both the country's and tennis's new king.

To say that Ríos' rise to the top of the tennis world is merely unlikely is to sell short the seemingly implausible thought that in a country obsessed with soccer, a scrawny nine-year-old could actually one day decide to pick up tennis and eventually reach the sports' upper echelons in a little over a decade. Ríos's parents sent him off to a sports academy at the age of fourteen which led to his turning professional at 16, just seven years removed from picking up a tennis racket for the first time. Ríos recounted the unlikelihood of such a story when saying after the Miami win that "being the best player in the world for Chile is not normal and I feel really proud. Maybe, at the moment, I'm playing better than anyone but I don't feel like I'm really good."[1] While the statement could be interpreted as falling somewhere between humble modesty and honest self-reflection, Ríos's physical gifts were not among the best the sport had ever seen. In fact, Ríos achieved the number one ranking without winning a Grand Slam singles title, having only even made one Grand Slam Final appearance. His serve was nowhere near as strong as Sampras and watching matches from that era, one could recount the names of more than a dozen brawnier ball strikers from the baseline than Ríos. What he lost in size and power of strokes, however, was made up for by his outstanding instincts and penchant to take the ball early that resulted in masterful and hard-to-read trajectories of his shots. Observers were quick to liken his game to former world number one John McEnroe, a fellow lefty known for his ability to out-think his opponent and use variety in his game to counterattack the bigger guys. Ríos and McEnroe shared the same coach, Larry Stefanki, who once said in praise of Ríos, and could just as easily have been attributed to McEnroe, "He has something that doesn't come around that often: a general awareness of the court and how to use it. He can create soft angles off hard balls, and generate velocity off slow balls. When he has time to turn on the ball, he can hit a winner from anywhere."[2]

The comparisons to McEnroe were not limited to playing style, as Ríos also possessed a certain attitude and fiery temperament that would become the thing which fans largely remember about him. "John was difficult," recalled Stefanki. "People said if I could last with him I can handle Marcelo."[3] *Sports Illustrated* confirmed Ríos' reputation as a hothead and difficult player when one of its story's title headings proclaimed Ríos to be the "Most Hated Man in Tennis." Ríos was accused of hurling insults at autograph seekers, being rude to tournament officials and players on the women's tour, and generally being curt in his dealings with the media. Ríos responded to such criticisms with statements such as, "Everybody can say whatever they want. I don't think I need to prove anything to anyone."[4] For all his alleged shortcomings, many welcomed the arrival of an interesting personality to shake up the sport and fuel some drama to the game. "It's more interesting for the fans to have a bad guy to root against than every player behaving exactly the same,"[5] McEnroe said.

Fans did not have ample opportunity to embrace his on-court excellence or refute his boorish behavior for long, as Ríos would lose the number one ranking six weeks later and never made another appearance in a Grand Slam final. Battling nagging injuries for most of the early 2000s, including recurring back trouble, Ríos retired at the young age of 28 in 2004. Upon making one last second-week run at a Grand Slam event at the 2002 Australian Open, Ríos provided one last glimpse of what made him so special as a player and the promise he showed in the late 1990s. Christopher Cleary of the *New York Times* wrote that "there is an ease to Ríos's tennis, a languid, loose-limbed, any-angle-is-possible quality that makes you realize how much the game has missed his game in the culminating stages of Grand Slam events. Touch players have not been the rule for too long, but Ríos still thrives or fades on touch, changing cadence and trajectories and ideas with a regularity that makes his ultra fit, full-swinging peers seem unimaginative."[6]

For his career, Ríos made 31 singles tournament final appearances, winning 18 of these matches, the last win coming in Hong Kong in 2001. At his July 2004 retirement press conference, Ríos professed that "It's very sad for me to accept that I have to give up tennis. It has been the great passion of my life. The truth is, I wanted to keep playing tennis. I think I could achieve so much more."[7] Ríos did achieve several notable feats on the tennis court, but more importantly, his impact on Chilean sports has been tremendous. Ríos was at the forefront of a wave of South American players who would go on to make an impact on the global tennis scene, including future Top-10 ranked Chileans Fernando González and Nicolás Massú. No doubt his place as the only Latin American to ever be the number one ranked player in the world on the ATP Tour showed countless South American children that success can be possible in other sports outside of soccer. Now married and a father to a young daughter, Ríos looks back fondly on his playing days. "Today I feel that I have lived through a lot, thanks to professional tennis and others things . . . I feel fulfilled. To be the best in the world at some point off the long career I had, I reached the top. I want to leave it like that."[8]

Notes

1. Chris Jones, "The New Superbrat," *The Evening Standard*, April 1, 1998.

2. Andrew Longmore, "The Ace Who Needs a Heart," *The Independent*, May 24, 1998.

3. John Roberts, "Mighty Mouth Rios Grows in Stature," *The Independent*, March 31, 1998.

4. Josh Young, "Rios'winning Flair Doesn't Convert Fans," *The Washington Times*, September 3, 1998.

5. "You cannot be se. . . rios, Mac backs Superbrat II," *Sunday Mirror*, June 21, 1998.

6. Christopher Cleary, "Rios Softens His Image but Retains His Touch," *The New York Times*, January 19, 2002.

7. "For the record," *Sports Illustrated*, July 26, 2004.

8. ESPN.com, "ESPN Hispanic Heritage Month: Marcelo Rios," ESPN Broad-band, http://sports.espn.go.com/broadband/video/clip?id=3593988&categoryid=null (accessed May 30, 2009).

7

LATINOS IN BOXING

by Richard Lapchick

I remember listening to my father talk about boxers when I was a boy. He would often talk about how different racial and ethnic groups seemed to dominate the sport at one time and how it helped them join mainstream America. Boxing also gave their community pride in being American. The Jewish community especially cheered for the likes of Max Baer and Ruby Goldstein. Jackie Flynn and Mick Ronan were among many Irish boxers in the early 20th Century. Italians followed Tony Galento, Giuseppe Antonio Berardinelli, who fought under the name of Joey Maxim, and Rocky Marciano and were disappointed by his early retirement. Joe Louis was a hero for African-Americans.

Latino boxers did the same for their communities both in their countries of origin and for their ethnic communities in the United States. The chapters that follow will highlight those men who include "Panama" Alfonso (Al) Brown, Gerardo "Kid Gavilán" González, Éder Jofre, José Nápoles, Rubén Olivares, Roberto Duran, Alexis Argüello, Salvador Sánchez, Julio César Chávez, and Oscar De La Hoya

"Panama" Alfonso (Al) Brown was a pioneer for future generations of Latino boxers when he became the first world boxing champion from Latin America in June 1929 when he captured the bantamweight title. Brown held the bantamweight title from 1929–1935. He fought in Brussels, Copenhagen, Havana, Paris, Montreal, Toronto, Marseilles, Milan, London, Algiers, Casablanca, Tunis, and Valencia, Spain in title bouts and non-title bouts, successfully defending his title 10 times. He lost the title to Spain's Baltazar Sangchilli in Valencia. In 1938, he regained his title from Sangchilli.

Cuban born Gerardo "Kid Gavilán" González dazzled the boxing world with his original "samba on the canvas" dance and shuffle combo. He is credited with inventing the bolo punch, a wide half hook and half uppercut punch that Gavilán said was a product of his years cutting sugar cane with his machete in Cuba. Muhammad Ali and "Sugar" Ray Leonard would later include the bolo punch in their arsenal. A fan favorite, he compiled a 107-30-6 record over a 16-year professional career during which he was knocked down only twice and never lost a fight by knockout.

In 1951, when "Sugar" Ray Robinson vacated the welterweight championship to move up to the middleweight division, Gavilán beat Johnny Bratton in 15 rounds to win the welterweight title. He made seven successful defenses of his title. In 1952, Gavilán, who was dark-skinned, successfully defended his welterweight title in front of more than 17,000 fans at Miami Stadium against Bobby Dykes in what was the first racially mixed bout in Florida.

Born in Sao Paulo in 1936, Éder Jofre started boxing as a boy and compiled an amateur record of 148-2 record before turning professional in 1956. He was so dominant that he didn't lose a fight for nearly nine years. Jofre beat Eloy Sánchez to win the bantamweight world title in 1960. From 1960 to 1965, he defended his title eight times. He had a career record of 72-2-4, with 50 knockouts and never suffered a knockout. In 1992 Éder was inducted into the International Boxing Hall of Fame.

Between 1963 and 1969, Cuban exile José Nápoles went 35-3 while fighting primarily in Mexico. He defeated Curtis Cokes for the welterweight title in 1969 and was the first Latino ever to be named the *Ring Magazine* Fighter of the Year. He successfully defended his welterweight title 13 times and retired at age 35 with a 79-7 career record in 1975 after he lost by technical knockout to John Stracey.

In 1990, Nápoles was inducted into the International Boxing Hall of Fame. In 2002, *Ring Magazine* recognized Nápoles as the 56th greatest fighter of the previous 80 years.

Rubén Olivares was raised in Mexico City. He was a power puncher who in 1969 became the world champ when he knocked out WBC and WBA bantamweight title holder Lionel Rose in five rounds. The victory also gave Olivares a 52-bout record of 51 wins (49 by knockouts) and one draw. On July 9, 1974, Olivares got his first chance at a featherweight world championship. He defeated Zensuke Utagawa of Japan to capture the vacated title. Olivares had just 13 losses in his career, of which eight came in his last 19 bouts. Olivares was inducted into the International Boxing Hall of Fame in 1991 with a career record of 88-13-3 that included 78 knockouts.

In the world of boxing, Roberto Durán was beloved for his willpower that guaranteed opponents' brutal battles and the audience an energy packed show. Born in Panama, he is considered one of the greatest boxers of all time. Roberto Durán was only the second boxer to fight in five decades. Durán won titles in four divisions: lightweight, welterweight, junior middleweight, and middleweight. In 2002, Durán was chosen as the 5th greatest figher by *Ring Magazine* of the last 80 years. His 69 wins by a knockout place him in a small group of boxers with 50 or more victories by knockout. Durán's career record was 104-16 and led to his induction into the World Boxing Hall of Fame on October 14, 2006, and the International Boxing Hall of Fame on June 10, 2007.

Alexis Argüello was born in 1952 in Managua, Nicaragua. He lost in his professional debut but then went on to win 36 of his next 38 bouts. At age 22, he beat Rubén Olivares to win the WBA featherweight title. In 1978, after four successful title defenses, Argüello won the super featherweight title by defeating Alfredo Escalera to become world champion in two divisions. In 1981 he won a title in the lightweight division. He just failed to win a fourth division title when he lost to undefeated future Hall-of-Famer Aaron Pryor, for the WBA World light welterweight title in 1982.

Argüello wanted to do more outside the ring and formed a personal mission to help the poor and young people in war-torn Nicaragua. He contributed to charities and spent time with children. After seeing one of his homes in Managua captured by the Sandinistas, his bank account seized, and one of his brothers killed fighting the Sandinistas, Argüello fought with the Contras in Nicaragua. Argüello was elected to the World Boxing Hall of Fame in 1991 and the International Boxing Hall of Fame in 1992.

At the age of 23, Salvador Sánchez had become one of the greatest boxers of all-time in a career that was tragically cut short after a car accident in August 1982.

He fought largely in obscurity before his February 1980 fight against WBC champion Danny López for the featherweight title. A heavy underdog, Sánchez won the title and then defended it against López. He then went up against undefeated Puerto Rican Wilfredo Gómez who was 32-0 with 32 knockouts. Gómez had moved up a division to fight Sánchez. It was a classic, and pitted Sánchez's Mexican fans vs. Gómez's Puerto Rican fans. Sánchez took control and the fight had to be stopped in the 9th round.

In 1981 Sánchez shared *Ring Magazine* Fighter of the Year honors with Sugar Ray Leonard. He was posthumously inducted into the International Boxing Hall of Fame in 1991. In 2002, Sánchez was ranked 24th in a list of the greatest fighters from the previous 80 years by *Ring Magazine*. One can only imagine what he could have done had his life not been tragically cut short.

Julio César Chávez won in three different weight classes over two decades, amassing 87 wins (75 knockouts) before his first draw or loss. Chávez finished his career with six world titles and the support of his own Mexico firmly behind him. More than 130,000 people came to watch him in Mexico. The president of Mexico joined a throng of 25,000 to watch his workout. His great work ethic helped him achieve a record of 107-6-2. At his peak, Chávez was often labeled by experts and fans alike as the "best pound-for-pound boxer in the world" as well as "hero" in his native Mexico. Today, the Chávez name is carried on in the sport by Chávez's son, Julio Jr., who is proudly following in his father's footsteps with no losses in his first 40 professional fights.

Oscar De La Hoya won the Olympic gold in 1992 after more than 200 amateur fights. De La Hoya ran off 31 straight victories to begin his pro career and would go on to win world titles in six different weight classes: super featherweight, lightweight, light welterweight, welterweight, light middleweight, and middleweight.

A superstar whose reputation transcends boxing, De La Hoya was considered one of the finest fighters in the world at any weight. At 36 years old, De La Hoya decided that he achieved what he wanted with his time in boxing and retired. By that time he had won 39 bouts in 45 attempts and earned just under $700 million dollars in revenue, more than any other fighter in the history of the sport.

With that taste of their careers, now you can read more about them in depth.

"Panama" Alfonso (Al) Brown

First Latino World Boxing Champion and Star of the International Boxing Hall of Fame

by Horacio Ruiz

"Panama" Alfonso (Al) Brown was a pioneer for future generations of Latino boxers as well as a true international fighter who rose to worldwide fame, only to fall, then rise, and fall back once more on the memories of his success. At 5-foot-11 and a spindly 120 pounds, Brown was one of the most imposing fighters of his time in the bantamweight division. A *London Times* article described Brown as "a bantamweight 71 inches tall, yet by some miracle of physique, perfectly proportioned."[1] He also had a reach measuring 76 inches. Brown was also gay, and in a time when homosexuality was rarely ever spoken of, let alone in the knockout, face-disfiguring sport of boxing, Brown was certainly ahead of his time. Reportedly fluent in seven languages, Brown first became involved in boxing when he saw American soldiers boxing when he was a clerk for the United States Shipping Board in the Panama Canal Zone. Encouraged by his boss to try the sport, Brown became an immediate sensation. On March 19, 1922 a 20-year-old Brown made his professional debut by winning a six-round points decision in his native city of Colón, Panama. In his seventh career fight, only nine months after his debut, Brown defeated Sailor Patchett to win the Isthmus Flyweight title.

With a far longer reach than his opponents and an effectively snappy jab, along with nimble footwork, Brown was built to dominate his era of bantamweights. In 1923, Brown won his first fight in the United States and from August 22, 1923–September 2, 1926, he fought exclusively in New York State, primarily in New York City while compiling a 42-5-3 record. By 1924, Brown was ranked the third-best flyweight by *The Ring* magazine, and after moving up in weight class he was ranked sixth in the bantamweight division by the magazine. In November of 1926, Brown traveled to Paris where he was under contract to box in three matches. The Parisians loved him so much—and he in return loving the Parisians and the nightlife —that Brown stayed for a little more than a year on his way toward winning seven fights, losing two and drawing one. Brown became a popular fighter in France where lighter weight classifications were a more popular draw than the heavyweight divisions. After fighting in France, Brown truly became an international fighter. He would travel back to France after winning four fights in the United States. In a 1929 fight in Paris, Brown was credited with what was at the time the fastest knockout ever outside of the United States. Brown and his opponent, Gustave Humery, agreed to do away with handshaking and Brown delivered a right to Humery's jaw five seconds into the fight. The referee counted Humery out 15 seconds into the fight.

The stage was set for Brown on June 18, 1929 for his first world championship title fight for the vacant bantamweight title. Against Gregorio Vidal, who entered the fight with a 29-3-4 record, Brown dominated while knocking Vidal down three times in the 13th round on his way to a unanimous 15-round decision in Long Island City, Queens, NY. With the victory, Brown became the first world boxing champion from Latin America.

Brown would hold the bantamweight title for six years from 1929–1935. He would fight in Brussels, Copenhagen, Havana, Paris, Montreal, Toronto, Marseilles, Milan, London, Algiers, Casablanca, Tunis, and Valencia, Spain in title bouts and non-title bouts. He successfully defended his title 10 times until squaring off with Baltazar Sangchilli, a Spaniard, in Valencia. Leading up to the fight, French boxing writer Georges Peeters wrote about the atmosphere in Valencia. "In the streets, in the cafes, on the quaysides, there was talk of nothing but Sangchilli-Brown," Peeters wrote. "The streetcars were entirely covered with posters about it. Lottery ticket sellers, florists and beggars were all peddling seats."[2] Sangchilli would win a 15-round decision against Brown and walk away as the new bantamweight champion of the world. Brown had stayed out late in the weeks preceding his fight by going to cabarets, drinking, and smoking. Peeters would write:

"By the time he got into the ring at the Valencia arena on Saturday evening, Panama Al Brown was unrecognizable. His eyes were hollow, his skin looked gray and his features were terribly drawn. As for Sangchilli, he was greeted by his countrymen with an ovation lasting nearly two minutes. Even before the first gong sounded, those who knew Brown were aware that they were going to be present at his crushing defeat. Time and again he had disposed of adversaries with the slickness of a conjurer making plaster eggs and bowls of goldfish disappear up his sleeve. But we were going to witness the end of the conjurer. He was a mere shadow of himself. His arms hung heavily, his every gesture betrayed physical distress."[3]

Brown insisted that despite his nights out on the town prior to the title fight, that he had been poisoned. He would fight once more in 1935 in a loss to the talented Pete Sanstol on Sept. 13, 1935 in front of 15,000 fans in Oslo. Brown retired for two years enjoying the nightlife in the French city of Montmartre before making a comeback in Paris in 1937. It was in Montmartre that Brown met French poet Jean Cocteau, who with no background in boxing, became one of Brown's inspirations for the comeback in what would become a second opportunity for Brown to recapture his glory. It was believed that Cocteau and Brown had a long-lasting romantic affair.

Beginning in September of 1937, Brown regained his form during warm-up matches in preparations for a rematch with Sangchilli. Brown fought five times before meeting Sangchilli, and won four out of the five by knockout. On the day of Brown's rematch with Sangchilli, Cocteau had a story published in a French magazine, excerpts of which read:

"Al Brown has been born: the shadow of himself. The 'black wonder,' as the journalists sometimes call him, is a fragile creature, slim, almost frail, and with the nobility of an icon. When I met him he seemed dead to me, poisoned during his stay in Valencia and halted in his course. It was his ghost I saw jump the ropes, his ghost that languished in Montmartre, and his ghost that I decided to persuade, despite its reluctance, to continue the work of Brown in flesh and bone. It was the incredulity of the crowd and of the profession that had to be overcome. He had to believe a poet, unversed in the field, and he had to advance from match to match and from K.O. to K.O. until he stood again face to face with Baltazar Sangchilli, the winner of that atrocious duel in Valencia where Brown abandoned the title of world champion, abandoned his fortune and abandoned boxing.

"Disgust and an enormous rebellion took the place of a first reflex of anger. I repeat, he had died. But an Al Brown does not die like a page in the court of Catherine de Medici. His race gives him an almost plantlike resistance. His ghost, his shadow, survive him. It is this shadow that I respect, that I am helping and that I now have the luck to see achieving its aim. Shall I lead Al Brown right to the goal? I believe I am not the only one to wish it with all my heart."[4]

In the Palais des Sports in Paris, celebrities from across France sat in the front-rows to watch their friend, Brown, make an improbable comeback. In his dressing room, Brown opened the last few remaining telegrams of well-wishers and he tucked away a small devotional medallion. By the 11th round, Brown had built up a points-lead that would be insurmountable unless he was to be knocked out. In the 12th, 13th, and 14th rounds Sangchilli came to life and nearly knocked out Brown who stubbornly stayed on his feet despite suffering a cut above the arch of an eyebrow. Brown hung on during the 15th round before the final bell signaled the end of the fight. When the decision came in, the referee lifted Brown's arms in victory and he was carried to his dressing room once more the bantamweight champion of the world.

After the fight, Cocteau wrote a letter to Brown pleading with him to retire from boxing. Brown agreed that he would retire after one last fight against Valentín Angelmann in Paris.

"For 15 years I have had to lead a life that agrees neither with my temperament nor with my tastes," Brown wrote back to Cocteau. "My dear Jean Cocteau, you are a true friend. You are right. I must leave the ring. I have no desire to follow the example of the old champions who hang on to their titles. How many times have I read in sporting journals, 'Make way for the young. We must bring new life into the ranks.' Well, I want to follow this advice.

"I have given everything to boxing, and boxing has given me everything. We are quits. I am now an old boxer, but I am still a young man. I want to leave the memory of a world champion who knew how to choose his own moment for retirement, who knew how to get out leaving an unspoiled name to the sporting world. On the evening of April 13, I shall leave the ring, I shall salute the public and I shall vault the ropes for the last time. My second life will begin."[5]

Brown would win his fight on April 13, 1938 against Angelmann with an eighth-round knockout. Many of the French media wanted to see Brown continue to fight, questioning what business a poet like Cocteau had in determining Brown's boxing future. But Brown heeded the advice of his friend and instead joined a successful circus act in which he was the star; shadowboxing himself and explaining to the crowd the secrets to his success. When his six-month contract with the circus expired and France on the brink of entering World War II, Brown was advised to leave France and go back to the United States.

He traveled back to the United States and fought twice in 1939. He would also fight eight more times in Panama, his final match coming as a 41-year-old on Jan. 25, 1944 in Panama City. Brown settled in Harlem where he bounced around from job to job. Near the end of his life, Brown was a sparring partner for boxers in a Harlem gym, earning one dollar per round. At the age of 48, Brown would sometimes leave the ring dazed from the sparring sessions. "Now I'm an old man," Brown said to Peeters during a brief reunion in 1950 between the boxer and the writer. "Ah, if I could only get back to Paris and see my friends. Life is too hard for me here. If I could find the money for the journey! But I have practically nothing. I've sold all my clothes. I've only kept three suits and this tuxedo that I wore at the Bal des Petits Lits Blancs in 1938. Paris seems so far away now."[6]

Thirteen months after his conversation with Peeters, Brown died on April 11, 1951 of tuberculosis after fainting on a New York street. Upon hearing about Brown's failing health, Cocteau mailed recordings to his friend from many years before, recounting their days together in France. Brown listened to the recordings on the day he died in New York's Sea View Hospital. Brown was buried in Harlem, but his remains were later moved to Panama. He finished his boxing career with a 134-19-13 record, never losing by knockout. In 2002, *Ring Magazine* selected Brown as the 46th greatest fighter of the previous 80 years. He was inducted into the International Boxing Hall of Fame in 1992.

Notes

1. William Detloff, "The First Hispanic World Boxing Champion," ESPN.com, September 15, 2008.

2. George Peeters, "How Cocteau Managed A Champion," *Sports Illustrated*, March 2, 1964.

3. Ibid.

4. Ibid.

5. Ibid.

6. Ibid.

Gerardo "Kid Gavilán" González

Star of the International Boxing Hall of Fame

by Horacio Ruiz

Before Muhammad Ali transformed the sporting landscape with his style and substance in the ring, Gerardo "Kid Gavilán" González graced the boxing ring with his original dance and shuffle combo. Some said Gavilán moved as if he were dancing the samba on the canvas. "He was a very pleasing performer," said Hank Kaplan, a boxing historian and a longtime friend of Gavilán. "He had a lot of ring charisma. He was kind of a whirling dervish in the ring. His flurries were very exciting. He fought the greatest fighters of his time. And the guy had that great chin."[1]

Gavilán was born in Camagüey, Cuba where he worked shining shoes at a street stand, selling newspapers on a street corner, and working at an ice factory to pay for his room and board while receiving boxing instruction. He is credited with inventing the bolo punch, a wide half hook and half uppercut punch that Gavilán said was a product of his years cutting sugar cane with his machete in Cuba. Ali and "Sugar" Ray Leonard would later include the bolo punch in their arsenal. Gavilán was one of the flashiest fighters of his time, a favorite of boxing fans for his showmanship and the flurry of punches he would throw in between his dancing around the ring. He compiled a 107-30-6 record over a 16-year professional career.

When Gavilán moved to Havana, he caught the eye of his future manager, Fernando Balido. Balido gave González the nickname "Kid Gavilán" after the fruit stand that Balido owned called "El Gavilán"—the Sparrow Hawk. The Kid, at 16 years of age, made his professional debut in 1943 after approximately 60 amateur fights. From 1943–46, Gavilán boxed primarily in Cuba and Mexico and compiled a 28-2-1 record. In 1947, Gavilán made the move to box primarily in the United States and had his first title shot against "Sugar" Ray Robinson in 1949 for the welterweight championship. Gavilán, who entered the contest against Robinson with a 41-5-3 record, would take the defending champion the full 15 rounds before losing by decision.

From May 26, 1950 to March 8, 1954, Gavilán enjoyed the most successful run of his career. In that time period he was nearly unbeatable while compiling a 40-2-2 record. In 1951, after Robinson had vacated the welterweight championship after moving up to the middleweight division, Gavilán beat Johnny Bratton in 15 rounds to win the welterweight title. He would make seven successful defenses of his title before losing in one of the most controversial decisions in boxing history when he lost to Johnny Saxton on October 20, 1954. Despite 20 of 22 ringside reporters scoring the fight in Gavilán's favor, Saxton was given the unanimous decision in 15 rounds. In his dressing room afterward, Gavilán told the press in tears, "I don't want nothing that I don't deserve, but I [won] at least nine rounds."[2] It is believed that Saxton's manager, who was a known mobster, influenced the outcome of the fight. Prior to the Saxton fight, Gavilán made an unsuccessful move up to the middleweight division when Carl "Bobo" Olson beat him on April 2, 1954 in Chicago. After nearly 120 professional bouts and coming off consecutive losses to Olson and Saxton, Gavilán was losing his speed and quickness as he compiled a 10-15-1 record from 1955 until his retirement in 1958. Nevertheless, Gavilán had made his mark and set a new standard for boxing. His 1952 fight against Gil Turner in Philadelphia, which Gavilán won with an 11th-round knockout, drew a gate of $269,667 which at the time was a record for a welterweight fight. In that same year, Gavilán, who was dark-skinned, successfully defended his welterweight title in front of more than 17,000 fans at Miami Stadium against Bobby Dykes in what was the first racially mixed bout in Florida. A full 34 of Gavilán's fights were televised due to his popularity. Gavilán, though not a knockout puncher, was universally regarded for his tough chin and flashy elusiveness as he was knocked down only twice in his career and never lost a fight by knockout.

There was nothing flashy about Gavilán in retirement. By 1958, Gavilán had squandered much of his $2 million in career earnings and moved back to Havana where he stayed for 10 years and endured constant pressure from the Cuban government. A devout Jehovah's Witness, Gavilán fell out of favor with Fidel Castro's government for preaching about his faith. In 1964, it was reported that Gavilán was sentenced to five years in prison for an unnamed political offense. In 1965, a short *Sports Illustrated* article on Gavilán reported that he was nearly blind from cataracts and that his liver was bothering him. Gavilán had been in out of jail half a dozen times, and was in danger of losing the farm he called Finca Margarita that he bought when he was still a top fighter in the United States. The article described Gavilán sitting on his porch on a rocking chair and his house and farm in the following words, "Now the house is eaten by termites. The grounds are unkempt. All the dollars and pesos are gone. There are two children."[3]

In 1968, the Cuban government took Gavilán's home and the former champion moved to Miami and became one of hundreds of thousands in the Cuban exile community. When he moved to Miami, the exile community raised enough money for Gavilán to have surgery for his cataracts. For the next few years he would toil with very little money and became estranged from his family. Opportunities would find their way to Gavilán but they were quickly squandered. He was hired to be a part of Ali's staff but the arrangement ended acrimoniously. He also became a trainer for younger fighters but struggled with alcoholism. By the 1980s, Gavilán was selling sausages to earn an income. In 1990, Gavilán was inducted into the International Boxing Hall of Fame but was penniless. By 1995, he was admitted into the assisted-living facility in Hialeah where he would live for the rest of his life.

Kaplan, the famed boxing historian dubbed the "Lord of the Ring," helped restore some of Gavilán's past glory. Kaplan set up public appearances for Gavilán across the United States where he earned pocket money. Kaplan took Gavilán on a yearly trip to the International Boxing Hall of Fame in Canastota, NY, where Gavilán signed hundreds of autographs and talked about boxing for hours with adoring fans. In 2002, Gavilán was listed as the 26th best fighter of the previous 80 years by *Ring Magazine*, and in 2007 the magazine ranked him the third greatest welterweight.

In 2003, Gavilán died of a heart attack at the age of 77. Boxing historian Bert Sugar said Gavilán was, "one of the heroes in the golden era of Friday-night fights."[4] There was nothing dazzling about Gavilán's grave which was marked by a bronze plaque 10 inches in circumference. The marker also used Gavilán's real name of Gerardo González. "No one there realizes that this was one of the greatest fighters of all time," said former lightweight champion Ray Mancini of Gavilán's resting place in the cemetery. "The Kid and other fighters of his era did not make the big money, but they paved the way for guys like me to do just that."[5]

In 2005, the Ring 8 Veterans Association, a non-profit organization started by Jack Dempsey and Sugar Ray Robinson in response to older fighters faced with financial and physical distress, along with a group of prominent boxing figures, raised money to move Gavilán's body from one part of the cemetery to another where they could erect a memorial headstone in recognition of his accomplishments. Mike Tyson covered most of the $15,000 cost with a $10,000 check. "We felt bad that someone who had done so much for his sport had been so overlooked," Shelly Finkel, Tyson's manager, said. "It is the least we could do."[6]

Notes

1. Steve Springer, "Kid Gavilan, 77; Flashy Boxer Held World Welterweight Crown in '50s," *Los Angeles Times*, February 15, 2003, California / Local section.

2. William Detloff, "More To Legendary Cuban Than Just The Bolo Punch," ESPN .com, May 16, 2008.

3. *Sports Illustrated*, "Scorecard: Remember The Kid?," March 8, 1965

4. *Sports Illustrated*, "For the Record: Died," February 24, 2003

5. Vincent Mallozzi, "No Rest Until Kid Gavilan Has Peace," *New York Times*, March 13, 2005, Sports section.

6. Ibid.

Éder Jofre

Star of the International Boxing Hall of Fame

by Chris Kamke

When a boy is raised in a boxing gym, one of two things will happen; he will spend his life either loving or hating the sport of boxing. Éder Jofre loved the sport and committed himself to be a great fighter. Jofre, a Brazilian of Italian descent, had the blood of a champion flowing in his veins. Both sides of his family tree branched into either the boxing or wrestling world. Jofre had an uncle who had held the European middleweight boxing championship title, another uncle had been the lightweight champion in Brazil, an aunt who was once one of Argentina's top female wrestlers, and a father who had been a lightweight boxer.

Born in Sao Paulo in 1936, Jofre got a young start at boxing. Very disciplined as a boy, he would stand before a mirror imitating the style and movements of the boxers he watched practice in the gym. When his father found him at age four with a pair of gloves on, he had little question what Jofre would be when he grew up. Jofre appeared in a public fight by age nine, defeating his cousin in the third round by knockout.

Jofre won his first amateur tournament at age 12 and continued his impressive amateur career for another eight years, amassing a 148-2 record. In 1956, he qualified for the XVI Olympiad in Melbourne, Australia as a member of the Brazilian boxing team. He would fail to medal, losing in the quarterfinals to Claudio Barrientos of Chile. Following his Olympic experience, Jofre turned professional. Over the course of his career, the 5'4" Sao Paulo native with a 66-inch reach would become a true fighting machine, leaving his opponents wondering how such a small package could deliver such a powerful blow.

Once he graduated to the professional ranks, there was no let off in Jofre's performance. Jofre won 10 of his 12 fights during his first year, with the two non-victories ending in 10 round draws. The following year he appeared in 11 bouts, recording 10 wins, seven by way of knockout. Again, his only non-victory resulted in a 10 round draw, his first fight abroad, against Ruben Caceres in Montevideo, Uruguay. After this draw, Jofre would not leave the ring as anything other than the winner until May 18, 1965 when he faced Masahiko "Fighting" Harada. In the 33 matches between the Caceres and Harada bouts, Jofre recorded another 18 knockouts, on his way to gathering 50 knockout victories in his career.

On February 19, 1960, Jofre fought Ernesto Miranda for the third time in his career, this time for the South American Bantamweight title. The battle lasted 15 rounds and Jofre won his first title as a professional. In November of that same year, Jofre would become NBA world champion. Jofre faced Eloy Sanchez for a chance at his first world title, the vacant NBA championship. In Los Angeles, Jofre emerged the victor by way of knockout in the sixth round. From 1960 to 1965, he defended his title eight times against top notch fighters including Piero Rollo, Jose Medel, Katsuyoshi Aoki, and Bernardo Caraballo. Jofre was recognized as WBA World bantamweight champion after the Medel fight and the WBC bantamweight champion after the Aoki fight.

It was around this time that people started to consider Jofre to be the greatest bantamweight champion of all time. Jofre's most remarkable quality as a boxer was his ability to adapt. He was a clever fighter who would change his style based on his opponent. Heading into the Harada fight there were rumors that Jofre had thoughts of retirement. However, due to his status as a national hero in Brazil, Jofre pressed on.

When Jofre finally lost in the bout against Harada, nobody could believe it. It hadn't happened during his first nine years as a professional and people had started to think it wasn't even allowed. There wasn't an aspect of the sport at which the Brazilian didn't shine. But in May of 1965, in front of more than 10,000 Japanese fans in Nagoya, Japan, the renowned boxer lost his bantamweight championship to Harada.

The fight was exciting and Harada was relentless in his attacks. In typical fashion, Jofre was studious in the early rounds, mapping his eventual assault. Anticipation grew for Jofre's offensive, but the moment never came. The vigorous Harada was punching all the time, seizing his chance for glory. Jofre never clawed his way back from his early round deficit and lost in a 15 round split decision.

Possibly shaken from his first defeat, Jofre's next match resulted in a draw. After that was a rematch with Harada. In May of 1966 he again suffered a defeat at the hands of Harada, this time by unanimous decision. After the match, Jofre retired.

The retirement would prove not to last. After a 26-month spell, Jofre decided he would make a comeback. In the history of boxing, comebacks are typically unsuccessful, especially for fighters as old as Jofre. However, he had proven before he was no run-of-the-mill fighter and his comeback would be a testament to that fact. After 26 months away from the ring and at an age much senior to that of his opponents, Jofre experienced the results he had before meeting Harada. This time boxing as a featherweight, Jofre reeled off 25 straight victories, including capturing the WBC featherweight title, before retiring for good in 1976.

With knockout power in both hands and great technical skill, Jofre totally dominated most opponents. Willing to put in the work to wear down his opponent before going for the knockout blow, "The Golden Bantam" was feared by many and finished with a career record of 72-2-4, including 50 knockouts. Also of note, Jofre never suffered a knockout. In 1992, Jofre was inducted into the International Boxing Hall of Fame. When questioned about when Jofre started boxing his father said, "When he was so small you could sit him in a glove."[1]

Notes

1. Bert Randolph Sugar, (2006). *Boxing's Greatest Fighters*. Delaware: Lyons Press.

José "Mantequilla" Nápoles

Star of the International Boxing Hall of Fame

by Horacio Ruiz

Boxing observers gave José Nápoles the nickname "Mantequilla," or butter, because of his buttery smooth style and superb footwork. What boxing observers were witnessing was one of the greatest welterweights of all-time. Born in Santiago de Cuba in 1941, Nápoles accumulated a remarkable 114-1 record as an amateur. He came from a line of great Cuban boxers that included Kid Chocolate, Kid Gavilán, Benny Paret, Ultiminio "Sugar" Ramos, and Luis Rodríguez. Nápoles was the next in line of a great Cuban tradition and turned professional in 1958, where he tallied an 18-1 record in Cuba. In 1961, the Cuban government, following Fidel Castro's military victory in 1959, banned professional boxing. With Nápoles' career in jeopardy, he left his home country and was able to gain political asylum in Mexico where he would live for the remainder of his life.

After 16 months of inactivity, Nápoles was back in the ring by 1962, where he won all four fights that year in Mexico. From 1963 to February 15, 1969, Nápoles went 35-3 while fighting primarily in Mexico before fighting for just the third time ever in the United States against Curtis Cokes for the welterweight title of the world. On April 18, 1969, in The Forum in Inglewood, Calif., Nápoles thoroughly out-boxed Cokes to claim his first-ever title when Cokes did not answer the bell in the 14th. The very next bout for Nápoles was a rematch with Cokes, and Nápoles again defended his title when Cokes did not answer the bell for the 11th round.

After his bouts with Cokes, Nápoles faced Hall of Fame fighter Emile Griffith in one of the more storied fights of his career. Griffith was aiming for a record-tying sixth world title and had defeated Cuban fighters Paret and Rodríguez earlier in his career. The losses by those Cuban fighters—that had, like Nápoles, left their home country—were not lost on Nápoles. Griffith was a big puncher, lacking the grace of his previous challengers, but still managing to punch his way to victory. In the first round, Nápoles coolly held back to study Griffith. At the end of the round he walked to his corner and told his manager, "I looked at his footwork, and I know he can't catch me."[1] From that point on, Nápoles dominated the fight, including a knock down of Griffith in the third round. Nápoles won in a unanimous decision leaving Griffith to say of Nápoles, "He is a great champion. I can't knock him. After all, he beat a good fighter tonight."[2]

Nápoles would successfully defend his title against Ernie López before being upset by Billy Backus when the fight had to be stopped due to a cut over Nápoles' left eye. Six months later, Nápoles would reclaim the welterweight title against Backus in Inglewood with a technical knockout in the eighth round. After the loss to Backus, Nápoles would run off a 12-0 record that included six title defenses. That led to a confrontation with legendary fighter Carlos Monzón, considered to be one of the top three middleweights in boxing history. Nápoles temporarily vacated his welterweight title to move up to the middleweight division to challenge Monzón for his title on February 9, 1974 in Paris.

It was anticipated that the quick Nápoles would be able to jab, counterpunch, and keep the much bigger Monzón chasing him around the ring. Angelo Dundee, Nápoles' trainer said the game plan was to "Slip and Rip." In the first round, Nápoles charged Monzón much more aggressively than expected and then continued his attack in the second round. But by the third round Monzón had asserted himself after containing Nápoles in the early going and would soon send a flurry of heavy rights and lefts. By the sixth round, despite a valiant effort by Nápoles, he was at Monzón's mercy and he retired as the bell sounded for the seventh round. "Nápoles was too old and short and light, though heartbreakingly brave,"[3] wrote *Sports Illustrated* writer Clive Gammon. "I can't see anything at all,"[4] Nápoles said at the end of the fight.

While the move up to the middleweight division was unsuccessful, Nápoles would go back into the welterweight division to defend his title against Hedgemon Lewis. While many thought that Nápoles had been through too many battles and the Monzón fight had signaled the end of a brilliant career, Nápoles responded with a resounding victory in the ninth round against the talented Lewis.

Nápoles continued to defend his welterweight title against Horacio Saldano and twice in consecutive bouts against Armando Muñiz. Since winning the welterweight title in 1969 up to his fight with John Stracey in December of 1975, Nápoles successfully defended his welterweight title 13 times and won the title twice. On December 6, 1975, after holding the welterweight title for six years, a 35-year-old Nápoles lost by technical knockout in six rounds to Stracey. After the fight, Nápoles announced his retirement to finish with a 79-7 career record that saw him go up against some of the greatest fighters of his time.

In 1990, Nápoles was inducted into the International Boxing Hall of Fame along with the original group of boxers that had been inducted into the now-defunct *Ring Magazine* Hall of Fame. In 1969, with his victory for the welterweight title, Nápoles was the first Latino ever to be named the *Ring Magazine* Fighter of the Year, a recognition that dates back to 1928. In 2003, *Ring Magazine* recognized Nápoles as the 73rd greatest puncher in history and in 2002 the magazine recognized him as the 56th greatest fighter of the previous 80 years. Nápoles is a beloved sporting figure in both Mexico and Cuba.

Notes

1. Jerry Kirshenbaum, "Jose Settles An Old Account," *Sports Illustrated*, October 27, 1969.

2. Ibid.

3. Clive Gammon, "Jose Was Attacked By The Entire Zoo," *Sports Illustrated*, February 18, 1974.

4. Ibid.

Rubén Olivares

Star of the International Boxing Hall of Fame

by Chris Kamke

A popular Mexican boxer during the 1960s, 70s, and 80s that competed at both bantamweight (118 pounds) and featherweight (126 pounds), many considered Rubén Olivares as one of Mexico's greatest fighter. Olivares was born in Mexico City on January 14, 1947 to parents Esperanza Ávila and Salomon Olivares. Olivares was one of the six children that survived from the original 12. While Olivares was still an infant, his father left the family to work on a construction site in Oregon. Olivares Sr. would eventually return to Mexico City, having learned the building business. Upon his return he invested in land and started building houses.

Early in his life, Olivares discovered his aptitude as a fighter. While growing up, Olivares missed school frequently due to suspensions for fighting. Olivares' decision to take up boxing at age 15 was sparked by friendships with two local fighters who competed regularly at the Arena Coliseo in Mexico City. "We didn't have a TV set at home," said Olivares, "So I remember paying a lady 25 centavos to allow me to watch one of my friends, Dumbo Perez, fight Chucho Hernandez. Dumbo was winning (the fight) until Hernandez knocked him out with a left hook in the last round, and that decided me on becoming a pro fighter."[1]

Olivares spent a little over a year in the amateur boxing ranks before making the move into the professional ring. Olivares began his professional boxing career with a first round knockout win over Isidro Sotelo. Olivares, a bantamweight boxer with a heavyweight punch, was an immediate sensation in Mexico. Fans loved the power he displayed in the ring as well as his easy going personality. Olivares would go on to tally 22 straight knockouts, using his left hook as his primary weapon, before winning by decision against Felipe González on March 3, 1967. Olivares commented on González, "I must have hit him a thousand times, but he wouldn't go down."[2] The first blemish on Olivares' perfect record came shortly thereafter as the 26-0 Olivares managed only a draw against Germán Bastidas after 10 rounds on July 27, 1967. This result did not sit well with Olivares and six months later, Olivares knocked out Bastidas in the rematch as he progressed toward his first title shot.

It was Olivares' punching power that brought him his first world title. Australia's Lionel Rose was the WBC and WBA bantamweight title holder. Rose was known for his willingness to travel to defend his titles, having successfully defended them in Japan, the United States, and Australia. On August 22, 1969, Rose went in the ring against Olivares at the Inglewood Forum in Los Angeles. Olivares proved too powerful and won easily in five rounds. After the bout Olivares showed his admiration. Hugging Rose in the dressing room he told him, "You gave me the chance, and I will never forget that. If you want another fight you can have it, it would be a pleasure to go into the ring again with a gentleman like you. My home in Mexico City is yours. Come whenever you want, you will always be my special guest."[3] With that win, Olivares established his place in history by becoming the WBC and WBA World bantamweight champion. The victory also gave Olivares a 52-bout record of 51 wins (49 by knockouts) and one draw.

Olivares was pound-for-pound the hardest puncher in boxing during the 1960s. During his career he was part of two great boxing trilogies, the first of which was against Chucho Castillo. The Castillo-Olivares showdown was one of the most important rivalries in the history of Mexican boxing. The rivalry featured the quiet and grim Castillo and an outgoing partygoer in Olivares. The combination of their differing personalities and the fact that both the WBC bantamweight and WBA world bantamweight titles were on the line in all three of their matchups made fans very involved in their fights. The trilogy of bouts with arch-enemy and countryman Castillo began with Olivares successfully defending his titles after 15 thrilling rounds by decision. They would meet again just six months later. This time Olivares would suffer a cut in the first round and the fight was stopped in the fourteenth round. Castillo, by way of technical knockout, was the winner and new owner of the WBC bantamweight and WBA world bantamweight titles. This match also ended Olivares' career undefeated streak at 61 fights, 54 by knockout. The third and final chapter of the rivalry took place in April 1971. It was not the thrillers of the previous two editions, but the crowd of 18,141 still got its money's worth as Olivares, thanks to his quick footwork and strong punches, won by decision after 15 rounds and recaptured the two titles that he previously held.

After defending his titles twice, Olivares lost them on March 19, 1972, when he was knocked out by Rafael Herrera of Mexico in the eighth round. Thereafter, Olivares fought as a featherweight. The move up in weight class made his punches become less deadly, which is not unusual, but Olivares was still able to find success due to his toughness. He started his campaign to the world featherweight title by defeating Walter Seeley on April 28, 1973. Olivares' next contest was against the unbeaten Bobby Chacón. Olivares was a far more experienced fighter than the younger Chacón and came away the winner in what would be the first installment of another boxing trilogy.

A year later on July 9, 1974, Olivares got his first chance at a featherweight world championship. The title had been vacated by the retirement of Ernésto Marcel and was now up for grabs between Olivares and Zensuke Utagawa of Japan. Olivares found glory in the seventh round by knocking Utagawa down for good to win the WBA World featherweight title. After two non-title wins, Olivares lost his title after being knocked out by Alexis Argüello. However, Olivares would not go without a title for long. On June 20, 1975, Olivares faced Chacón for a second time, this time with the WBC featherweight title on the line. Something about this matchup inspired Olivares to train hard, something he was not known for, said Armando Muñiz, a friend and U.S. welterweight champion. Muñiz said, "Olivares is training at about 80%, and that is 25 percent more than he has ever done."[4] The contest lasted only two rounds as Olivares won with a technical knockout. However, just three short months later, in his 86th career fight, Olivares became an ex-champ again, suffering a defeat by way of points after 15 rounds to David Kotey of Ghana.

Olivares fought for a few more years but his only notable victory was against future WBC lightweight champion José Luis Ramírez. Olivares lost to Chacón in their third and final meeting and the defeats continued to accumulate. Olivares had just 13 losses in his career of which eight came in his last 19 bouts.

He fought for the WBA World Featherweight title against Eusebio Pedroza on July 21, 1979, but the fight was stopped in the 12th round and Olivares left empty-handed. Olivares retired after losing to Margarito Márquez in the winter of 1981. However, he would return briefly in 1986 and in 1988 for exhibition fights. As one of Mexico's most celebrated boxers of all-time, Olivares always had the ability to draw a big crowd for his fights. Olivares' knockout streaks of 22 and 21 still stand as two of the longest streaks in boxing history. A four-time world boxing champion at bantamweight and featherweight, Olivares' career peaked in his early 20s, yet lasted on and off until his 40s. Considered one of the top five bantamweight boxers of all-time, Olivares was inducted into the International Boxing Hall of Fame in 1991. Posting a win-loss-draw record of 88-13-3 that included 78 knockouts, Olivares participated in 595 rounds during his long career. In 2002, *Ring Magazine* ranked Olivares number 29 in their list of the 80 greatest boxers of the last 80 years. In 2003, *Ring Magazine* also placed Olivares at number 12 in their list of the 100 greatest punchers of all time. Always willing to fight anyone, Olivares fearlessly said, "I'll give anybody a chance. I'm a fighting champion."[5]

Notes

1. Rob Snell, (2008). "Ruben Olivares," Boxing Biographies. http://boxingbiographies.com/bio/index.php?option=com_content&task=view&id=252&Itemid=29 (accessed April 30, 2009).

2. Ibid.

3. Ibid.

4. Pat Putnam,(1975). "Chacón Was From Hunger," *Sports Illustrated*, June 30.

5. Rob Snell, (2008). Ruben Olivares. Boxing Biographies. http://boxingbiographies.com/bio/index.php?option=com_content&task=view&id=252&Itemid=29 (accessed April 30, 2009).

Roberto Durán

Star of the International Boxing Hall of Fame

by Chris Kamke

In the world of boxing, Roberto Durán was beloved for his will-power that guaranteed brutal battles and the audience an energy packed show. Considered one of the greatest boxers of all time, Durán's career spanned five decades. Born in Panama City, Panama on June 16, 1951, Durán would become a four division champion at lightweight, welterweight, junior middleweight, and middleweight. The child of a Panamanian mother and Mexican father, Durán grew up in the tough parts of Panama, forcing him to learn to fight at a young age. Durán didn't receive a traditional education as he was kicked out of elementary school. Durán's schooling came on the streets and in the gyms of Panama and it was there where his natural fighting ability was developed.

Durán competed briefly at the amateur level with promising results. He was propelled to the professional ranks because of the income a successful boxing career could offer. In 1967, at 16 years of age, Durán made his professional debut. Quickly, he adjusted to this level of competition and found success against more experienced fighters. He was able to put together a streak of 21 victories without much in the way of guidance. During this winning streak, his raw talents were recognized by a wealthy landowner, Carlos Eleta, who bought Durán's contract and hired Ray Arcel as his trainer. On June 26, 1972 in Madison Square Garden, Durán received his first title shot against WBA Lightweight Champion Ken Buchanan. Durán's winning streak would hit 29 that night by defeating Buchanan in the 13th round. This victory marked Durán's first world title.

Over the next several years Durán defined his seat on top of the lightweight boxing world. He fought many challengers and success-fully defended his title 12 times, 11 of which were by way of knock-out. Additionally, Durán engaged in 20 non-title bouts during this time. In his last title defense Durán had the opportunity to unite the WBA and WBC lightweight titles. During this bout, the third against Esteban De Jesus, Durán won the fight by knocking out De Jesus.

Durán gave up the unified lightweight title in February 1979 when he decided to move up in weight class to welterweight. Durán's first title chance in the welterweight division came against the then-undefeated Sugar Ray Leonard. Dubbed "The Brawl in Montreal," Durán fought Leonard in Montreal's Olympic Stadium, where Leonard had won Olympic gold medal at the 1976 Summer Olympics. Durán entered the bout with a 73-1 record. He walked away with his 74th victory and third world title by out-boxing Leonard in a 15-round unanimous decision. The two would enter the ring again just five months later for a rematch. This match, however, was not as glorious for Durán. In the eighth round, a seemingly unscathed Durán shocked the world when he gave up, supposedly saying the now famous words, "No más" (no more). The controversy around this bout is still discussed as some believe Durán fixed the fight for the large payday.

This one act had a devastating impact on Durán's career and his perception among his countrymen. "I said to myself, Durán, you must demonstrate to the world that you're not finished,"[1] Durán said. For 22 months he focused only on the day he would get the chance to redeem himself. He committed himself to do what great ones do; he started a successful comeback. Since walking out on Leonard, Durán had been abandoned by everyone, countrymen included, because of that single reckless act. He took time off to recover from the Leonard fight, gaining weight for a shot at the WBC world junior middleweight title.

Durán seemed to have turned this career around when he met up with Mexico's Pipino Cuevas, a former WBA welterweight champion. At the time both men were on skids. The recommitted Durán entered the bout in the best shape he had been in a long time and caught Cuevas in the fourth round, relentlessly pounding him. Cuevas did not escape the round. Durán was on his way back, his next stop would be a title shot against WBA World light middleweight champ Davey Moore. Back home in Panama, where Durán had been disgraced there was rejoicing; he had been welcomed back by his countrymen.

The Durán-Moore title bout took place in Madison Square Garden on Durán's 32nd birthday. Durán drew upon all his experience and initiated the attack, serving as the fight's conductor. Whatever Moore threw at him, Durán shook off and returned twice as much to Moore's body. Moore's size and speed advantage amounted to nothing. Over the course of eight rounds, Durán administered such a beating to the champion that some believe Moore's career was nearly finished. By the end of the seventh round Moore had been reduced to little more than a punching bag. During the break between rounds, Durán's trainer instructed him to finish Moore off. Just over two minutes into the eighth round Moore's trainer threw in a blood-splattered white towel, surrendering the match. "Ah, he was an artist," said Ray Arcel, after the match with Moore. "That performance could be compared to that of any great fighter who ever lived. It was masterful."[2] Durán had claimed a world title in his third different division. The man who once said, "No más," was back on top. With this victory, Durán joined six others as triple division title-holders. "I was born again," he said. "I've returned to be Roberto Durán. It's been a long time."[3]

Durán immediately followed up the Moore fight by meeting World middleweight title holder Marvin Hagler. However, the result of this match was not grand as Durán suffered the loss after a full 15 rounds by unanimous decision. In June 1984, Durán lost his WBC light middleweight title to Thomas "Hitman" Hearns, after a second round knock-out loss to Hearns. Durán did not fight for a title until 1989 when he faced WBC middleweight champion Iran Barkley. In what would be named the 1989 Fight of the Year by *Ring Magazine*, Durán made possibly his greatest achievement, claiming his fourth different divisional title. In a tough fight that showcased back and forth fighting, Durán put the icing on the match by knocking the bigger and stronger Barkley down in the 11th round. This knockdown proved to be a pivotal point in the match as Durán won the 12-round bout by split decision.

In a fight that Durán described as "the greatest of my life," Barkley said of Durán afterwards, "It was his heart, it just wouldn't go."[4] Perhaps even more astonishing than defeating Barkley was that the win came nearly 22 years after his first professional fight. "I am like a bottle of wine," Duran said. "The older I get, the better."[5]

Just as with the rest of his career, Durán decided to try and conquer another division and moved up in weight class again, this time to super middleweight. His first bout was his third clash against

Sugar Ray Leonard, then the WBC super middleweight champion. Durán lost in a 12-round decision. Whether it was the shear difficulty of fighting in his fifth weight class or the aging of his body, the Barkley match marked the peak of Durán's career. After losing to Leonard, Durán's career started to decline. He would fight his final match in 2001; 33 years after his career began.

In 2002, Durán was recognized by *Ring Magazine* as the 5th greatest fighter of the previous 80 years. He held world titles at four different classifications as a lightweight, welterweight, junior middleweight, and middleweight. He is also just the second boxer to fight in five different decades. After battling to a career record of 104-16, he was inducted into the World Boxing Hall of Fame on October 14, 2006, and the International Boxing Hall of Fame on June 10, 2007.

As a lightweight, welterweight, junior middleweight, and middleweight world champion, Durán fascinated the boxing world and was an emblem for Latinos because of his willingness to face adversity. Durán would say, "Getting hit motivates me. It makes me punish the guy more. A fighter takes a punch, hits back with three punches."[6]

Notes

1. William Nack, (1983). "He That Was Lost Has Been Found," *Sports Illustrated*, June 27.

2. Ibid.

3. Ibid.

4. Monte D. Cox, "Roberto Duran,'Hands of Stone,' . . . Born to be Champion," Cox's Corner. http://coxscorner.tripod.com/duran.html (accessed June 30, 2009).

5. Bruce Newman, (1989). "Stonehands Rules Again,". *Sports Illustrated*. March 6.

6. Barbara Haberman, (2009). The Official Website of Roberto Duran. http://www.cmgww.com/sports/duran/ (accessed June 30, 2009).

Alexis Argüello

Star of the International Boxing Hall of Fame

by Chris Kamke

Boxing was the one area of Alexis Argüello's life where he controlled all aspects. It was outside the ring where Argüello at times struggled to find his place in the world.

Argüello was born into dismal poverty on April 19, 1952 in Managua, Nicaragua. When he was just nine years old, his family could no longer afford his schooling. Argüello dropped out and left home to work on a farm. Almost a year had passed before his father found him and begged him to return home. He would leave home again, this time at 13 to find work in Canada. He was absent for a year before he returned to Managua. Upon his return, he handed his parents a thousand dollars he saved while working two jobs. At age 14 Argüello found boxing. He devoted himself to perfecting the art of boxing in hopes of escaping a life plagued by poverty.

Argüello was dominant while in the amateur ranks, compiling a win-loss record of 58-2 which included 48 knockouts, before he turned pro at the age of 16. During his first five years as a professional, Argüello fought exclusively in his home town of Managua. After Argüello, "The Explosive Thin Man," suffered a loss in his professional debut, he went on to win 36 of his next 38 bouts. At age 21 Argüello made his first title appearance against the WBA World featherweight champion Ernesto Marcel. Marcel's strategy of staying out of range of Argüello's dominant punches allowed Marcel to fight his way to a unanimous 15-round decision. Marcel retired after that bout, never giving the young Argüello a chance to avenge his loss.

Impervious to this setback, Argüello began another impressive winning streak. Nine short months later, Argüello earned another featherweight title shot, this time against Mexican great Rubén Olivares, who won the WBA featherweight title that was vacated by Marcel. The fight turned out to be a classic battle with Olivares leading on the scorecards through 12 rounds. However, the tide changed in the 13th round when a commanding left hook by Argüello sent Olivares to the ground. Although Olivares got up from that blow,

Argüello quickly finished him off and at age 22, Argüello was a world champion for the first time.

Argüello successfully defended his title four times before moving up weight classes for a chance at a super featherweight title. His chance came against Alfredo Escalera on January 28, 1978 in Bayamon, Puerto Rico. Escalera had survived 10 title defensives before his encounter with Argüello. In a fight that became known as "The Bloody Battle of Bayamon," fight referee Arthur Mercante called it "the most brutal fight I have ever witnessed."[1] Both men suffered beatings during the bout. Escalera had his ears, nose, and mouth busted but managed to rally in the later rounds until Argüello landed a vigorous strike that finished off his opponent in the 13th round. Argüello was now a two-time world champion.

Argüello believed that boxing should provide more than just brutality. He believed boxing should serve a greater purpose than just two men trying to annihilate one another. He formed a personal mission to help the poor and young people of war-torn Nicaragua. He contributed to charities and spent time with children. Before and after matches he abstained from mocking his opponent. Argüello thought he was more than just a man with two powerful weapons. "I'm not a fighter," he said. "I'm an artist. Boxing should be beautiful . . . It should be like ballet dancing."[2]

Argüello's reign as WBC super featherweight champion saw him fend off eight challengers including Escalera in a rematch, as well as former world champions Bobby Chacon and Rafael Limón. Argüello seemed invincible as a super featherweight. Physically stronger than much of the opposition, he also maintained the dominant punch that had made him such a spectacular featherweight. In 1981, Argüello decided to attempt something only achieved by few great fighters, to become a triple-crown champion.

In just his fourth fight after moving up to the lightweight division, Argüello got his shot at a title. The opportunity came in England, in front of a ravenous home crowd of world lightweight champion Jim Watt. Although Watt endured all 15 rounds, Argüello dominated the southpaw, winning by a unanimous decision. On June 20, 1981, Argüello joined Bob Fitzsimmons, Barney Ross, Tony Canzoneri, Henry Armstrong, Emile Griffith, and Wilfred Benítez as boxing's only three division champions.

Argüello attempted to differentiate himself among all his boxing peers by making history in becoming the first world champion in four different weight classifications. On November 12, 1982, he met 31-0 and future Hall-of-Famer Aaron Pryor, for the WBA World light welterweight title at the Orange Bowl in Miami, Florida. The fight would go down in boxing history as one of the sport's supreme battles. On a night when his legs were not fully with him, Argüello still brought all he had to the ring. After the fight, Argüello would say, "I fought only on guts."[3] Pryor was a fast and powerful boxer that had the strength to withstand almost anything. As predicted, Pryor opened the fight quickly but Argüello tolerated the force and pace as they exchanged solid punches through the early rounds. During the mid to late rounds, Argüello appeared to have solved Pryor's attack method and closed the gap in points. Controversy would set in between the 13th and 14th rounds. During the 13th round, Pryor was impaired sufficiently by a blistering right cross from Argüello. During the break in rounds, Pryor's trainer, Panama Lewis, who would later be banned from boxing for cheating, had Pryor drink from a "specially mixed" bottle. Pryor came out of the minute-long intermission with renewed energy and was able to force Argüello against the ropes. Guts were all that kept Argüello on his feet for one of the longest unanswered assaults in boxing history. Argüello was hammered with 23 consecutive punches before collapsing. After feeling the 23rd punch from Pryor make contact with his skull, Argüello lay on the canvas unconscious for four minutes while doctors checked his pulse and gave him oxygen before he opened his eyes again.

The controversy clouding the fight forced the WBA to sanction a rematch. Ten months later, Argüello had his second chance at history. This time held in Las Vegas, the fight had a similar outcome to the first edition. Pryor's fast-paced style wore Argüello down and ultimately resulted in a 10-round knockout victory for Pryor. After the fight, Argüello stated, "The carnival is over."[4] Argüello would retire from boxing never obtaining that fourth divisional world title.

After boxing, Argüello struggled to fit into a world void of the sport he had known so well. In that boxing world he knew so well, choices and results seemed clean and clear. Punch or be punched. Stand or fall. Outside of the ring life wasn't as simple.

For a brief time during the 1980s Argüello fought with the Contras in his native Nicaragua. This commitment came after seeing one of his homes in Managua captured by the Sandinistas, his bank account seized, and one of his brothers killed fighting the Sandinistas. His commitment appeased a feeling that had been missing since his retirement.

In 1984, Argüello was sitting on his boat one morning staring down the shaft of a loaded pistol. His son A.J. sat across from him begging him not to pull the trigger. Argüello cried too. After looking at his son for a long time, he laid the gun down. His son had just extended his life. After that incident, Argüello slowly started turning his life around from the dead end street he had started down.

He made a brief boxing comeback in the late 1980s and early 1990s before retiring again, this time for good in 1995. Dignified and commanding in the ring with complete control of his movements, Argüello was a Samaritan to each of the men he faced. Argüello's career produced an amazing record of 82 wins, 8 losses, and 65 knockouts.

Argüello was elected to the World Boxing Hall of Fame in 1991 and the International Boxing Hall Of Fame in 1992. In 2002, *Ring Magazine* named Argüello 20th on its list of the 80 best fighters of the previous 80 years. In 2003, *Ring Magazine* again named Argüello 20th on its list of the 100 greatest punchers of all time. In 2008, he was selected as Nicaragua's flag-bearer for the Opening Ceremony of the Beijing Olympics. Argüello became mayor of Managua, his home town and capital of Nicaragua in the November 2008 elections.

Shortly after, Argüello, the newly elected mayor of Managua, was found dead on July 1, 2009 from a gunshot wound to the chest in an apparent suicide. Thousands of Nicaraguans lined the capital's streets as the former champion's hearse passed by on the way to his funeral. They stood to say goodbye to a man that held a place in the hearts of some many of his countrymen. Argüello's daughter, Dora, sat against his casket without moving to stare at him one last time as mourners shuffled by. Nicaraguan President Daniel Ortega canceled attending the inauguration of Panamanian President-elect Ricardo Martinelli to be at Argüello's funeral. Ortega described Argüello as "an extraordinary human being full of truth."[5]

Argüello was proof that through hard work, discipline, and persistence a person could escape poverty and become respected, a symbol many Nicaraguans treasured. The heartfelt loss of Argüello was not limited to his homeland. "I felt sad receiving the news and still find it hard to believe," said retired boxer Oscar De La Hoya. "Alexis was my idol. When I was young, I heard so much about him and his fights and loved his style in the ring. In my opinion he was one of the biggest and most influential fighters boxing has ever produced."[6]

Notes

1. Monte Cox, "Alexis Argüello, The Explosive Thin Man . . .'One of the Greatest Ever,'" Cox's Corner. http://coxscorner.tripod.com/Argüello.html (accessed May 8, 2009).

2. Gary Smith, (1985). "Adrift In A Sea Of Choices," *Sports Illustrated*, October 21.

3. Ibid.

4. Pat Putnam, (1983). "Good Night, Sweet Prince," *Sports Illustrated*, September 19.

5. *Associated Press.* 2009. "Arguellos' Death Reported as Suicide," July 2. http://sports.espn.go.com/sports/boxing/news/story?id=4299144 (accessed September 2, 2009).

6. Ibid.

Salvador Sánchez

Star of the International Boxing Hall of Fame

by Horacio Ruiz

Already at twenty three years of age, Salvador Sánchez had become one of the greatest boxers of all-time. On July 21, 1982 Sánchez defeated Hall of Fame fighter Azumah Nelson in a classic showdown at Madison Square Garden. Twenty-two days later Sánchez was driving his Porsche in the early morning of August 12, 1982 on an open Mexican highway. He was in training for a rematch against Juan Laporte, a fighter he had beaten two years earlier by unanimous decision. His life and career were ahead of him, he spoke about moving up from the featherweight division to the lightweight division to challenge world champion Alexis Argüello. By all accounts it would have been a fight for the ages. "I want him very much. I have the weaponry to beat him,"[1] Sánchez said of a match up with Argüello.

Sánchez would say he learned to fight before and after school when other kids would pick on him because of his small stature. They would steal his books and pencils. The final straw for him was when the bullies called him a little girl. Sánchez began to fight back and soon found that he liked to hit others while defending himself. He began taking boxing classes and his potential for greatness was apparent after just a few sparring sessions. Even as a 23-year-old world champion, Sánchez was still learning his craft, but he would forever stay in his youth. As Sánchez was speeding in the darkness of the highway, his white Porsche collided with two trucks and he was killed instantly.

His premature death left the boxing world stunned. But his seven-year career was one that all of Mexico would eternally be proud of. Fighters are remembered for their style and for the fights that defined them. For Sánchez, no fight was too big for his technical skills and explosive counterpunches to silence his opponents. Sánchez had a brief amateur career, taking part in 14 fights, all of which he won. In 1975 at the age of 16, he turned pro and accumulated a 32-1-1 record in relative obscurity before gaining recognition in 1979 by *Ring Magazine* as the 8th ranked featherweight in the world.   On Februarty 2, 1980, Sánchez challenged WBC champion Danny López for the featherweight title. Many had never heard of Sánchez and predicted that López would make easy work of his challenger. López was 42-3 going into the fight and had fought against the toughest opponents of his time. In a nationally televised fight, it was clear that López was no match for Sánchez. By the ninth round, Sánchez had closed López's left eye, and in rounds six and seven, the fight had to be stopped for doctors to look at a deep gash above López's right eye. In the 13th round, the fight was stopped and Sánchez announced his arrival to the rest of the world by capturing the WBC belt. López was able to get a rematch, confident that Sánchez had beaten him due to beginner's luck. Their second fight, however, would play out the same as the first.

In his first title defense, Sánchez defeated Rubén Castillo in a deeply-contested 15-round fight which Sánchez won in the later rounds. *Sports Illustrated* dubbed him the "Mexican Machine" after the fight. No fight would lift Sanchez into Mexican boxing lore like the fight against Puerto Rican Wilfredo Gómez. Gómez was known for his vicious power and had devastated through the super-bantamweight division. Gómez, with a 32-0-1 record that included 32 consecutive knockouts, moved up to the featherweight class to challenge Sánchez. Gómez was not short on trash-talking. He insulted Sánchez's masculinity and promised that he would knock out Sánchez in the opening rounds. "During the whole run up to the fight, Gómez was talking so much trash, it was unbelievable," said Hall of Fame fighter Carlos Palomino, who was hired as a translator for both fighters. "I was fed up. Sánchez was very quiet. He never said anything except, 'I'm ready, I trained hard,' and, 'We'll see.' After the weigh-in, I talked to Sánchez and asked him how he felt about all the trash-talk. He told me, 'I'm not going to knock him out, I'm going to punish him.'"[2]

In a sold-out Caesar's Palace Sports Pavilion fans were waving Puerto Rican and Mexican flags. The two fighters stepped inside the ring in what was considered the biggest fight between the two boxing-loving nations. From the opening round, Sánchez took control by delivering a right-left combination. He would also buckle Gómez's knees with a right cross within the first three minutes.

"The fight was over," Palomino said, referring to the first round. "He backed off after Gómez got up and he let him recover and then he just started pounding him for eight rounds. It was the worst punishment I've seen a guy take in a one-sided fight. Sánchez was just dominant and just punished him. That's exactly what he said he was going to do."[3] Sánchez would eventually close both of Gómez's eyes, and in the eighth round he knocked Gómez down with a flurry of punches. Gómez would beat the count but the referee mercifully stopped the fight. Gómez finished the fight with a fractured right cheekbone. "The reaction of the Puerto Rican people to that fight was like losing a war, like a president being shot," said Jorge Pérez, a sports writer for *El Nuevo Día*, a daily newspaper in Puerto Rico. "It was like an earthquake of disappointment for the whole island. Gómez was the idol, the most acclaimed athlete on the island at that time, and he was loved."[4]

A wave of euphoria swept over the Mexican crowd. "[Gómez's] famous line before the fight was that he would rather die than lose to Sánchez on his knees," Perez said of Gómez. "The fight photo showed Gómez on his knees (at the end) with his face transformed because of punches by Sánchez. People more or less never forgave him for that loss, even though he kept on winning."[5]

Sánchez would go on to win against Olympic bronze medalist Patrick Cowdell. He would also emerge from a tough 15-round decision versus Jorge "Rocky" García. The fight against García was the first fight between featherweights to be televised on HBO. With his reputation as one of the finest boxers in the world, Sánchez was now getting commercial attention. With his final fight against Nelson, Sánchez gave the boxing world his final masterpiece. At the time of their fight, Nelson was unknown outside of his native Ghana. After taking Sánchez to 15 rounds Nelson gained the respect of the boxing spectators. Sánchez nearly knocked Nelson out of the ring with a left cross only a few seconds before the fight was stopped by the referee. Sánchez raised his arms in victory and was hugged by the men in his corner. In victory, Sánchez appeared calm and stoic even after being pushed to the end by Nelson who would go on to have a glittering Hall of Fame career.

The night after his victory over Nelson, Sánchez was in a Manhattan hotel celebrating the fight and thinking about his future. "Salvador Sánchez will triumph in New York again," Sánchez told a reporter about his upcoming rematch with Laporte at Madison Square Garden. *"Mi horizonte es muy negro* (My future is very black),"⁶ Sánchez joked with a grin, knowing full well that his future was burning bright. Friends of his patted him on the back in recognition of the joke. In three weeks he would die in the car crash. Gómez, the foil to Sánchez's most memorable fight, and who was training to defend his super bantamweight title against Roberto Rubaldino, traveled to Mexico to offer Sánchez flowers. Sánchez finished his career with a 44-1-1 record. Nine of his final ten fights were title defenses, all of which he defended successfully. Sánchez won the final 24 fights of his career.

In 1981 Sánchez shared *Ring Magazine* Fighter of the Year honors with Sugar Ray Leonard. He was posthumously inducted into the International Boxing Hall of Fame in 1991. In 2002, Sánchez was ranked 24th in a list of the greatest fighters from the previous 80 years by *Ring Magazine*, and in 2003, he was ranked the 88th greatest puncher of all-time by the magazine. In anticipation of fighting Argüello, Sánchez said, "I will win because I promised, and because of the faith and the confidence I have in Salvador Sánchez." Even though the mega match up would never occur, Sánchez had already won the hearts of the world and the people of Mexico.

Notes

1. Jerry Kirshenbaum, "Scorecard: Death Of A Champion," *Sports Illustrated*, August 23, 1982.

2. Robert Morales, "We Meet Boxing: Rivalry Between Puerto Rican, Mexican Boxers—Renewed With Tonight's Cotto-Margarito Fight—Hit Its Apex With 1981 Gomez-Sanchez Battle," *Daily News*, July 26, 2008, Sports section.

3. Ibid.

4. Ibid.

5. Ibid.

6. Jerry Kirshenbaum, "Scorecard: Death Of A Champion," *Sports Illustrated*, August 23, 1982.

Julio César Chávez

Star of the International Boxing Hall of Fame

by Charlie Harless

> "And he went up and down among the lions, he became a young lion: and he learned to catch the prey, he devoured men."
>
> —Ezekiel 19:6

Julio César Chávez, "The Lion of Culiacán," instilled fear in his boxing opponents like few men in history have ever done. A tenacious fighter in three different weight classes, Chávez won his first 87 bouts before his first draw or loss, 75 of the fights ending in a knockout. With a career spanning over two decades, Chávez finished with six world titles to his name and an entire nation firmly behind him. Boxing promoter Don King once said of Chávez, "Americans are just starting to learn and realize the icon, the god he is in Latin America, Mexico specifically. He's the biggest star there is in boxing. More than 130,000 people came to watch him in Mexico not long ago, and 25,000 came to watch his workout, including the president of Mexico."[1] Chávez himself once conceded that "I have come from the poorest house in a poor place to wealth and to walk with presidents. But I remain one of the people and they know it."[2] Chávez traveled a long and arduous road to boxing glory from the railroad car he occupied as a young child in Culiacán. The hard knocks of his childhood and humble surroundings helped cultivate the fighting spirit that would lead him to become one of the greatest sporting icons in Mexican history.

Learning the meaning of hard work from a young age, Chávez spent his childhood in the 1960s and 1970s selling newspapers, washing cars, vending taco stands, and painting houses among many jobs. Chávez once reflected on the work ethic he was instilled with at a young age, saying, "My father, Rodolfo, worked as a train conductor and that's how we came to live in the railway car. The Government owned it and we paid rent on it. Back then I would wake up at 4 in the morning and run through the streets, selling newspapers . . . I'd run six miles through the streets. I'd be up that early to beat the competition."[3] In between earning these small wages to help support his parents and his nine siblings, he learned to box from his older brothers. During his teenage years, he spent time at a local gym sparring against more seasoned fighters and entered his first amateur tournament at the age of sixteen. Confident in his physical abilities, the young fighter told his mother that "I was going to become a world champion and buy her a home."[4]

Chávez would deliver on that promise, winning fight after fight upon turning professional in 1980 and accumulating the earnings to build his parents a house on the land the railroad car sat upon. Chávez seized upon the first chance he had to claim a world title when he TKO'ed Mario Martínez in eight rounds in a 1984 fight to claim the WBC super featherweight title and extend his record to 45-0. Chávez spent the remainder of the 1980s winning new titles and knocking out opponents left and right, yet he remained a virtual unknown outside of Mexico. Michael Wilbon of the *Washington Post* once wrote that "he always fights on the undercard, early in the evening while the cameras are being set up and the high rollers with the ringside seats are just leaving the pool to get dressed. By the time the seats filled for Leonard or Tyson or Holyfield, Chávez was gone, on a plane, back to Mexico to be worshiped. Only two or three times has he been the headliner, the main event, the pay-per-view attraction . . . He is to the lighter weight classes what Tyson and Ali and Louis were to the heavyweight division when they were at their very frightening best. But to the average American sports fan, even the average boxing fan, Chávez is a whisper, a clip on the highlights on a slow news night."[5]

While Chávez could have been as celebrated as these other fighters, Chávez made it very clear on repeat occasions that international superstardom, particularly in America, was not the reason he fought. While several of his international counterparts learned English or took up residence in the United States to train with greater resources, Chávez put his head down and focused on perfecting his craft and increasing his stature within the Mexican community. Chávez once said that "When I fight, all the eyes of Mexico are upon me. It's a big responsibility. Sometimes it seems I am defending the nation."[6]

Chávez defended Mexico with a steely tenacity and nearly untarnished record throughout his career. While other lightweight boxers would dance around to avoid being hit, Chávez became notorious for his ruthless fighting style, willing to stand in front of his opponent and take a punch before offering a rebuttal of brutal counterpunches that would quickly wear down an opponent before a devastating final blow ended the fight. Typically all business, Chávez was generally not one to engage in dramatic theatrics or controversial chatter to promote a fight, but those who insulted or challenged Chávez probably wished they had not opened their mouth once they were knocked out. Prior to a 1993 fight, Chávez's opponent, Greg Haugen, told Chávez in a pre-match press conference that the guys Chávez had beat were not that good, many the equivalent of Mexican cab drivers. Chávez, reportedly infuriated over the remarks, proceeded to demolish Haugen in five rounds, forcing Haugen to state after the fight that "Okay, so they were tough cab drivers."[7]

A loss to Frankie Randall in 1994 would be the first setback of his career, with Chávez falling in a twelve round split decision. Chávez would win a few more fights over the remaining years of his career, but he was clearly past his prime as the once perfect fighter lost several more showdowns as well. Yet there was little room for regret when considering the 107-6-2 record Chávez accumulated and the legacy he left behind for the sport. Chávez at his peak was often labeled by experts and fans alike as the "best pound-for-pound boxer in the world" as well as a "hero" in his native Mexico. Today, the Chávez name is carried on in the sport by Chávez's son, Julio Jr., who is proudly following in his father's footsteps with no losses in his first 40 professional fights.

The Chávez name is one that will continue to be revered by the Mexican community and the history books, although Chávez himself was once modest when asked to speculate about his place in the sport and in Mexican history. "I'm not the one to say about myself. That is for others."[8] Clearly, Chávez needs to say little, as his actions and words have cemented his remarkable legacy as one of the hungriest and toughest fighters boxing has ever seen.

Notes

1. Michael Wilbon, "Out From Under Card, Perfect Chavez Storms Prime Time," *The Washington Post*, September 9, 1993.

2. Jeff Powell, "An Assassin with a Gentle Touch," *Daily Mail*, September 6, 1993.

3. Phil Berger, "Chavez has Pounded His Way to the Top," *The New York Times*, September 10, 1992.

4. Ibid.

5. Michael Wilbon, "Out From Under Card, Perfect Chavez Storms Prime Time," *The Washington Post*, September 9, 1993.

6. Ibid.

7. Ibid.

8. Jay Searcy, "A Nation Roots for its Fading Boxing Legend," *The Philadelphia Inquirer*, June 6, 1996.

Oscar De La Hoya

Future Hall of Famer

by Chris Kamke

Competing at 132 pounds in the 1992 Olympics in Barcelona, Spain, Oscar De La Hoya earned the nickname "The Golden Boy" as the 19-year-old fighter was the only U.S. boxer to win gold. Even at the young age of 19, De La Hoya was an experienced fighter, having competed in over 200 amateur fights. Born into a boxing family on February 4, 1973, De La Hoya put on his first pair of boxing gloves at age six.

De La Hoya's road to greatness was ignited on the streets of East Los Angeles. He once said, "I was a little kid who used to fight a lot on the street and get beat up. But I liked boxing. So my dad took me to the gym."[1] De La Hoya, a third generation boxer, had great support at home. "One of my strengths is family power," De La Hoya says. "There are many fighters who have no family help. When I fight, there are uncles, aunts, cousins cheering for me."[2] Perhaps his biggest supporter was his mother, Cecilia.

In October 1990, while De La Hoya was training for the upcoming Olympic Games, his mother passed away from breast cancer. His mother often told De La Hoya to go to the gym rather than spend time with his friends, reminding him that with hard work he would be a champion. Before she died she had one request of her son, to win an Olympic gold.

De La Hoya's path to gold would not be an easy one. He endured and faced Marco Rudolph in the gold medal round. De La Hoya dominated the fight from start to finish, working Rudolph for the entire three rounds. De La Hoya won gold for his mother by defeating Rudolph in a 7-2 decision. After the fight, De La Hoya said, "The most important thing I've done in my life was winning the Olympic gold medal for my mother."[3] At the medals ceremony, De La Hoya carried two flags. "The American flag was for my country; the Mexican flag was for my heritage."[4] When he returned home he paid tribute to his mother by laying his gold medal on her grave.

The Olympic Games served as a spring board for a splendid professional career. A megastar whose reputation transcends boxing,

De La Hoya is considered one of the finest fighters in the world at any weight. De La Hoya would go on to win world titles in six different weight classes.

De La Hoya made his professional debut just a little more than three months following the Olympics with a first-round knockout of Lamar Williams. That victory was the first of 31 straight victories to begin his career. In his twelfth professional fight, De La Hoya won his first world title by technical knockout over Jimmy Bredahl to capture the WBO junior lightweight title. He successfully defended that title once before jumping up weight classes.

In his first lightweight fight he defeated Jorge Páez with a second round knockout to win the WBO lightweight title. In his sixth and final lightweight title defense he defeated Jesse James Leija in the second round of a 12 round fight. Still undefeated, De La Hoya looked to further the evidence of his greatness by moving up weight classes again.

This time De La Hoya would have to wait until his second fight at his new weight class for a title shot. His chance came in 1996 against Mexican legend Julio César Chávez for the WBC Light Welterweight championship. At this point De La Hoya was still undefeated but some in the boxing world felt like he was largely untested. Entering the match as the underdog, De La Hoya was filled with liveliness and hammered Chávez by the fourth round, earning the WBC super lightweight title. Yet again, after just one successful title defense, De La Hoya moved up weight classes.

On March 12, 1997, De La Hoya fought one of the best pound for pound fighters in the world, Pernell Whitaker and won the WBC welterweight title in a 12 round decision. De La Hoya ruled the welterweight division, defending his title seven times, until September of 1999 when he met with up with the 35-0 Félix Trinidad. The fight was one of the most anticipated fights during the 90s. De La Hoya built up a lead but was not able to maintain it in the late rounds and Trinidad was awarded the decision after 12 rounds. The loss was De La Hoya's first and there would never be an opportunity for a rematch.

De La Hoya would go on to fight as welterweight three more times before moving up to light middleweight. His first bout was a title shot against WBC light middleweight champion Javier Castillejo in the MGM Grand Casino in Las Vegas, Nevada. Although De

La Hoya would only emerge as the fight's victor by way of decision, he dominated the fight, winning almost every round on his way to attaining his fifth different division title. De La Hoya would not fight for 15 months following the Castillejo match. His next match would be a unification bout against Fernando Vargas with three titles on the line. With a preexisting distaste, the months leading up to the fight added to the tension between the two fighters. The match finally took place on September 14, 2002 and had been labeled "Bad Blood." The first half of the match featured even fighting. De La Hoya started to take control in the seventh round and kept the pressure on by seriously damaging Vargas in the tenth. Vargas was knocked down in the following round and though he managed to regain his feet, De La Hoya trapped him in the corner and unleashed a beating that forced the fight to be stopped moments later. De La Hoya's win in this scintillating fight is considered one of the biggest in his career.

Two fights later, De La Hoya would lose his unified title to Shane Mosley by a slim margin in a rematch from De La Hoya's welterweight days dubbed "Retribution." De La Hoya then moved up weight classes again, this time to challenge Felix Sturm for the WBO world middleweight title. De La Hoya defeated Sturm by decision in 12 rounds to solidify his place in boxing lore. He became the first boxer to win major titles in six different weight classifications.

One of De la Hoya's last matches was another unification bout, this time against Bernard Hopkins with four titles on the line. Both fighters were in the later portions of their careers and each had successfully married their name with the sport of boxing. De La Hoya entered the ring on September 18, 2004 a large underdog. Fighting with a cut on his left hand, De La Hoya was still ahead 77-75 on some scorecards as late as the ninth round. It was then that a left hook from Hopkins knocked De La Hoya to the canvas, marking the first time in De La Hoya's career that he lost by knockout. Though beaten, De La Hoya lost no prestige as he had proved his motivation to fight the best.

After that match the time between De La Hoya's matches increased. In the final four years of his career he fought in four more matches, winning two of them. In what would be his final match on December 6, 2008 he faced Manny Pacquiao in the MGM Grand Casino, a place that had become a home away from home for him.

Pacquiao was widely recognized as the best pound-for-pound boxer in the world. Some thought Pacquiao was competing at a weight class—147 pounds—far above his natural build, which made De La Hoya the favorite due to his size advantage. De La Hoya lost the fight in a dominant nine-round performance by Pacquiao. One of a boxer's greatest challenges is to decide when to retire. At 36 years old, De La Hoya decided that he achieved what he wanted with his time in boxing. Over a16-year career, De La Hoya captured titles at super featherweight, lightweight, light welterweight, welterweight, light middleweight, and middleweight; in addition to an Olympic gold for his mother. With 39 wins in 45 fights against the best competition in the world, and earning just under $700 million dollars in revenue, De La Hoya has proven what family support can do.

Notes

1. Golden Boy Promotions. 2006. Oscar De La Hoya: Golden Boy.
2. Richard O'Brien, 1992. Arriving With a Bang. *Sports Illustrated*. December 7.
3. Golden Boy Promotions. 2006. Oscar De La Hoya: Golden Boy.
4. Robert Winters, 2004. *Oscar De La Hoya: Notable Sports Figures*. Michigan: The Gale Group, Inc. 2004.

8

LATINOS IN MAJOR LEAGUE SOCCER
AND PROFESSIONAL AMERICAN SOCCER

by Richard Lapchick

The fact that American national teams have World Cup championships in their sights speaks to how far American soccer has progressed in the last few decades. Legendary Latino players like those discussed in this section on Latinos in Soccer have helped shape the country's soccer teams into ones capable of competing with the world's best. World Cup championships are becoming a little easier for American fans to see.

With such a large Latino population in the United States, and with the tremendous popularity of soccer in the Latino community, the future of US soccer depends disproportionately on Latino fans helping to produce more star players as every level, including Major League Soccer. While other chapters show that every major professional sports league gets and embraces the importance of the Latino community, MLS has that "ingrained in its core" according to Maria Burns Ortiz who writes for *ESPNsoccernet*.

This is a no brainer for the MLS and Don Garber, its commissioner who says that the Latino market is part of the MLS DNA. In 2009, 40 percent of those at MLS matches were Latino. According to Ortiz, a full 85 percent of the 47 million Latinos in the US can trace their families back to countries where soccer is by far the number one sport.

MLS works at tapping that market. The *2009 Major League Soccer Racial and Gender Report Card* shows the highest percentages of Latino professional employees at the League Office and team levels. Latinos Gabriel Brener, Jorge Vergara Madrigal, Antonio Cue, Javier Leon, and Oscar de la Hoya are part of the MLS

Board of Governors which is, in effect, the ownership group. At headquarters, 27 percent of the professionals are Latino. Major League Baseball was second at 16 percent. In 2008, 23 percent of the head coaches were Latino (MLB had 13 percent) while 17 percent of the team Presidents/CEOs were Latino (no other sport has a Latino in this position). Of the team senior administrators, 14 percent were Latino while 22 percent of all team professionals were Latino. MLB has eight and five percent Latinos in these roles.

Forty-three percent of the radio and TV broadcasters are Latino vs. 17 percent in MLB. Not to be confused, MLB is doing well with Latino employees. But MLS is setting the standard with the demographic. MLS also works the youth market where there are so many potential players and fans. MLS Futbolito youth tournaments were in 13 communities in 2009. MLS teams also promote soccer for Latino youth in many of their markets including Washington, DC, Los Angeles, and Dallas.

MLS efforts have resulted in a 33 percent Latino fan base that is double that of any other pro sport according to *ESPNsoccernet*'s Burns. The NBA is a distant second with 16 percent. In an April 24, 2009 interview with Chicago Spanish-language weekly, *Éxito*. Commissioner Garber said that the future of MLS lies with soccer talent surfacing in second-generation Latino immigrants and the love of soccer prevalent in the growing Latino community. He emphasized that the MLS will contract less stars from Latin America and rely more on the "first generation of Latinos born in this country."

With the explosive growth of Latinos in the United States, MLS will continue to work with the community at all levels. But like all the other sports covered in *100 Campeones*, it is the players who make the biggest potential impact.

Throughout his career, Hugo Pérez boosted the U.S. national team. He played in 73 total matches and scored 13 goals with the national team and was a member of the 1984 Los Angeles Olympics and the 1988 Seoul Olympic teams. Pérez was a reserve on the 1994 World Cup team. That team is widely believed to have brought soccer onto the national stage as a result of its success in reaching the quarterfinals and losing to eventual-champion Brazil. Pérez also played with professional teams in France, Sweden, El Salvador, and Saudi Arabia, and with the Los Angeles Salsa of the American Professional Soccer League. Pérez was the U.S. Soccer Athlete of the Year in 1991 and was inducted into the National Soccer Hall of Fame in 2008

Born in Uruguay, Tabare "Tab" Ramos moved to New Jersey when he was 10. He was a three-time All-American at North Carolina State before he left school to play on the 1988 Olympic team and one year later signed with the U.S. men's national team. After playing in Spain, Ramos played an historic role in the development of Major League Soccer when he became its first drafted player in February, 1995. He spent all seven years with the MetroStars. Twice an MLS All-Star, he retired in 2002 as the last member of the original team. Ramos was elected to the National Soccer Hall of Fame in 2003.

Marcelo Balboa played soccer at San Diego State University and led the team to the NCAA Division 1 National Championship game in 1987. He became one of the most famous players in the history of Major League Soccer and is well known as a world-class defender, as a participant on three World Cup Teams, and for his legendary bicycle kicks. Balboa was the first player in the history of the MLS to play 100 games for the same team and was named U.S. Soccer Athlete of the Year in 1992 and 1994, one of the 11 best players in the history of Major League Soccer, and in 2005, was elected to the National Soccer Hall of Fame.

Claudio Reyna is considered one of the greatest soccer players the United States has ever produced. He had a great career at the University of Virginia and in Germany, Scotland, and the English Premier League. Reyna finished his career in Major League Soccer with the New York Red Bulls. Reyna is also famous for his contributions to the U.S. national team. He represented the United States in the 1994, 1998, 2002, and 2006 World Cups and then with the 1992 and 1996 Olympic teams. He was the first American voted to the FIFA World Cup All-Star First Team in 2002.

Major League Soccer has created so many opportunities for soccer players in the United States. In becoming the first Latino Commissioner of any major American sports league, Cuban-born Doug Logan helped launch MLS in 1996; he was also President and CEO. MLS started strong with first-year average attendance at more than 17,000 fans per game and two games attended by more than

85,000. In addition, Logan worked to generate more than $120 million in corporate sponsorships from companies like Nike, Honda, and AT&T. In July, 2008, Logan was named at the new Commissioner of USA Track and Field.

The following are the full stories of the stars who bolstered Logan's chances of giving birth to MLS.

Hugo Pérez

Star of the National Soccer Hall of Fame

by Jared Bovinet

The fact that many people consider Hugo Ernesto Pérez the most underrated soccer player in the history of the United States, even after all of his awards and accolades, is a testament to just how great he was during his playing years. In the 1980s and 1990s, Pérez established himself as one of the country's most deft ball-handlers and one of the U.S. national team's most reliable players.

Pérez was born into a soccer family in El Salvador on November 8, 1963 and started playing the sport when he was four. Both his grandfather and father played for C.D. FAS, a professional team, in El Salvador. The family moved to the United States when Pérez was 11.

As a midfielder, he became famous for his ball-handling and playmaking skills. Pérez began his professional career in 1982 with the Tampa Bay Rowdies of the North American Soccer League (NASL). The following season, he went to the San Diego Sockers and played several years with the team. He was voted most valuable player when they won the Major Indoor Soccer League (MISL) Championship in 1988.

Throughout his career, Pérez proved an invaluable addition to the U.S. national team. He started with the team in the 1984 Los Angeles Olympics and helped it qualify for the Olympics in Seoul four years later. Pérez did not play in the 1992 Olympics due to injury but did play as a reserve on the 1994 World Cup team, a team largely credited for bringing the sport to the national forefront due to its success in reaching the quarterfinals and losing to eventual-champion Brazil. Pérez represented the United States in 73 total matches and scored 13 goals with the national team. Along with playing with the national team and MISL, Pérez played with professional teams in France, Sweden, El Salvador, and Saudi Arabia, and with the Los Angeles Salsa of the American Professional Soccer League.

One reason for Pérez's success, and why so many fans think he is underrated, is because of his ability to beat his opponents with just one foot. California Victory head coach Glenn Van Straatum commented, "He can do everything with his left foot-inside, outside, whatever—and you would think, 'Why doesn't he use his right foot?' He can still do it with his right, but he can do everything twice as good with his left."[1]

Pérez has received numerous awards. He earned U.S. Soccer Athlete of the Year honors in 1991, the first Honda Award as the most outstanding player on the U.S. national team, and was inducted into the National Soccer Hall of Fame in 2008.

He has stayed active in the world of soccer after retiring from the professional ranks in 1999. After his last professional game, he looked to start coaching the game he loves. His new focus seemed like a perfect fit for him. A fellow coach said of Pérez, "Considering his pedigree, his playing experience and his qualities as a human being, I think he's a great role model. He's ready to make (coaching) a full-time thing."[2]

Pérez first worked to establish soccer camps at the University of San Francisco, where he emphasizes basic skills to young children. When asked why he believes the U.S. has struggled in World Cup play, he said, "We need to develop [children] into good, technical players. That is what's lacking in youth soccer."[3] The creation of these camps directly addresses this need.

He also coached the University of San Francisco men's soccer team for several years and the California Victory, a United Soccer League expansion franchise. Currently, he coaches teams with the Novato Youth Soccer Association and with the U.S. Soccer Federation, working with soccer academies on the West Coast to prepare players for the national team.

Pérez has a goal of coaching one of the U.S. national teams. He said, "I would like to do it here in America because that's where I played. I still have the belief that we can be better. We've progressed so much but we still can get better. Maybe I'm crazy but I think one of these days we can win the whole thing (World Cup)."[4]

The fact that American national teams have World Cup championships in their sights speaks to how far American soccer has progressed in the last few decades. Legendary players like Pérez have helped shape the country's soccer teams into ones capable of competing with the world's best. And with Pérez coaching soon-to-be national team players, those World Cup championships are becoming a little easier to see.

Notes

1. Dave Albee "From Novato Youth to High-level Pros, Hugo Perez Still Setting Goals in the U.S.," *Marin Independent Journal.* May 2, 2007.

2. Ibid.

3. "Back to Basics: Former Start Says Fundamentals Key to U.S. Competing on World Stage," *The Spokesman-Review*, July 1, 2006.

4. Dave Albee, "From Novato Youth to High-level Pros, Hugo Perez Still Setting Goals in the U.S.," *Marin Independent Journal*, May 2, 2007.

Tabaré "Tab" Ramos

Star of the National Soccer Hall of Fame

by Jared Bovinet

When he was 12 years old, Tabaré "Tab" Ramos got a D on a midterm paper and as a result missed three straight weekends of playing soccer. This punishment—to take him away from the one thing he lived for—proved to be a huge teaching tool. "That was very, very hard for me—and it never happened again," he said. "I've been living almost the life of a professional soccer player since I was 12 years old because that's what I wanted so badly."

Soccer was the lifeblood of Ramos' childhood. His father, Julian Ramos, moved the family to Harrison, New Jersey from Montevideo, Uruguay when Ramos was 10. Ramos made friends easily on the playground, where he displayed his remarkable ball-handling skills for a child his age. He soon joined local leagues and met his lifelong coach and friend, Phil Santamessina, who led Ramos to enroll in St. Benedict's School.

During his high school years at St. Benedict, Ramos scored 161 goals in 80 games. In addition to playing at his school, he played club soccer with Thistle United, along with future United States national teammates Tony Meola and John Harkes. Also during high school, Ramos was named a two-time high school All-American and *Parade Magazine*'s National High School Player of the Year in 1983.

Ramos played with the New Jersey All-Star team and received an invitation to try out for the country's Under-20 national team when he was just 16. Despite his young age, he earned a spot. From high school, the New York Cosmos of the North American Soccer

League (NASL) drafted him. But because of the uncertain future of the league, friends instead encouraged Ramos to attend North Carolina State University. He ended up making a wise decision, as the NASL shut down six months later.

At North Carolina State, Ramos earned All-ACC honors all four years and was a three-time All-American. He left school to play on the 1988 Summer Olympic team and one year later signed with the U.S. men's national team. He played many incredible matches for the national team, helping it place fourth at the 1995 Copa Mundial. Two years later, he scored what historians call one of the most important goals in U.S. soccer history against Costa Rica in a World Cup qualifier.

Ramos played with the New Jersey Eagles of the American Soccer League and then with the Miami Sharks for the next season, for which he was chosen as a league all-star yet again. Throughout his career, Ramos earned spots on many all-stars teams by differentiating himself from his teammates through his amazing skills. A *New York Times* article offered why Ramos is considered the best American player ever and what he offered when he played:

> A mastery of the ball that is almost uncanny. It's on view in the deft, quick touches that take him and the ball around the legs of opponents; in passes to teammates that, whether short or long, arrive exactly where the teammate would like them; and in a cracking hard shots so powerful that it seems impossible it could come from the 5-foot-6-inch, 140-pound body. [1]

After having played for the United States national team after the 1990 FIFA World Cup, Ramos played with the Spanish club, Figueres, which bought his contract from the United States Soccer Federation. One year later, he moved to another Spanish club, Real Betis, which he helped win the division championship and continued with another season. During that second season with Real Betis, however, he did not play a game because he was injured during a World Cup game against Brazil. Brazilian player Leonard elbowed Ramos in his skull, sending him to a three and a half month stay in the hospital to recover.

Ramos played a historic role in the development of Major League Soccer when he became its first drafted player in February

272 Part 1: Professional Sport

of 1995. He spent all seven years with the MetroStars and earned All-Star honors in 1996 and 1998. Ramos played until the end of the 2002 season and retired as the last member of the original team. He was elected to the National Soccer Hall of Fame and received a star in the U.S. Soccer Star Plaza at the Home Depot Center in Carson, California, in 2003.

Off the soccer field, Ramos remained dedicated to his education and earned his degree from North Carolina State through correspondence courses. Along with valuing education, Ramos values the importance of community involvement and understands the impact sport can have in society. He serves as the President and Founder of Tab Ramos Soccer Programs, which holds camps and clinics for players in New York, New Jersey, and Pennsylvania. He also serves as the President and Founder of the New Jersey Soccer Academy and of the Tab Ramos GOAL! Foundation, a non-profit organization that helps disadvantaged children to learn life lessons through sports.

Notes

1. Lawrie Mifflin, "Doing a Star Turn for the Home Team, at Last," *The New York Times*, August 18th, 1996.

Marcelo Balboa

Star of the National Soccer Hall of Fame

by Jared Bovinet

Courtesy of San Diego State Athletics Media Relations.

Marcelo Balboa is one of the most famous players in the history of Major League Soccer. He is well known for many things, including his career as a world-class defender and his participation in three World Cups with the U.S. national team. But when most people think of Balboa, the first thing that comes to mind is his legendary bicycle kicks.

These kicks took years to perfect. In an interview with Captain U, Marcelo explained how he became so well known for them. "I used to practice on mom and dad's bed, on my bed with a balloon. I used to go out after practice. I would stay a half-hour, forty minutes with other guys that were crossing balls . . . that's the way you develop your skills."[1] Years later, balloons became real soccer balls in professional games and Balboa became synonymous with amazing bicycle kicks. In a 2000 Colorado Rapids vs. Columbus Crew game, he scored with a bicycle kick, a goal later voted MLS Goal of the Year and to this day considered the most famous goal in the league's history.

A famous Balboa bicycle kick in the 1994 World Cup helped launch Major League Soccer a few years later. Denver businessman Phil Anschutz, a potential investor in the league, saw the kick and was so impressed that he insisted on having Balboa play in the league if he were to invest. "I mean, without too much exaggeration, that we might not have a league without Marcelo Balboa,"[2] said Ivan Gazidis, deputy commissioner of MLS. Anschultz got his wish and Balboa was a part of the inaugural Rapids team.

Born in Chicago on August 8, 1967, Balboa grew up in Cerritos, California and participated in the American Youth Soccer Organization program. He also played baseball and football, but was most passionate about soccer and "always had a smile on his face" when he was playing.[3] His father, who was a professional player in Argentina and with the Chicago Mustangs of the North American Soccer League, coached his son's team. Balboa went on to play soccer at San Diego State University and led the team to the NCAA Division I National Championship game in 1987.

He spent his first two professional years playing with the Mexican League team León, and then with the Colorado Foxes, San Francisco Blackhawks, and San Diego Nomads, all pre-MLS teams. He signed with the Colorado Rapids, who he played with for six seasons and then with the MetroStars in 2002 but was injured shortly after joining the team. He considered a comeback after injuring his knee but decided against it, explaining, "It's not worth me trying something that I can't give 100 percent to . . . Nobody's going to remember me for being old, slow, and couldn't do the job."[4]

In addition, Balboa represented the United States in the 1990, 1994, and 1998 World Cup competitions. He ended his U.S. national team playing years with 128 appearances and 13 goals, and his MLS career with 151 games, including 24 goals and 23 assists. He was the first player in the history of the MLS to play 100 games for the same team. Balboa was named U.S. Soccer Athlete of the Year in 1992 and 1994, one of the 11 best players in the history of Major League Soccer, and in 2005, was elected to the National Soccer Hall of Fame.

After he retired from soccer, Balboa worked in the front office of the Rapids and served as a soccer announcer for ESPN, ABC, and MLS games on HD Net. In addition, he was an NBC Sports analyst for soccer at the 2008 Summer Olympics. In 2007, he created From the Pitch, a radio show broadcast through Colorado devoted to soccer. He now works with the Boulder County Force Soccer Club as a Technical Advisor, which involves running training sessions and providing feedback to the team's players and coaches.

As he explained later in the Captain U interview, Balboa's personal career highlight was being a member of the 1994 World Cup team. The entire team lived and practiced together for 18 months. It was the first time the United States had hosted the World Cup, so there was immense pressure on the team, but he relished the opportunity to play in a World Cup in his own country and grow so close with his teammates.

Later in the interview, he offered an interesting perspective on what soccer programs in the United States must do to nurture players capable of beating the world's elite. "I think there's too much coaching going on sometimes. I think our kids are a little too structured on how they play. We're missing that one key element that other teams have but we don't . . . We don't have that creativity in the United States."[5] He continued by explaining that the best soccer practices are the ones in which coaches step aside and let children have fun and figure out how best to play, and that this style of practice may very well create players who are fundamentally sound and also creative enough to outplay any team in the world.

The coming years may reveal if Marcelo Balboa's recommendation to improve U.S. soccer is correct. More creativity and less-structured practices certainly can improve our teams, but thousands of young soccer players across the country practicing bicycle kicks on their beds certainly could help, too.

Notes

1. "Marcelo Balboa: The Interview on Role Models," Captain U. http://www.captainu.com/buzz/273-marcelo-balboa-the-interview-on-role-models

2. Alan Peace, "MLS Pays Homage to Balboa on Retirement," *Rocky Mountain News*, April 3, 2003. (Accessed September 1, 2009).

3. Marcelo Balboa: The Interview on Role Models," Captain U. http://www.captainu.com/buzz/273-marcelo-balboa-the-interview-on-role-models

4. Alan Peace, "MLS Pays Homage to Balboa on Retirement," *Rocky Mountain News*, April 3, 2003. (Accessed September 1, 2009).

5. Marcelo Balboa: The Interview on Role Models," Captain U. http://www.captainu.com/buzz/273-marcelo-balboa-the-interview-on-role-models

Claudio Reyna

Future Star of the National Soccer Hall of Fame

by Jared Bovinet

The first American player to be named to the FIFA World Cup All-Star First Team, Claudio Reyna is considered one of the greatest soccer players the United States has ever produced. He enjoyed an illustrious career as a college standout and in Europe before he returned to the United States to finish his career in Major League Soccer.

Reyna was born on July 20, 1973 in Livingston, New Jersey. His father played professional soccer in Argentina and moved to New Jersey in the late 1960s, where he met Claudio's mother. Their son started playing soccer when he was young and attended Saint Benedict's Preparatory School, famous for its soccer program. During his years at the school, the soccer team went undefeated in 65 games. Reyna earned *Parade Magazine*'s National High School Player of the Year award twice (the only player to do so), and was named the Gatorade National Player of the Year.

Beginning in 1991, Reyna attended the University of Virginia on an athletic scholarship. He played on its soccer team for three years and helped the team win the Atlantic Coastal Conference and the NCAA National Championship each year. Reyna won the Hermann Trophy, given to the country's top male college soccer player, and was named the Missouri Athletic Club's Player of the Year and *Soccer America* magazine's Player of the Year in 1992 and 1993. The same magazine also named him to its Team of the Century.

After his time at the University of Virginia and playing in the 1994 World Cup, Reyna looked to play in Europe because professional soccer did not yet exist in the United States. He signed with the German club Bayer Leverkusen but only made five appearances with the team. He then was loaned to VFl Wolfsburg of the same league and saw more playing time. With VFl, he became the first American to be named captain of a European club. In 1999, he moved to Scotland to play with the Glasgow Rangers and helped them win their 11th league title in 12 years. In addition, he played in the English Premiership with Sunderland and Manchester City.

Reyna returned to the United States in 2007 and played with the New York Red Bulls, whose coach, Bruce Arena, coached at the University of Virginia when Reyna played there. In an interview with *The New York Times*, Reyna reflected on his time in Europe and what he would miss. "I've done more than I ever dreamed of in Europe. I've lived away so long that just being back on home soil is a great feeling." He continued by saying, "Are there things I'll miss? I guess the atmosphere is definitely one of them. The excitement of playing in a big derby, which doesn't exist here, yet."[1]

Reyna's career with the New York Red Bulls did not last as long as he would have liked due to hamstring and back injuries that prevented him from playing at full-strength. He announced his retirement on July 16, 2008, after having played 27 matches over two seasons. At the announcement, which took place at St. Benedict's, he made sure everyone understood he would not return, saying "there's not going to be any Brett Favre situation here."[2]

Reyna's career had a huge impact on the world's perception of American soccer players. In playing at such a high level for so many years in Europe, Reyna proved that Americans could play with the world's best. Jeff Agoos, Reyna's teammate on the U.S. national team said, "There were players that went over to Europe before [Reyna], but what Claudio did was raise the bar for what an American player is and should be."[3]

Reyna is also famous for his contributions to the U.S. national team. He represented the United States in the 1994, 1998, 2002, and 2006 World Cups and then with the 1992 and 1996 Olympic teams. In his time with the national team he served as captain twice, scored eight goals in 112 appearances and was among 16 players voted to the FIFA World Cup All-Star First Team in 2002.

After he retired, Reyna announced the creation of the Claudio Reyna Soccer Academies in Brooklyn and Newark, New Jersey. The goal of the Academies, an initiative of the Claudio Reyna Foundation, is to work with low-income young soccer players to help them achieve both academic and social success. In addition to playing soccer, children focus on schoolwork and volunteer with community projects. The Foundation plans to expand to Harlem and the Bronx this fall.

Reyna currently lives in New York with his wife Danielle, who played for the U.S. women's national soccer team. They have three children together. He serves on the Board of Trustees at St. Benedict's Preparatory School, which allows him to give back to the school that helped mold him into one of the greatest American soccer players of all time.

Notes

1. "Red Bulls Midfielder Claudio Reyna on His Homecoming," *The New York Times*, February 2, 2007.

2. David Porter, "Former US National Team Captain Claudio Reyna Announces Retirement," *APWorldstream*, July 16, 2008.

3. Ibid.

Douglas "Doug" Logan

First Latino Commissioner of a Major American Sports League and First Commissioner of Major League Soccer

by Jared Bovinet

Leading the 1996 launch of Major League Soccer in the United States was no small task. Introducing a new league in a country dominated by football, basketball, and baseball took strong strategic insight and creativity that is not easily found. Doug Logan, the MLS' first Commissioner, President, and CEO, had the leadership and vision to ensure the league got off to a strong start.

Logan understood the importance of the MLS for the United States. Ten years earlier, the North American Soccer League folded, and as a result there was significant amount of pressure on MLS leadership to ensure that this new league remained viable while harnessing the sport's popularity. In a *Washington Times* article, he emphasized how much he welcomed the challenge,

> I have observed [soccer] as a fan, as a sport executive and as an international, almost universal idiom that transcends languages, borders and cultures in just every sport spot in the world. To finally bring that level of soccer to the United States is a fascinating challenge and a chance to make a little bit of history.[1]

Major League Soccer officials recruited Logan because of his extensive marketing and experience in promotions. Prior to joining MLS, he worked with an entertainment company in Mexico City, where one of his responsibilities was operating the Mexico Aztecas with the Continental Basketball Association. He later became owner but sold his ownership when he started with the MLS. Following his work with the Mexico Aztecas, Logan worked with Ogden Entertainment Services, a company in New York that works in facility management and concessions. Some of his prior work experience included concert promotions in Mexico and in facility management in Illinois, where he promoted the first Arena Football League game in 1985.

Major League Soccer experienced significant successes under Logan's tenure as Commissioner, with first-year average attendance at more than 17,000 fans per game and two games attended by more than 85,000. In addition, Logan worked to generate more than $120 million in corporate sponsorships from companies like Nike, Honda, AT&T, and PepsiCo. His impact on the MLS continued with five-year television broadcasting agreements with ABC, ESPN and Univision. The number of televised MLS games doubled as a result of these agreements.

His tenure at MLS was not completely harmonious, however. Although the league's first year was quite successful, during his five years there, the league lost a total of $250 million. Even with more televised games, the league's television audience had not expanded and MLS investors began to seek a replacement.

After parting ways with Major League Soccer in 1999, Logan created Empresario, LLC, a business that specializes in sports consulting and entrepreneurship in North America, Central America, and Spain. He also worked as a consultant to the National Rugby League. In July of 2008, Logan was named the new Commissioner of USA Track and Field. His major objectives with this organization include restructuring its board of directors, increasing television programming, and identifying new sponsors.

Working in track and field matches Logan's athletic interests; he is a lifelong runner and has completed several marathons. Logan was born in Cuba in 1943 and then moved to the United States. He attended Manhattan College and the University of Baltimore Law School. He also served in the 101st Airborne Division Vietnam and received two Bronze Stars for his service.

In many ways, Logan is not your typical commissioner. He is considered one of the most approachable and candid leaders in sports and actively maintains a blog called "Shin Splints," which details his work at USTAF and the progress it is making. From reading the blog, it is clear that Logan is excited to improve the organization and that he embraces the challenges it currently faces. One of these challenges involves increasing the number of Latinos on the U.S.A Track and Field team. A recent Associated Press review found that only four percent of its members, 24 individuals, are Latino.[2] In acknowledging this fact and recognizing room for growth, Logan said, "We have to do more to take the fine young athletes that exist among new Americans and find some way of creating opportunities for them. They are underrepresented."[3] With his breadth of experience, from working in both Mexico and the United States and serving as Commissioner of Major League Soccer, Doug Logan gives us good reason to hope for progress in increasing Latino participation in track and field.

Notes

1. Steven Goff, "MLS Names a Soccer Novice, Doug Logan, as Its Commissioner," *Washington Times*, November 22, 1995. (Retrieved July 17th, 2009.)
2. "Few Hispanics on Olympic Squad," *The Latino Journal*. http://thelatinojournal .blogspot.com/2008/08/few-hispanics-on-us-olympic-squad.html, August 8th, 2009, (accessed April 17th, 2009).
3. Ibid.

9

LATINOS AND HORSE RACING

by Richard Lapchick

Horse racing was not a sport I thought of regarding Latinos when I first conceived of writing this book. I tried to think back at watching the Triple Crown races as a boy with my mom and dad. We never missed one of the big races. But a Latino presence? I was not conscious of it then. Now thinking back some of the names I heard often were Pincay, Cordero, Baeza, and Ycaza. I just did not know they were Latino or even think about it.

A year after I was born in 1945, 17-year-old Ángel Valenzuela came back from Mexico to ride in the United States. Although Ángel was born into a large family in McNary, Texas, he went to Porvenir, Mexico as a child and learned to handle and ride cow horses at his father's ranch. He moved from there to riding at bush league tracks. In 1952, he was riding at California's Hollywood Park. Many say that even though his career was not spectacular, he opened the door for other Latino jockeys.

He was soon joined on the US horse racing stage in 1957 by 18-year-old Panamanian Manuel Ycaza who then led the way for Latino jockeys in the late 1950s and early 1960s by becoming the first successful Latino jockey in the United States. He became known as an aggressive rider with fervor to win. He style led him to be suspended for nearly 250 days in his first two seasons. Ycaza believes he was unfairly targeted because of his success, ethnicity, and his status as a new arrival on the racing scene.

Ycaza's 1959 season included a victory in the Washington, D.C. International, at the time the only international horse race in the

United States that drew the best horses from the United States and Europe. Ycaza would again win the International in 1960 and in 1967.

In 1964, Ycaza broke through in a big way by winning his first and only Triple Crown Race by capturing the Belmont Stakes. He kept on winning but made yet another mark when forced into retirement by an injury when he sued Hialeah Racetrack in 1970 for negligence and won an unprecedented $225,000 settlement. In 1964, he was awarded the George Woolf Memorial Jockey Award, given to the jockey who demonstrates high standards of personal and professional conduct, on and off the racetrack. He finished with nearly $20 million in career earnings, 2,367 victories and was inducted into the National Museum of Racing and Hall of Fame.

Avelino Gómez became a sensation in the Canadian-riding circuit and was Canada's top jockey from 1956–1960 and again in 1964 and 1966. After his victories, Gómez would jump off his horse while raising his arms in the air and then walk along the grandstands so he could interact with his fans.

As a result of his physical and mental approach, Gómez won each of Canada's Triple Crown races at least twice. In 1966, Gómez had a banner year by leading all North American jockeys in wins with 318, and becoming the first Canadian jockey ever to win 300 races. With a winning percentage of 32 in 1966, Gómez set a record for a North American champion that still stands to this day.

He retired several times during the mid-1970s, but on June 21, 1980, Gómez's horse broke down with a back leg fracture that caused a three-horse accident. One of the horses behind him jumped over him and then landed on Gómez, who was the only jockey ever to be killed at Woodbine Racetrack. With 4,081 career wins, in 1982 he was inducted into the National Museum of Racing and Hall of Fame in Saratoga, NY.

A racing star in Panama, Braulio Baeza came to the United States for a new challenge where he became famous for both his substance and style. Baeza rode 65-1 long shot Sherluck to victory at the 1961 Belmont Stakes, the final leg of horse racing's Triple Crown. In celebration, Baeza plucked the carnations from the blanket of flowers draped over Sherluck and tossed them to the crowd. With the victory at Belmont, Baeza became one of the first foreign-born Latino jockeys to ever win a Triple Crown race.

In the early 1960s, *Sports Illustrated* called it the "Latin Invasion" when Baeza and Ycaza and a group of other Latino riders were making their presence felt in the United States. They were not welcomed by some of the establishment but ultimately talent trumped racial injustices. Baeza and other Latino jockeys of his generation would get to ride on the best horses and inspire the next wave of Latino jockeys.

Baeza was the leading money winner between 1965–1969, including the 1967 season in which he was the first jockey ever to have winnings over $3 million. In 1969, Baeza staked claim to his third Belmont victory on Arts & Letters, who would go on to win the United States Horse of the Year Award. In 1975, Baeza would again be the top money winner with earnings of $3,674,398. He finished his career with 4,013 lifetime victories in the United States and Panama.

Ángel Cordero Jr. started his professional career at the age of 17 in Puerto Rico. Two years later in 1962, he was riding in New York where he became a dominant jockey. Cordero would win 13 Saratoga titles, including 11 straight titles from 1976–86.

In 1974, Cordero won the Kentucky Derby for the first time. It is the most famous American race and the first leg of the Triple Crown. He won it again in 1976 and in 1985 becoming only one of seven jockeys to win the Derby three times. He also won the Belmont Stakes in 1976 and the Preakness Stakes in 1980 and 1984, joining an exclusive club of jockeys that have won all three of the Triple Crown races.

With the victories came the accolades. He was the leading money-winning jockey in 1976, 1982, and 1983. Cordero won all the major awards. In 1988, he was elected into the National Museum of Racing and Hall of Fame. As of this writing, Cordero is sixth on the all-time wins list with 7,057 and with career earnings of $164,570,627. It was Cordero whose name I heard most often growing up.

Laffit Pincay Jr. was the most recognizable name in the industry in 1970s, winning four Eclipse Awards for Outstanding Jockey and being the top earner six times in the decade. In 1973, he was the first jockey ever to break $4 million in earnings and then the first to break $8 million in 1979. His dominance did not stop and he led all United States jockeys in earnings in 1985, becoming the first jockey to break the $13 million mark and winning his fifth Eclipse Award for Outstanding Jockey.

On December 10, 1999, aboard Irish Nip, Pincay broke the career victory mark previously held by legendary Willie Shoemaker with his 8,834[th] win, becoming the winningest jockey ever. He did not stop until he won his 9,530[th] win. As of this writing, only three other jockeys won more than the $237,120,625 he amassed.

Now for the stories of the men who paved the way for generations of Latino jockeys in the United States . . . Ycaza, Gómez, Baeza, Cordero, and Pincay.

Manuel Ycaza

Star of the National Museum of Racing and Hall of Fame

by Horacio Ruiz

"He was the Spanish [jockey] who opened the door for all the others," said Ángel Cordero, Jr., of Manuel Ycaza. "He made a name for himself that's always gonna be in people's minds."[1] One look at today's horse racing landscape and one would think that Latinos always enjoyed popular numbers among the ranks of jockeys, but that wasn't always the case. Ycaza led the way for Latino jockeys in the late 1950s and early 1960s by becoming the first Latino jockey to be successful in the United States. He paved the way for jockeys like Braulio Baeza, Cordero, and so many others after him. At the same time, he became one of the most controversial jockeys of his time. "I told my mother when I was young," said Hall of Fame Panamanian jockey Jorge Velázquez, "I wanted to be like (Braulio) Baeza and (Manny) Ycaza. But Ycaza would put you over the rail just to win a race. He would do anything to beat you."[2] Ycaza made his permanent move to the United States in 1957, and by 1963, five of the top U.S. stables employed Latino jockeys. Ycaza had such an influence that Hall of Fame rider Baeza, a fellow Panamanian, was signed in the United States after Ycaza told a prominent agent that Baeza had the talent to succeed in the U.S. and that Panama was the cradle of the greatest jockeys in the world.

One of nine children, Ycaza learned to ride ponies at the age of six and began riding in Panama and Mexico. He became a professional rider when he was 14 years old. Ycaza rode with the desire to win and was a keen observer for what worked and didn't work on the track. He was also an avid sports fan, playing such sports as baseball, swimming, biking, and soccer where he developed his ambidextrous abilities that would later transfer into his riding style. In Panama, he raced against jockeys from Chile, Peru, and Cuba, and they all had distinct styles that Ycaza would pick out and also incorporate in his own style. "Ever since I was little I was very observant," Ycaza said. "I experimented with both hands because others wouldn't do it. When I started to ride—with what I experimented—

the good that came I accepted it, and the bad, I didn't. As a result, I created a unique riding style."[3] In 1957, as an 18-year-old, Ycaza transitioned into racing in the United States on a permanent basis, bringing with him the tough and unique style he had developed earlier in his career.

But Ycaza claims that with his desire to win came a concerted effort by track officials and rival jockeys to take advantage of his aggressive riding style. "Any rival wanted any edge," Ycaza says, "and I was no different. But what they wanted to do was dishearten me. They would claim unjust fouls against me because of my reputation. I was under a microscope throughout my entire career. But I made an impact."[4] Ycaza would make a name for himself in the Golden Gate Fields Racetrack and at the Santa Anita Racetrack, and word was spreading of his skills, but so were the suspensions. Ycaza entered a racing group where all-time great Eddie Arcaro was the perennial king and all the other top jockeys protected their turf. When Ycaza beat Arcaro in a race, it was not welcomed by all the riders. Ycaza incurred so many fines and fouls from the beginning that it nearly ended his career in the United States. In 1957, he was suspended 130 days for fouls and in 1958 he was suspended 110 days. Ycaza said that while some claims by rival jockeys may have had some legitimacy, he was overly and unfairly targeted because of his success, ethnicity, and his status as a new arrival on the racing scene. While the competition among the jockeys was fierce and meant to intimidate Ycaza, he did not back down and refused to be pushed around. As a result he kept up his relentless riding style accompanied by his victories, though they did not come without controversy.

But Ycaza's talents were obvious enough for owner Harry F. Guggenheim to hire him as a contract rider for his Cain Hoy Stable. Guggenheim, who once was the American ambassador to Cuba and spoke Spanish fluently, took Ycaza under his wing. For Ycaza, the signing with Cain Hoy Stable made him feel like he was a part of a family. It also catapulted his career into a Hall of Fame career. "Guggenheim for me was a great influence in my career and in my life," Ycaza said. "He was a great person that with me was very direct and honest and he was a positive influence in my life. He had a stable that had good results before I was there, but once I started with their stable they had some very formidable results."[5] For Cain

Hoy Stable, the signing of Ycaza coincided with becoming the leading money-winning stable in 1959 with earnings of $742,081.
Ycaza's 1959 season included a victory in the Washington,
D.C. International, at the time the only international horse race in the
United States that drew the best horses from the United Sates and
Europe. The race was so prestigious that during the 1960s, at the
height of the Cold War, Russian owners would send their horses to
compete. Ycaza would again win the International in 1960 and in
1967. "I used to want to win so much that I got excited when any-
thing interfered, and I would lose my temper," Ycaza said in 1960.
"Now I still have the same temper, but I know I've got to hold it."[6]

With a newfound sense of direction, Ycaza became a fan favorite. He publicly said he raced for the $2 bettors, the common men
and women who he said kept horse racing alive. During post-race
parades Ycaza would pass by the railbirds—racing enthusiasts who
watch races from the outer rail of the track—and they would coo at
him. He'd smile back at them. "He dismounts with gymnastic verve,
helmet at a rakish tilt, his step jaunty,"[7] wrote Joe Val of the *New
York World-Telegram* and *Sun.*

In 1962, Ycaza was involved in one of the most famous races
in history at the Travers Stakes at the Saratoga Race Course in
Saratoga Springs, NY. Riding the favored Ridan, Ycaza lost by a
bob of a nose to Jaipur and all-time great Bill Shoemaker. The race
is listed in the 2006 book *Horse Racing's Top 100 Moments* and the
outcome of the race determined which horse would be named 1962
U.S. Champion 3-Year-Old Horse. Years later, at the time of Shoemaker's death, Ycaza remembered when Shoemaker would pull up
his horse on purpose only to say 'See you later' and burst away from
his closest competitor.

"When I rode Ridan and [Shoemaker] beat me in the 1962 Travers with Jaipur, I told him, 'I think I got you.' He said, 'I think you
did, too.' Then, they put his number up," Ycaza said, referring to
Shoemaker's famous victory. "In the 1967 Washington D.C. International at Laurel, I was on Fort Marcy and he was on Damascus
and [he] pulled that 'See you later,' thing again. Only this time, I got
really down on my horse and got there at the wire. I told him, 'I
nailed you.' He said, 'I don't think so,' but my horse won by a
nose."[8]

The 1963 racing season would be another big one for Ycaza. Riding Canebora, Ycaza won the Queen's Plate, North America's oldest thoroughbred horse race, and the most famous race in Canada. He would later win the Breeders' Stakes, the third leg of the Canadian Triple Crown, also with Canebora. In 1964, Ycaza broke through in a big way by winning his first and only Triple Crown Race by capturing the Belmont Stakes. That year, he was awarded the George Woolf Memorial Jockey Award, given to the jockey who demonstrates high standards of personal and professional conduct, on and off the racetrack. In 1968, Ycaza rode Dark Mirage to the first-ever Filly Triple Crown. "The satisfaction is short because you need to continue," Ycaza said of even the biggest victories in his career. "If you have seven or eight mounts, and you win your first mount, you need to put that behind you because you still have more races to run. You have to have your mind set on what you are going to do next."[9]

Ycaza retired in 1971 because of persistent ankle and knee problems due to an accident at Hialeah Racetrack in 1970. Ycaza would sue the racetrack for negligence, unheard of at the time, and win a $225,000 settlement. He would be the Panamanian Consul General to New York in 1973 and 1974. He returned to race briefly in 1983 before retiring permanently. He finished with nearly $20 million in career earnings, 2,367 victories, and a 22.4 winning percentage. In 1977, he was inducted into the National Museum of Racing and Hall of Fame. "All the races were my favorites," Ycaza said. "I rode in more than 10,000 races and I rode equally as hard in each one of them. Each one of them was my Derby and I had a desire to win every single one. I finished with a winning percentage near 23 percent, and for me, that wasn't enough."[10] In addition, Ycaza held the summer record for single-season victories (41) at Saratoga for more than 40 years. Ycaza currently resides in the Forest Hills area of Queens, NY, where he is a big baseball fan and cheers for both the Yankees and the Mets. He once threw the ceremonial opening pitch during a Mets game at Shea Stadium.

Latinos are a prevalent force in horse racing as evidenced in the 2009 Kentucky Derby where 11 out of the 19 jockeys were either Latino or Latino-American. "Today, it's a great satisfaction to see the percentage of Latino jockeys in and winning all of these big races," Ycaza said. "There were Latinos that came before me with great ability and dreams of conquering, but they had to pack it in and they gave up because of the pressures and discrimination they faced during that era. I went through that and worse. But it's more than just physical ability. You also need to have mental fortitude and perseverance. I could've returned to my country like the others before me. I wasn't accepted and had to overcome many obstacles but I persevered. It is great satisfaction to me seeing so many Latino jockeys competing at the highest level and making a living for themselves and having success."[11]

Notes

1. Keith Marder, "Chasing A Legend," (1988). *Albany Times Union*, August 28.
2. Ibid.
3. Manuel Ycaza. Interview with the author, September 7, 2009.
4. Ibid.
5. Ibid.
6. "To Wish Is a Big Thing," *Time*, April 25, 1960.
7. William Leggett, "Manuel Is Their Darling," (1960). *Sports Illustrated*, June 13.
8. EquineSearch, "Shoemaker Remembered," http://74.125.93.132/search?q=cache :SZ3WirPRLnkJ:equisearch.com/equiwire_news/shoemaker101603/+1962+travers+st akes+ridan+ycaza&cd=13&hl=en&ct=clnk&gl=us. (accessed August 3, 2009).
9. Manuel Ycaza. Interview with the author, September 7, 2009.
10. Ibid.
11. Ibid.

Avelino Gómez

Star of the National Museum of Racing and Hall of Fame

by Horacio Ruiz

Avelino Gómez considered it his job to be part-entertainer and part-competitor. He lived up to both parts with equal bravado. Gómez became a sensation in the Canadian-riding circuit, becoming Canada's top race-winning jockey from 1956–1960 and again in 1964 and 1966. After his victories, Gómez would jump off his horse while raising his arms in the air. For the crowd, Gómez would walk along a fence next to the grandstands where he could interact with his fans and even with those who booed him. It was all part of the show for one of Canada's most revered jockeys. "He was fearless, he was strong, and he had a talent that came about naturally," said Lou Cavalaris, a longtime trainer and friend. "He towered above the local riders at the time."[1]

Born near Havana, Cuba, in 1928, Gómez worked as a stable hand for two years before riding in his first race at the age of 13 in 1943. In 1944, Gómez rode his first winner in Mexico City at the age of 14. From 1945–55, Gómez rode in Mexico, Cuba, the United States, and Canada, before moving full time to Canada. His first major victory came in 1951 when he captured the Hawthorne Gold Cup Handicap in Stickney, Illinois. In time, he would come to be known as one of the best jockeys, along with carrying a fiery temper and a burning desire to win. Earning the nickname "El Perfecto," Gómez would go on to win every major stakes race in Canada. He became the first jockey, and is part of an exclusive three-jockey club to win four Queen's Plate races, North America's oldest thoroughbred race, and the most prestigious in Canada.

Gómez and his family made their home in Toronto, Ontario and Gómez raced primarily at Woodbine Racetrack in Toronto. Gómez dominated many of the most prestigious races held at the Woodbine Racetrack where he still holds the most wins by a jockey at the Autumn Stakes, Victoria Stakes, Shady Well Stakes, Coronation Futurity Stakes, and Plate Trial Stakes. Gómez is a nine-time winner of the Plate Trial Stakes, considered one of the most important prep races for the Queen's Plate. Gómez's intensity during racing season was described by his son, Avelino Jr.

"When he was at home, he'd have his dinner, he'd watch his television and he did not want any other distractions," Avelino Jr. said. "He was very intense that way."[2] But Gómez would use his persona as a ploy in the jockey's room. "He would walk into the jockey's room and rub shoulders with the guys," said Avelino Jr. of his father. "He would have a nap. It was all part of his bag of tricks. The other guys would see my dad and think his guard was down. It wasn't. He read other riders. He would read the racing form and he loved to say, 'You're going to the lead today.' He had a way of getting guys to ride the way he wanted them to ride, not the way that was best for them."[3]

As a result of his physical and mental approach, Gómez won each of Canada's Triple Crown races at least twice. Gómez captured the Prince of Wales Stakes in 1959 and 1964, and he captured the Breeders' Stakes in 1959, 1966, and 1967 in addition to his four triumphs at the Queen's Plate. In 1966, Gómez had a banner year by leading all North American jockeys in wins with 318, and becoming the first Canadian jockey ever to win 300 races. With a winning percentage of 32 in 1966, Gómez set a record for a North American champion that still stands to this day.

Gómez had memorable moments on the track aside from his victories. In 1960, on his way toward his second Queen's Plate victory, Gómez stood high in his irons down the backstretch and peering behind him to see if anyone was close. Gómez was daring a crank caller that had threatened to shoot him down during the race. In another race in the early 1960s, Gómez took a spill from his horse during a multiple-horse accident. Al Coy, one of Gómez's rivals also involved in the crash, went back to see if he could help Gómez. Gómez, faking that he was badly injured jumped at Coy and punched him thinking that Coy had caused the crash.

Through the late 1950s and the 1960s Gómez dominated the Woodbine Racetrack as the leading jockey in 1956, 1957, 1960, 1966, and 1967. Woodbine was where Gómez reigned supreme. In 1971, battling weight problems, Gómez retired from racing. He tried training horses, but he returned to racing in 1972. He would again retire and return to training horses in 1974, before deciding to return once again in 1976. "As a ride, I'm the chief!"[4] Gómez proclaimed. In 1977, Gómez earned two of the greatest honors of his career. He won the Sovereign Award for Outstanding Jockey, the most prestigious award for a jockey in Canada, and he was inducted into the Canadian Horse Racing Hall of Fame. In 1978, Gómez was recognized with the Sovereign Award of Merit for his lifetime contribution to horse racing. But the sport had taken a toll on Gómez's body, and after several short-lived retirements, those close to him began to question Gómez's motive for putting his health at risk. Prior to the Canadian Oaks race at Woodbine, Mickey Gómez, Gómez's brother and long-time agent pressed Gómez about his desire to continue racing. "Why do you continue to do this? What do you need it for?" Mickey asked his brother. "My brother said to me, 'If I'm going to die, this is the best way.' I couldn't argue with him. He loved to ride. He was a determined person who wanted nothing else but to win."[5]

On June 21, 1980, Gómez was racing in the Canadian Oaks at his beloved racetrack, when his horse broke down with a back leg fracture that caused a three-horse accident. One of the horses behind him jumped over him and then landed on him. "You've seen him in a whole lot of falls and you say, 'He'll get back up, it's Avelino. What the hell can happen to him?'"[6] Cavalaris remembers thinking.

"When I saw him in the ambulance he was in pain but he was talking," said Hall of Famer Sandy Hawley, also in the race. "I thought to myself, 'That's Avelino, he'll be fine.' His brother Mickey had been talking to the doctor. They said he'd be okay but he'd be out of action for a while."[7] Later that night while he was out at dinner with his wife and friends, Hawley received news that Gómez had died at the age of 51. He was stunned. Gómez was the only jockey ever to be killed at Woodbine. "Being the athlete he was, you thought he was invincible," Hawley said of Gómez.

For his career, Gómez finished with 4,081 career wins and a winning percentage of 24. In 1982, he was inducted into the National Museum of Racing and Hall of Fame in Saratoga, NY. In 1984, the Avelino Gómez Memorial Award was established in his honor. The Award is a Canadian thoroughbred horse racing honor given annually to a jockey who is Canadian-born, Canadian-raised, or a regular in the country for more than five years, who has made significant contributions to the sport.[8] In 1990, Gómez was posthumously inducted into Canada's Sports Hall of Fame. In his memory, there is a statue of Gómez at Woodbine holding two fingers up. "The rub," wrote Jim Coleman, Canada's premier sports columnist, "is the certain knowledge we shall never see his like again."[9]

Notes

1. Slam! Sports. "Almost Invincible," http://slam.canoe.ca/Slam/Columnists/Ulmer/2005/06/19/1095335-sun.html (accessed August 5, 2009).
2. Ibid.
3. Ibid.
4. Canadian Horse Racing Hall of Fame. "Avelino Gomez," http://www.canadianhorseracinghalloffame.com/jockeys/1977/Avelino_Gomez.html (accessed August 3, 2009).
5. Slam! Sports. "Almost Invincible," http://slam.canoe.ca/Slam/Columnists/Ulmer/2005/06/19/1095335-sun.html (accessed August 5, 2009).
6. Ibid.
7. Ibid.
8. Bloodhorse.com. "Loseth Wins Avelino Gomez Award," http://www.bloodhorse.com/horse-racing/articles/4352/loseth-wins-avelino-gomez-award?id=4352. (Accessed December 3, 2009).
9. Ibid.

Braulio Baeza

Star of the National Museum of Racing and Hall of Fame

by Horacio Ruiz

Braulio Baeza began working out thoroughbreds in Panama when he was five years old. By the age of 15, he was riding professionally, having learned the craft from his father and grandfather, who were both jockeys. One of Baeza's early experiences training horses involved a stubborn horse that refused to break out of the gate. During a training session, as he sat on top of the horse and the gate opened, the horse broke out unexpectedly. A young and unprepared Baeza was thrown to the ground. It was a lesson he would carry with him for the rest of his career; things will not work out as planned. In his first professional race in 1955, Baeza came in last place, but making the needed adjustments, he won his first professional race two mounts later. Even after his initial victory, Baeza would struggle in his first two years as a rider in Panama. Baeza, however, would continuously work on his craft and by 1958 he was riding on some of the best horses in Panama. In 1959, Baeza rode 309 winners on 112 racing dates, such an astonishing rate that it ceased to be news in Panama. Looking for the next challenge, a 20-year-old Baeza moved to the United States in 1960.

In the United States, Baeza became famous for both his substance and style. In the post-race parades, Baeza would sit up tall and straight, attracting the crowd's attention. Baeza gained the respect of his peers for his understated elegance as both a jockey and a person. In 1961, Baeza rode 65-1 long shot Sherluck to his first career win in the Belmont Stakes, the final leg of horse racing's Triple Crown. In celebration, Baeza plucked the carnations from the blanket of flowers draped over Sherluck and tossed them to the crowd. With the victory at Belmont, Baeza became one of the first foreign-born Latino jockeys to ever win a Triple Crown race. "Sherluck, that was a very important day for me in my career because I was just a year from coming from Panama, and I was second in the Derby, third in the Preakness," Baeza said. "It was a very emotional time and it was a great highlight for my career at the time."[1] In the winner's circle, former President Dwight Eisenhower spoke to Baeza in Spanish during the presentation.

In the early 1960s, Baeza, along with Manuel Ycaza and a group of other Latino riders, led what *Sports Illustrated* termed the "Latin Invasion." But, as foreign-born Latino jockeys were making their presence felt in the United States racing circuit, they were not welcomed by some of the establishment. "The racial prejudice that has held back Negroes in other sports has been directed in riding against Latin-Americans by their peers,"[2] wrote *Sports Illustrated* writer Frank Graham Jr. Ultimately, it was talent that trumped race, and Baeza along with the other Latino jockeys of his generation

Courtesy of Braulio Baeza.

would get to ride on the best horses and inspire the next wave of Latino jockeys.

"Braulio Baeza is no bum," Baeza said to a reporter in early 1962. "He is no liar and no fool. There are two things that he wants from his career. The first is to win the 1962 Kentucky Derby and become the hero of his Panama. The second is to become the most successful jockey that ever lived."[3] Baeza would not accomplish his first goal in 1962, when he finished ninth in the Kentucky Derby. The outcome was different in the 1963 Derby when Baeza won with Chateaugay. "He just seemed to fit the horse,"[4] trainer Jimmy Conway said of Baeza's ride on Chateuagay. For Baeza, the Derby victory was the greatest of his career. Only four years after leaving Panama, and with Kentucky Derby and Belmont Stakes victories under his belt, Baeza was already a national hero in Panama and was well on his way toward leaving his mark as one of the greatest jockeys ever.

From 1965–1969, Baeza was the leading money winner, including the 1967 season in which he was the first jockey ever to have winnings over $3 million. In 1969, Baeza staked claim to his third Belmont victory with the horse Arts & Letters, which would go on to win the United States Horse of the Year Award. In 1975, Baeza

Courtesy of Braulio Baeza.

would again be the top money winner with earnings of $3,674,398. Another one of Baeza's most memorable races came in the United Kingdom's 1972 Benson & Hedges Gold Cup, now known as the International Stakes. Filling in as the replacement jockey for a horse named Roberto—named after baseball Hall of Famer Roberto Clemente—Baeza rode Roberto to an upset victory over the heavily favored and until then unbeaten Brigadier Gerard at York Racecourse. It would be the only loss in the 18-race career of Brigadier Gerard, who was previously considered unbeatable. With Baeza as jockey, "Roberto was out of the stalls like a bat out of hell,"[5] and took the lead from the very beginning without looking back and setting what was then a course record time in the mile and a quarter race. As Baeza was riding back to the unsaddling area, he tipped his cap to Queen Elizabeth II, who stood up and waved back at him for a job well done.

In 1972, and again in 1975, Baeza was awarded the Eclipse Award for Most Outstanding Jockey. In 1968, Baeza was awarded the George Woolf Memorial Jockey Award by Santa Anita Park in Arcadia, California as the thoroughbred jockey in North America whose career and personal character earn recognition for the individual and the sport of thoroughbred racing. Throughout his racing career, Baeza had endured a number of injuries and confronted weight issues. In the summer of 1976, Baeza woke one morning to find that after having jogged in a plastic suit the previous day, he still had eight pounds to lose before the start of the race day. Tired of the toll the weight constraints were taking on his body, Baeza retired from horseracing that day. "Racing is what I had done all my life, and I did it with all the effort I had," Baeza said. "But I couldn't keep on fighting with weight issues. The retirement wasn't planned, it was forced. I couldn't control the weight any longer."[6]

He finished his career with 3,140 victories in the United States, and combined with his 873 wins in Panama, Baeza closed the door on his career with 4,013 lifetime wins. As a website says, "He was pure poetry on a horse: efficient, elegant, and always spectacularly in rhythm with the horse."[7] In the same year as his retirement, Baeza was inducted into the National Museum of Racing and Hall of Fame in Saratoga, NY.

After retirement, Baeza switched to training horses before accepting a job in 1995 with the New York Racing Association as the assistant clerk of scales. It would not be easy for Baeza who was indicted in late 2004 on charges of misrepresenting jockeys' weights before races. Baeza was fired from his post in 2005 and was unable to find work with a revoked license. The charges were widely viewed as flawed and the unfair actions of then-attorney general Eliot Spitzer, who would later be disgraced as New York's governor. On September 17, 2007, a judge tossed out a 291-count indictment and all charges against Baeza were dismissed.

"For three years, I have been stall-walking," Baeza said of his ordeal. "It is a happy ending, but the damage is already done. You can't take back those three years."[8] Many of his friends in the racing circle helped pay his attorney's fees, but when Baeza tried to find work, for one reason or another there was always an excuse not to hire him. Today, Baeza lives in West Virginia where he lives with his wife, Janice, and spends his free time traveling to visit his friends and family.

Notes

1. Braulio Baeza. Interview with the author, September 3, 2009.
2. Frank Graham, Jr., "Tall In the Saddle," 1966. *Sports Illustrated*, April 11. 3 William Leggett, (1962)."The Latin Invasion," *Sports Illustrated*. February 5.
4. Frank Graham, Jr., (1966). "Tall In the Saddle," *Sports Illustrated*. April 11.
5. Wikipedia.org. "Roberto (horse)." http://en.wikipedia.org/wiki/Roberto_(horse) (accessed June 28, 2009).
6. Braulio Baeza., Interview with the author, September 3, 2009.
7. Braulio Baeza website. "Biography: United States." http://www.brauliobaeza.com/usa.html (accessed June 28, 2009).
8. Braulio Baeza website. "Current Events." http://www.brauliobaeza.com/current-events.html (accessed June 28, 2009).

Ángel Cordero, Jr.

Star of the National Museum of Racing and Hall of Fame

by Horacio Ruiz

In a 1976 *Sports Illustrated* article, Ángel Cordero Jr., was called the most controversial jockey of the day. He was called the jockey New Yorkers loved to hate, and even Cordero would say that he would hear boos from the grandstand after his mounts. But it didn't bother Cordero because as much as New Yorkers loved to hate him, they had to love him because he was the best bet on the track. Known for his extremely aggressive racing style, Cordero would take chances on his horses that few others would, making dangerous passes seem effortless, and sometimes winning by what some opponents called questionable tactics. Cordero kept himself in top shape while earning a reputation as one of the fiercest competitors. "If a horse has four legs and I'm riding it, I think I can win,"[1] he once said.

Cordero learned his trade from his father, Ángel Sr., who was a successful rider and trainer in Puerto Rico. Cordero started his professional career at the age of 17 in Puerto Rico, winning his first race at El Comandante race track in Puerto Rico in 1960. In 1962, he moved to New York as a 20-year-old to begin his career in the United States. In time, Cordero would become the dominant rider in the New York racing scene at the Saratoga Race Course in Saratoga Springs, NY. In 1968, he was the leading winner of races. Cordero began winning many of the major stakes on the New York circuit, including the Woodward, Suburban, the Jockey Club Gold Cup, Coaching Club American Oaks, and the Matron. Cordero would win 13 Saratoga titles, including 11 straight titles from 1976–86.

"It is such a good feeling to win a big stakes race when everybody crowds into the winner's circle and they drape a horseshoe of flowers around your horse's neck and the jockey gets a trophy and the owners take you to dinner to tell you how great you are," Cordero said. "Nothing compares to that."[2]

In 1974, Cordero won his first Kentucky Derby, the most famous American race, and the first leg of the Triple Crown. He would go on to win the Derby again in 1976 and in 1985. He is one of seven jockeys to win three times at the Kentucky Derby since the event inaugurated in 1875. Cordero counts his win at the 1976 Belmont Stakes as his most memorable because it came while riding Bold Forbes, the champion two-year-old in Puerto Rico in 1975. In 1976, Cordero would ride Bold Forbes to victories at the Derby and at the Belmont. Bold Forbes would go on to be named the U.S. Champion three-year-old Male in 1976. Cordero would claim victories at the Preakness Stakes in 1980 and 1984, joining an exclusive list of jockeys that have won all three of the American Classic Races.

With the victories came the accolades. He was the leading money-winning jockey in 1976, 1982, and 1983. In 1972 he was the recipient of the George Woolfe Memorial Jockey Award for outstanding achievement both on and off the track. In 1982 and 1983 he was the winner of the Eclipse Award for Outstanding Jockey. In 1992, he received the Mike Venezia Memorial Award for exemplifying excellent sportsmanship and citizenship. In 1988, when Cordero had already amassed $132 million in winnings, he was elected into the National Museum of Racing and Hall of Fame. On July 29, 1987, Cordero became the fourth jockey ever to win 6,000 races. Cordero became the first New York-based rider to reach 6,000 victories, but he didn't stop there. He tallied his 7,000[th] victory on October 17, 1991, to become only the third jockey to reach that milestone.

All the winning, however, came at a price. In 1978, Cordero fractured a vertebra when his horse broke down and he was thrown off the saddle. In 1986, he lacerated his liver, broke his arm, and a bone underneath his left knee when he was thrown from a horse and trampled by four oncoming horses, and in 1992, he suffered a broken left elbow, three broken ribs, torn intestines, a damaged kidney, and the removal of his spleen. Doctors gave Cordero only a few days to live after the accident, but he was able to survive. Taking his health and his diminishing strength into consideration, Cordero retired as jockey following his 1992 accident and began a new career as a trainer.

"Riding has been my life," Cordero said at the time of his retirement. "But after long pain, after consulting my doctors, I have decided to quit riding but to stick with racing as a trainer. I only hope that I accomplish as much as a trainer."[3] It was a tough decision for Cordero since he did not finish his career on his terms. The temptation to race proved too strong and Cordero returned in 1995 to ride briefly in the Breeders' Cup. In 2005, Cordero again proclaimed he would make a one-day comeback to ride the filly Indian Vale at the Cotillion Handicap at Philadelphia Park on October 1, 2005. Cordero announced that he would donate 25 percent of his winnings to support Hurricane Katrina relief efforts. Cordero was greeted with a large ovation as he walked toward the paddock. He would ride Indian Vale to a fifth-place finish, but was gracious in defeat. "That was a very touching welcome," Cordero said. "The fans still remember."[4] He was asked if he would attempt to make any other comebacks, saying, "No, this is it. I'm honored and thank God for the opportunity to do this. I'm happy I made it and right now just want to go home, relax and get myself a bite to eat."[5] On his way to the jockey's room he was cheered one last time by the adoring fans.

Through May 2009, Cordero is sixth on the all-time wins list with 7,057 and with career earnings of $164,570,627. He won 18.3 percent of his mounts and fellow jockey Steve Cauthen, the last jockey to win the Triple Crown, called Cordero "the elite stylist of the last fifty years."[6] Cordero is still very active on the racing scene, working as an exercise rider for trainer Todd Pletcher, and working as the agent for fellow Puerto Rican jockey John Velázquez.

Notes

1. "Puerto Rico Profile: Angel Cordero, Jr.," *Puerto Rico Herald*, July 6, 2001. http://www.puertorico-herald.org/issues/2001/vol5n27/ProfCordero-en.html.

2. Dave Feldman, "An Angelic Talk with Cordero," *Chicago Sun Times*. December 4, 1988.

3. Joseph Durso,"Horse Racing; Cordero Says His Reluctant Goodbye To Racking," *New York Times*, May 8, 1992.

4. Keith Jones, "Nothing But Fun Wins Dramatic Photo in Cotillion,"Philadelphia Park, http://www.philadelphiapark.com/Racetrack/press_box.php?load_id=884.

5. Ibid.

6. "Puerto Rico Profile: Angel Cordero, Jr," http://www.puertorico-herald.org/ issues/2001/vol5n27/ProfCordero-en.html. *Puerto Rico Herald*. July 6, 2001.

Laffit Pincay, Jr.

Star of the National Museum of Racing and Hall of Fame

by Horacio Ruiz

What's the hardest part of horse racing? For jockeys, it can be the dieting restrictions they put on themselves to make weight for their mounts. Jockeys have long been known for their extravagantly poor diets. Some have been known to eat nothing but eggs for an entire year, while others would eat one or two leaves of lettuce for dinner after drying them out in the sun. There are stories of jockeys walking in the middle of summer wrapped in wool coats, taking potent laxatives, and even swallowing pills with the egg of a tapeworm in them.

During a transcontinental flight, Laffit Pincay Jr., winner of 9,530 races, refused the flight attendant's meal, but accepted a bag of peanuts. Pincay opened the bag and took out one peanut. He split the peanut in half, ate one half for dinner, and later in the flight ate the other half for dessert. It was Pincay's way of keeping his competitive edge, of keeping what was meant to be a 140-pound body, a 115-pound model of horse racing efficiency. The battle to keep his weight down would cause him to collapse of exhaustion, to hallucinate, and to become dizzy, sick, and depressed. However, Robert Kerlan, a renowned sports physician based out of Los Angeles, once remarked that Pincay had the best body of any athlete he had ever seen.

It's possible that the dieting is not the hardest part of horse racing; the act of racing a horse is exhausting. Laura Hillenbrand writes in the book *Seabiscuit*, "To pilot a racehorse is to ride a half-ton catapult. It is without question one of the most formidable feats in sport. The extraordinary athleticism of the jockey is unparalleled: A study of the elements of athleticism conducted by Los Angeles exercise physiologists and physicians found that of all major sports competitors, jockeys may be, pound for pound, the best overall athletes."[1] Even when riding on such powerful and unpredictable horses, jockeys had to contend with banging against rails or walls and into one another.

Hillenbrand goes on to write that, "The only thing more danger-ous than being on the back of a racehorse was being thrown from one."[2] Pincay was up to the task of becoming a dominant jockey. He was such a dominant rider that only nine years after moving to the United States from Panama, he was inducted into the National Mu-seum of Racing and Hall of Fame in 1975, long before many of his greatest career accomplishments. In 1984, he won his first and only Kentucky Derby after 10 unsuccessful attempts. From 1982–84 he won three consecutive Belmont Stakes, becoming the second jockey ever to do so. His fitness rivaled that of any world-class athlete, even his large biceps muscles made an impression on those inspecting the 115-pound Pincay. He earned a reputation as the best finisher in rac-ing by muscling his horses down the stretch.

The injuries were difficult, too. They would eventually cause Pincay to end his career before he was ready to leave the sport.

But the most difficult part of horse racing for Pincay was re-claiming the desire to ride again. In January 1985, Pincay received a phone call from his daughter as he was getting ready for the ninth race at Santa Anita Park. "Dad? My . . . my . . . my mom shot her-self," Lisa Pincay told her father. She was home when she heard Linda, Pincay's wife of more than 17 years, shoot herself in the head. Linda was the same woman that had carried Pincay through his difficulties early in his career when he abused alcohol and looked for fights. She put an ultimatum on him to stop or else their marriage would disintegrate. He agreed and in return begged her not to try and commit suicide; Linda had made three previous attempts that Pincay knew about, and she promised that she would stop.

"She can't do this! She can't do this!" Pincay screamed in the jockey's room. "I felt like a hole opened up and swallowed me," Pincay said. "I didn't care whether I rode or not. I know people were saying, 'He won't come back.' I didn't think I would come back, ei-ther."[3] Weren't the demands of his chosen profession enough to con-tend with? Pincay was the most recognizable name in the industry, winning four Eclipse Awards for Outstanding Jockey in the 1970s. Six times he was the leading money winner in the 1970s, including five consecutive seasons from 1970–74. In 1973, he was the first jockey ever to break $4 million in earnings and then the first to break $8 million in 1979. In 1971, he led all United States jockeys in wins.

Pincay couldn't help but blame himself for Linda's death. But he figured he needed to race again—he needed to stay busy—and much later he realized he wasn't to blame. "I got a hold of myself," Pincay said, "and I talked to myself and I said to myself, 'I've got this one life.' I had seen so many people go down because of one thing that bothered them and I said, 'I have been tough all my life with my profession, with my self-discipline, and I'm not going to let this happen to me.'"[4]

"I never had any doubt in my mind that Laffit would keep riding," said Bill Shoemaker, a horse racing legend. "There has never been any rider who is more dedicated to his profession—not me, or Arcaro, or anyone. I don't care who he is."[5]

With the rest of the 1985 season ahead of him, Pincay would dominate like he hadn't before. He again led all United States jockeys in earnings in 1985, becoming the first jockey to break the $13 million mark. He would go on to win his fifth Eclipse Award for Outstanding Jockey.

On December 10, 1999, aboard Irish Nip, Pincay broke the career victory mark previously held by Shoemaker with his 8,834[th] win, becoming the winningest jockey ever. That year he won the Eclipse Special Award for his achievement. It seemed that there was no end in sight to how many victories Pincay could tally, but in April 2003, he was thrown from a horse that would also land on him. Days after the spill, he would find out that he had broken three bones in his neck. He felt discomfort in his neck for several days, but continued his training routine. He was lucky that the muscles in his neck were strong enough to support his broken bones and prevent paralysis.

The specialists told him he should never ride again. He refused to listen to the doctor, but ultimately his friends and family convinced him to retire, including Shoemaker. Pincay finished his career with 9,530 victories, at the time horse racing's winningest jockey in the world. It would not be until December 1, 2006, that jockey Russell Baze passed Pincay on the all-time win list. Pincay won 19.66 percent of his mounts and finished with $237,120,625 in career earnings, the fourth-most ever through May 2009. Looking back on his career, Pincay was happy to have persevered through the tough times, through the most difficult parts of being a jockey. Today, Pincay is considered the greatest ambassador for horse racing. The

Laffit Pincay Jr. Award was established in his honor, given annually by Hollywood Park Racetrack in Inglewood, Calif., to someone who has served the horse racing industry with integrity, dedication, determination and distinction.[6] It is presented on Hollywood Gold Cup Day, a race which Pincay won a record nine times.

"There have been so many times I thought about quitting, I thought about giving up, but because of my love for the game, I kept hoping things would get better," Pincay said. "And they did. I'm glad I didn't give up."[7]

Notes

1. Laura Hillenbrand, *Seabiscuit* (Random House: New York. 2001) p.66.
2. Ibid., p. 67.
3. William Nack, "Scaling New Heights," November 17, 1986, *Sports Illustrated*.
4. Ibid.
5. Ibid.
6. Wikipedia.org. "Laffit Pincay, Jr. Award". http://en.wikipedia.org/wiki/Laffit_Pincay,_Jr._Award. (accessed December 3, 2009).
7. Cindy Pierson Dulay, "Laffit Pincay Retires," April 30, 2003. About.com. http://horseracing.about.com/cs/trainersjockeys/a/aa043003c.htm

10

LATINOS IN THE NHL AND NASCAR

by Richard Lapchick

Latino Players in the NHL

There have been only three Latinos in the history of the NHL but if they were on the same team, they would be a strong offensive force. Among them are a regular NHL All-Star and U.S. Olympian, a two-time Stanley Cup Champion and Calder Trophy winner, and a power forward with a deadly shot. Bill Guerin, Scott Gómez, and Raffi Torres' collective success may spur growth within in the Latino community not usually associated with the sport of hockey.

All three were in the NHL before it was finally clarified who was the first when the League celebrated "Hockey is for Everyone Month" in 2004. The NHL attributed the confusion to their surnames.

It had been widely believed that Alaskan-born Scott Gómez was the first Latino to skate in the NHL when he entered the league less than 10 years ago. A center with New York Rangers since 2007, he stepped on the ice for the New Jersey Devils in 1999. On www .latinosportslegends.com, Gómez is quoted as saying, "It's an honor being the first Latino to play in the NHL, I'm sure there will more to follow."

But Bill Guerin, the current team captain of the New York Is-landers, played for the New Jersey Devils in the 1991–92 season. The son of a Nicaraguan mother and an Irish father, Guerin was the first Latino in the league. When Hurricane Mitch devastated his mother's homeland of Nicaragua in 1998, Guerin teamed with the Edmonton Red Cross to raise $250,000 to help the recovery in Nica-ragua. He was playing for the Edmonton Oilers after a six-year stint with the New Jersey Devils. Gradually, his humanitarian efforts helped illuminate his ethnic background and the fact that he was in the NHL for seven years before Gómez.

The NHL published interviews with Guerin and Gómez in 2004. "People don't assume I am Hispanic, because my last name is Irish," Guerin explains. "I thought it was great when I heard that Gómez was coming into the league. He's got the name, he's got the looks, and all the attention he gets is great for hockey."

"Guerin always gives me crap [about getting so much attention for being a Latino in the NHL]" says Gómez. "He says I steal his thunder."

"It's all in fun," explains Guerin, now with the Dallas Stars.

"Latinos are definitely proud of their own," says Gómez. "A couple of guys came up to me almost in tears to tell me how proud they were. That hits the heart."

In any case, the first Latino in the NHL came more than three decades after Willie O'Ree became the NHL's first Black player in 1958. Fifty one Black players have followed Willie O'Ree.

Guerin played for the Oilers until joining the Boston Bruins from 2000–2002. He was the Most Valuable Player in the 2001 NHL All-Star Game with three goals and two assists and played in three other All-Star games. While playing for the St Louis Blues in the

Courtesy of Boston College Media Relations.

summer of 2006, Guerin was named to the 2007 All-Star game.

During his NHL career Guerin also played on the 2002 United States Olympics team helping the U.S. win the silver in Nagano. Guerin also played on the 1998 and 2006 U.S. Olympic Hockey teams.

Scott Gómez, whether he was the first or second Latino in the NHL, has had a terrific career on the ice. He started big, winning the Calder Trophy as the rookie of the year after accumulating 19 goals and 51 assists. Scott's father is Mexican-American and his mother is Colombian American. He played for the 2006 United States Olympic team, was an NHL All-Star in 2002 and 2008, and helped New Jersey win the coveted Stanley Cup in 2000 and 2003.

His career has enabled him to work on behalf of children through his foundation which helps children who cannot afford to play hockey to get into the game. The Foundation was motivated by his own upbringing. His father took him to see a hockey game when he was only five years old and that made Scott Gómez want to play. However, his parents could not afford the equipment so his Dad got in line when the local Boys and Girls club handed out free equipment. The rest, as the saying goes, is history. Part of the history was racism which he encountered before he became a pro.

He was the only Latino on the "Select 16 USA Team." It was with that team that he first encountered racist comments from opposing players. Gómez's mother had to tell him what it meant after a player of Asian descent called him a "Spic." He shook off the hurt because he was focused on going far in hockey.

Guerin and Gómez got company. Born in Canada of Mexican and Peruvian descent, Raphael "Raffi" Torres was drafted with the fifth overall selection by New York Islanders in the 2000 NHL Draft. To date, he has played for the Edmonton Oilers (2003–04, 2005–08) and the Islanders in 2001–02 and 2002–03. The Oilers made the Stanley Cup finals in 2005–06 where they lost to the Carolina Hurricanes in seven games. Torres was traded to the Columbus Blue Jackets in July of 2008.

Waiting in the wings to be the fourth Latino to play in the NHL is Al Montoya, who is Cuban-American. Montoya starred at the University of Michigan before being drafted by the New York Rangers in 2004 as the sixth player picked in the draft. To date, he has only played in the AHL for the Hartford Wolf Pack and the San Antonio Rampage. He is battling for a spot on the Phoenix Coyotes for the 2008–09 season.

So what about the future for Latinos in the NHL? Now that there are at least three notable Latino role models in the NHL, hockey's growth in Latino communities will be largely based on increased resources and opportunities.

Disney GOALS is a program that involves thousands of low-income youth annually through a combination of athletics, after school educational enrichment, and community service and is believed to be the largest program involving ice hockey in the United States for people of color. Nearly 2,000 youth, mostly Latino, participate in the Disney GOALS program annually. The NHL uses pioneer Willie O'Ree to try to impact communities where hockey has not been popular or accessible. At 72, 50 years after he broke the color barrier in the NHL, O'Ree still conducts up to 15 clinics a year. He is a regular hockey ambassador visiting schools and local organizations. While he has impacted more Black communities, he has also touched Latino communities.

Hockey in Mexico is another area where the sport can experience growth. Youth hockey programs, Spanish-language sports programming on TV and radio, the popularity of inline hockey, and the globalization of sport in general have helped hockey grow where it did not exist until recently. The popularity of inline skating in California helped increase support for ice hockey programs and teams in California. Latin American sports leaders believe the same can happen for them. Gordon Young, the referee-in-chief for the Federation International De Roller Sports travels extensively all over the world to promote and referee inline and ice hockey. He says that Latin Americans don't just root for the NHL's three Latino stars, but they also pull for U.S., Canadian, and European hockey players. They are becoming fans of the game. Young acknowledges that hockey needs another decade to fully develop in Latin America but he sees it happening.

Gómez, Guerin, and Torres are pleased to help lead the cause. Gómez said, "It's an honor to help open doors for Latinos. I am proud of who I am and I'd love to see another Gómez in the NHL soon."

I do not think he will have to wait too long.

Latinos in NASCAR

While NASCAR's Drive for Diversity program might be perceived as an effort to draw more African-Americans into professional racing, the reality is that the campaign is aimed at developing a full range of minority and female drivers, crew members, and to expand its fan base in numerous directions. And so far, among Hispanics, NASCAR is making strides.

The program is helping produce promising Latino drivers. Michael Gallegos, who was born in Colorado, finished 17th in the 2007 NASCAR Camping World West Series standings in his third season in the program. And Jesús Hernández, a second-generation Mexican born in Fresno, CA., finished 12ᵗʰ in the 2007 NASCAR Camping World East Series standings in his fourth season in the program. Several drivers, including Ruben Pardo, Rogelio López, and José Luis Ramírez, were born in Mexico. The elder statesman among Latino drivers might be Carlos Contreras, the first Mexican-born driver to compete in any NASCAR national series. Contreras, 38, broke through in 1999 when he joined the NASCAR Craftsman Truck Series and finished 14ᵗʰ in his first race—the NAPA Auto Parts 200 at California Speedway.

"Most people expected me to go to CART (Championship Auto Racing Teams), which was very popular at the time in Mexico, but I chose NASCAR," Contreras said. "I wanted to be the first Hispanic in NASCAR, to open doors in Mexico and with Hispanics to NASCAR racing. I feel I have definitely opened doors for others to follow, including Ruben Pardo. We now have a NASCAR series in Mexico, and the races are broadcast in Spanish throughout the U.S. and Mexico. I feel that what I did started everything."

According to the Simmons National Hispanic Consumer Survey, about 8.9 percent of NASCAR fans are Latino. There was a 10 percent increase between 2001 and 2005, when the most recent survey was taken.

There are Latino team members, drivers, and a team owner in the NASCAR Sprint Cup Series, Nationwide Series, and Camping World Series. Felix Sabates, born in Cuba, has owned a NASCAR team since 1987 and was instrumental in making a Mexico City race part of the NASCAR Nationwide Series circuit. Armando Fitz, owner of Fitz Motorsports, has been a Nationwide Series team owner for seven years. Joe Nava, owner of Performance Motorsports, competes in the Camping World West Series. Alba Colón, from Puerto Rico, is General Motors' top engineer for its NASCAR Chevrolet racing program and was one of *Hispanic Business* magazine's 20 Elite Women last year. Phil Jiménez is a race engineer for the No. 84 Red Bull Toyota team.

But drivers are the faces of the sport. Aric Almirola, who is of Cuban descent, drives for DEI (Dale Earnhardt Inc.) in the NASCAR Spring Cup Series.

"When fans have someone they can relate to, identify with,

and cheer for, they become emotionally invested in the sport," said Max Siegel, president of DEI. "I am proud to be able to support Aric's career, and hopefully have a direct impact on the growth of our sport."

There are obstacles, however, and some in NASCAR spoke openly about the challenges they have faced in trying to reach the top of the sport. Asked if he faced racism, Contreras said, "a little."

"The new Mexican guy stood out sometimes, especially to some people in the garage who had never been out of the South," said Contreras, who competed in two races last year in the NASCAR Nationwide Series for Fitz Racing. "I can say, though, that with time, I was seen by most as a regular guy in the garage, and I made lots of friends."

The bigger obstacle is attracting sponsors, Contreras said, because corporate America doesn't really rush to sponsor Hispanic or other minority drivers.

"If sponsors want the Hispanic market, they will go to soccer or music," he said. ". . . Give me a good car and I will get around the track as good or better than any driver. Why should I be limited with my sponsors because I am Hispanic? It's really not fair."

Ruben Pardo, who drives for Fitz Motorsports, said Contreras helped open doors for him. "If there aren't big pockets behind you, you just can't go racing," he said. "I am eager to race, but support for me to continue my career is not there right now. I really have to work twice as hard as the next guy. Companies need to support Hispanic drivers. If you had a Hispanic driver competing with a high-profile team or sponsor, I am sure that fans would flock to their support. . . . It is tough for a Mexican company to spend this kind of money, and U.S. companies hesitate to sponsor a minority. My résumé should impress most anyone, but once they see I am Hispanic, I am cast aside as a Hispanic driver, instead of being seen as a NASCAR driver who has won races and championships."

Clearly, the talent is there. But the sport still needs more top Latino drivers at all levels. And the corporate sponsors still need to fully understand that embracing diversity is a business imperative and that the Latino market has not been fully engaged. Understanding that could be the real fuel that propels the Latino community even further in the world of motorsports.

COLLEGE
SPORT

COLLEGE SPORT

By Richard Lapchick

Bobby Cavazos, a Mexican-American football player at Texas Tech, led his team to a 10–1 season and the 1954 Gator Bowl championship. During the time he played, Mexican-Americans could not use public toilets. Tech professor Jorge Iber believes that Cavazos helped local fans rethink their stereotype that Mexican-Americans were "lazy and dirty." This is what sports is supposed to do on a regular basis. It surely did that for African-American student athletes who were hardly seen on college teams in 1954.

According to the *2008 College Racial and Gender Report Card*, the percentage of African-American Division I college student-athletes soared to 24.7 percent for men and 15.7 percent for women. More than five decades after Cavazos, several factors have prevented similar rates of participation among Latino student athletes. The percentage of Latino male Division I college student-athletes was only 3.8, and 3.7 for Latinas. The highest concentration of Latino athletes was in baseball with 5.4 percent, a number slightly smaller than the one for African-Americans in college baseball, at 6.0 percent. In Major League Baseball, Latinos outnumber African-Americans three to one.

Many hope that young Latinos, who make up the nation's largest ethnic group, will play sport both for physical fitness and for educational opportunities. But for now, the gap between the sport participation rates of the nation's two largest ethnic groups is startling, especially among student-athletes. African-American males in Division I basketball made up more than 60.4 percent of total players while Latino men accounted for 1.8 percent. In Division I football (IA and IAA combined), African-American student-athletes comprised 45.9 percent while Latinos held only 2.2 percent.

The percentage of African-American women playing Division I basketball reached an all-time high of 47.4 percent while only 1.8 percent of players were Latina. On Division I women's cross country and track teams, African-Americans comprised 23.7 percent and Latinas made up 4.0 percent.

Overall, the percentage of white male student-athletes at the Divisions I, II, and III combined were 72.2 percent, 18.3 percent for African-American males, 3.9 percent for Latinos, 1.6 percent for Asian men, and 0.3 percent for American Indian/Alaskan Natives males. The percentage of white female student-athletes at the Divisions I, II, and III combined were 78.8 percent, 11.2 percent for African-American females, 3.6 percent for Latinas, 2.1 percent for Asian females, and 0.4 percent for American Indian/Alaskan Native females.

In Divisions I, II, and III, white male student-athletes comprised 64.2, 66.5, and 83.1 percent of the total male student-athletes, respectively. In Division I, white female student-athletes comprised 72.1 percent of the total female student-athlete population. In Division II, they made up 76.7 percent and in Division III, 87.4 percent. In Divisions I, II, and III, African-American male student-athletes made up 24.7, 23.7, and 9.1 percent of total male student-athletes, respectively while Latinos made up 3.8, 5.5, and 3.1 percent, respectively and Asians comprised 1.7, 1.2, and 1.7 percent, respectively. Native Americans made up 0.4, 0.4, and 0.2 percent, respectively.

In Divisions I, II, and III, African-American female student-athletes comprised 15.7, 12.8, and 5.3 percent of the total female student-athlete population, respectively, while Latinas made up 3.7 5.3, and 2.5 percent, respectively, and Asians comprised 2.3, 1.7, and 2.1 percent, respectively. Native Americans made up 0.4, 0.6, and 0.3 percent, respectively.

The star Latino student-athletes highlighted in this section are inspirational figures who hopefully will encourage more Latinos to play competitive sport in the future.

Uncomfortable with his Hispanic heritage as a boy, Tony Casillas became proud of it through sports. He was a consensus first team All-American for the Oklahoma Sooners in 1984 and 1985 and won the Lombardi Award in 1985 as the nation's top lineman. The National Football Foundation named him the College Defensive Player of the Decade for the 1980s. Casillas then played 13 seasons in the NFL, serving as a defensive tackle for Atlanta, the New York Jets, and Dallas. He helped the Cowboys win Super Bowls XXVII and XXVIII. In 2004, he was the second Latino inducted into the College Football Hall of Fame (the first being Jim Plunkett). Casillas was active in Dallas' Hispanic community, especially with youth, during his time playing professional football.

Brenda Villa, a Stanford All-American and three-time Olympian, is regarded as one of the best offensive players in water polo and one of the greatest Latina athletes in U.S history. Villa finished her Stanford career as the second leading scorer in school history with 172 goals in just three seasons. She was chosen as captain for the 2008 Beijing Olympics and guided the American team to a silver medal after winning the silver and bronze, respectively, in 2000 and 2004. In 2009, Villa captained her team to a third FINA World Championship, setting a women's water polo record among all nations.

Lisa Fernández is arguably the best pitcher and all-around softball player in U.S. and Olympic history. Her incredible ability, intense drive, and relentless commitment both on and off the field transformed softball into a premier U.S. sport and paved the way for future generations of athletes to achieve their dreams. Fernández compiled a 93-7 record for UCLA from 1990 to 1993. With 74 shutouts and 784 strikeouts, she led the Bruins to two national championships in 1990 and 1992. In 1991 and 1993, they finished second. Fernández boasted a 0.22 ERA, which ranks her second in NCAA history. She was also an offensive star and ranks fifth in all-time batting average and fourth in hits at UCLA. Fernández is a three-time Olympic Gold Medalist, leading Team USA to victories in the 1996, 2000, and 2004 Olympic Games.

A fierce competitor with a big heart, Eduardo Alonso Nájera is currently the only Mexican professional basketball player in the NBA, where he plays as a reserve forward for the New Jersey Nets. Nájera is the second Mexican-born player to be drafted and to play for the NBA, after Horacio Llamas. Nájera starred at the University of Oklahoma, where he led the Sooners to four consecutive NCAA tournament appearances while finishing in Oklahoma's all-time top ten in nine categories. He won the Chip Hilton Player of the Year

Award for his great character in 2000. Nájera is very active in encouraging young people to achieve their goals and has become one of Mexico's most popular and recognizable athletes.

Between 1999 and 2002, Jessica Mendoza was a four-time first team All-American at Stanford. She has also been an outfielder for the United States National softball team since 2001 and was inducted into the International Latin Sports Hall of Fame in 2006. That same year, she was also named the USA Softball Female Athlete of the Year and two years later was chosen as the Women's Sports Foundation Sportswoman of the Year. She is very active with the Foundation and with the ISF's "Back Softball" campaign for Olympics reinstatement.

Off the field, Mendoza, who is of Mexican descent, has been nothing short of amazing. Mendoza passionately speaks at schools nationwide about the importance of education and has helped secure million-dollar grants to "Close the Achievement Gaps" in education for disadvantaged and minority students. She has been active on the global stage and has done community work in Afghanistan, South Africa, the Czech Republic, Guatemala, and the Dominican Republic.

Amy Rodríguez became a national team soccer player while competing in high school and college at the University of Southern California. In 2005, she was named to the full U.S. Women's National team as the youngest player and only high school athlete on the roster. One month later, Rodríguez became the second Latina to ever play on the senior team, earning her first two caps at the Algarve Cup. By 2008, Rodríguez became a mainstay on the team, tallying her first two international goals at the Four Nations Cup. She has now appeared 38 times for the U.S. women, scoring six international goals, and tallying six assists. In 2009, the Boston Breakers professional team used their number one pick to draft Rodriquez.

Stephanie Cox, formerly Stephanie López, became the first Latina to play on the United States Women's Soccer National Team, becoming a pioneer in women's soccer in the process. She is considered one of the best soccer defenders in the world and was a three-time NSCAA All-American selection at the University of Portland. In 2005, Cox earned a position with the Women's National Team and became the youngest player on the squad. In 2008, she helped the United States win a gold medal at the Beijing Olympic Games.

Cox is currently playing professionally for the Los Angeles Sol. Cox has done missionary work alongside her family all her life. In 2005, she was part of a team that created a Hurricane Katrina fundraiser and recently she became a spokesperson for Casey Family Services, the country's largest foster care organization.

Coaches

According to the *2008 College Racial and Gender Report Card*, recent opportunities for Latino coaches at the college level were minimal, which brings up an issue that remains below the radar screen. While there have been regular stories about the lack of opportunities for African-American head coaches since the 1990s, especially in football, there has been hardly any interest to date in the even worse lack of opportunities for Latino head and assistant coaches. Most of the Latino coaches are in baseball, with 2.9 percent of the head coaching positions across all three Divisions.

In the 2007–08 year, only 1.6 percent of the head coaches of men's teams in Division I were Latinos. On women's Division I teams, 1.3 percent were coached by Latino men and .8 percent by Latinas. In Division II, 3.8 percent of the head coaches of men's teams were Latinos and .1 percent were led by Latinas. On women's Division II teams, 2.2 percent were coached by Latino men and .6 percent by Latinas. Among Division III schools, 1.5 percent of the head coaches of men's teams were Latinos. On women's teams at that level, a mere .9 percent were coached by Latino men and .3 percent by Latinas.

Latinos should not hold their breath waiting for opportunities to advance past the assistant to the head coach position. Latinos barely have a presence as assistant coaches in the first place. In the 2007–08 year, only 1.7 percent of the assistant coaches of men's teams in Division I were Latinos. On women's Division I teams, 1.7 percent of the assistant jobs were held by Latino men and 1.0 percent by Latinas. In Division II, 3.6 percent of the assistant coaches of men's teams were Latinos and .6 percent were held by Latinas. On women's Division II teams, 2.8 percent were coached by Latino men and 2.0 percent by Latinas.

Among Division III schools, 1.4 percent of the assistant coaches of men's teams were Latinos. On women's teams at that level, a mere 1.1 percent were held by Latino men and .5 percent by

Latinas. All of this data makes the stories of the coaches we are profiling here even more remarkable.

August "Augie" Garrido, Jr., is the all-time winningest baseball coach in NCAA Division I history with more than 1,600 career victories. As head coach at the University of Texas at Austin since 1996, he has led the Longhorns to five appearances in the College World Series and the National Championship in 2002 and 2006. He was named National Coach of the Year six times and was the first coach to lead teams from different schools to national titles (Texas and Cal State Fullerton). He is one of three coaches to win five or more national championships. He has coached three National Players of the Year and 44 All-Americans. Among his many awards, Garrido has been inducted into the Latin American International Sports Hall of Fame.

Joe Kapp became the first Latino Head Coach at a Division I-A school when he accepted the job at the University of California, Berkeley. He earned national coach of the year honors two years later. He was a standout college and NFL player who later both acted in and produced movies. Kapp was the 1969 NFL Player of the Year and became a symbol for players' rights after he signed a contract in 1970 with the Boston Patriots, which made him the highest paid NFL player at the time. When the year ended, Commissioner Pete Rozelle demanded that Kapp sign a Standard Player Contract. Kapp refused and ended up in an antitrust lawsuit with the NFL. Although he was not awarded any damages, the rules in question in his case were later revised, which dramatically increased the earning potential for future athletes.

Barry Álvarez took over what had been a terrible football program at the University of Wisconsin in 1990. The team had compiled a 9-36 record during the previous four seasons. Nineteen years later, the Wisconsin name is golden. Álvarez is now Director of Athletics and had been the winningest coach in school history with a record of 118-73-4. Álvarez was named one of the "100 Most Influential Hispanics" by *Hispanic Business* in 2001. He is one of only four Latino ADs as of this writing.

Leticia Pineda-Boutté is entering her fifth season as head softball coach for Washington University in St. Louis. The team won at least 25 games and went to the NCAA tournament in her first four seasons while compiling a 124-42 overall mark. A college star at Arizona, Pineda-Boutté is the only Division I athlete to be named first team All-America at three different positions (catcher, third base, and first base.) Her teams went to the College World Series all four years and won two National Championships and three Pac-10 Conference titles. Pineda-Boutté is also a community leader and role model for younger Latinas.

Mario Manuel Cristóbal became the first Cuban-American head football coach when he was selected at Florida International University. He is a Miami native and former University of Miami player and assistant coach. While working hard to turnaround FIU's football program, Cristóbal has also been living up to the promises he made to the South Florida community by giving a great deal of his time to make dozens of appearances, and speaking to civic groups, professional and youth organizations. As a player at the University of Miami from 1988–1992, he competed in four bowl games with the Hurricanes, helping the team to National Championships in 1989 and 1991 and earning All-Big East honors as an offensive tackle during his senior season.

Athletic Directors

At the time of this writing, there are four Latino ADs, slightly higher than the number of Latinos among FBS coaches. The ADs are Daniel G. Guerrero at the University of California, Los Angeles; Pete García at Florida International University; Rick Villarreal at the University of North Texas; and Barry Alvarez at Wisconsin.

In the 2007–08 year, only 1.6 percent of the athletics directors in Division I were Latinos and .3 percent were Latinas. In Division II, 3.0 percent of the athletics directors were Latinos and there were no Latinas. There were no Latino or Latina ADs at Division III schools.

As with coaches, Latinos should not hold their breath waiting for opportunities to move up from being the assistant or associate AD to the athletics director posts. Latinos barely have a presence as assistant or associate ADs. In the 2007–08 year, only 1.4 percent of the assistant or associate ADs in Division I were Latinos and .8 percent were Latinas. In Division II, 3.0 percent of the assistant or associate ADs were Latinos. There were no Latinas in this position in Divisions II and III. Among Division III schools, .6 percent of the assistant or associate ADs were Latinos. All of this data makes the stories of the athletics directors we are profiling here even more amazing.

Dan Guerrero has been a dear friend since the 1980s. A former UCLA baseball player, he was named as UCLA's athletic director in 2002. Under his leadership, UCLA teams have won an amazing 18 NCAA team titles in 11 different sports. He also expanded a culture that is more committed than ever to providing resources to encourage the academic development and community involvement for its student-athletes. From the start, Guerrero has emphasized diversity, gender equity, and commitment to public service.

Recently, Guerrero increased his profile on the national stage by becoming the chair of the NCAA Division I Men's Basketball Committee and second vice-president of the National Association of Collegiate Directors of Athletics (NACDA). He was on both the *Hispanic Business* magazine's 2004 list of the "Top 100 Most Influential Hispanics" and *Sport Illustrated's* 2003 ranking of the "101 Most Influential Minorities in Sports."

Rudy Dávalos was the University of New Mexico's Athletics Director for over 13 years, the third-longest tenure of any athletic director at the school. Retiring in 2006, he left behind a long legacy as an AD with previous AD positions at the University of Houston from 1987–92 and at the University of Texas-San Antonio for nine years starting in 1975. As the son of Mexican-born parents, Dávalos showed a strong commitment to achieving diversity among his staff and for supporting the youth and minorities in his community. In 2002, *Sports Illustrated* named him one of the 101 Most Influential Minorities in Sports. He hopes this accomplishment will be an inspiration to young people of all backgrounds to pursue their goals.

When Irma García was named Athletic Director of St. Francis College in 2007, she became the country's first Latina AD. García was a basketball player at St. Francis and then came back in 1988 as the eighth women's basketball coach in school history. The 27-year-old was one of the country's youngest Division I coaches. Over the next 11 years, García's players received many individual honors with 12 named to postseason Northeast Conference (NEC) teams. In addition, García's teams were among the NCAA elite in academics.

The 1998–99 team was honored by the WBCA for having the fourth highest team grade point average out of approximately 300 Division I women's basketball teams in the country. Rick Villarreal became the Director of Athletics at the University of North Texas in 2000. During his tenure, there have been 12 Sun Belt Conference championships and North Texas finished among the top three in the SBC all-sports championship standings six out of eight years. Under his watch, the school built an academic center for student-athletes and experienced a ten percent increase in student-athlete graduation rates. Villarreal oversaw the building of an $8 million athletic facility that contains a state-of-the-art training suite, administration and football offices, and brand new locker rooms.

Pete García has been the Director of Athletics at Florida International University since the fall of 2006. Born in Havana, Cuba, García's family migrated to Miami in 1967 and García has been loyal to South Florida ever since. After his arrival at FIU in the fall of 2006, he dedicated himself to giving back to the community and realized the best way to accomplish this was to build up the local college sports program. He began turning around FIU Athletics by instilling a commitment of excellence with his coaches, department staff, and student-athletes, and striving for success on the field, in the classroom, and in the community. Prior to FIU, García had worked for the Miami Dolphins and the Cleveland Browns for almost 15 years.

II

STUDENT ATHLETES

Tony Casillas

Star of the College Football Hall of Fame

by Cara-Lynn Lopresti

Courtesy of University of Oklahoma Athletics.

Tony Casillas has long been proud of his Latino heritage, but there was a point in his life where he felt the need to disguise it. Born in Tulsa, Oklahoma, on October 16, 1963, Casillas grew up in a large family of nine at a time when "being Spanish wasn't cool."[1] He lived in a primarily white neighborhood and rarely encountered different ethnic groups. While growing up, Casillas questioned whether he came from non-Latino descent because his parents opted to use the Anglo pronunciation of their name as Ca-SILL-as. Casillas commented that he "always thought our name was different than all my other relatives because their last name was pronounced Ca-SEE-yas. I asked my dad and my family, but never really got an answer. They simply didn't want to expose us to anything negative."[2] Casillas's father was indeed Spanish and his mother was Irish and Indian. However, when Casillas looks back at his childhood he remembers, "there were words in Spanish that [his] mother and father didn't want us to know, so we really didn't speak Spanish," Casillas said. "To this day, Spanish is a struggle for me."[3]

His sheltered youth is one of the "reasons he is thankful his career in football has given him a chance to be a role model for kids, demonstrating that regardless of race, color, or religion, they can achieve anything if they are determined and willing to work hard enough."[4] Casillas was an All-State football player for Tulsa East Central High School. He played baseball in the summer and threw the discus 170 feet and the shot put 60 feet as a senior in high school. He also won the state high school power lifting meet as a senior and finished the competition with a 600-pound dead lift.

In high school, Casillas disguised the pronunciation of his name, and tried to hide his ethnicity by growing a thick mustache and covering his face. However, whatever uneasiness about his ethnicity existed before, was eliminated once he went to play college football for Oklahoma University. At first, Casillas was sensitive to the racial slurs and banters that occurred in the locker rooms. However, Oklahoma's head coach and current Hall of Famer Barry Switzer, was "a master of mixing personalities and talent, no matter what ethnicity."[5] Casillas soon became comfortable with his background and was proud to represent his Hispanic heritage on the football field. He also changed his name back to the proper pronunciation of Ca-SEE-yas.

Casillas excelled both academically and athletically during his time at Oklahoma. In 1984 and 1985, he earned consensus first team All-American honors, and in 1985 won the Lombardi Award, given to the nation's top lineman. As much as opponents tried, Casillas was a force to be reckoned with. Entrenched in the middle of the Sooners' defensive line, Casillas pushed his opponents around, prompting Switzer to call him "perhaps the greatest Sooner defensive lineman ever."[6] Casillas won a national championship in 1985, and earned UPI National Lineman of the Year and Big Eight Conference Defensive Player of the Year honors. Casillas was also a strong student and was an Academic All-American in 1985 while earning a degree in public relations. After graduating from Oklahoma, the National Football Foundation named Casillas the College Defensive Player of the Decade for the 1980s. In 2004, he was inducted to the College Football Hall of Fame.

After his collegiate career, the National Football League scouting report on Casillas had nothing but positive remarks. He was known for finishing the plays, "never giving up even in a game that is out of hand,"[7] and loving to work. The Atlanta Falcons quickly jumped on the opportunity to add Casillas to their lineup by selecting him as the second overall pick in the 1986 NFL Draft. Casillas played 13 seasons in the NFL, serving as a defensive tackle for Atlanta, the New York Jets, and Dallas Cowboys. He was twice named All-Pro and helped the Cowboys win Super Bowls XXVII and XXVIII. Casillas was active in Dallas' Hispanic community during his time playing professional football. He started a college scholarship program, and spoke several times at high schools, offering Cowboys tickets to students who improved their attendance and grades. However, assisting the community was nothing new for Casillas, as he was involved with the Fellowship of Christian Athletes (F.C.A) all throughout high school. He still talks to charity groups when possible and especially enjoys being involved with disabled children. His dad is legally blind, so helping disadvantaged people has been important to him.

After his NFL career, Casillas continued to set a good example in his community. He served as president of T.C. Oil and Gas Company in Flower Mound, Texas and owns part of a company that represents business firms owned by minorities and women. In 2006, Casillas hosted the Golf Classic, which was a benefit tournament for the Dallas Can! Academy. Casillas was inducted into the Oklahoma Sports Hall of Fame in 2008 and in 2009 he opened his first restaurant, Agave Tex-Mex Grill, which reflects his wife Lisa's long history of serving Tex-Mex cuisine. However, despite all of his accomplishments, Casillas always puts everything in its proper perspective. He credits his success not to his

Courtesy of University of Oklahoma Athletics.

hard work, but instead to the people around him and to the people who believed in him. It is this humble personality that will forever earn Casillas respect and admiration within the sports community.

Notes

1. "Tony Casillas." *Jim Thorpe Foundation.* 2009. http://www.jimthorpeassoc.org/index.php?option=com_content&view=article&id=176&Itemid=6
2. Rohde, John. "Tony Casillas Shares Memories." *News OK.* August 19, 2008. http://newsok.com/tony-casillas-shares-memories/article/3285404
3. Rohde, John. "Tony Casillas Shares Memories." *News OK.* August 19, 2008. http://newsok.com/tony-casillas-shares-memories/article/3285404
4. "Tony Casillas." *Jim Thorpe Foundation.* 2009. http://www.jimthorpeassoc.org/index.php?option=com_content&view=article&id=176&Itemid=6
5. Rohde, John. "Tony Casillas Shares Memories." *News OK.* August 19, 2008. http://newsok.com/tony-casillas-shares-memories/article/3285404
6. "Casillas Receives On-Campus Salute." *The National Football Foundation and Collegiate Hall of Fame, Inc.* September 10, 2004. http://www.footballfoundation.com/news.php?id=457
7. Eskenazi, Gerald. "Pro Football; Jets' Casillas Seems to be in Right Frame of Mind." *New York Times.* October 21, 1994. http://www.nytimes.com/1994/10/21/sports/pro-football-jets-casillas-seems-to-be-in-right-frame-of-mind.html
1. "Tony Casillas," *Jim Thorpe Foundation.* 2009. http://www.jimthorpeassoc.org/index.php?option=com_content&view=article&id=176&Itemid=6
2. John Rohde, "Tony Casillas Shares Memories," *News OK.* August 19, 2008. http://newsok.com/tony-casillas-shares-memories/article/3285404
3. Ibid.
4. "Tony Casillas," *Jim Thorpe Foundation.* 2009. http://www.jimthorpeassoc.org/index.php?option=com_content&view=article&id=176&Itemid=6
5. John Rohde, "Tony Casillas Shares Memories," *News OK.* August 19, 2008. http://newsok.com/tony-casillas-shares-memories/article/3285404
6. "Casillas Receives On-Campus Salute," *The National Football Foundation and Collegiate Hall of Fame, Inc.* September 10, 2004. http://www.footballfoundation.com/news.php?id=457
7. Gerald Eskenazi, "Pro Football; Jets'Casillas Seems to be in Right Frame of Mind," *New York Times.* October 21, 1994. http://www.nytimes.com/1994/10/21/sports/pro-football-jets-casillas-seems-to-be-in-right-frame-of-mind.html

Brenda Villa

Water Polo All-American and U.S. National Team Captain

by Cara-Lynn Lopresti

Courtesy of Stanford University Media Relations.

"Every once in a while, somebody comes along to remind the sports world that performance is not always about muscle tone and chiseled abs."[1] As a 5'4", 162-pound world-class athlete, Stanford All-American and three-time Olympian, Brenda Villa is that somebody for the sport of water polo. Although the shortest and perhaps the stockiest player on the United States National Women's Water Polo Team, Villa is an incredibly quick swimmer, an intelligent passer, and skilled decision maker on defense. However, perhaps what she is best known for is her phenomenal scoring ability. When Villa is "anywhere in the attacking zone, she's a goal waiting to happen,"[2] and for this reason she is regarded as one of the best offensive players in water polo and one of the greatest Latina athletes in U.S history.

Twenty years ago Villa's parents, Ines and Rosario Villa, young apparel industry workers from Mexico, moved to the United States to raise their family. Villa and her two brothers grew up in Commerce, California just minutes from the Commerce Aquatorium, an internationally recognized swimming center that has produced numerous Olympians over the years. Villa's older brother, Edgar, was the first to take swimming and water polo lessons at the aquatorium and excelled almost immediately in both. At the age of six, Villa knew she wanted to follow in her brother's footsteps and take up water polo. Villa's mother was very reluctant at first, having never swam in her life and knowing how fast-paced, grueling, and violent the sport could be. Two years later, Villa finally got her chance, but she had to play with boys because there were not enough girls to form a team. However, going up against boys taught Villa "mental toughness and aggressiveness" and "anytime the boys would make fun of her, she would go one-on-one and put them to shame."[3] Once she went to Bell Gardens High School, Villa played with the boys' team again and was a three-time First-Team All-CIF and four-time girls First-Team All-American.

In 1998, Villa earned a scholarship to Stanford as the "most highly-sought-after female water polo player in the country."[4] However, since she was also a member of the United States National team at the time, she decided to red shirt in 1999 and 2000 to train for the Olympics. In 2001 she competed as a freshman and was named the NCAA Women's Water Polo Player of the Year, tallying a team-high 69 goals for the season. She also led her team to a second place finish at the first ever Women's Water Polo NCAA Championship. In 2002, Villa had another great season for the Cardinals with 60 goals, including 19 multiple goal games, and a NCAA Women's Water Polo Championship. She was also awarded the Peter J. Cutino Award as the top female college water polo player in the United States and was a finalist for the Women's Sports Foundation Sportswoman of the Year. In 2003, Villa was the Mountain Pacific Sports Federation Player of the Year, finishing her Stanford career as the second leading scorer in school history with 172 goals in just three seasons. Villa graduated in 2003 with a degree in Political Science.

As a member of the U.S. Senior National team since 1996, Villa has also been a strong presence at the international level, "boasting a quick and powerful shot that is known throughout the water polo world."[5] In 2000, Villa competed in her first Olympics in Sydney, Australia, which was also the first ever Women's Water Polo Olympic games. The U.S won the silver medal during the inaugural event and Villa led the team in scoring with nine goals. She also netted in the tying goal against Australia in the championship match, but ended up losing after Australia scored the winning goal with one second remaining in regulation.

In December of 2002, Villa was the United States Olympic Committee Player of the Month after helping the U.S. National Team to the 2002 FINA Women's Water Polo World Cup championship game. She led the 2002 World Cup Tournament in scoring with nine goals. In 2003, she had a team-high 13 goals to guarantee the U.S. the gold medal at the FINA Water Polo World Championship. In the 2004 Olympic Games in Athens, Villa scored four goals against Hungary and two against Russia to win a bronze medal. She led her team in scoring again with 16 goals during the 2005 FINA World Championships, making her the second highest scorer in the tournament. In 2007, Villa captained the team in three gold medal finishes including the 2007 World Championships, 2007 Pan American Games, and 2007 FINA World League. She put home 11 goals during the 2007 Pan American Games including three in a win over Venezuela. Villa was chosen as the U.S. team captain for the 2008 Beijing Olympics and guided them to the finals after scoring three goals, including the game-winner, in a 9-8 victory against Australia. The United States took home the silver medal, marking Team USA's third medal in the last three Olympics and making them the only nation to medal in all three Olympics featuring women's water polo.

Most recently, Villa captained her team to a third FINA World Championship in 2009, a record among all nations with women's water polo. Villa scored one goal in the 7-6 gold-medal win over Canada and threw in eight others during the six preliminary matches of the tournament. To Villa this victory was especially meaningful because she was "able to demonstrate what USA water polo has become in the last 10 years."[6]

Depending on the time of year, Villa also plays professionally in Italy and serves as the assistant women's coach at Cerritos College in California. However, "always attentive to her roots, Villa spends as much time as she can at her home club," serving as a "role model and hero to Latina athletes."[7] Villa also supports the Women's Sports Foundation, and is dedicated to giving women from every walk of life the opportunity to play sports and live a healthy lifestyle.

Notes

1. David Leon Moore, "Standing Tall in the Water," *USAToday*, June 23, 2004. http://www.usatoday.com/sports/olympics/athens/pool/2004-06-23-villa-water-polo_x.htm

2. Ibid.

3. David Davis, "Jumping In: Brenda Villa Proved that she Could Play with the Boys. Now She Wants to Win Olympic Gold.(Sports)(sportswoman)," *Los Angeles*, (2004), http://www.highbeam.com/doc/1G1-117450706.html

4. Wendy Lewellen, "Brenda Villa: The American Saint of Water Polo," *Women's Sport Foundation*. July 7, 2008. http://www.womenssportsfoundation.org/Content/Articles/Athletes/About-Athletes/B/Brenda-Villa-saint-of-Water-Polo.aspx

5. "Brenda Villa," 2008. *USAWater Polo.* http://www.usawaterpolo.org/National
Teams/PlayerBio.aspx?ID=33

6. "USA Women Officially World Champions; Canadian Protest Denied," *USA
Water Polo.* August 1, 2009. http://www.usawaterpolo.org/SingleNews/09-08-01/USA
_Women_Officially_World_Champions_Canadian_Protest_Denied.aspx?ReturnURL
=%2fpress.aspx

7. Wendy Lewellyn, "Brenda Villa: The American Saint of Water Polo," *Women's
Sport Foundation.* July 7, 2008. http://www.womenssportsfoundation.org/Content/Ar
ticles/Athletes/About-Athletes/B/Brenda-Villa-saint-of-Water-Polo.aspx

Lisa Fernández

College Softball and U.S. National Team Legend

by Cara-Lynn Lopresti

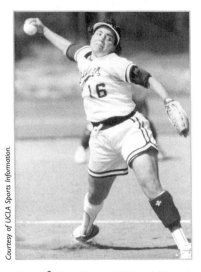

Courtesy of UCLA Sports Information.

One day at Collins Elementary, Lisa Fernández's teacher clipped a newspaper article about a softball player and wrote, "Your name will appear at the top of articles like this someday."[1] This statement could not have been more fitting as Lisa Fernández is one of the most recognizable names in softball and arguably the best pitcher and all-around softball player in U.S. and Olympic history. However, more importantly, Fernández is a "pioneer in the world of softball competition."[2] Her "incredible ability, intense drive, and relentless commitment"[3] both on and off the field transformed softball into a premier U.S. sport and paved the way for future generations of athletes to achieve their dreams.

Both Fernández and her older sister grew up watching their mother play softball in the housewives league in Lakewood, California. However, Fernández "was the one most infected with the diamond bug."[4] At four years of age Fernández was already making pitching motions and diving in the dirt. Fernández became so absorbed in the sport that "she turned the living room into a stadium, making balls out of socks and begging her parents to throw them just out of reach so she could dive for them."[5] She started playing competitively at eight years old, but struggled initially. In her first game she lost 28-0 and walked in 20 players. However, slowly but surely she developed into the outstanding player, coach, and mother she is today.

Fernández competed for UCLA from 1990 to 1993. With a 93-7 record, 74 shutouts, and 784 strikeouts Fernández led the Bruins to two national championships in 1990 and 1992 and two runner-up finishes in 1991 and 1993. She boasted a 0.22 ERA, ranking second in NCAA history. In her junior and senior seasons, Fernández had the lowest ERA in the nation with a 0.14 ERA in 1992 and a 0.25 ERA in 1993. She also finished the 1992 season with a perfect 29-0 record. Fernández threw 11 career no-hitters, two of them in the 1993 College World Series. What was even more incredible about Fernández was that she was "just as powerful at the plate" as she was with pitching, "batting .382 with 15 home runs and 128 runs batted in."[6] In her junior season she owned a .401 batting average, but "eclipsed that mark by more than 100 points in her senior campaign, batting an NCAA-best .510 with 11 homers and 45 RBI."[7] Fernández broke seven school records and ranks in the UCLA Top 10 in numerous offensive categories, including fifth in average and fourth in hits.

Fernández's outstanding performance during her collegiate career did not go unnoticed. She was a three-time winner of softball's Honda-Broderick Award, and become the first softball player to win the overall award as the top woman college athlete in the country in 1993. Fernández was also a four-time, first-team All-American, All-Region and All-Pac-10 first-team, and a three-time Pac-10 Player of the Year. In 1995, Fernández completed her degree in psychology, and in 2003 became the eighth softball player inducted into the UCLA Athletics Hall of Fame.

In addition to her prolific collegiate career, Fernández is also a three-time Olympic Gold Medalist, leading Team USA to gold medals in the 1996, 2000, and 2004 Olympic Games. During softball's inaugural appearance in the 1996 Olympics, 25 year-old Fernández posted a .47 ERA and recorded the final three outs in the United States' 3-1 gold-medal win over China. However, her impact during the first Olympics was more than just from her performance on the field. Fernández was just as intense promoting the sport as she was playing it. She "carrie[d] the heart and soul of the game upon her shoulders,"[8] and sold the sport of softball to the world.

In the 2000 Sydney Games, Fernández pitched in both the semifinal victory over Australia and the gold-medal game against Japan, and finished with a 0.47 ERA and 52 strikeouts for the Olympic tournament. Her 25 strikeouts versus Australia broke an Olympic

single-game strikeout record. In 2004, Fernández pitched the final
out of the gold-medal contest in a 5-1 victory over Australia. She
was also Team USA's leading hitter and pitcher, batting .545 (12-
for-22), which marked another Olympic record. Fernández was
chosen as an alternate for the 2008 Summer Olympics.

In 2009 Fernández entered her 11th season on the UCLA Bru-
ins coaching staff as an assistant coach. Under her direction, the
Bruins have claimed a 482-117-1 (.804) record and have won
NCAA Championships in 1999, 2003, and 2004, and Pac-10 titles in
1999 and 2002. Fernández also guided six Bruin pitchers to ten All-
American awards.

Away from softball, Lisa Fernández has been staying busy
with her family. Fernández has been married to her husband, Mike
Luján since August 2002. The couple has been devoted to raising
their three-year-old son, Antonio, in Long Beach, California.

Notes

1. Pamela Lewis, "It has Been a Family Affair for U.S. Softball's Lisa Fernández," *Knight Ridder/Tribune News Service*. 1996. http://www.highbeam.com/doc/1G1-1844 8781.html

2. "Lisa Fernández," *Real Women in Sports*. (2009). http://www.realwomeninsports .com/Fernández.php

3. Pamela Lewis, "It has Been a Family Affair for U.S. Softball's Lisa Fernández," *Knight Ridder/Tribune News Service*. 1996. http://www.highbeam.com/doc/1G1-1844 8781.html

4. "Lisa Fernández16.com," *Lisa Fernández*. 2006. http://www.lisaFernández16 .com/

5. Ibid.

6. "Lisa Fernández." *CBS Interactive*. (2009). http://www.uclabruins.com/sports/w -softbl/mtt/Fernández_lisa00.html

7. Ibid.

8. Pamela Lewis, "It Has Been a Family Affair for U.S. Softball's Lisa Fernández," *Knight Ridder/Tribune News Service*. 1996. http://www.highbeam.com/doc/1G1-1844 8781.html.

Eduardo Nájera

Chip Hilton Player of the Year Presented by the Naismith Memorial Basketball Hall of Fame

by Cara-Lynn Lopresti

A fierce competitor with a big heart, Eduardo Alonso Nájera is currently the only Mexican professional basketball player in the NBA, playing reserve forward for the New Jersey Nets. Originally from Chihuahua, Mexico, Nájera is the second Mexican-born player to be drafted and to play for the NBA, after Horacio Llamas. Over the years, Nájera "has become one of Mexico's most recognizable athletes" and "is revered among Mexico's biggest sports celebrities, up there with the great boxer Julio Cesar Chavez and former major league pitcher Fernando Valenzuela."[1] His NBA games are regularly aired on television, and he is often featured in local sports pages. Nájera is also an "athlete whom marketers in the United States and Latin America see as someone who can bridge demographics."[2] Before Nájera's success, few Mexicans were found in the history of the NBA, but now the league has become a melting pot with athletes from all over the world. Nájera has helped make this happen through his strong commitment to supporting youth minorities, giving them opportunities to succeed, and showing them that any dream is achievable if they work hard enough.

Nájera had a very successful college basketball career at the University of Oklahoma. As a major star on the team from 1997–2000, Najera led the Sooners to four consecutive NCAA tournament appearances and finished in Oklahoma's all-time top ten in nine categories, ranking "third in minutes played (3,853), fourth in steals (193), fifth in rebounds (910), sixth in blocked shots (89), seventh in field goal attempts (1,423), eighth in points scored (1,646), ninth in field goals (612), 10th in free throws (337), and 10th in free throw attempts (504)."[3] Nájera finished second in Big 12 Freshman-of-the-Year voting and was a First-Team All-Big 12 and Big-12 All-Defensive Team selection. He was also an AP Third-Team All-American and was honored with the Chip Hilton Player of the Year Award from the National Basketball Hall of Fame, an award given to a player who has demonstrated personal character both on and off the court.[4] While in college, Nájera also played for the Mexican team in the 1997 World University Games and helped them to a fourth place finish in the 1999 World University Games. Nájera was also a strong student, graduating from the University of Oklahoma with a degree in sociology.

Before being drafted into the NBA, Nájera received many promising reviews from scouts, who especially raved about his quick first step and extraordinary rebounding and scoring ability. In the 2000 NBA Draft, Nájera was initially selected in the second round (38th overall) by the Houston Rockets, but was then acquired by the Dallas Mavericks. In his first two seasons with Dallas, Nájera saw significant playing time and recorded consistent numbers. He quickly emerged as a fan favorite "because of his fearlessness and never-surrender approach."[5] He was the "6-8 fireball answer to the Mavericks' big man woes because he is the kind of player who gets under your fingernails, irritates you, and pokes and prods you."[6] However, recurrent knee injuries and arthroscopic knee surgery limited his action in his last two years in Dallas, as he missed a total of 57 games.

In 2004, Nájera was traded to the Golden State Warriors and then again to the Denver Nuggets in February of 2005, where he played well despite more injuries and another knee surgery. During the 2004–2005 season, Nájera appeared in 68 games, including 26 with Denver. He averaged 5.2 points per game and 3.6 rebounds per game in 17.4 minutes on the year and 6.9 points per game and 4.8 rebounds per game in 22.1 minutes with the Nuggets. He also scored in double figures 11 times, eight with Denver. The following year, Nájera appeared in 64 games with the Nuggets, scoring in double digits nine times and grabbing 10 rebounds or more seven times. Nájera's attempt to break up a fight in the December 2006 Knicks–Nuggets brawl was a true testament to his character.

After playing for the Nuggets, Nájera signed a four-year, $12 million contract with the New Jersey Nets. The 33 year-old is the oldest player currently on the team's roster. Serving as a team leader, Nájera is committed to developing the young New Jersey team and has stayed true to these convictions, despite offers for better pay and a chance to return to Oklahoma.

Despite all the glory that Nájera has achieved in his college and professional career, he will never forget "his roots or his fellow countrymen."[7] The moral values that he has "learned from his family and friends since his childhood" have motivated him to help "the people that are less fortunate, that continue to struggle through life."[8] Since joining the NBA, Nájera has held more than 30 basketball clinics throughout Mexico, organizing events in several cities including Monterrey, Mexico City, Guadalajara, and in the state of Chiapas. While with the Mavericks, he participated in numerous basketball clinics for the Dallas School District and the Hispanic Boys and Girls Club. In 2001, Nájera served as the United Nations Drug Control Program Goodwill Ambassador for Sports Against Drugs. Prior to the 2004–05 season, he launched the Eduardo Nájera Foundation for Latin Achievement, which gives college scholarships to underprivileged Latino children who have demonstrated outstanding academic achievement. The Foundation's motto is "In 100 years, it won't matter the car you have, the house you own, the amount of money in your bank account, it will only matter the impact that you made on a child's life," and is Nájera's "personal attempt to give back to the community by helping children discover their leadership potential through sports."[9] For several summers Nájera has hosted a basketball charity event in his hometown of Chihuahua.

In 2004, Nájera particpated in the first Basketball Without Borders Americas tournament in Rio de Janeiro, and helped to open an NBA Reading and Learning Center in an impoverished Brazilian neighborhood. He has also trained with the best young players from countries across Latin America and the Caribbean and joined with the NBA, UNICEF, and Pier 1, to raise money and awareness for children in Afghanistan. In 2006, Nájera received the Chopper Travaglini Award for his strong commitment and dedication to community service while with the Nuggets.

Notes

1. Ridgell, Patrick. "Eduardo Najera: You Can't Keep a Good Man Down: Forward for the Dallas Mavericks," (Main cover: Eduardo Najera)(Cover Story)." *Latino Leaders*. 2002. *HighBeam Research*. (July 26, 2009). http://www.highbeam.com/doc/1G1-113053361.html

2. Ibid.

3. " Uno en Uno con Eduardo Najera," NBA. http://www.nba.com/espanol/najera_transcript_010312.html

4. "Eduardo Najera," NBA. 2009. http://www.nba.com/playerfile/eduardo_najera/bio.html

5. "Mavericks'Najera Loses His Ssoft Tag With Hard Work," *The Dallas Morning News* (via Knight-Ridder/Tribune NewsService). 2002. *HighBeam Research.* (July 26, 2009). http://www.highbeam.com/doc/1G1-120561963.html

6. Ibid.

7. Almonte, Mayerlin, "Paying it Forward: A Chat with Eduardo Najera: Reserve Forward, NBA's Denver Nuggets.(OPEN INTERVIEW)(Interview)(Company overview)." Latino Leaders. 2007. *HighBeam Research.* (July 26, 2009). http://www.highbeam.com/doc/1G1-165936268.html

8. Ibid.

9. Ibid.

Jessica Mendoza

College Softball All-American and U.S. National Team Member

by Cara-Lynn Lopresti

Jessica Mendoza is an elite softball player of Mexican descent that was born in Camarillo, California on November 11, 1980. She has been an outfielder for the United States National softball team since 2001 and was inducted into the International Latin Sports Hall of Fame in 2006. That same year, Mendoza was also named the USA Softball Female Athlete of the Year and in 2008 she was chosen as the Women's Sports Foundation Sportswoman of the Year.

Mendoza started playing softball at the age of ten. In 1998 she graduated from Camarillo High School where she was named NFCA first-team All-American and Los Angeles Times Player of the Year as a senior. Mendoza was also first-team All-Ventura County, all-league, and a scholar-athlete all four years of high school and was Female Athlete of the Year in 1997 and 1998.

Courtesy of Stanford University Media Relations.

Mendoza continued to excel in softball at the collegiate, club, and national levels. From 1999–2002 she was a four-time first team All-American at Stanford, where she received a bachelor of arts in American studies and later a master's degree in Social Sciences and Education in 2003. During her sophomore year Mendoza was named Pac-10 Player of the Year, becoming the first Stanford player to earn the honor. She led the Cardinal to their first NCAA Women's College World Series appearance in 2001 and is currently the all-time team leader in batting average (.475), hits (94), doubles (70), triples (9), stolen bases (31), runs (71), and home runs (50).

Mendoza received her first gold medal as a member of the United States National team in 2001 at the U.S. Cup. The following year she was a gold medalist at the ISF World Championships where she hit .313 (10-32) with eight runs and seven RBI. Mendoza won another gold medal in 2003 at the Pan American Games and made her Olympic debut during the 2004 Athens Olympics. The U.S. team won the gold medal and Mendoza started every game in left field and went 5 for 20 (.250) with 5 runs scored and 5 RBI. In 2005, Mendoza took home three more medals, one gold and two silver medals, at the Pan Am qualifier, World Cup, and the Japan Cup, respectively. In 2006, she was a World Cup Champion, hitting 11-for-18 (.611) with a double, three homeruns, and 16 RBI. She was also a gold medalist at the ISF World Championships while going 16-for-32 (.500) with five home runs, 16 RBI, and a slugging percentage of .969.

During the 2008 pre-Olympic tour, Mendoza set a hitting record with a .495 average, 102 hits, 107 RBI, and 21 home runs. In August, Mendoza appeared in her second Olympic games in Beijing, with her team taking home the silver medal. She was the third batter for which Olympic coach Mike Candera noted 'to hit third in our order is quite an honor.'[1] She averaged .333 in 24 at bats, including four home runs and tied for first in stolen bases. She also ranked second in home runs and third in RBI.

Outside of softball, Mendoza prides herself on her closeness to her family. Mendoza's father, Gil, who played football for Fresno State, mother Karen, and three siblings mean the world to her. She is also deeply in love with her husband, Adam Burks, a U.S. Marine, whom she married in 2006. Some of Mendoza's fondest memories are when her entire family comes "together after months of not seeing one another and we laugh so hard we cry and our cheeks go numb."[2] For her those moments were the "best kind of laughter."[3]

In addition to her family, Mendoza also enjoys being involved in the community and especially helping children. She loves to "look in a child's eyes" and see that she has made a "difference in their life."[4] Mendoza credits her passion for volunteerism to her father, who, after getting in trouble as a child, had his life changed because a coach took him under his wing and introduced him to sports. After hearing this story, Mendoza developed a "you never know who you can help philosophy and found an outlet to apply it."[5] Mendoza now passionately speaks at schools nationwide about the importance of education and has helped provide grants totaling in the millions to close gaps in education for disadvantaged students throughout the United States. As a board member on the Women's Sports Foundation, Mendoza helped introduce GoGirlGo! programs in Chicago and San Antonio. GoGirlGo! "helps inner-city girls get active, stay healthy, and learn skills such as leadership, confidence, body image, and self-esteem."[6] She is also on the athlete advisory council for the Bay Area Women's Sports Initiative and a board member for the National Education Association. Mendoza is also known for her involvement in politics. Mendoza helped create awareness and supported an end to the genocide in the Darfur region of Sudan. In 2008, she was one of five Olympians chosen for the U.S. Army Goodwill Tour of Afghanistan, to visit soldiers and hospitals in Afghanistan.

Mendoza has also been playing a crucial role in promoting the sport of softball, especially following the decision to remove the sport from the 2012 Olympic Games. Mendoza has traveled across the globe as a softball ambassador to areas where it is rarely played. As the president of the Women's Sports Foundation, she has also served as an athlete ambassador for the ISF's "Back Softball" campaign for Olympics reinstatement. Most recently, though, Mendoza has been dedicated to taking care of her newborn son, Caleb.

Notes

1. "Women's Sports Foundation Honors Athletic Achievement at Its 29th Annual Salute to Women in Sports." *U.S. Newswire.* 2008. http://www.highbeam.com/doc/1P2-19316449.html

2. "Jessica Mendoza," *USASoftballI. 2009.* http://www.usasoftball.com/bios.asp?uid=7803Ibid.

4. Ibid.

5. Jeff Latzke, "Making a pitch for softball." *The Boston Globe.* 2009. http://www.highbeam.com/doc/1P2-20407016.html

6. "Jessica Mendoza," *USASoftballI. 2009.* http://www.usasoftball.com/bios.asp?uid=780

Stephanie Cox (formerly Stephanie López)

College Soccer All-American and First Latina to Play on U.S. Women's National Team

by Cara-Lynn Lopresti

Stephanie Cox, formerly Stephanie López, is recognized as a pioneer in women's soccer. With her distinguished college and international career, Lopez-Cox is now considered one of the best soccer defenders in the world and is the first player of Latin descent to play on the United States women's national team. However, what is perhaps more incredible than her soccer skills is how "easy, down-to-earth, and caring"[1] of a person she is. Born on April 3, 1986 in Los Gatos, California, Cox's parents raised her while serving as foster parents to 90 children. Despite their responsibilities at home, the

Courtesy of University of Portland Athletics.

López's were dedicated to bettering the world as missionaries. The family made several trips to Mexico to serve meals to American missionaries that were working there. Cox and her family served meals to American missionaries in Mexico, helped paint an orphanage in Egypt, and traveled to the Bahamas to clear land for a new learning center. Inspired by these childhood experiences, Cox "emerged as a grounded . . . compassionate and selfless woman," which "translates on the soccer field,"[2] as she is one of the most composed and skilled leaders on the field.

As a standout defender at Elk Grove High School, Cox guided her soccer team to league championships in 2001

and 2002. She was an all-section team her junior and senior years, won the NSCAA youth All-American award, and was a *Parade* Magazine All-American.

In 2003, Cox attended the University of Portland where she had a legendary college career as a four-year starter for the Pilots. While leading the team to a 76-11 record, Cox was a three-time NSCAA All-American selection, four-time First-Team All-West Coast Conference selection, and a two-time WCC Defensive Player of the Year. In 2008, she was also named the Bill Hayward Female Amateur Athlete of the Year for 2007 at the 56th annual Oregon Sports Awards.

Cox had an outstanding freshman campaign at Portland, playing a key role in the team's defense being ranked second nationally in shutouts with 16 and ninth nationally in goals against average, (0.58). After red-shirting her sophomore year to compete at the U-19 FIFA World Championships, Cox led Portland to an undefeated record of 23-0-2 and a 2005 NCAA Championship. The following year, she started in 13 games and scored her first collegiate goal. In 2007 she missed half the season while helping the U.S. to a third-place finish at the World Cup. Cox had the opportunity to forgo her remaining collegiate eligibility and become a salaried player with the national team, but prior commitments brought her back to Portland to finish her senior season. Staying true to her values, Cox commented on the decision stating, "I have my whole life to earn money . . . It's important to be loyal to the program."[3] After returning to the team she led the Pilots to an undefeated run in conference play, the WWC title, and an NCAA playoff berth. Cox also scored two goals and two assists, and helped establish a school record with nine consecutive shutouts.

Cox was also exceptional off the field, graduating with a 3.77 cumulative grade-point average as a psychology major despite her numerous calls to the national team throughout her collegiate career. She was a three-time West Coast Conference All-Academic Team and made the Dean's List seven times. In 2007, Cox was honored as the Lowe's Senior CLASS Award winner, for her leadership and achievements in the classroom, the community, and on the playing field.

Cox had been in the national team system since the age of 14. She gained a reputation for her durability and saw extensive playing time at an elite level. Cox made her debut with the U.S. Under-21 National Team in 2005 while playing every minute of all four games in the Nordic Cup, helping the U.S. claim the championship. She captained the U-20 squad at the 2006 FIFA U-20 Women's World Championship to lead the U.S. to a fourth place showing.

In 2005, Cox was selected to the full Women's National Team and became the youngest player on the squad. She earned her first cap at the 2005 Algarve Cup in Portugal where she played in the third match of the tournament against Denmark. The following year she earned her second and third caps at the 2006 Algarve Cup, where she also made her first career start, going 90 minutes in a 4-1 victory over France.

Cox eventually earned a consistent starting slot on the national team in 2007 with her role becoming even more important after Heather Mitts went down with a torn ACL. She started 18 of the 21 games she played, "developing into an impact player on the back line."[4] She started all six games at the 2007 FIFA Women's World Cup, her first world championship at the senior level. She played all but 45 minutes of the tournament helping the team to win the bronze medal. In 2008, she played in 13 matches for the USA heading into the Olympics, starting eight. As "an experienced, battle-tested defender,"[5] Cox helped the Women's National Team win a gold medal at the 2008 Beijing Olympic Games. Cox and teammate Amy Rodríguez, made history during the 2008 Games as the first two women of Hispanic origin to represent the United States in Olympic soccer competition.

Similar to her dedication to soccer, Cox is also very committed to helping individuals and organizations in need. In addition to her missionary work with her family, Cox has served as a volunteer cook at a Ronald McDonald House in the Portland area. In 2005 she assisted with the creation of a Hurricane Katrina fundraiser and recently serves as a spokesperson for Casey Family Services, a foster care organization that serves seven states throughout the U.S.

Following the Olympics, Cox returned to her hometown as a hero and spoke to the students at Markofer, the elementary school she had attended, about perseverance, the importance of family, and how to perform well in school.

Cox now lives happily in Gig Harbor, Washington with her husband, Brian Cox, whom she married in December of 2007. Brian was also a standout athlete having played baseball for Portland University. Currently, she plays professionally in the Women's Professional Soccer League for the Los Angeles Sol.

Notes

1. "Of Girls and Goals," *Latina Style*. (2009). http://www.latinastyle.com/currentissue/v11-5/f-wearing.html

2. Marlen Garcia, "USA Soccer's López is Well-grounded," *USAToday*. August 10, 2007. http://www.usatoday.com/sports/soccer/2007-08-10-López_N.htm

3. Ibid.

4. "Stephanie López," *U.S. Soccer Federation*.2009. http://www.ussoccer.com/bio/index.jsp_10962.html

5. John Philip Wyllie, "U.S. Hopes in China May Rest with Their Depth," *La Prensa San Diego*. 2008. http://www.highbeam.com/doc/1P3-1549156271.html

Amy Rodríguez

College Soccer All-American
and U.S. National Team Member

by Cara-Lynn Lopresti

Soccer sensation Amy Joy Rodríguez was born on February 17, 1987, on the same birthday of her childhood sports idol, Michael Jordan. Today the striker from Lake Forest, California has even more in common with Jordan, as they both share a similar "passion and desire to compete and win at the highest levels"[1] of their respective sports. Whether it was leading the University of Southern California Trojans to the 2007 NCAA Championship or providing the game-winning assist in the 2008 Olympic gold-medal match, "Rodríguez consistently showcases her skills on the game's biggest stages."[2] At the young age of 22, Rodríguez has achieved things that most athletes could only ever dream of, and what is even more remarkable is that her career is just beginning.

In her earlier playing days, Rodríguez was named the 2005 Gatorade National Player of the Year and the National Player of the Year by *Parade* Magazine, EA Sports, and NSCAA after scoring 17 goals for her high school in her senior season. The *Orange County Register* and the *Los Angeles Times* both recognized her as the Girl's Soccer Player of the Year. In 2005, she won her second national championship with her club, Laguna Hills Eclipse.

Following high school, Rodríguez went to play for USC as the nation's top recruit. She was initially attracted to the school because her family lived an hour away and USC women's soccer coach Jim Millinder had known Rodríguez's mother since high school. However, most of all, Rodríguez wanted to play for the team because she saw it as an "opportunity to build something new, to create a foundation of success for the future."[3] Rodríguez lived up to her promise, transforming the Trojans into a National Champion just three years after one of the worst seasons in USC soccer history. In her freshman year, Rodríguez was the Pac-10 Freshman of the Year and was the first USC player on the NSCAA All-American team since fellow Trojan Isabelle Harvey earned the distinction in 2000. In

2006, Rodríguez missed USC's first four games while competing internationally, but gained her starting spot quickly after her return, scoring the game-winning goal in USC's upset victory against Santa Clara in the NCAA's First Round. Rodríguez appeared in all 25 games as a junior, starting in 21 matches, with her team winning the NCAA championship. She also led the Trojans in scoring that year, with 10 goals and three assists for 23 points. By her senior year Rodríguez emerged as a lethal weapon on the front line. She had an "unmatched explosiveness and dangerous scoring ability" that was "coupled with an astute knack for setting up her teammates to generate USC's offensive strikes."[3] With eight goals and four assists, Rodríguez made it to the third-round of the 2008 NCAA championship in her final season with the Trojans. She ended her collegiate career with 31 goals, including nine game-winning goals, 17 assists, and 79 total points.

While playing in high school and college, Rodríguez quickly rose up the ranks of the Women's National Soccer teams, eventually becoming the first USC soccer player to win an Olympic medal. In 2004, she was a late addition to the junior national team that competed in the under-19 FIFA World Championship in Thailand. In her first international match at that level, she scored a goal and an assist in a 3-0 victory over South Korea. After starting most of the tournament and finishing with two goals and two assists, Rodríguez worked her way up to the under-21 national team, playing in the 2005 Nordic Cup championship team in Sweden. Soon after, she was named to the U.S. Women's National team as the youngest player and only high school athlete on the roster. One month later, Rodríguez became the second Latina-American woman to ever play on the senior team, earning her first two caps at the prestigious Algarve Cup in Portugal. Rodríguez admitted that she was intimidated playing for the team, stating it was tough "playing against these girls and proving yourself"[4] to a whole new set of people. However, by 2008 Rodríguez became a mainstay on the team, tallying her first two international goals at the Four Nations Cup in China. She also scored winning goals against Brazil in the Peace Queen Cup and in the Olympic send-off match in Commerce City, Colorado. Rodríguez now stakes "her claim as one of the United States' best goal scorers."[5] According to Abby Wambach, the U.S. team's leading scorer who broke her leg before the 2008 Games, Rodríguez is "one of the fastest players on our team, and I think as long as we can keep putting her in positions to score goals for us she'll continue to do so . . . when she gets those opportunities and chances, she capitalizes on them."[6] Rodríguez did capitalize on her chances during the 2008 Beijing Olympics when she made the game-winning assist in the finals to win the gold medal. She has now appeared 38 times for the U.S. Women´s Team, scoring six international goals and six assists. In the spring of 2009 Amy "A-Rod" Rodríguez embarked on another journey as a forward for the professional soccer team, the Boston Breakers. Rodríguez has played a key role for the Breakers since being selected with the No. 1 overall pick in the Women's Professional Soccer (WPS) inaugural draft. She notched her first goal in a 2-0 win over the Chicago Red Stars in June and it is only a matter of time before she will add a WPS championship to her long list of accomplishments.

Notes

1. Sean Grybos, "Goal.com Profile: Boston Breakers' Amy Rodriguez," *Goal.com*. April 22, 2009. http://www.goal.com/en-us/news/66/united-states/2009/04/23/1224394/goalcom-profile-boston-breakers-amy-rodriguez

2. Ibid.

3. Jeffrey Treem, "Rodriguez to Join USC Soccer After Becoming Youngest U.S. Team Member," *University Wire*. 2005. http://www.highbeam.com/doc/1P1-107486083.html.

4. "Amy Rodriguez," 2009. http://usctrojans.cstv.com/sports/w-soccer/mtt/rodriguez_amy00.html

5. Wyllie, John Philip. "Rodriguez Hopes to Make Impact at Summer Olympics," La Prensa San Diego.2008. http://www.highbeam.com/doc/1P3-1574487171.html

6. Lucas Shaw, "Amy Rodriguez is 'A-Rod'of U.S. Soccer," *Los Angeles Times*. August 5, 2008. http://articles.latimes.com/2008/aug/05/sports/sp-olyrodriguez5

7. Ibid.

LATINO COACHES IN COLLEGE SPORT

August "Augie" Garrido

College Baseball Groundbreaker

by Jared Bovinet

Courtesy of Cal Poly Athletics Media Relations.

With more than 1,600 career victories, August "Augie" Edmun Garrido, Jr. is the all-time winningest baseball coach in NCAA Division I history. His storied career ranks him in national baseball lore, as his list of accomplishments demonstrates. As the head coach at the University of Texas at Austin since 1996, he has led the Longhorns to five appearances in the College World Series, four Big 12 Conference Championships, three league tournament titles, and the National Championship in 2002 and 2006. He has earned National Coach of the Year honors six times and made headlines for becoming the first coach to lead teams from different schools to national titles (Texas and Cal State Fullerton) and one of three coaches to win five or more national championships.

While he has always valued all aspects of baseball, it is his emphasis on the mental side of the game that differentiates Garrido from so many other coaches. He has always placed importance on the process of failing and how his teams can become mentally stronger because of losses. He also highlights the necessity of understanding the game. He claims that "no corked bat or tainted ball has ever been as potent a weapon on the field of play as the mind of a knowledgeable ballplayer."[1] No one can argue with this strategy, as Garrido's career wins speak for themselves. And despite his amazing success on the field, he places more emphasis on helping his players learn life lessons through baseball. In addition, he challenges players to pursue what they love, whether it is baseball or another interest, and to find balance in the pursuit. Garrido reflected, "I want to help (players) themselves become what they want to be through the fundamentals of baseball. Baseball is nothing more than another classroom in the educational process. Really, baseball is a metaphor for life."[2]

Garrido's interest in baseball formed long before he started coaching. As a child growing up in Vallejo, California, he could very well have followed in his father's footsteps by working at the local shipyard. The young Garrido took an interest in baseball, however. When he told his father about his goal of playing college baseball, his father was skeptical and doubted his ability to play in college. His son responded by growing more determined than ever.

He realized his dream when he enrolled as a player at Fresno State University in the late 1950s. While there, he earned all-conference honors and played in the 1959 World Series. Following college, Garrido signed to play with the Cleveland Indians and played six seasons in the minor leagues.

Garrido began his coaching career at a high school in California in 1966 and his collegiate coaching career at San Francisco State three years later. He then coached at Cal Poly San Luis Obispo for three seasons, where he also earned a graduate degree in education. After his three years at Poly San Luis Obispo, Garrido arrived at Cal State Fullerton where he left an indelible mark by leading the university to the College World Series and defeating the University of Southern California, a five-time national champion, along the way. He led the team to four national titles and a .694 win percentage during his 15 seasons.

In 1988, Garrido accepted the head coaching job at the University of Illinois. In Champaign, the team won two Big Ten titles and twice went to the NCAA Tournament. He returned to Fullerton in 1990, where he helped the program win its third national championship and compile a 57-9 record.

When Garrido arrived in Austin in 1997, he had the responsibility of following Cliff Gustafson, another legend in his own right. The Longhorn baseball team is sometimes referred to as the New York Yankees of college baseball, with 71 conference championships and five national championships. Garrido welcomed the challenge. Although the team struggled in its first two seasons, his persistence paid off and the team has since made nine NCAA tournaments and five College World Series appearances.

Garrido's influence is not limited to the realm of baseball; he has touched the lives of many outside America's pastime as well. When Texas women's basketball coach Gail Goestenkors had to make the difficult decision between remaining at Duke University or becoming the head coach at Texas, she consulted with Garrido. "He is a person very much in the moment, in the present. He speaks from the heart."[3] Goestenkors ended up joining Garrido at the University of Texas at Austin.

Friendships in Garrido's life extend to Hollywood. His longtime friend, Kevin Costner, invited him to play the role of the New York Yankees manager in the 1999 movie *For Love of the Game*. The two met when Garrido coached at Cal-State Fullerton and the Texas premiere of the movie took place at a fundraiser on the campus of the University of Texas to benefit the UT baseball program.

Among his many awards, Garrido has been inducted into the Latin American International Sports Hall of Fame, the Texas Sports Hall of Fame, and the Titan Athletics Hall of Fame in California. Furthermore, he was inducted into the Fresno State Hall of Fame in 1993 and named Alumnus of the Year in athletics in 2002. The Major League Baseball Directors of Player Development named him one of the nation's top three baseball teachers, as evidenced by his having coached three National Players of the Year, 44 All-Americans, 135 All-league selections, and 82 professional players.

What people find even more inspiring than all his wins and accomplishments is the humility and wisdom which define Garrido as a coach and leader. "The winning doesn't belong to me . . . No general ever won a war by himself,"[4] he said. Garrido is currently writing a book that includes much of the wisdom he has learned in his more than forty years of coaching. Given his tremendous level of success, there will surely be great demand to discover the life of a champion both on and off the baseball field.

Notes

1. University of Texas Sports, "Augie Garrido," http://www.texassports.com/sports/m-basebl/mtt/garrido_augie00.html.

399 Ibid. ??Where did this come from??

2. Michael Freer, "Garrido Sets Wins Record with Passion for Teaching," *ESPN .com.* July 3, 2007. http://sports.espn.go.com/ncaa/news/story?id=2922813.

3. Ibid.

Joseph "Joe" Kapp

First Latino Football Head Coach at Division I-A School

by Cara-Lynn Lopresti

Joseph Kapp has had many illustrious careers in his storied life as a Latin American. He was a standout college and professional football player, actor and movie producer, head college football coach, and most recently a business entrepreneur and motivational speaker. However, Kapp is perhaps most known for his long successful history in sports. He was the 1969 NFL Player of the Year, the 1982 National College Coach of the Year, and became a member

Courtesy of Joe Kapp.

of the Laredo Latin American International Sports Hall of Fame in 2001. He is also "the only player to quarterback in an NFL Super Bowl, CFL Grey Cup and NCAA Rose Bowl games, and is the last quarterback to throw seven touchdown passes in an NFL game."[1] In addition, Kapp's unprecedented accomplishments as a Latino athlete, coach, and businessman have also broken down barriers and opened doors for future minorities.

Kapp was born March 19, 1938 in Santa Fe, New Mexico, but moved often as a child from New Mexico to San Francisco to Salinas and then to Newhall, California. When Kapp's parents moved to California, they looked "to find any work that they could get"[2] so they could support the family. His father primarily worked in sales, while his mother took a position in the food service industry. Kapp's Latino heritage comes from his mother who is of Spanish and Mexican descent. His father has a German background, but actually speaks better Spanish than English.

Sports became a part of Kapp's life at a very early age because it was immersed in the culture of his neighborhood. According to

Kapp, "if you were not working you were playing sports."[3] The boys especially enjoyed boxing, football, and basketball and also idolized their favorite professional teams and players. Listening on the radio to the much-anticipated Friday night fights with boxer, Joe Lewis, was among the most popular activities. By seventh grade Kapp really started thinking seriously about pursing a career in sports. During that year, Kapp went on a trip to the University of California, Berkeley with his teacher, Pamelina Brunelli, and friend, Everett Alvarez. Alvarez and Kapp immediately fell in love with the university and vowed that they would play football there one day. Alvarez was "the first American POW in Vietnam, enduring more than eight years of captivity and torture."[4] However, Kapp's dream to play for the Golden Bears did become a reality.

While at Berkeley, Kapp quickly "became a great leader" on the team and "intimidated Cal's opposition by running over opposing linebackers and calling out anyone who dared talk or take a cheap shot at his teammates."[5] He led the Golden Bears football team in passing and total offense for three straight years (1956–58), and was named Most Valuable Player for California in 1958. Kapp was also named first-team All-American by *Football News* and *Time* Magazine. As a senior, Kapp led the Golden Bears to the Rose Bowl following a 1-9 season, making it one of the biggest season turnarounds in college football history. When asked about Kapp's athletic abilities, John Ralston, an assistant coach on the California Rose Bowl team and now working with the College Football Hall of Fame said, "In fifty-some odd years being around some top-level players in the NFL and college, Joe Kapp was the one guy who could start in all 22 positions in college football . . . that tells you how competitive he was"[6] While at California, Kapp also competed on the varsity basketball team, playing on Pete Newell's NCAA Championship basketball team in 1959. He graduated from the University of California that same year.

After being drafted by the Washington Redskins in the 1959 NFL draft, Kapp opted to play in Canada with the Calgary Stampeders of the Canadian Football League (CFL). In his second year with the team, Kapp led Calgary to their first playoff appearance in years. In 1961, the BC Lions entered into a major trade with the Calgary Stampeders, trading four starting players for Kapp. In 1962, after an extensive rehab program for his knee and under new head coach Dave Skrien, the Lions finished the season with a 7-9 record. Kapp had an excellent year, throwing 28 touchdowns and passing for 3279 yards. He also added 183 rushing yards on 51 carries. However, the trade really paid off for the Lions the following two years when Kapp guided the team to a Grey Cup appearance in 1963 and to their first Grey Cup victory in 1964. After the 1963 season, Kapp became the first B.C. Lion to receive the Jeff Nicklin Memorial Trophy as the Most Valuable Player of the Western Conference. He was also named to the CFL All-Stars on offense in his championship season. Kapp played a total of eight years in the CFL, passing for 22,925 yards, and leading the league in passing yardage from 1962 to 1965.

In 1967, Kapp decided to return to the United States to play professional football. Many NFL teams were heavily pursuing him at that time as the 6'2, 215-pound Kapp had proven he was now a reliable quarterback, fierce competitor, and a great leader. Kapp eventually signed with the NFL's Minnesota Vikings in a multi-player trade between the CFL and NFL teams. In 1968, he took the team to their first ever playoff appearance and the following year Kapp led the Vikings to a 12-2 record, and a trip to Super Bowl IV.

During the 1970 season, Kapp signed the most lucrative contract in the league with a four-year deal for the Boston Patriots. At the end of the year the NFL commissioner, Pete Rozelle, tried to require that Kapp sign a Standard Player Contract. However, Kapp, not "wanting to accept certain aspects of how "they", the NFL did business,"[7] refused to sign the contract. In 1971 Kapp's 12-year professional football career came to an end. Soon after he engaged in a multi-million dollar anti-trust lawsuit against the NFL claiming the standard NFL contract was a restraint of trade. The 9th circuit court in California ended up granting Kapp a summary judgment, indicating that the NFL's actions had indeed violated antitrust laws. By challenging the NFL, Kapp was instrumental in increasing the earning potential for future athletes and opened the doors for the "powerful contracts that players now enjoy today."[8] The lawsuit also led to the NFL changing their rules surrounding free agency.

After his professional football career, Kapp went to Hollywood and became a popular character in major films and TV shows. He continued his acting career until the mid 80s, appearing in shows and movies, such as *Adam-12*, *Medical Center*, *Two-Minute Warning*, *Breakheart Pass*, *The Frisco Kid*, and *Climb an Angry Mountain*. Kapp's most notable role was the bully prison guard in the box-office hit movie, *The Longest Yard*, where he also served as the Technical Coordinator on set.

In 1982, Kapp was hired as the head football coach at the University of California, Berkeley. In his first year as head coach at his alma mater, he was voted the Pac-10 Coach of the Year. During that year Kapp also orchestrated one of the greatest plays in the history of college football in a victory over archrival Stanford. "The Play" was a five-lateral kickoff return by California to score the winning touchdown in the final 4 seconds of the Big Game. After witnessing the determination and teamwork among his players that day, Kapp coined the phrase, "The Bear will not quit, the Bear will not die!"[9] Kapp finished his career as California's head coach in 1986 with another victory over the Cardinal, ending with a Big Game record of 3-2.

During his tenure as quarterback, college coach, and business leader, Kapp compiled a number of awards and honors. In 1969 he was given the Vince Lombardi Award and the F.C.A Hall of Fame Award. The following year *Sports Illustrated* dubbed Kapp "The Toughest Chicano" on a cover of its weekly magazine. In 1985, 1993, and 1999 he joined the Canadian Football, the University of California Sports, and the British Columbia Sports Hall of Fames, respectively. In 1993 he earned the City of Hope Cancer Center's "The Spirit of Life Award." Kapp followed that with the 1997 Society of Hispanic Professional Engineers (SHPE) Award and the 1999 National "Breaking the Barriers" Award by the Hispanic Employee Association. Most recently, Kapp was honored by the National Council of La Raza and its Board of Directors with the 2003 Roberto Clemente Award for Sports Excellence "because of his renowned excellence in the world of sports and commitment to the advancement of Hispanic America." However, even with all these accomplishments and awards, the one thing Kapp is most proud of about his life is "his love and care for his family."[10] He has three wonderful children and currently resides in Los Gatos, California with his wife. Kapp and his brother, Larry, own Kapp's Pizza Bar & Grill in Mountain View, California, which was established in 1984 and contains memorabilia from Kapp's career and the infamous "Big Play."

Kapp also spends time as a motivational speaker and spokesperson, delivering messages "about life and leadership and the football skills that can be applied to living a successful life outside of the playing fields."[11] One of Kapp's topics of speeches is dedicated to the impact of Latinos on American sports and society. He is also currently the director of the "What Do You Want To Be Foundation." The goal of the foundation is to "share with young people the opportunity to be what they want in life."[12]

Notes

1. "Joe Kapp.com.," 2009. http://www.joekapp.com/home.html
2. "Joseph Kapp." Interview with author, November 20, 2009.
3. Ibid.
4. "Golden Oldie," November 12, 2009. http://sports.espn.go.com/travel/news/story?id=4647075
5. "50 Greatest Golden Bears—Joe Kapp," *Tightwad Hill*. January 3, 2007. http://tightwad-hill.blogspot.com/2007/01/50-greatest-golden-bears-2-joe-kapp.html
6. "Joe Kapp—Quarterback—B.C.Lions—1961–66," *British Columbia Lions*. April 12, 2004. http://www.geocities.com/cfl_historical/Kapp.Joe.htm
7. "Joseph Kapp." Interview with author, November 20, 2009.
8. Ibid.
9. "Joe Kapp—Quarterback—B.C.Lions—1961–66," *British Columbia Lions*. April 12, 2004. http://www.geocities.com/cfl_historical/Kapp.Joe.htm
10. "Joseph Kapp." Interview with author, November 20, 2009.
11. Gavin McMeeking, "Pizza, Football, and Joe Kapp." *The Daily Californian*. November 15, 2000. http://www.dailycal.org/article/3928/pizza_football_and_joe_kapp
12. "Joseph Kapp." Interview with author, November 20, 2009.

Barry Álvarez

College Football Groundbreaker

by Cara-Lynn Lopresti

Courtesy of University of Wisconsin Athletics.

When Barry Álvarez arrived at the University of Wisconsin in 1990, the Badgers football team had compiled a 9-36 record during the previous four seasons and attendance at Camp Randall Stadium had plummeted to 54 percent of its capacity. The program was in dire need of change and obtained that change when Álvarez joined the staff as the head football coach and later as the Director of Athletics. Initially, Álvarez "had to overcome a losing mentality and a roster laden with players better suited for the Division II and Division III level."[1] However, over the next 19 years, Álvarez's "tremendous work ethic" and "charismatic leadership"[2] revitalized Badger Athletics. He became the winningest coach in school history with a record of 118-73-4, and coached four of the five winningest teams in school history. As Athletic Director, Álvarez has now "made a lasting impression on the [entire] Wisconsin sports scene," transforming "the culture of athletics at the UW."[3]

Álvarez's parents, Anthony and Alvera, were Spanish immigrants who settled in a small mining town in western Pennsylvania. The family lived modestly in a house no larger than Álvarez's current office. However, despite their poor living situations, Anthony and Alvera were committed to supporting and motivating their son, so that he could make a better life for himself. In 1965, Álvarez was able to "escape the dreary realities of his rough-hewn, small-town world"[4] when he was recruited to play college football at Nebraska. From that point on, he was devoted to achieving excellence and vowed that he would never need to return home and work in a steel mill like the majority of the other residents did. Álvarez achieved his goal of excellence during his three seasons at Nebraska, leading the team to a 25-7 record and playing in both the Sugar and Orange

Bowls. In 1967, he was the leading tackler for the Cornhuskers, who were the top defensive unit in the country that year. Álvarez was equally motivated with his academics, earning his bachelor's degree from Nebraska in 1969 and then a master's degree two years later. After a brief NFL tryout with the Minnesota Vikings, Álvarez changed paths and decided to become a coach. His first coaching position was as an assistant coach at Lincoln Northeast High in Nebraska. He remained there for three years before he was finally given his opportunity to take on the head coach role at Lexington High from 1974–75. His final head coaching position was at Iowa's Mason City High where he was head coach from 1976–78, capturing a 4A state title in his final year. Álvarez received his college coaching start in 1979 as Iowa's assistant coach under Hayden Fry. In the eight years that Álvarez was with the Hawkeyes, Iowa appeared in six bowl games and went 61-33-1. Álvarez left Iowa after the 1986 season to become the linebackers coach at Notre Dame under Lou Holtz. Álvarez was promoted three times in three seasons and helped the Fighting Irish to a 32-5 overall record and national title in 1988.

After learning of Álvarez's success at Notre Dame, the former Wisconsin Director of Athletics Pat Richter decided to hire him as Wisconsin's new head football coach. Álvarez "always had a vision of what [he] wanted to do, and at what level"[5] and it was at Wisconsin where he would achieve these dreams. During Álvarez's inaugural season, the Badgers still struggled, ending the season with a 1-10 record. However, Wisconsin was within striking distance entering the fourth quarter in 10 games, and had the third-best attendance gain nationally. The following season, Wisconsin improved its win total by four games, the fourth-largest improvement in the NCAA. By 1993, the Badgers were Big Ten co-champions, defeated UCLA in the Rose Bowl, and finished ranked in the Top 5.

The newfound success of the football program under Álvarez's leadership "ignited and heightened the interest in Badger sports" and allowed "the school's entire athletic department to blossom into one of the nation's finest and most respected organizations in college sports."[6] Over the next 12 seasons, the football team continued to soar during a time of dominance known as the Álvarez era. In 1998, the team had its best season in school history to that date, with an 11-1 record and a 38-31 victory over sixth ranked UCLA at the Rose Bowl. The following season the team went 10-2, finished a

consensus fourth in the polls and defeated five ranked teams for the first time in its history. The Badgers won their final eight games and led the Big Ten in scoring offense and scoring defense. In 2005, the Álvarez era ended in fashion with a stunning 24-10 upset win over seventh-ranked Auburn in the Capital One Bowl. The victory also marked Álvarez's 195th game as a Badger head coach.

Álvarez closed out his final year with the highest bowl winning percentage of all-time (8-3, .727). He became the 10th coach in Big Ten history with 100 or more wins at one conference school. For his team's accomplishments, Álvarez was named National Coach of the Year in 1993, Big Ten Coach of the Year in 1993 and 1998, Victor Award's 1999 National Coach of the Year and 2004 AFCA Region 3 Coach of the Year. Álvarez was also a finalist for ESPN's College Football Coach of the Decade Award in 1999.

In 2000, Álvarez was named Associate Athletic Director, and then became Wisconsin's Director of Athletics in 2004, operating in a dual role as both football coach and Athletic Director. Álvarez retired from coaching at the conclusion of the 2005 season, so he could concentrate on running Wisconsin's athletic program. Under the new leadership, Wisconsin has experienced success in a variety of its sports, winning 10 team national titles and 20 Big Ten regular-season or tournament championships. In his first year working exclusively as Director of Athletics, Wisconsin won four national titles. The following year the Badger student-athletes recorded the highest cumulative grade-point average for a fall term in department history. Wisconsin continued the tradition of excellence by winning two more national titles and finishing 16th in the 2006–07 NACDA Directors Cup standings, the program's highest finish since 1993–94.

Although most of his day is consumed with his responsibilities as Athletic Director, Álvarez is still devoted to spending time with his family and helping the community. He is a loving husband, father, and grandfather to his wife, Cindy, daughters, Dawn and Stacy, son, Chad, and grandchildren Joe, Jake, Jackson, Grace, Scarlett, and Barry. In 2000, Álvarez and his wife made a quarter-million dollar contribution to the school's foundation by endowing a football scholarship at Wisconsin. The two were also co-campaign chairs in the effort to bring a Gilda's Club to Madison, a free support center for families dealing with cancer, which opened in the fall of 2008. That same year Álvarez was appointed as one of the chairs of the NCAA's Football Academic Enhancement Group, which was formed to review and recommend improvements for the Academic Progress Report rating. He also serves on the NCAA Football Issues Committee and on the Board of Directors of the Midwest Athletes Against Childhood Cancer Fund. For his impact on Wisconsin Athletics and the greater community, Álvarez was named one of the "100 Most Influential Hispanics" by Hispanic Business in 2001 and "Person of the Year" by the Big Ten Club of Southern California in 2008.

Notes

1. Jeff Potrykus, "Barry Álvarez at Wisconsin; So Long Coach," Álvarez Looks Back at His Tenure at UW, Where he Took a Program From the Lowest Depths to Great Highs," *The Milwaukee Journal Sentinel.* 2006 http://www.highbeam.com/doc/1P2-6376083.html

2. Associated Press, "Barry's New Mission; Álvarez Looks to Take Thriving UW Athletic Department to Next Level," *Telegraph—Herald*, 2005. http://www.highbeam.com/doc/1P2-11183854.html

3. "Barry Álvarez.," University of Wisconsin—Madison, Division of Intercollegiate Athletics,(2009). http://www.uwbadgers.com/bios/?staffid=100

4. Andy Baggot, "Return to His Roots Barry Álvarez has Come a Long Way From His Native Western Pennsylvania," SPORTS)." *Wisconsin State Journal.* 2003. http://www.highbeam.com/doc/1G1-107152882.html

5. "Will Barry Coach Again? Never Say Never: Q & A with Barry Álvarez," (SPORTS)(Interview)." *The Capital Times.* 2006. http://www.highbeam.com/doc/1G1-140494671.html

6. "Barry Álvarez," University of Wisconsin—Madison, Division of Intercollegiate Athletics.(2009). http://www.uwbadgers.com/bios/?staffid=100

7. Ibid.

Leticia Pineda-Boutté

College Softball Groundbreaker

by Cara-Lynn Lopresti

Courtesy of Washington University Athletics.

Entering her fifth season as head softball coach for Washington University in St. Louis, Leticia Pineda-Boutté "stands as one of the most prolific players in the storied history of Arizona softball."[1] As the only Division I athlete to be named first-team All-America at three different positions; catcher, third base, and first base, Pineda-Boutté guided her team to the College World Series each of her four years, winning two National Championships and three Pac-10 Conference titles. Pineda-Boutté is among the short list of Latina athletes who have not only excelled in their sport, but who are also community leaders and role models for younger Latinas. She has coached at clinics and camps, particularly those aimed at minority girls. She often returns to her former high school to offer words of encouragement to the current players. Pineda-Boutté enjoys being a "role model that these athletes can relate to" and hopes that she will "inspire them"[2] to work toward their dreams.

Growing up, Pineda-Boutté was the youngest of four children. Her mother was an immigrant from Juárez, Mexico, a small border town of El Paso, Texas, and her father was an Arizona native. Although Pineda-Boutté's family struggled financially, the parents made many sacrifices so their children would have the same opportunities as any other family. Pineda-Boutté's mother was a stay-at-home mom and her father worked for the city of Tucson and also played in a baseball league, which was where Pineda-Boutté first started falling in love with the game. Growing up as a daddy's girl, Pineda-Boutté would tag along with her father to his games and practices and throw the ball with him on the sidelines. However, Pineda-Boutté's father eventually decided to give up playing baseball so that he had more time to coach his daughters. From that point on Pineda-Boutté and her sister "lived and breathed softball."[3]

Every Christmas the only present that they would ask for was to attend a softball camp or to get softball equipment. Although Pineda-Boutté started playing softball at age five she was not old enough to compete in a league. For three years she "became practice buddies with her sister mimicking everything she did."[4] Once Pineda-Boutté was eight years old, she and her sister played together all through the year, with their goal to earn a college scholarship.

Pineda-Boutté soon emerged as a standout player at Tucson's Desert View High School. In 1994, she became the first student-athlete at her high school "to get a Division I letter of intent"[5] when she signed with the University of Arizona. Being awarded a scholarship was a huge honor for Pineda-Boutté, who had attended a high school that was comprised primarily of minorities and was surrounded by naysayers, who said earning a scholarship was impossible. Now that Pineda-Boutté proved these people wrong she expects that it will bring "hope for other minorities" and will "make them realize that they can accomplish anything that they put their minds to."[6]

Pineda-Boutté had a "highly decorated collegiate career at perennial softball power Arizona,"[7] becoming a three-time all-region and All-America honoree in 1996, 1997, and 1998. She connected for 52 home runs in her career, the 10th highest tally in NCAA history, and finished with a .375 batting average and a .687 slugging percentage, which ranks among the NCAA top 20. Pineda-Boutté's 240 career RBI also ranks eighth on the all-time NCAA list.

Courtesy of Washington University Athletics.

Her sophomore year at the University of Arizona was particularly memorable, as she brought home her first National Championship and second Pac-10 title with a team that was considered to be in a rebuilding year at the start of the season. She also had 96 runs batted in that season, a feat that has only been topped by four players in Division I history. Pineda-Boutté finished her college career in 1998 with a 20 home run mark, which ranks among the NCAA top 20.

In 2004, Pineda-Boutté was honored for her outstanding accomplishments as a Wildcat when she was inducted into the Arizona Sports Hall of Fame. In addition to her athletic recognition, she also earned the Hughes Missile Systems Company's Sportswoman of the Year award in 1997 and the Courage and Leadership Award from the National Hispanic Women's Corporation in 1998. That same year, Pineda-Boutté became the first member of her family to finish college when she graduated from Arizona with a bachelor of arts degree in Humanities. This was another meaningful accomplishment that she hoped would have a lasting affect on younger Latina athletes and their pursuit for higher education.

Upon graduation, Pineda-Boutté spent one season playing professionally for the Tampa Bay Firestix of the Women's Professional Softball League. She then moved on to the University of Colorado—Colorado Springs, where she served as interim head coach. Boutté finished the 1999–2000 season with a record of 21-26, and led the Mountain Lions to postseason play for the first time in four years. The following year, Pineda-Boutté worked as a consultant for the United States Air Force Academy's club softball team before accepting the assistant coaching position at Creighton University in Omaha, Nebraska in 2002. For two seasons, "Coach Let, as she [was] affectionately called,"[8] worked primarily with the pitchers, catchers, and hitters and helped lead the Bluejays to two NCAA berths. In 2004, Pineda-Boutté coached the Bluejay hurlers to an outstanding 0.99 ERA, which ranked sixth in the nation, and a .718 winning percentage which ranked 20th in the nation. The team also went 44-17-1, finishing third in its NCAA Regional bracket. Following her stint at Creighton, Pineda-Boutté briefly served as the assistant coach at Purdue University for one season before taking on her current head coaching position at Washington University in St. Louis in 2006.

In four seasons as Washington University's head coach, Pineda-Boutté has guided the Bears to a 124-42 overall mark and a .747 winning percentage. The team has also had four straight seasons with 25 or more victories, and have won four UAA titles and made four NCAA Tournament appearances. Pineda-Boutté's first season was her winningest season so far on the Danforth Campus. That year she was named UAA Coaching Staff of the Year and had a 37-7 record and a .841 winning percentage. However, Pineda-Boutté really made her mark in 2007 when she became the National Fastpitch Coaches Association (NFCA) Midwest Region Coach of the Year after leading the Bears to a 35-7 overall record and their first-ever trip to the College World Series. In 2008, she was named UAA Coaching Staff of the Year for the second time, and in 2009 Pineda-Boutté led the team to a 27-13 record and a third place finish at the NCAA Midwest Regional.

Pineda-Boutté especially enjoys working at Washington University in St. Louis because it allows for a healthy work-life balance. She loves being a wife to her husband, Shawn, and mother to their three-year-old daughter, Lorin. Pineda-Boutté has also had time to work on her Master of Arts degree in Management and Leadership, and is expected to graduate in December of 2009. When asked about her future goals, Pineda-Boutté may want to go into athletic administration some day, but she expects to continue "coaching softball for as long as she is physically able to,"[9] as she could not be happier with what she is doing right now.

Notes

1. "Head Coach Leticia Pineda-Boutte," (2009). http://bearsports.wustl.edu/soft-ball/softballcoach.html

2. Leticia Pineda-Boutté. Interview with author, August 13, 2009.

3. Ibid.

4. Ibid.

5. "Latina Athletes Extraordinaire," *USAToday*. March 29, 2005. http://www.usatoday.com/sports/2005-03-29-leading-hispanic-athletes_x.htm

6. Leticia Pineda-Boutté. Interview with author, August 13, 2009.

7. "Leticia Pineda-Boutte," CBS Interactive. 2009. http://www.purduesports.com/sports/w-softbl/mtt/pinedaboutte_leticia00.html

8. Ibid.

9. Leticia Pineda-Boutté. Interview with author, August 13, 2009.

Mario Cristóbal

First Cuban-American Football Coach at Division I-A Program

by Cara-Lynn Lopresti

Born on September 24, 1970, Mario Manuel Cristóbal is currently the second head football coach in Florida International University's history and the first ever Cuban-American head football coach. As a Miami native and former University of Miami player and coach, Cristóbal "embodies the culture, sophistication, and attitude of the City of Miami."[1] He also knows firsthand the meaning of work ethic and perseverance, having witnessed his parents juggling multiple jobs growing up to support the family. Cristóbal now

Courtesy of Samuel and Micki Lewis.

demands nothing less than excellence of himself and of others, and, with his roots "embedded in arguably the nation's most talent-rich area for football,"[2] is committed to making FIU one of the premier programs in the country. However, more importantly, he is dedicated to making an impact far beyond football. On his first day at FIU, Cristóbal established his vision for the program and has since been committed to achieving success not only on the field, but also in the classroom, in the community, and in life.

Prior to coaching at FIU, Cristóbal played on the University of Miami football team from 1988–1992. He competed in four bowl games with the Hurricanes, helping the team to National Championships in 1989 and 1991 and earning All-Big East honors as an offensive tackle during his senior season. While in Coral Gables, Cristóbal also served as a spokesperson for D.A.R.E. and the University of Miami's "Join A Team, Not A Gang" initiative. He graduated in 1993 with a degree in Business Administration and added his Masters degree in Liberal Arts in 2002, both from the University of Miami.

In 1994, Cristóbal signed with the Denver Broncos as a free agent and participated in preseason camp. He then spent a brief stint in Europe, playing on the Amsterdam Admirals team from 1995 to 1996. However, at the end of the second year Cristóbal officially retired from playing and instead decided to start moving up through the coaching ranks. In 1998, Cristóbal joined the Miami Hurricanes as a graduate assistant where in three seasons he helped Miami to a 29-8 record, three bowl victories, and two Big East Conference titles.

From 2001–2003, Cristóbal was a tight end and offensive line coach at Rutgers University under former Miami defensive coordinator, Greg Schiano. While there, Cristóbal became a part of one of the biggest turnarounds in modern-day college football. Under his supervision, Rutgers steadily improved from records of 2-9 and then 1-11, to a 5-7 record in 2003, the team's best showing since 1998. It was during his time at Rutgers when "Cristóbal put the first notches in his belt as a full-time coach and that his talent as a coach and recruiter were recognized."[3] From 2004-2006 Cristóbal spent a second stint at Miami as tight end and offensive line coach. The Hurricanes went 24-12 in that time with appearances in the Chick-fil-A Peach Bowl and the Micron PC Bowl.

On December 19, 2006, Cristóbal was named the head football coach at Florida International University as the second-youngest football coach in Division I-A. FIU Athletic Director Pete García could not have been more confident in his decision to hire Cristóbal as he knew he would "lead [the] program in a manner that [the] University, alumni, and the South Florida community [would] be proud."[4] During his first months at FIU, Cristóbal started re-

vitalizing a program that had just finished the 2006 season 0-12. He introduced "intensity . . . discipline and accountability,"[5] transforming the Golden Panthers into a, "whatever-it-takes kind of team."[6] Cristóbal also worked hard to change the image of the program by increasing the team's visibility in the community and strictly enforcing high academic standards and responsible behavior among the players.

Although FIU still struggled in 2007, the Golden Panthers did break a 23-game losing steak with a 38-19 victory over North Texas in the team's last game of the season. FIU made more progress during Cristóbal's second year as head coach, with a new on-campus stadium and state-of-the-art fieldhouse. The Golden Panthers had an upset win over Toledo in their fourth contest of the season, followed by two more conference victories against North Texas and Middle Tennessee State. FIU was two wins away from a bowl game before falling out of contention after a 57-50 OT loss to Florida Atlantic. The team finished the year with a much-improved 5-7 record, tying a school record for most victories.

In preparing for the 2009 season, Cristóbal validated his reputation as "one of the top recruiters in college football,"[7] when he attracted an impressive recruiting class of 23 student athletes, many of which were highly sought after by top BCS football programs.

These athletes went to FIU because they believed in Cristóbal and wanted to be a part of the legacy that he will create for himself and the program.

While working hard to turnaround FIU's football program, Cristóbal has also been living up to the promises he made to the South Florida community. In his free time "he has made dozens of appearances, speaking to civic groups, professional and youth organizations including the Latin Builders Association, FIU Student Government, the Brian Jenkins Camp, and the Night of Champions."[8] In 2007, he was honored as a mentor for the 5000 Role Models of Excellence, a program that motivates kids to live responsible and healthy lifestyles and to pursue their dreams. Cristóbal also participated in the 4th Annual FIU Relay For Life in support of the American Cancer Society's Relay For Life campaign. Most recently, he served as the keynote speaker at the Baptist Hospital's South Miami Hospital Men's Health Day to promote healthy living.

Notes

1. "Mario Cristobal," *Florida International University*. 2009. http://www.fiusports.com/ViewArticle.dbml?DB_OEM_ID=11700&ATCLID=727585

2. Ibid.

3. Ibid.

4. "Golden Panthers Name Mario Cristobal Head Football Coach," *Florida International University*. December 19, 2009. http://www.fiusports.com/ViewArticle.dbml?DB_OEM_ID=11700&ATCLID=727586

5. "New FIU Coach Knows How to Recruit, Discipline and Win," *South Florida Sun-Sentinel 2007*. http://www.highbeam.com/doc/1G1-168101490.html

6. "Mario Cristobal Q & A Part 3," *The Miami Herald*. 2007. http://miamiherald.typepad.com/fiusports/2007/07/mario-cristob-2.html#comments

7. "Golden Panthers Name Mario Cristobal Head Football Coach," *Florida International University*. December 19, 2009. http://www.fiusports.com/ViewArticle.dbml?DB_OEM_ID=11700&ATCLID=727586

8. "Mario Cristobal," *Florida International University*. 2009. http://www.fiusports.com/ViewArticle.dbml?DB_OEM_ID=11700&ATCLID=727585

13

LATINO ADMINISTRATORS IN COLLEGE SPORT

Dan Guerrero

Groundbreaking Athletic Director

by Charlie Harless

There is perhaps no other university as synonymous with winning as the University of California Los Angeles (UCLA). Having become the first school to win 100 NCAA team championships after the women's water polo clinched its fifth title in 2007, the expectation to be the best remains an intrinsic part of the ethos of UCLA faculty, students, and supporters. In 2002, after Peter Dalis announced his decision to retire from the UCLA athletic director post he held for almost two decades, UCLA found itself at a critical crossroads to find a leader that would continue UCLA's winning heritage, and take the university in a fresh direction to greater heights. The hiring of Dan Guerrero, a former UCLA baseball player returning to his alma mater, was questioned by some critics who were not sure if this athletic director from a football-less school in UC Irvine had the experience necessary to survive and flourish at UCLA. Yet in just over seven years since his hire, Guerrero has supplied the support and leadership to win an astounding 18 NCAA team titles in 11 different sports and ushered in a culture that is more committed than ever to providing the resources to encourage the academic development and community involvement of its student-athletes. Whatever initial reservations critics professed has clearly been erased as Guerrero has established himself and the university as winners in every sense of the word.

When Guerrero took the athletic director job at UCLA, he immediately understood that his success at the position was dependent on building upon, and in some cases, reestablishing the winning tradition of its 24 sports. Despite this pressure to be the best, Guerrero has always been resolute in his stance that winning would not come at the price of compromising his personal code of ethics and way of conducting business. Guerrero said shortly after his hire that, "I want to run a program with integrity, one that's committed to things that are important to me—issues of diversity, gender equity, and commitment to public service. In other words, it's not about winning at all costs. You can cite examples of universities all across the country that have won, but I would not say they've won it the right way. I think that at UCLA the challenge is to win, but win the right way."[1] Richard Lapchick, author of this book, once said of Guerrero that, "Dan is a model in terms of the values involved with college athletics and what sports can do in the broader society."[2]

Guerrero's ascent to the high-profile post at UCLA has caused many to view him as a trailblazer in the field of college athletics, where currently only four Latino men serve as athletic directors. In overcoming challenges on the strength of his hard work, Guerrero has displayed a resiliency that is enviable to anyone looking to become a leader. Guerrero himself followed the example set by his father, a blue collar worker who labored for three decades at a California oil refinery so that he could help support his family and his son's dream of playing baseball. Of his father, Guerrero said that "With no more than a ninth grade education, my father, Gene Guerrero, taught me more about the important things in life than any person I have ever known. A promising athlete from Tucson, Arizona, his aspiration to become a professional baseball player came to a screeching halt when he completely lost his sight in one eye due to a serious traffic accident . . . He was a hard charger, a task master in many ways. He taught me how to work and more importantly, taught me the value of work. He emphasized the importance of education, but also the relevance of knowing who you are and from where you came. He often reminded me that some of the smartest or richest men in the world don't know how to roll up a garden hose. It was his way of reminding me that I should always re-

Courtesy of UCLA Athletics.

main humble no matter how successful I might become later in life."[3]

Guerrero put in the hard work and soon developed into the star baseball player that his father never had the chance to become. Guerrero looks back fondly on his college playing days with UCLA, as he describes how the experience carried deep personal and professional meaning. "The first day I put on the UCLA uniform in the fall of 1969 was the day I was intrinsically linked to Jackie Robinson. Growing up, I learned about Jackie Robinson and UCLA from my father. We grew up as a family rooting for UCLA because of my dad's admiration for Jackie Robinson as a player and a person. As minorities, the role of the underdog was all too familiar to us. To be triumphant as an underdog was not only a blessing, but a revelation. No one personified this more than Jackie Robinson. My dad always told me as a young boy that UCLA was a great university and that because of Jackie Robinson it was a university "for the people." What he meant was that a person of color was not only welcome at UCLA, he could also succeed at UCLA. It didn't take long for me to accept an athletic scholarship to UCLA when it was offered. It was my destiny."[4]

Guerrero lettered in each of his four seasons at UCLA where he was known by teammates and fans as the "Warrior" due to his fighting spirit, but a torn hamstring in his senior year severely hindered any chance of seriously being considered for opportunities in the major leagues. Faced with the prospect of moving onto life beyond playing baseball, Guerrero worked in Los Angeles in the late

1970s with nonprofit organizations aimed at community development. Soon however, Guerrero realized that the career he wanted for himself would be in athletic administration. Of his career shift, Guerrero said that "entering the field of athletic administration at age 32, I chose to leave a successful career in community development because of my love for sports, education, and competition. An administrative career in college athletics allows an individual to walk onto a university campus everyday and work with a committed hard working staff, coaches who possess great pride in their craft and student-athletes who are bright, ambitious, and competitive. While the challenges are significant, the rewards are greater. The athletic experience changes lives. It provides opportunities for student-athletes to grow as people, to find their voices, and to lay the foundation for the rest of their lives."[5]

Laying the foundation for the rest of his professional life, Guerrero earned a Master's degree in Public Administration from Cal State Dominguez Hills while simulataneously serving as a volunteer in the athletic department. Guerrero's hard work and proven commitment to do everything from moving ticket inventory to selling concessions led him to be named the school's athletic director in 1988. After gaining five years of experience, Guerrero left to take on the athletic director role at UC Irvine. His leadership was essential in building $38 million worth of new athletic facilities over a five-year stretch and providing the resources to build conference-championship programs. Petrina Long, a fellow staff member at UC Irvine during Guerrero's 10-year tenure, said that "we (UC Irvine) faced some heavy problems with few resources. When Dan came here, he rolled up his sleeves and went to work. I don't think I ever heard him say 'obstacle.'"[6]

By the time UCLA came calling in 2002, Guerrero had put in the time and shown through his achievement that he earned an opportunity to tackle the challenges of one of the most high-profile jobs in athletics. Alluding to the special qualities that has made him successful and his heritage that has made him a vanguard for Latinos in college sports administration, Guerrero stated that "there's a saying in Spanish: 'Por eso luchamos,' or 'That's why we struggle.' I worked hard to get the chance to prove what I can do. I expect to do well because I want young people to say, 'That guy looks like me, and look at where he is.'"[7]

Looking at where Guerrero is today, it is clear that this accomplished athletic director, dedicated husband, and father of two daughters, is still driven and passionate about being the best and setting examples for others. Guerrero has accepted opportunities on the national stage by becoming the chair of the NCAA Division I Men's Basketball Committee and second vice-president of the National Association of Collegiate Directors of Athletics (NACDA). Additionally, Guerrero has been recognized for his tremendous work by earning accolades such as NACDA's Division I West Region Athletic Director of the Year in 2007 and inclusion on both the *Hispanic Business* Magazine's 2004 list of the "Top 100 Most Influential Hispanics" and *Sports Illustrated*'s 2003 ranking of the "101 Most Influential Minorities in Sports."

For all that Guerrero has achieved in life, he remains true to the personal value system that has guided him toward becoming one of the most powerful and respected sport administrators in the country. Guerrero believes that in order to maintain excellence, "a core ideology has to stay in place and you can't waver from that. That ideology is based on integrity. We have to do things the right way. You have to work hard and you have to work smart . . . You have to love what you do."[7] Guerrero has shown that he is many things, whether it is being an athlete, servant to the community, academic reformer, role model, or athletic leader, but above all else, Guerrero is a winner.

Notes

1. Billy Witz, "First 100 days AD Guerrero Wants it Done His Own Way," *Daily News*, October 3, 2002.

2. David Davis, "Tough Guy: New athletics Czar Dan Guerrero is Giving UCLA a Welcome Jolt," *Los Angeles Magazine*, December 1, 2003.

3. Dan Guerrero, E-mail interview by author, October 27, 2009.

4. Ibid.

5. Ibid.

6. David Davis, "Tough Guy: New Athletics Czar Dan Guerrero is Giving UCLA a Welcome Jolt," *Los Angeles Magazine*, December 1, 2003.

7. Ibid.

8. Jill Painter, "UCLA Thinks New AD has the Right Stuff," *Daily News*, April 27, 2002.

Rudy Dávalos

Groundbreaking Athletic Director

by Cara-Lynn Lopresti

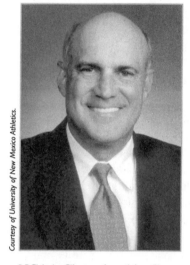

Courtesy of University of New Mexico Athletics.

Rudy Dávalos was the University of New Mexico's Athletics Director for more than 13 years, the third-longest tenure of any athletic director at the school. While operating in that role, "Dávalos undeniably elevated the Lobos' program academically, competitively, and fiscally."[1] In addition, as one of the original athletics directors of the Mountain West Conference, "Dávalos' influence has reverberated throughout Division I athletics."[2] He has been a part of numerous conference and national committees, including the NCAA Championship Competition Cabinet, the NCAA Committees for men's basketball, women's basketball and baseball, Chairman of the Executive Board of the New Mexico Bowl, and the Executive Committee for the National Association of Collegiate Directors of Athletics. He also received the Dr. Albert C. Yates Distinguished Service Award in 2006, which is given to an individual who successfully supported, promoted, and exemplified the ideals of the Mountain West Conference or a member institution.

Dávalos has also been recognized repeatedly throughout his career for supporting the youth and minorities in his community. In 1976 he was given the Catholic Youth Organization's "Man in Youth" award and has served as a chairman of the San Antonio Summer Youth Games, the board of director for San Antonio Boys Club of America, and the San Antonio YMCA, among others. In 2002, Dávalos was recognized nationally by *Sports Illustrated* as one of the 101 Most Influential Minorities in Sports and hopes that this accomplishment "will be an inspiration to young people of all backgrounds to pursue their goals."[3]

A native of San Antonio, Texas, Davalos' emerged as a standout early on in his sports career. At Southwest Texas State, Davalos was an All-American point guard and team captain, and led his team to an NAIA national title. In 1960 he earned his degree in Education and two years later added a Master's degree in Education from Georgetown College. Dávalos was honored on numerous occasions for his athletic career, having been elected to the NAIA Basketball Hall of Fame, the Southwest Texas State Hall of Fame, the Texas High School Basketball Hall of Fame, and the San Antonio Sports Hall of Fame.

After Dávalos' playing days ended, he began an illustrious career as a basketball coach. From 1961–1970 Dávalos served as an assistant coach at three different schools; Georgetown College, Kentucky, and Auburn. In 1970 he entered into his first head coaching position as the head men's basketball coach at the University of the South in Sewanee, Tennessee. In his final season with the University of the South, Dávalos' Tigers captured the College Athletic Conference championship with a 23-4 record, the best in school history. Dávalos then spent three years working in the NBA, serving as an assistant coach and Director of Player Personnel for the San Antonio Spurs.

Dávalos' administrative career began in 1975 when he was named the athletics director at the University of Texas-San Antonio. After nine years leading the Roadrunner athletics department, Dávalos returned to San Antonio for another year to serve as the director of community relations for the Spurs. He also worked as a television and radio commentator for the team during that time. In 1987 Dávalos was hired as the Athletics Director at Houston. Dávalos was credited with the procurement of gift-in-kind donation to the Cougar athletics department in excess of $32 million. He was responsible for establishing state-of-the-art athletics facilities at Houston, spearheading projects such as new baseball stadium, tennis courts, and renovation of departmental offices. The Cougar program also enjoyed enormous success under Dávalos' leadership. In 1989, the Houston football program produced Heisman Trophy winner, Andre Ware.

On November 16, 1992, Dávalos was named New Mexico's 11th Athletics Director and served in that role until 2006. During his tenure, Dávalos set a high standard for the program and the 21 sports he presided over. As the son of Mexican-born parents, Dávalos also

382 Part 2: College Sport

showed a strong commitment to achieving diversity among his staff. He was proud to "provide a place that welcomes and acknowledges personal ability and experience" and emphasized that New Mexico's "diversity is not by design, but rather because [he] hired the best people for those positions."[4]

Dávalos was also known for placing "a well-rounded, across-the-board emphasis [on] all sports from an academic and athletics standpoint."[5] With Dávalos at the reins, the Lobos student-athletes compiled a GPA of 3.0 or higher for eight straight terms, including a school-record 3.05 GPA during the 2004 fall semester. That same year, there were 86 Mountain West Conference Scholar-Athletes, and sixteen student-athletes were named to the academic All-America team. In addition, more than 100 student-athletes received national academic recognition since 1993.

From an athletic standpoint, "Dávalos' leadership has served as the cornerstone for success at UNM."[6] In the decade before him, only five sports had combined to win or share 10 conference titles. Once Dávalos took over, New Mexico was transformed into a premier athletics institution with eight teams winning or sharing nearly 40 regular-season or postseason conference championships. Under his guidance, New Mexico was represented at NCAA postseason competition more than 115 times and more than 150 student-athletes earned All-America recognition for their athletic achievements. Eight of the Lobos's 11 NCAA Tournament appearances in men's basketball and all of the NCAA Tournament showings for the women's basketball program came while Dávalos was at New Mexico. In addition, men's and women's basketball ranked in the top 15 in national attendance average nine times. In football, half of New Mexico's total bowl appearances took place between 1997–2004 and season attendance records were broken seven times. With the excellent performances within these sports, New Mexico became one of 11 schools to have its football team play in a bowl game and its men's and women's basketball teams appear in the NCAA Tournament. In 2004, the Lobo program claimed its first national title when the ski team won the NCAA championship. Also, during the 2004–05 season, New Mexico finished 48th nationally in the Sports Academy Director's Cup, the second-best ranking in school history, and a school-record 15 teams represented UNM at NCAA postseason competition. In 2005, the Lobo men's soccer team was national runner-up and was among the nation's leaders in attendance, along with women's soccer.

Dávalos left a legacy of unparalleled financial success for the institution. During his term he increased the athletics department's operating budget from $9.4 million to more than $22 million. Dávalos turned New Mexico's marketing, promotions, and fund-raising into nationally-respected programs, with them producing greater than $6 million each year. This was an incredible feat especially considering just 12 years ago the funds generated by the athletic department was less than $2 million and corporate sponsorships were non-existent. Dávalos established longstanding relationships with the state's governors and legislators, local businesses and private contributors, enabling New Mexico to improve upon nearly every one of its athletics facilities. The most recent expansion included a $4.2 million basketball practice facility, and improvements at Lobo Field for softball and at the UNM track.

Dávalos retired from his position as Director of Athletics in the summer of 2006. Although, the university lost a great leader in Dávalos, the "intercollegiate program [was] poised for a sustained period of greatness."[7] This was because he left New Mexico "competitive as it's ever been and stronger academically and financially because of the talented and high integrity coaches and staff Rudy recruited to UNM."[8] Following retirement, Dávalos was added to the National Invitation Tournament (NIT) LLC Selection Committee. He has also had the opportunity to spend more time with his wife, children, and grandchildren, who live in various parts of the country. His son, Doug, is entering his third season as Head Men's Basketball Coach at Texas State University. Dávalos has been a great supporter of Texas State and the Men's Basketball program as a 6th man member.

Notes

1. "Rudy Davalos," *CBS Interactive*. (2009). http://www.golobos.com/genrel/davalos_rudy00.html

2. "Rudy Davalos, New Mexico Athletics Director, Named Dr. Albert C. Yates Award Recipient For 2006," *CBS Interactive*. April 24, 2006. http://www.themwc.com/genrel/042406aaa.html

3. Carolyn Gonzales, "UNM Athletic Director Davalos Makes *Sports Illustrated* List," *University of New Mexico Public Affairs Department. May 2, 2003.* http://www.unm.edu/news/Releases/03-05-02davalos.htm

4. Ibid.

5. Greg Remington, "Director of Athletics Rudy Davalos Announces Retirement," *UNM Today*. October 1, 2005. http://www.unm.edu/~market/cgi-bin/archives/000857 .html

6. "Rudy Davalos, New Mexico Athletics Director, Named Dr. Albert C. Yates Award Recipient For 2006," *CBS Interactive*. April 24, 2006. http://www.themwc .com/genrel/042406aaa.html

7. Greg Remington, "Director of Athletics Rudy Davalos Announces Retirement," *UNM Today*. October 1, 2005. http://www.unm.edu/~market/cgi-bin/archives/000857 .html

8. Ibid.

Irma García

Groundbreaking Athletic Director

by Cara-Lynn Lopresti

Irma García knew at a very young age that she wanted to run a sports program. Thirty years later, against significant odds, García achieved her childhood goal when she was named Athletic Director of St. Francis College. However, on that day, García had achieved an even greater accomplishment because she also became the first Latina responsible for the management of a NCAA Division I Athletics Program. Although she never had imagined that she would be breaking barriers when she finally achieved her goal, García is "proud of [her] Latina heritage" and "hope[s] her success helps more Latinas rise to realize their dreams."[1] Aside from her influence on the Latino culture, García is also proud to serve in a position rarely held by a woman, as she was just one of 30 females to lead a Division I athletic programs at the time of her promotion. As of 2008, the number of women directing Division I programs were six among BSC schools, 10 at Division I championship sub-division schools, and 14 at Division I colleges without football programs. To her, if "becoming AD serves as inspiration to even one other woman" then that makes "this position even more important"[2] and she hopes that her success will "ease the path for other women who want to break into college athletics."[3]

Courtesy of St. Francis College Athletics.

García was born in Brooklyn, New York, in a community that served as a melting pot of many different ethnic groups. Her parents were Puerto Rican immigrants and raised García along with her seven sisters and one brother. García was the natural athlete in the family and a tenacious competitor having grown up playing various sports on the streets with the local boys. By her junior year at St. Angela High School, she decided to try organized basketball. Although she struggled at first, García improved quickly and by her senior year she made captain and averaged 27 points a game. Soon after, she was offered a basketball scholarship, something that would have been unimaginable a few years earlier. From there, her 22-year relationship with St. Francis College began, starting with her playing for the women's basketball team. During her four years as a student-athlete, St. Francis won 48 games, finishing just under a .500 record.

After obtaining her undergraduate degree at St. Francis, García became a physical education teacher and female basketball coach at St. Joseph by the Sea on Staten Island. She returned to her alma mater in 1988 to take the position as St. Francis College's head women's basketball coach. At the age 27, García was one of the youngest coaches in Division I.

In the next 11 years, García's players received many individual honors, including five players who were inducted into the St. Francis Hall of Fame. She also coached Carolyn Harvey, the first St. Francis women's basketball player to play professionally.

García maintained strict academic standards for her teams, with great success. Her 1998–99 team was honored by the WBCA for having the fourth highest team grade-point-average among Division I programs. The 1997–1998 team notched the 23rd-best GPA in the country. After the 1997–98 season, García was honored for her guidance both on and off the court as the Northeast Conference Coach of the Year.

While coaching, García gained administrative experience when she served as the Department of Athletics Senior Woman Administrator (SWA). In that role she was responsible for overseeing financial aid for the student-athletes and was acquiring the necessary funds needed to build a new women's basketball locker room. In 1999, García officially ended her coaching career and became the St. Francis College Associate Director of Athletics, where she managed large parts of the athletic department, including budgeting and purchasing.

In 2001, García earned a master's degree from Brooklyn College in Sports Administration and four years later she was inducted

into the St. Francis Athletics Hall of Fame. This "was a well deserved honor" as her "leadership, compassion and dedication to the St. Francis College Department of Athletics has touched"[4] countless people over the past two decades. In 2007, García's hard work was further rewarded when she took over as Director of Athletics after serving in the position on an interim basis. St. Francis president Dr. Frank Macchiarola said his decision to hand her the reins "was a no-brainer" because of her "can-do motto" and her "demonstrated leadership, integrity and loyalty."[5] As Director of Athletics, García now presides over a staff of 50 and is dedicated to helping her athletes "perform better in the classroom and in the community."[6]

García has also been keeping herself busy participating in activities outside of St. Francis College. She is an active member of the Women's Basketball Coaching Association and the National Association of Collegiate Women Athletic Administrators. García has been featured in the *USA Today*, *New York Daily News*, *NCAA News*, ESPN.Com, and American Latino, a nationally syndicated TV show. Most recently, García was honored at the White House, as a 2008 Las Primeras Award Recipient by MANA, a national Latina organization. García received the award for being a pioneer in Division I athletics and has since become dedicated to bringing "more women along the path to success."[7] With García's "high-energy buzz," driven attitude, and "competent . . . friendly, open and direct demeanor"[8] she certainly will be able to achieve this goal and the many other goals that she has set for herself and for St. Francis College.

Notes

1. "Irma Garcia Featured on National TV Program," *St. Francis College*. July 13, 2009. http://www.stfranciscollege.edu/newsDetail.aspx?Channel=%2FChannels%2FAdmissions%2FAdmissions+Content&WorkflowItemID=b521e305-52c0-4e92-8eb8-3767b7412021

2. "Irma Garcia Named St. Francis (NY) Director of Athletics," *The Northeast Conference.* August 29, 2007. http://www.northeastconference.org/news/general/2007/8/29/sfny-garciaadrel.asp?path=general

3. Mira Wassef, "Unheralded Heights: St. Francis AD Irma Garcia is Division I pioneer," *Daily News.* December 4, 2007. http://www.nydailynews.com/sports/college/2007/12/04/2007-12-04_unheralded_heights_st_francis_ad_irma_ga.html

4. "Irma Garcia." *St. Francis College Athletics.* 2009. http://sfcathletics.com/bio.asp?staffid=2

5. Mira Wassef, "Unheralded heights: St. Francis AD Irma Garcia is Division I pioneer," *Daily News.* December 4, 2007. http://www.nydailynews.com/sports/college/2007/12/04/2007-12-04_unheralded_heights_st_francis_ad_irma_ga.html

6. George J. Tanber, "St. Francis AD had a Vision for Her Future," *ESPN.* September 15, 2008. http://sports.espn.go.com/espn/hispanicheritage2008/news/story?id=3574645

7. "St. Francis (NY) Athletic Director Irma Garcia To Be Honored At White House," *The Northeast Conference.* September 24, 2008. http://www.northeastconference.org/News/stfranny/2008/9/24/sfny-garciawhitehouserel.asp?path=stfranny

8. George J. Tanber, "St. Francis AD had a Vision for Her Future," *ESPN.* September 15, 2008. http://sports.espn.go.com/espn/hispanicheritage2008/news/story?id=3574645

Rick Villarreal

Groundbreaking Athletic Director

by Cara-Lynn Lopresti

Rick Villarreal has worn many hats in his illustrious career. He has had previous successes as a coach, football administrator, private businessman, and as an Associate Athletic Director and key fundraiser at Southern Mississippi. Most recently he has been serving as the Director of Athletics at the University of North Texas. In just eight years leading North Texas' athletic department, Villarreal "has brought to fruition a dream of the Mean Green community—an administrator who can raise money, build facilities, direct championship teams with quality coaches while helping develop the lives of student-athletes."[1] Villarreal's vision is for UNT to be "the best in the Sun Belt Conference and continue to elevate the SBC."[2] This goal involves not only advancing its athletics program, but also branding UNT into an elite institution and leader in athletics, education, and in the community.

    Born and raised in Gulfport, Mississippi, Villarreal was a 1975 graduate of St. John High School and received his bachelor's degree in Coach and Sports Administration from Southern Mississippi in

1989. While in school, Villarreal also owned and operated an eight-unit Domino's Pizza group in Decatur, Alabama, and served as President of the Southeast Region Franchise Association from 1984 to 1986. In this role, Villarreal proved he was a gifted businessman that was capable of achieving strong returns, as he generated annual sales that exceeded $5 million and his stores ranked in the top 20 percent in the country.

From 1988 to 1997 Villarreal pursued a career in football as a coach and then administrator. He received his first coaching positions under Curly Hallman at Southern Mississippi, working for two years as a student assistant, a graduate assistant, and as wide receivers, running backs, and special teams coach. From 1991 to 1995, he served again on Hallman's coaching staff, this time at Louisiana State University. He took on several different positions at LSU, starting as Director of Football Operations and Recruiting Coordinator and later coaching tight ends. Villarreal then became the Director of Football Operations and Assistant Athletic Director at Texas Christian University from 1995 to 1997 under Coach Pat Sullivan.

Villarreal's last stop before the University of North Texas was back to his alma mater, the University of Southern Mississippi, where he worked as Associate Athletic Director for three years. In that position, Villarreal "served as a leading force in major gift fundraising."[3] He initiated the Circle of Champions, a group of donors that gives at least $100,000 each, which now has over 60 members. He also spearheaded a number of fundraising projects, resulting in more than $8 million in added funds, and the construction of a new athletic center, a new baseball clubhouse, and a women's softball stadium. Villarreal also played a key role in the plans for a future football stadium and renovation of the basketball arena.

On April 4, 2001, Villarreal was hired to take over the University of North Texas athletic department. When President Norval Pohl announced Villarreal's selection, he stated that "his enthusiasm is contagious. He knows how to articulate a vision in a way that literally makes you want to get involved because you know the outcome will be special. He will reach out to our alumni and students alike. He understands the economic development aspects of athletic events and will work cooperatively to build loyalty in the local community. He is right for North Texas."[4]

Villarreal was clearly the right choice for the university, as under his leadership UNT has accomplished things "that have been unparalleled in the previous 20 years of Mean Green athletics."[5] So far in his tenure, there have been 12 conference championships and North Texas has finished among the top three in the Sun Belt Conference all-sports championship standings six out of eight years. Although the football program has struggled, Villarreal expects 2009 will be a turnaround year due to the coaching changes he has been implementing, including the addition of the strength and conditioning position. The Mean Green now has a mature and experienced coaching staff and veteran players that are proven and explosive.

UNT has also made significant progress in academics. During Villarreal's tenure, graduation rates have improved by 50 percent to over 60 percent for student-athletes and the department's current overall GPA is the highest of his tenure. He was responsible for the development of an academic center for student-athletes.

Villarreal has similarly made a commitment to improving the fan participation and athletic facilities, so that the University of North Texas can "compare favorably to the elite collegiate athletic programs in the nation."[6] In an effort to expand the school's visibility, Villarreal has worked to broadcast local games in the Dallas-Forth Worth market and has secured a 100,000 watt radio station. It is his goal to increase game attendance by servicing the fan and creating the very best experience for them, whether it is through the Website, during game days, or on chat boards.

With regards to facilities, Villarreal oversaw the building of an $8 million athletic facility that contains a state-of-the-art training suite, administration and football offices, and brand new locker rooms. He also facilitated the acquisition of additional property and the renovation and construction of new venues for basketball, soccer, softball, golf, and volleyball. As part of a joint strategic plan with the University, Villarreal was also instrumental in the fund raising, design, and construction of a $3 million tennis facility. These new facilities as well as other resources have contributed to the recent success of women's sports, which were previously ignored. As a result, the Penn State Gender Equity Report Card has recognized the university as the No. 1 program in the country the last two years.

Villarreal has also made an impact outside of the immediate

North Texas community. He was on the Sun Belt Conference Executive Committee that concluded in 2008 and also recently completed terms with the NCAA Division I Managment Council and the NCAA Membership Committee. He currently serves as the Sun Belt representative on the board of NCAA Football and was just appointed to a three-year stint on the NCAA Championships Committee. Rick and his wife D'Lynn are also the proud parents of three children; Kimberly, Justin, and Tony and have one grandson, Jayden Tyler.

Notes

1. "Rick Villarreal," *University of North Texas*. 2009. https://www.nmnathletics.com/ViewArticle.dbml?SPSID=9509&SPID=581&DB_OEM_ID=1800&ATCLID=68013

2. "Recap Of Live Chat With Athletic Director Rick Villarreal," *University of North Texas*, July 22, 2009. http://www.meangreensports.com/ViewArticle.dbml?DB_OEM_ID=1800&ATCLID=204763275

3. "Rick Villarreal Named UNT Athletic Director," *Inhouse@UNT*. 2001. http://www.unt.edu/inhouse/april62001/newad.htm

4. "Rick Villarrea,." *University of North Texas*. 2009. https://www.nmnathletics.com/ViewArticle.dbml?SPSID=9509&SPID=581&DB_OEM_ID=1800&ATCLID=68013

5. Ibid.

6. Ibid.

Pete García

Groundbreaking Athletic Director

by Cara-Lynn Lopresti

Pete García has been the Director of Intercollegiate Athletics at Florida International University for three years. He was originally expected to be the successor to University of Miami Athletic Director Paul Dee, but opted to go to FIU because he wanted the chance to develop an athletic program. Most of all, he accepted the position because it was an opportunity for him "to further his career without leaving the community he loves."[1] Born in Havana, Cuba, García's family migrated to Miami in 1967 and García has been loyal to South Florida ever since. After his arrival to FIU in the fall of 2006, García became dedicated to giving back to the community and realized the best way to accomplish this was to build up a college sports program that the local residents could enjoy supporting. So, he began turning around FIU athletics by "instilling a commitment of excellence with his coaches, department staff, and student-athletes"[2] and striving for success on the field, in the classroom, and in the community. Although it will be a difficult challenge, García is capable of achieving a level of success for FIU that South Florida can be proud of.

Prior to FIU, García attended the University of Miami. He then accepted a position with the Miami Hurricanes in 1990 and worked there for ten years as the football program's recruiting coordinator. In 2001, García followed former Miami head coach Butch Davis to the Cleveland Browns, becoming the team's director of football development and subsequently vice president of player personnel and football development. Davis said that bringing "García with him was an easy decision" as he "is meticulously organized, and has outstanding people skills."[3] In 2005, García returned to Miami as the senior associate athletic director for external operations. In that position he was responsible for supervising the school's media relations, ticket sales, marketing, and corporate sponsorships.

On October 10, 2006 García accepted his current position as FIU's Director of Intercollegiate Athletics. The Golden Panthers administration had been looking for someone to take its struggling sports programs to the next level and aggressively recruited García because of his "outstanding reputation in the world of sports administration."[4] Upon his hiring, García immediately tackled the challenge of revitalizing FIU athletics by evaluating its sports programs and improving his coaching staff. With his "keen eye for detail,"[5] "tremendous vision,"[6] "personable"[7] leadership style and "excellent recruit[ing]," skills[8] García was able to attract proven winners to the school, including baseball's Henry "Turtle" Thomas, softball coach Beth McClendon, who was named Sun Belt Coach of the Year in her first season, and football coach Mario Cristóbal who brought valuable experience from Rutgers and Miami. Most recently, in 2009, García hired NBA Hall of Famer Isiah Thomas to lead the men's basketball team. With such legendary athletes and coaches at the helm of the Golden Panther staff, there is no doubt that FIU will rise to the highest level of athletic competition.

Although he has been instrumental in improving FIU athletic programs, García's number one priority will always be "to ensure that all of our student-athletes have the resources and support necessary to graduate, get their degrees, and be ready for the outside world."[9] In an effort to enhance the academic performance of the Golden Panther athletes, García added advisors, tutors, and computers to the academic support program and hired additional compliance officers, including the first known APR specialist in the country. The following year, García's efforts yielded positive results as FIU graduated 59 student-athletes, the highest number of athletic graduates in the history of the program. The improvements continued in 2009 as five teams—women's cross country, women's golf, women's soccer, women's tennis, and women's softball—earned perfect yearly scores of 1,000 in the Academic Progress Rate reported by the NCAA, and 10 others, including men's basketball and football, saw noticeable academic improvement.

García has also been involved in developing state-of-the-art athletics facilities at FIU. He headed the construction and operation of FIU's new on-campus football stadium. The 18,000-seat stadium has an expected future expansion to 45,000 and is the only Division I on-campus football stadium south of Orlando in Florida. García was also responsible for the creation of a new two-story fieldhouse, which features a 14,000-square foot clean-span weight room that will better accommodate strength and conditioning needs of FIU's student-athletes.

García has already taken great strides toward turning FIU into an "elite sports program that the community can rally behind."[10] He has assembled a staff capable of producing winning programs and attracting promising athletes, revamped the academic support program, its resources and its personnel, and has added facilities to create the best conditions for the players and fans. With progress continuing at this pace, it is only a matter of time when "FIU will [truly] thrive under [García's] leadership"[11] just as former Miami coach Butch Davis predicted.

Notes

1. "Pete Garcia," *Florida International University.* 2009. http://www.fiusports.com/ViewArticle.dbml?DB_OEM_ID=11700&ATCLID=747735

2. Ibid.

3. "FIU Names Pete Garcia Athletics Director," *Sun Belt Conference.* October 11, 2006. http://www.sunbeltsports.org/ViewArticle.dbml?DB_OEM_ID=4100&ATCLID=649398

4. Ibid.

5. Omar Kelly, "Miami's Garcia Moving Across Town: Golden Panthers Likely to Announce AD's Hiring Today," *South Florida Sun-Sentinel.* October 10, 2006. http://www.highbeam.com/doc/1G1-152578482.html

6. Ibid.

7. "FIU Names Pete Garcia Athletics Director," *Sun Belt Conference.* October 11, 2006. http://www.sunbeltsports.org/ViewArticle.dbml?DB_OEM_ID=4100&AT-CLID=649398

8. Harry Coleman, "Garcia Ready to Build Program,." *South Florida Sun-Sentinel.* 2006. http://www.highbeam.com/doc/1G1-152696315.html

9. "Pete Garcia," *Florida International University.* 2009. http://www.fiusports.com/ViewArticle.dbml?DB_OEM_ID=11700&ATCLID=747735

10. Ibid.

11. "FIU Names Pete Garcia Athletics Director," *Sun Belt Conference.* October 11, 2006. http://www.sunbeltsports.org/ViewArticle.dbml?DB_OEM_ID=4100&ATCLID=649398

INTERNATIONAL
SPORT

THE OLYMPICS AND LATINOS SUPERSTARS ON THE INTERNATIONAL STAGE

by Richard Lapchick

South America will finally have its big Olympic moment in 2016 when the Rio de Janeiro Olympics take place. Rio won the bidding process in September 2009 over Chicago, Madrid, Tokyo, and Prague. A winning bid from South America was a long time coming and many believed that in addition to the strong bid package by Rio, the fact that no games have ever been held in South America or Africa helped carry the day.

Nonetheless, athletes from Latin American nations have not been acknowledged with the acclaim that went to other regions of the world. The awarding of the 2016 Olympics to Rio was thought, in part, to be recognition of that oversight. In fact, the widely watched Olympic Torch Relay never went through a Latin American nation until 2004 when it finally landed in Rio, more than 100 years after the first Latino athlete won an Olympic medal.

From Rio, the flame came to Mexico City where the Games were hosted in Latin America for the first and only other time in 1968. Enriqueta Basilio was the first woman to ever light the flame in Mexico in 1968 and she was a torchbearer in 2004. Basilio was an Olympic hurdler from Mexico.

Part of the lack of recognition can be attributed to a relative poor record as a region in winning Olympic medals. In Beijing, no South or Central American nation finished among the top 25 nations in medals per capita. Jamaica, with superstar Usain Bolt, finished first; Cuba was 11th and Trinidad and Tobago was 13th. All three were from the Caribbean. Before Beijing, counting all the Olympics from Athens in 1896 to Athens in 2004, athletes from Latin

America and the Caribbean won less than four percent of all the medals awarded winning 490 medals out of the 12,550 won. Cuba has had a remarkable record for such a small island nation, winning 63 of the region's 126 gold medals. Cuba won 24 in Beijing. I will try to highlight the successes of Latino athletes in the 20th Century Olympic Games in this introduction. The experience of Latinos in the Olympics goes back almost as far as it could to the second modern Olympic Games in Paris in 1900 where Cuba's Ramón Fonst Segundo became the first Latino athlete to ever win an Olympic gold medal which he captured in fencing. He is profiled in this section.

Twenty-four years later after the first medal and back in Paris, Joe Salas became the first Latino from the United States to capture a medal in boxing as a flyweight. In those same games the soccer team from Uruguay began its dominance by winning the first of two consecutive gold medals. In the 1928 Amsterdam Games, athletes from Argentina and Spain won medals in boxing and in equestrian including the first three gold medals won by Latinos in boxing and team show jumping.

In Los Angeles, Juan Zabala from Argentina won the marathon while his fellow countrymen won four more boxing medals. American Miguel de Capriles took a fencing bronze.

The 1936 Berlin Olympic were meant to be Adolf Hitler's propaganda festival to showcase the Nazi regime. The Germans tried to conceal their racist, anti-Semitic, militaristic character as the host and tried to sell an image of a peaceful, accepting nation. Before the Games there was a proposed boycott by the United States and several European nations. Spain was not one of the nations that were close to a boycott and the Latin American nations were not involved in the discussion in any impactful way. United States Olympic Committee president Avery Brundage made the case that politics had no place in sport and defeated the boycott attempts. When the Games ended, Hitler rapidly proceeded toward the extermination of the Jews across Europe and the start of World War II. Some historians believe that if we had boycotted the Games there might have been more international resistance to German intentions, and World War II and the Holocaust might have been avoided.

The polo and basketball teams from Mexico won that nation's first medals. Argentina continued to show its strength among Latin

American nations when Jeanette Campbell medaled in swimming. There were, of course, no Games in 1940 and 1944 while World War II raged. The 1948 London Olympics were a stage for the success of athletes from Mexico in diving and equestrian and Panama in track and field. Juan Venegas won Puerto Rico's first ever medal in boxing where he won the bronze in the bantamweight.

Four years later in the Helsinki Games, Brazil and Venezuela dominated the triple jump with the gold going to Brazil's Adhemar F. de Silva and the bronze to Venezuela's Asnoldo Devonish. Likewise, Argentina and Uruguay's rowing teams dominated double sculls winning the gold and bronze.

There were not many highlights for Latin American athletes in the next three Games in Melbourne, Rome, and Tokyo. Chile's Marlene Ahrens won a silver in the javelin in 1956 and Cuban Enrique Figuerola took the silver in the 100 meters in 1964. Ahrens remains the only woman athlete from Chile to win an Olympic medal. In 1960, Venezuela's Enrico Forcella won a bronze with the small bore rifle event and Spain's field hockey team captured the bronze.

Mexico City in 1968 marked the first Olympics in a Latin American country. It was marked by political events that were national and international. Shortly before the Games were to begin, students poured into the streets to protest and ran into the Mexican army and police. More than 300 students were killed. The International Olympic Committee went ahead with the games in spite of the atmosphere in Mexico City.

The Olympic Project for Human Rights, led by Dr. Harry Edwards, had attempted to have a boycott of the Games by African-American athletes to protest racism in both the United States and in South Africa. The boycott was eventually called off but it was widely believed that something would be done by African-American athletes during the Games. What happened shocked the sports world and became the lasting image of the Mexico City Games. Tommie Smith and John Carlos won the gold and bronze medals in the 200 meter race. During the medal ceremony, they came to the podium barefoot and raised their black gloved fists during the playing of the national anthem. IOC President had Smith and Carlos banned from the Olympic Village. For years they had a difficult time getting jobs. It was one of the largest controversies ever at a sports event. Four decades later, Smith and Carlos are viewed mostly as courageous heroes. They certainly are that and more to me as they helped launch the athletic revolution.

But the Games went on and the riots and the actions by African-American athletes were eventually, if temporarily, put in the background. Host Mexico won four boxing medals and Felipe Muñoz, their star swimmer, won a gold medal in the 200 meter breaststroke. Cuba and Brazil captured the silver and bronze, respectively in the 4 × 100 meter men's relay.

The politics of the Games not only continued but the death toll included 11 Israeli athletes who were killed by Palestinians who kidnapped the athletes. They died in what has become known as the Munich Massacre. But once again the games went on and boxers from Latin America and the Caribbean began to march to the victory stand more often. Athletes from Cuba, Columbia, Mexico, and Spain won 11 medals in 1972. It was the launch of the Olympic career of the brilliant Cuban heavyweight, Teófilo Stevenson. Stevenson is one of the athletes highlighted in the section. His countrywomen won the bronze in the 4 × 100 meter relay.

There was a boycott by the African nations in 1976 after the IOC refused to ban New Zealand after its national rugby team competed in South Africa in 1976. The Peoples Republic of China and Taiwan also did not compete because of political debates over which team should represent China.

Cuba continued to show its athletic power by winning a volleyball bronze, gold in the men's 400 and 800 due to Alberto Juantorena's domination, and a host of boxing medals. Juantorena is another of the athletes highlighted in the section. In all, Latino boxers from Mexico, Puerto Rico, and Venezuela in addition to Cuba won 12 medals. Daniel Bautista from Mexico won the 20 kilometer walk.

Boycotts continued in 1980 and 1984. In the 1980 Moscow Olympics, 61 nations pulled out after US President Jimmy Carter called for a protest against the Soviet invasion of Afghanistan. In the 1984 Los Angeles Games, 14 Soviet allies pulled out citing "security" reasons. It was an apparent retaliation for the US-led boycott of the Moscow Games.

But once again, both Games went on. In Moscow, Cuban boxers swept 10 medals while countrywoman María Colón became the first Latina to win a gold when she captured the javelin. Colón is another of the athletes highlighted in the section. Brazil, Guatemala, and Spain won bronze, silver, and gold, respectively in the 4 × 200 women's freestyle, the equestrian three day event, and the Flying Dutchman yachting competition.

The absence of the Cubans who boycotted Los Angles changed the events they had dominated, especially boxing. The Dominican Republic's Pedro J. Nolasco took a silver bantamweight title. Paul González of the USA won the light flyweight gold. Fellow countryman Pablo Morales swept three swimming medals. Morales is another of the athletes highlighted in the section. Mexico won three medals when walkers Raúl González and Ernesto Canto took two gold medals and a silver in the 20 and 50 kilometer walks, respectively.

The medal count was again affected when Cuba and Ethiopia stayed home from the 1988 Seoul Olympics in support of North Korea when the IOC did not allow them to be co-hosts of the 1988 Games. Two Latinos from the United States won medals when Tracie Ruiz-Conforto and Michael Carbajal both won silver in synchronized swimming and boxing's light flyweight division. Ruiz-Conforto is another of the athletes highlighted in the section. Argentina men's team and Peru's women's team won the bronze and silver respectively in volleyball. Aurelio Miguel won the gold in the half-heavyweight class in judo. He was from Brazil.

In Barcelona in 1992, the Cubans were back and finished fifth in the total medal count with 15 gold medals and 31 medals overall. Host Spain was sixth with six golds and 22 overall medals. U.S. team members Oscar de La Hoya and Trent Dimas won the gold in boxing and gymnastics, respectively. Pablo Morales won two gold medals. De La Hoya and Dimas are also featured here.

In the 1996 Atlanta Olympics, Cuban boxers won seven medals to dominate this Olympic sport while their baseball team took the gold. Ecuador's Jefferson Pérez won the gold in the 20 KM walk, while Mexico's Bernardo Segura takes the bronze. Brazilian swimmers won two bronze and a silver in the freestyle events. Latina-Americans Beatriz "Gigi" Fernández and Mary Jo Fernández captured the gold in women's tennis doubles.

Now we can meet the Olympians who we have selected from this long list of possibilities.

Summer Olympics

Ramón Fonst Segundo became the first Latino athlete to win Olympic Gold when he did so at the 1900 Games in Paris. While the Cuban's name is not particularly well known today, his 1900 victory coupled with three more gold medals in fencing at the 1904 Olympics, helped launch Cuba as Latin America's winningest nation at the Olympics.

Born in Los Angeles, featherweight boxer Joe Salas was the first American-born Latino to compete on a United States Olympic team. He won the National Amateur Featherweight title in 1924, which qualified him for the Olympics where he lost in the gold-medal match. Following the Olympics, Salas continued to fight professionally for five years, retiring in 1929 with a 42-6 record.

Considered the father of Mexican diving, in December of 1956, Joaquín Capilla Pérez capped off his third Olympic games by winning the 10 meter platform dive in the pools of Melbourne. Prior to the 1956 Games, Capilla dominated the 1951 and 1955 Pan American games by capturing the gold in the platform and springboard competitions at both events.

With triumphs at the 1972, 1976, and 1980 Olympic Games, Teófilo Stevenson became the first boxer to win three consecutive Olympic gold medals in the same weight division. At 17, he won his first Cuban national heavyweight title and after a loss to Duane Bobick at the 1971 Pan American games, Stevenson utterly dominated the sport as he did not drop a match in international competition over the next decade. Stevenson recorded only 19 losses in his career while on the way to winning three Olympic gold medals, three world titles, and 11 national championships.

World class sprinter Alberto Juantorena rewrote the record books by becoming the first athlete to ever win the elusive double gold in the 400m and 800m at the same Olympic Games. Juantorena stunned the sporting world with his utterly amazing effort at the 1976 Games in Montreal. Juantorena left behind a legacy that will forever be treasured in the track and field world and in his native Cuba.

At 22 years of age, Cuban María Colón won the javelin throw at the 1980 Olympics in Moscow, becoming the first Latina to win an Olympic gold medal. After finishing eighth at the World Championships in 1983, she threw a personal best 69.06 meters a few months before the 1984 Games in Los Angeles. However, because of the Cuban boycott of the 1984 Games and 1988 games in Seoul, South Korea, Colón never got the opportunity to defend her Olympic gold medal.

Born in Honolulu, Tracie Ruiz-Conforto started synchronized swimming as a 10-year old and quickly emerged as a dominant competitor. When synchronized swimming made its debut as an Olympic medal sport during the 1984 Los Angeles Games, Ruiz-Conforto won two gold medals. In the 1988 Olympics in the solo event she won silver. During her 16-year career, Ruiz-Conforto was a six-time U.S. national champion and was awarded 41 overall gold medals. She was inducted into the International U.S. Synchronized Swimming Hall of Fame and the International Women's Sports Hall of Fame. Ruiz-Conforto was also named "Synchronized Swimmer of the Century" in 2001 by the International Swimming Hall of Fame.

Pablo Morales, known as one of the greatest swimmers and coaches in United States history, owns an NCAA record of 11 individual titles while swimming for Stanford University from 1983–1987. He also helped lead the Cardinal to three consecutive NCAA titles. As an Olympic swimmer, Morales won three gold and two silver medals in the 1984 and 1992 Games. After his swimming career ended, Morales served in various coaching roles before taking his current position as the Head Swimming and Diving coach at Nebraska in 2001

As a young boy, Félix Savón marveled as Stevenson became a national boxing icon. Savón later went on to match Stevenson's mark of three gold medals by winning gold at the 1992, 1996, and 2000 Olympic Games, joining Stevenson as one of Cuba's all-time great fighters. A Cuban boycott of the Seoul Games delayed then 21-year-old Savón's march towards history at the 1988 Olympics. While Savón spent the 1990s achieving at the highest amateur levels of boxing, there was great pressure from people outside of Cuba telling him to leave his homeland and fight at the professional level in the United States. Savón responded by saying that he would never abandon his country.

Trent Dimas became the only American gymnast to win an individual gold medal on the horizontal bar in the 1992 Barcelona

Games. He is the only Latino to ever win a gold on the horizontal bar. No other male gymnast from the United States has won a gold medal in an Olympics played outside the United States.

Swimmer Claudia Poll won Costa Rica its one and only Olympic gold medal at the Summer Olympics in Atlanta in the women's 200 meter freestyle. She was the first Central American woman to win a gold medal. At the 2000 Summer Olympics in Australia, she won two bronze medals in the 200 and 400 meter freestyle events. Poll was named *Swimming World Magazine*'s best swimmer in 1997, Costa Rican Sportswoman of the Year five times, and Costa Rica's Athlete of the Century in 1999.

Steven, Diana, and Mark López are a unique family of taekwondo athletes coached by their older brother, Jean, who was a member of the 1996 U.S. National team with Steven. At taekwondo's Olympic debut in 2000, the then-21-year-old Steven López won the featherweight before winning the welterweight class at the 2004 Olympics in Athens. At the 2005 World Championships, López won his third straight title while Mark and Diana won their divisions as well. This marked the first time in any sport that three siblings earned world titles at the same event. Steven, Diana, and Mark López made history again in the 2008 Beijing Olympics as the first three family members to represent the United States at the Olympics since 1904. They were also the first U.S. siblings to win medals at an Olympic Games.

Irving Saladino won Panama's first Olympic gold medal when he captured the long jump at the 2008 Beijing Summer Games. He came home to a hero's welcome because he was also the first Central American man to win a gold medal. He dreamt of replicating fellow Panamanian and New York Yankee Mariano Rivera's path but instead found his fame in track.

The 2004 Argentina Men's Basketball team shocked the world of sport at the Athens Games by winning the gold medal. They knocked out the usually dominant United States team which had won 13 of the 17 gold medals awarded over seven decades. Manu Ginóbili's 29 points led his team to an 89-81 victory in the semifinals and then won the gold against Italy, 84-69. The gold was Argentina's first Olympic medal in basketball.

Alberto Salazar was a great cross country student-athlete at Oregon and made the US Olympic team that never went to the boycotted Moscow Games in 1980. That was when he made the fateful choice to become a marathon runner. He won three consecutive New York Marathons in 1980, 1981, and 1982. In 1981, he set a then world-record time of 2:08.17. He also won the Boston Marathon in 1982. He made the 1984 Olympic marathon team but did not win a medal.

Winter Olympics

A standard joke about the Winter Olympics was that the snow was not the only thing that was white. When 23 African-American, Latino, and Asian Americans made the 211 member United States team for the Turin Winter Games in 2006, it was two times the number who made the 2002 team for the Salt Lake City Games and four times the number on the 1998 and 1994 U.S. teams.

Geography and climate, of course, have not helped athletes from Latin America and the Caribbean to be great competitors in the Olympics. United States born athletes have fared better but there has also not been as much interest in winter sports as is summer sports.

Jennifer Rodríguez won 12 world championships as a roller skater before switching to speed skating. The Cuban-American became the first Latina-American medalist when she won the bronze in the 1000 and 1500 meter events in the 1998 Nagano Games. Since then she has won more than 45 international medals and has won several world championships.

Mexican-American Derek Parra became the first Latino-American to win a Winter Games gold medal in 2002 where he captured the 1500 meter event as well as a silver medal in the 5000 meter event. Like Rodríguez, he was a champion roller skater who switched sports. Parra was the U.S. speed skating coach for the 2010 Vancouver Olympics.

The Winter Games remain a largely exclusive club. In the summer games, 200 nations bring more than 10,000 athletes. In the 2004 Athens Olympics, athletes from 75 nations climbed the victory stand. The 2006 Winter Games in Turin hosted on 87 nations and 2500 athletes. Only 24 nations made a similar climb to the victory stand and they all came from North America, Europe, Asia, and Australia.

The Winter Olympics are a slow work in progress for Latino athletes, especially for those from outside the United States.

Latino Superstars on the International Stage

Edson Arantes do Nascimento, with the nickname Pelé, has become synonymous with fútbol much like Ruth with baseball, Jordan with basketball, and Ali with boxing. Having scored a total of 1,281 goals throughout his 22-year career, Pelé is the only player to have played on three World Cup championship teams. His agility, tempo, and ball-handling skills revolutionized soccer as he scored five goals or more per game on six occasions, four goals in 30 games, and finished his career with 92 hat trick games.

Argentinean Alfredo di Stéfano played scoccer for Columbian club Los Millionarios as the leading scorer with 267 goals in route to three Columbian Championships in four years. Continuing his career with Real Madrid, di Stéfano scored an astonishing 307 goals in competitive club matches. Real Madrid won eight Spanish League titles, five European cup titles, and the inaugural World Club Cup championship in 1960. In 1997, di Stéfano was inducted into the International Football Hall of Fame.

Brazilian soccer star Manuel "Garrincha" dos Santos' first international appearance for Brazil came at the 1958 World Cup with fellow rookie Pelé. Brazil never lost a game in which both Pelé and Garrincha started together. Tested at the 1962 World Cup when Pelé suffered a hamstring injury, Garrincha stepped up by becoming the leading goal scorer for the entire tournament as Brazil won a second straight World Cup title.

Soccer star Hugo Sánchez is revered by Mexican fans although Mexico never won a World Cup. In 1999, the International Federation of Football History and Statistics placed Sánchez as the 26th best soccer player of all-time and the greatest ever to come from the North America and Central America region. Sánchez left the game in 1997 with a total of 239 goals in the Spanish leagues and competed in three World Cups for Mexico.

Diego Maradona scored five goals in seven contests at the 1986 World Cup, leading his Argentinean national team to the title. Playing for FC Barcelona from 1982–1984, Maradona scored 22 goals in his 36 appearances. During the years of 1984–1991, Maradona led his new club team, SSC Napoli, to the Serie A Italia Championships for the first time ever in 1986 and the prestigious UEFA Cup in 1989.

Selected three times as the world's best goalkeeper in 1995, 1997, and 1998, José Chilavert played for his native Paraguayan national team as well as clubs in Argentina, Spain, and France. In the 1998 World Cup, Chilavert relinquished just two goals in four games for Paraguay, shutting out Spain and Bulgaria and pushing eventual champion France to double overtime before being eliminated.

Cuba's Ana Quirot won both the 400 meter and 800 meter events at the 1986 Central American and Caribbean Games and the 1997 Pan American Games. She won the 800 meter world championship in 1989. Almost killed in a fire, Quirot came back to win the world championships in 1995 and 1997 and won a silver medal at the 1996 Olympics in Atlanta.

Ana Guevara's first major track and field victory came in the 1999 Pan American Games where she won gold for Mexico in the 400 meters. In 2001, Guevara garnered bronze in the World Championships before winning the 2003 World Championships. Guevara won gold in her event in the Pan American Games in 2003 and 2007. Following her silver medal finish in the 2004 Olympics in Athens, Guevara won bronze at the 2005 World Championships.

Argentinean Juan Manuel Fangio joined the Formula One racing circuit in 1950. Throughout seven full Formula One seasons, Fangio won five championships. In 1990, he was inducted into the International Motorsports Hall of Fame, the only Latino in the Hall of Fame and the first from Latin America.

Considered one of Brazil's most beloved sports heroes, Ayrton Senna finished his career with three Formula One world championships, 41 career victories, and 65 pole qualifiers. In 2000, he was posthumously inducted into the International Motorsports Hall of Fame after he died when his race car crashed at the San Marino Grand Prix in Italy in 1994. Brazil declared three days of mourning.

Now we can meet these legendary superstars.

14

SUMMER OLYMPICS

Ramón Fonst

First Latino to Win Gold Medal at Summer Olympics

by Charlie Harless

We assume that if someone becomes the very first to do something of note, then like clockwork the recognition and adulation for this achievement will come pouring in. When Ramón Fonst Segundo became the first Latin American athlete to ever win an Olympic gold medal, there was undoubtedly celebration as he returned home from the 1900 Games in Paris to his native Havana. Yet in the century that has passed since Fonst's monumental victory, few journalistic accounts detailing his winning performance in the épée fencing competition have survived the course of time. Early 20th Century American writers largely overlooked his accomplishments and Cuba did not have much in the way of organized journalism, as Fonst's accomplishments took place two years before Cuba became an independent republic. In a way, it almost seems as if history has forgotten Fonst.

While indeed little is known about the mindset and personal story of this history making man, Fonst can never be truly forgotten when understanding the precedent his victory set. Not only would Fonst win three more gold medals in fencing at the 1904 Olympics, but his wins were the start of an impressive Cuban Olympic movement that over the last century has had athletes accumulate 67 gold medals and made Cuba the winningest Latin American country in

Olympic history. Fonst's victory was even more remarkable considering the discrimination he faced from European judges and Olympic officials. In a translation of an interview he gave shortly before his death in 1959, Fonst recalled that the 1900 Olympic officials saw him not only as a 17-year-old foreigner, but also viewed him as "un intruso," or an intruder.[1] Thus, Fonst's performance was so special that he was able to overcome biases to claim gold and truly make the second modern Olympic Games a world affair. Even more importantly, by "intruding" on the Olympic sport scene, Fonst opened the doors for all future Latin American athletes to feel that they too had a legitimate shot at Olympic gold if they showed that they were the best in the world.

In the years following the 1900 and 1904 Olympic Games, Fonst remained active in not only fencing, but competed in boxing, cycling, and shooting. From 1941–1946, he gave back to his home nation by serving as the president of the Cuban Olympic Committee and overseeing the development of aspiring Olympic athletes. Today, Fonst continues to hold onto a century's old record as the only male athlete to have won two individual épée gold medals. Cuba has also honored this first gold medalist by naming one of its primary indoor sports facilities after him in Havana. While there are few words out there that shed light on the man behind the record, the name Ramón Fonst will be forever written as the first line in the continually growing story of Latin American achievement in sport.

Notes

1. Miguel Ernesto Gómez Masjuán,. "Ramón Fonst, ni siquiera el aire pudo tocarlo," *Emisora Habana Radio*, May 30, 2008. Accessed online, August 24, 2009, from http://www.habanaradio.cu/singlefile/?secc=19&subsecc=19&id_art=20080520111215.

Joseph "Joe" Salas

First Latino-American to Compete in Summer Olympics

by Cara-Lynn Lopresti

Born in Los Angeles, Joe Salas was a featherweight professional boxer that competed in the 1920s. He was also the first Latino-American to compete on a United States Olympic team.

Salas always considered himself "very fortunate to have such a wonderful family"[1] and a pleasant childhood. He was the youngest of 11 children, with seven girls and four boys. His father worked for the city of Los Angeles planting trees, while his mother was busy keeping the household together. Salas also considered many of his neighbors as part of his family as they played a crucial part in his life after his father passed away. His neighbors also taught him about the importance of diversity, as he was able to witness early on how many people of different backgrounds can live together and support one another.

Salas worked as a newspaper delivery boy before taking up boxing in 1920. He became interested in boxing after watching one of his neighbors, Joe Rivers, train in his backyard. Rivers was an outstanding professional boxer and one of the first locals to make a name for himself. Salas thought that "if he can do it, I can do it,"[2] and so he started to practice on the bags with him. Soon after, Salas became involved in organized training at the Los Angeles Athletic Club at the age of 14.

Salas' boxing career took off after he won the National Amateur Featherweight title in 1924, which qualified him for the Olympics. Salas's good friend, and fellow Los Angeles Athletic Club boxer, Jackie Fields was also chosen to represent the United States Olympic team. There were four boxers from Salas's hometown that competed in the 1924 Paris Olympics. Salas commented that when they all "got together, it was like family."[3] The boxing competition at the 1924 Olympics lasted five days. Both Fields and Salas won their preliminary matches in the featherweight, 126-pound class. In the first round, Salas defeated Agnew Burlie of Canada. He then went on to beat Bruno Petrarca from Italy and Jean Devergnies from Belgium to reach the finals against Fields.

The gold medal fight took place "at a time when Olympic competitors from the same country were permitted to face each other" and "was an emotional contest for both boxers."[4] Later Salas reflected on his memories of this Olympic showdown, stating that they had to dress in the same room and when the officials "knocked on the door, we looked at each other and started to cry, and we hugged each other. Ten minutes later, we were beating the hell out of each other."[5] It was a very close fight, but Fields, only 16 at the time, was given the decision after the final round. Salas's loss in that gold-medal match was his first defeat of his amateur career. However, "after the verdict was given the two fighters embraced in the ring while two American flags were raised,"[6] with Salas winning the silver and Fields the gold medal. Another member of the Los Angeles Athletic Club, Fidel La Barba, also won a gold medal in the flyweight division. Salas and La Barba lived five blocks apart from each other as children and grew up playing together.

Once the two boxers returned home from Paris, public interest demanded another fight between the friends. In response, Fields and Salas turned professional and debuted against each other in late 1924 in Vernon. Fields was victorious again in a 10-round decision. Salas continued to fight professionally for five years under the guidance of his two managers, George Blake and Gig Rooney. He traveled all over the United States competing and earning a good living. However, Salas's professional career was plagued by frequent hand injuries due to his aggressive punching style, which forced him to retire in 1929 with a 42-6 record.

Following retirement, Salas became a role model to young athletes, having spoken to youngsters at different clubs about his boxing experiences. He also owned a liquor store and worked as a handyman in his free time. In 1932, Salas was invited to work as a training assistant for the American Olympic boxing team. He built a house in East Los Angeles that same year and lived there with his high school sweetheart the rest of his life. Salas and his wife had two sons, Joe Jr. and Robert, and some wonderful grandchildren. Salas passed away on June 11th, 1987 at the tender age of 83, eight days after his former rival, teammate and friend, Jackie Fields.

Notes

1. "Joseph Salas 1924 Oympic Games Boxing." *Amateur Athletic Foundation of Los Angeles*. 1988. http://www.la84foundation.org/6oic/OralHistory/OHSalas.pdf

2. Ibid.

3. Ibid.

4. Michael Janofsky & Thomas Janofsky, Robert McG. "Sports World Specials; Memorable Showdown," *New York Times*. (Late Edition [East Coast]). July 22, 1987. P. C. 2.

5. Earl Gustkey, "The Day in Sports; COUNTDOWN TO 2000 / A Day-by-Day Recap of Some of the Most Important Sports Moments of the 20th Century: July 20, 1924; Gold Medal Turns Friends Into Enemies; [Home Edition]" *Los Angeles Times*. Los Angeles,. July 20, 1999. P. 8.

6. "Joe Salas." *Sports Reference LLC*. 2000–2009. http://www.sports-reference.com/olympics/athletes/sa/joe-salas-1.html

Joaquín Capilla Pérez

Summer Olympic Gold Medalist

by Charlie Harless

The third time's the charm; practice makes perfect; if at first you don't succeed, just try, try again. These idioms are repeated so frequently in the English language that their usage can feel hackneyed even if they accurately describe someone's successes or shortcomings in achieving their dreams. Yet when considered in the context of Joaquín Capilla Pérez's Olympic career, all three expressions somehow become more pertinent and make one believe that they could have very easily been conceived with the Mexican diver in mind.

In December of 1956, Capilla capped off his third Olympic games by winning the 10-meter platform dive in the pools of Melbourne, Australia, becoming the first Mexican diver to ever win a gold medal in the sport. The 27-year-old Capilla had to be perfect to knock off a vaunted United States contingent, led by rival Sammy Lee. As the two-time defending gold medalist in the 10-meter platform whose previous performances only allowed for Capilla to take silver in 1952 and bronze in 1948. While Lee surprisingly finished out of medal contention in 1956, Capilla's improved technique and resiliency to never let go of his gold medal ambitions combined to give him just what he needed to record a three-hundredths of a point edge in the final scorecard at the 1956 games. This margin of victory over American silver medalist Gary Tobian was the slimmest ever in the sport of Olympic platform diving and represented the thin line that separates the best athletes from the rest in the eyes of history. Capping off his third Olympic games with his first medal, a bronze, in the three-meter springboard competition, Capilla cemented his place as Mexico's all-time greatest diver.

Even without the Olympic gold medal in 1956, Capilla's other amateur performances had already shaped his indelible legacy in Mexico. At the 1951 and 1955 Pan American games, Capilla was a perfect 4 for 4, capturing golds in the platform and springboard at both events. While there should have been little surprise that Capilla had the talent to win an Olympic diving gold, his actual achievement of beating the Americans and winning the previously unattainable gold medal set a frenzy off in Mexico. Capilla was treated to a hero's welcome upon his arrival home from Melbourne, as nearly 10,000 Mexican fans, including many of the country's biggest politicians and entertainment stars, overflowed the area in and around the airport to congratulate the diver. The new celebrity could not go anywhere without being recognized and lauded by his fellow citizens, as it took a security motorcade of 14 motorcycles to safely escort Capilla from the airport celebration to his home in Mexico City. Although on the outside everything appeared to be golden for Capilla, the diving great soon hit a rough patch as he tried to cope with life in the public bubble. Capilla, reflecting on some of his tougher days, said of his adjustment to newfound fame that "how is one going to be ready? Fame, women, money . . . we get lost!"[1] After failing to make any more Olympic games, including the 1968 games held in his native Mexico City, Capilla was devastated at his inability to compete and the lack of consideration he received from the Mexican Olympic delegation. Capilla recalled that at the 1968 Olympics, "I thought that I'd be lighting the torch. Then I thought I'd give the oath, but no, what I did was crash my car at Barranca del Muerto and have the story come out in the police section of the newspaper, all due to alcohol."[2] Capilla's alcoholism contributed to many problems in his life, including the aforementioned car crash, the loss of friends, and a diminished level of respect from many of his fans.

Capilla went through a great portion of his adult life without much success, as he had lacked the skills needed to find a job after his athletic career had come to an end. As fellow diver Luis Niño de Rivera surmised, "people love the medals, but what are they worth if you have nothing to fall back on?"[3] Although there was a long stretch of isolation and sadness in his life, Capilla eventually found the road to recovery by building a stronger commitment to his church and faith. Today, Capilla is rightfully revered in his Mexico for his amazing athletic achievements and role as a standard bearer for which almost all other Mexican sporting figures are measured up against. Mexican diving star Paola Espinosa, a 2008 Olympic bronze medalist in the 10-meter synchronized platform dive, has said of Capilla's influence that, "I don't just want to be an Olympic medalist . . . I want to transcend, to be like Joaquín Capilla and become the best female diver."[4] In 2008, at the dedication ceremony of a new pool named after Capilla at the "Centro Deportivo Olímipico Mexicano," diver Jesús Mena, who followed in Capilla's footsteps and earned the bronze medal at the 1988 Olympic games, said of Capilla that "if I feel grateful about anything in my life, it is belonging to the family of divers. It is an honor to be in the same discipline as people like Joaquín Capilla."[5]

Rightfully seen as the father of Mexican diving, Capilla's impact will not be forgotten as his winning legacy is remembered by other divers who carry the Mexican flag and seek to duplicate his incredible success. Although no Mexican diver has won a gold medal since Capilla did so in Melbourne, perhaps future generations of Mexican divers could achieve success by adhering to the principles of those familiar idioms that were embodied by Capilla. Better yet, the next generation of divers should not forget a familiar Mexican idiom that could also speak to their journey to follow in Capilla's large footsteps. This idiom reads "poco a poco se anda lejos," or "little by little one goes far," sound advice when attempting to emulate the greatness of Capilla, a true giant of diving and of Mexico.

Notes

1. "El precio del Olimpo: Joaquin Capilla lo paga," *Vanguardia*, August 18, 2008. Retrieved online August 20, 2009 from http://www.vanguardia.com.mx/XStatic/van guardia/template/content.aspx?se=deportes&su=beijing&id= 210454&te=nota.

2. Gerardo Mendoza, "El premio mayor es Joaquin Capilla," *Excelsior*, July 15, 2008.

3. "El precio del Olimpo: Joaquin Capilla lo paga," *Vanguardia*, August 18, 2008. Retrieved online August 20, 2009 from http://www.vanguardia.com.mx/XStatic/van guardia/template/content.aspx?se=deportes&su=beijing&id= 210454&te=nota.

4. Villanueva, Rosalia. "Paola Espinosa no se conforma y desea hacer historia, como Joaquin Capilla," *La Jornada*, October 14, 2008.

5. "Joaquin Capilla recibe homenaje" *Es Mas*, July 2, 2005. Retrieved online August 20, 2009 from http://www.esmas.com/deportes/otrosdeportes/457067.html.

Teófilo Stevenson

Summer Olympic Gold Medalist

by Charlie Harless

To listen to the words and rags-to-riches success story of Cuban boxer Teófilo Stevenson, you would believe he was the wealthiest man in the world. Stevenson does not have the fame and millions earned by the Muhammad Ali's, George Forman's, and Mike Tyson's of the world, yet Stevenson is none the poorer for his decision to remain an amateur in the sport and rebuff promises of the luxuries that come with being a great professional boxer. A loyal Cuban, Stevenson rejected the temptation to defect to the United States and was handsomely rewarded with the love and adoration of a nation. Stevenson once said, "I will not leave my country for one million dollars or for much more than that. What is a million dollars against eight million Cubans who love me?"[1] Another great Cuban athlete held in high esteem by his home country, track star Alberto Juantorena, indicated that the love affair between Stevenson and the people of Cuba was mutual when saying, "There is really nobody like Teófilo. He is such a good person, very humble, very easy going. He occupies a special place in Cuba."[2]

Stevenson occupies a special place in the history of the sport of boxing as well, becoming the first pugilist to ever win three consecutive Olympic gold medals in the same weight division with his triumphs at the 1972, 1976, and 1980 games. Yet long before he was demolishing opponents in the ring, Stevenson had a lengthy road to travel from his humble beginnings. Stevenson's fighting spirit was instilled at a young age, as he was not born into riches or prosperity. Stevenson's father, originally from the Caribbean Island of St. Vicent, earned less than a dollar a day as a worker in the sugar mills of Delicias while supporting a wife and five children. In search of a better life and to utilize his natural athletic talent, Stevenson left his hometown of Puerto Padre as a teenage boy to develop his boxing skills at the national sports complex in Havana.

Although Stevenson would one day grow into his imposing 6'5", 200 pound-plus frame, he took his lumps as an amateur learning the intricacies of timing and strategy. Stevenson would later recall that "I lost 14 of my first 20 fights. I hated getting hit. What happened was that I decided I hated losing even more."[3] The young boxer's aversion to losing soon became apparent in his results in the ring, as at seventeen he would win his first Cuban national heavyweight title and showcased an intimidating right hook that often intimidated opponents before they stepped in the ring. After a loss to Duane Bobick in the 1971 Pan American games, Stevenson would utterly dominate the sport as he failed to drop a match in international competition over the next decade. As his reputation as a great knockout fighter grew, more and more of his matches would end in forfeit, as competitors did not want to get pummeled. Stevenson responded to this by saying that, "When I am training and sweating, I do not like to think about the forfeits. I must be prepared to fight every bout because if I am not ready, they will see it and suddenly everyone will be anxious to fight."[4]

For all his preparation, nothing could ready Stevenson for the challenge he would face in attempting to win Cuba's first gold medal in boxing. At the 1972 games in Munich, he would encounter Bobick in the quarterfinal round. Although many considered the American Bobick to be the favorite, Stevenson knocked him down three times in the final round of the bout to avenge his loss in the 1971 Pan American Games. What made the result even more impressive in retrospect was the fact that Stevenson won that match and eventually the gold medal while fighting with a fractured hand. Stevenson refused to allow any doctors to examine him so as not to expose his injury and risk being told to pull out of contention and derail his Olympic dream. His performance as defending champion at the 1976 Olympics was even more dominant, recording three straight knockouts before a 3 round TKO over Romania's Mircea Simon for his second gold medal.

As dominant as Stevenson had become, there were questions as to whether he could do the same damage at the professional level. Among those who sought to find out the answer to this question were international agents and fight promoters, who by the time Stevenson had earned his second gold medal had already made multiple million-dollar offers in attempts to lure the prized fighter away from his native Cuba. Observers such as Bob Surkein, a head referee at the Olympic games with more than three decades of experience once said that, "Stevenson is the best. Better than Foreman or Frazier and as good as Ali, but Ali fought as a light heavy in the Olympics. Stevenson has quick hands and he already moves almost as well as Ali—and he's bigger. He is a classic boxer, like all the Cubans. He has a strong jab and a punishing one."[5] With the hyperbole and anticipation for a dream Ali-Stevenson match in full swing, Stevenson responded on multiple occasions with a firm 'no' out of respect for his country and his distaste for the idea of professional sports by saying, "if you are a professional, you are not an athlete."[6] Yet the competitor inside Stevenson did not stop his mind from contemplating the outcome of such a dream showdown. "Of course, I would like to have seen what would have happened against Ali. The feeling you have when you think about it is that you will be the one getting the victory."[7]

Although Stevenson never got the chance to earn a win over the famed Ali, Stevenson would end his storied career at the age of 36 with an outstanding 312 victories to his name. Even more impressive was the fact that Stevenson recorded only 19 losses in his career while on the way to winning three Olympic gold medals, three world titles, and 11 national championships. Upon his retirement, Stevenson made good on his promise to begin coaching amateur talent in Cuba to pass on his expertise to young hopefuls. Stevenson put his career in perspective when saying, "sports has its different phases. You grow, you develop, and then you become a champion. I was a champion, and now I've decided to go on to other tasks."[8] Stevenson's accolades set the bar high for future pugilists and undoubtedly inspired future Cuban greats like Félix Sávon to measure their greatness against his record of achievement. Although his records will likely be matched and broken in the future, Stevenson will always be treasured by his country and boxing fans everywhere for being the utmost professional amateur boxer.

Notes

1. Tex Maule, "He'd Rather be Red than Rich," *Sports Illustrated*, March 18, 1974.
2. Eugene Robinson, "The Cuban Ali," *The Washington Post*, June 10, 2001.
3. Ibid.

4. Thomas Boswell, "The National Treasures, Juantorena, Stevenson Stand Alone in Cuban Sport," *The Washington Post*, April 8, 1978.

5. Tex Maule, "He'd Rather be Red than Rich," *Sports Illustrated*, March 18, 1974.

6. John Papanek, "A New Bunch Punches In," *Sports Illustrated*, July 23, 1979.

7. Peter Alfano, "For Cuba's Stevenson, Quest Goes On," *The New York Times*, November 23, 1982.

8. Bill Brubaker, "The Enigma of Teofilo Stevenson," *The Washington Post*, February 21, 1989

Alberto Juantorena

Summer Olympic Gold Medalist

by Charlie Harless

"A man must be crazy to live so that one day a year, or one day every four years, is the most important in his life."[1] World class sprinter Alberto Juantorena understood the veracity of his statement when looking back on the crazy feat he undertook in the 1976 Olympic Games in Montreal. The muscular Cuban, blessed with a beautiful 9-foot stride and a physique that towered over most of his opponents on the track, rewrote the record books when he became the first athlete to ever win the elusive double gold in the 400 meter and 800 meter at the same Olympic games. In a combined 2:27.76 minutes, comprised of a 400 meter time of 44.26 seconds and a 800 meter world record time of 1:43.50 minutes, Juantorena stunned himself and the sporting world with his gargantuan effort. Looking back, Juantorena has said that "I can scarcely believe even now that I won both events. No one seriously considered me in the 800. The 400 was the only race I really knew. I was even a little afraid of the 800 for that reason. I entered it only for fun."[2]

Running became an exciting endeavor for Juantorena later in life, after the 6' 3" athlete realized that his dreams of basketball glory would not come true. Juantorena had spent the majority of his childhood away from his hometown of Santiago de Cuba and instead developed his athletic skills in Havana at the Higher School of Athletic Improvement. Juantorena would recall that "I loved basketball, but the basketball coach said I had no further chances in basketball and the coach wanted me to join him."[3] Track coach Zygmunt Zabierzowski would help mold Juantorena into a track star in a relatively short time. Just a little over a year after the two began working together, Juantorena qualified for the 1972 Olympics and went on to give a respectable showing, falling in a semifinal heat of the 400 meter race.

After this introduction to the Olympics, Juantorena quickly burst onto the international scene. While many observers of the time considered him to be a raw talent, lacking an understanding of race strategy that comes with experience, Juantorena had an innate ability to intimidate and use his enormous stride to compete and win many races. Written at the peak of Juantorena's dominance, *Washington Post* writer Thomas Boswell observed that "he was a running machine so inexorably efficient that it was both magnificent and oppressive. Combining the speed of the dashes and the stamina of distance runners, he seemed a hybrid, not a human."[4] Juantorena was so physically dominant and rewrote human records with such ease that his competitors soon nicknamed the track star "El Caballo," or the Horse. Juantorea would retort that "I've never seen myself run, but I think I look more like an ostrich than a horse. I think I seem to be floating, but I'm actually going fast."[5]

The nearly two and half minutes of glory in Montreal that would come to cement his legacy in the sport almost did not happen for El Caballo. Juantorena, a 400 meter runner, was coaxed into running 800 meters during practice sessions as a means to increase his endurance. When told by his coach in early 1976 that he should run both the 400 meter and 800 meter at the Olympic Games to be held later that summer, Juantorena initially rebuffed this suggestion. Juantorena expressed concern that he would not have the stamina to run the 400 meter race after putting his energy into the 800 meter. "I said, no way. My coach was running behind me for two weeks, trying to convince me to do it."[6] Soon, the 25-year-old Juantorena would have a change of heart and take on the challenge to shock the sporting world by doing what no athlete had ever done before, and as of this publication, has never since been done: winning both the 400 and 800 meter distance at one Olympic Games. After accomplishing this feat and setting a world record in the 800 meter race along the way, Juantorena humbly confessed that "Until recently, I never even thought about running the 800. It wasn't until a few months ago that I was fast enough to win a medal here in the 800. But a world record? That was really surprising. I had hoped to get a world record in the 400."[7]

Immediately following the Olympics, Juantorena continued to race, winning events and earning accolades that would warrant him a hero's following in Cuba. However, in a sport where the window for success is often brief, Juantorena soon began to slow down. While dealing with nagging foot injuries in the late 1970s and early 1980s, Juantorena continued to try and push himself to compete and tackle new obstacles. Yet in this race against time and his body's limitations,

Juantorena could never again reclaim the magic of 1976, as he ran to a disappointing fourth place finish in the 400 meters at his last Olympic Games in 1980. A keen observer of both his talent and his place in the hearts of his fans, Juantorena retired on his own terms in 1984. "I had begun to lose speed," Juantorena later said. "I couldn't do what I used to do . . . I realized I must take care of my image. One must understand when is the correct time to say 'goodbye' in sports. I was losing ground and this was the moment to say 'goodbye.'"[8]

Juantorena left behind a legacy and record breaking performance that will forever be treasured in the track and field world and in his native Cuba. Journalist Dave Stubbs detailed that "he (Juantorena) is revered in Cuba, a genuine hero to a people for whom sport is a way of life, and perhaps something to soften the hard times born of food rationing, gasoline shortages, and political turmoil."[9] Juantorena echoed a similar sentiment when stating that "sports for us is a matter of pride and health for Cuba," and he continued to make Cuba proud by serving in leadership roles for the country's national sports governing body.[10] Overseeing the development of other young Cuban talent, perhaps Juantorena will provide the resources and support to take another dreamer and mold him into a world class athlete and the face of a nation. Given Juantorena's track record, one would be unwise to count him out of any challenge he undertakes.

Notes

1. Thomas Boswell, "Juantorena: Mythic Steed Moon-bound," *The Washington Post*, July 9, 1979.

2. Dave Stubbs, "Juantorena a Pparadox in Track Spikes," *The Gazette*, July 29, 1991.

3. Joseph Treaster, "Juantorena Joins Cuba's Executive Suite," *The New York Times*, July 2, 1985.

4. Thomas Boswell, "Juantorena: Mythic Steed Moon-bound," *The Washington Post*, July 9, 1979.

5. Joseph Treaster, "Juantorena Joins Cuba's Executive Suite," *The New York Times*, July 2, 1985.

6. Tom Weir, "Bids for double gold not all that unusual" *USAToday*, July 31, 1996.

7. Pat Putnam, "Holy Moses, What a Dandy Race," *Sports Illustrated*, August 2, 1976.

8. Joseph Treaster, "Juantorena joins Cuba's Executive Suite," *The New York Times*, July 2, 1985.

9. Dave Stubbs, "Juantorena a Paradox in Track spikes," *The Gazette*, July 29, 1991.

10. Christine Brennan, "Juantorena Doesn't Fault U.S. Shuttle," *The Washington Post*, August 10, 1991.

María Colón

First Latina to Win Gold Medal in Summer Olympics

by Jared Bovinet

When María Colón arrived at Lenin Stadium in Moscow for the 1980 Olympics, a journalist described her as a "lioness running away from her cage."[1] At the brink of her historic breakthrough, the young javelin thrower found herself worlds away from her native Cuba and a long shot to win the javelin competition. Her personal best up to that point ranked her seventh in the world and in Moscow she faced five of the six women ranked ahead of her. Despite this, Colón proved to be the fiercest competitor and soon found herself receiving global accolades.

It did not take Colón long to make history after she entered the stadium. She had six throws during the competition but focused her energy on the first; viewing it as an all-or-nothing opportunity to show her opponents she had come to win. Colón's plan paid off as her first attempt proved to be her longest and resulted in an Olympic record. None of her 11 opponents beat the throw and she became the first Latina to win an Olympic gold medal. The historic significance of the moment could not be overemphasized, and Colón felt as if every one of her fellow Cubans stood with her during that night in July. "Ten million Cubans threw the javelin 68.40 meters with me that night,"[2] she said.

All the excitement and emotion of the night took root years before when Colón was growing up in Cuba. Born in March of 1958 in Baracoa, Colón was a natural athlete who excelled in many sports. She realized her potential as a track and field athlete after she competed in an event composed of a 60-meter sprint, a high jump, an 80-meter hurdle, and a javelin throw. She performed so well that she was selected to attend a series of schools that specialized in training promising, young athletes to perform at the next level. Her routine there consisted of academic classes in the morning followed by training under her coach, Miguel Ángel Justiz.

Her coach saw great potential in her and was impressed that she had such a strong arm for being so petite. Colón then earned the opportunity to travel to Mexico City, where she took first place in the javelin throw in an international track and field competition. Cuban national coaches soon took notice of the girl who showed much promise to bring home an Olympic medal one day.

When she was 19, Colón qualified to participate in the Central American and Caribbean Games, where she set a competition record with a throw of 63.40 meters. That same year, she won the javelin throw at the Pan American Games in Puerto Rico and was primed for success going into the Olympics.

Colón continued to win following the 1980 Olympics. After finishing eighth at the World Championships in 1983, she threw a personal best 69.06 meters a few months before the 1984 Games in Los Angeles. She never got the opportunity to defend her Olympic gold medal, however, because of the Cuban boycott of the 1984 Games and 1988 games in Seoul, South Korea.

Since retiring from track and field, Colón has worked tirelessly to promote women's involvement in sports across the world. She served as the Chairperson of the National Olympic Women's Committee and Sport Commission and was a member of the International Association of Athletics Federations Women's Committee along with the Pan American Women and Sport Commission. Colón has also worked to expand youth sport leagues around the world. In 2009, the International Olympic Committee awarded her the Women and Sports Award in recognition of her efforts to strengthen women's sport participation across the globe.

Notes

1. "María Caridad Colón," http://www.cuba-sport.com/en/stars/mariacaridad.asp /
2. "María Caridad Colón Ruenes-Elle fue la primera," Cuba-Atenas 2004. http://www.bohemia.cubasi.cu/cuba-atenas2004/maria-caridad.html

Tracie Ruiz-Conforto

Summer Olympic Gold Medalist

by Cara-Lynn Lopresti

When synchronized swimming made its debut as an Olympic sport during the 1984 Los Angeles Games, Tracie Ruiz-Conforto surfaced as the star. Her two gold medals in Los Angeles gave synchronized swimming unprecedented attention, and "for the first time, spectators saw the sport as something other than an obscure and seemingly unathletic little endeavor."[1] By the end of her career, Ruiz-Conforto captured more than two dozen international and national gold medals. Referred to as the "pioneer of U.S. Synchronized Swimming,"[2] Ruiz-Conforto is one of just three athletes to win four consecutive U.S. national titles and is the only athlete to win six solo national titles. If there is "a queen of the sport, [Ruiz-Conforto] is it . . . although she only modestly acknowledges her accomplishments."[3]

Born in Honolulu, Hawaii, Ruiz-Conforto started synchronized swimming as a 10-year-old and quickly emerged as a dominant competitor. At the University of Arizona, Ruiz-Conforto and teammate Candy Costie were instrumental in winning AIAW Championships for the Wildcats in 1981 and in 1984. She also captured the gold and silver medal at the 1982 World Championships and in 1984 she won her first Olympic gold medal as a soloist, and another gold medal in the duet with Costie.

After the Olympics, Ruiz-Conforto temporarily retired from synchronized swimming competition and decided to turn "her amateur talent into a promising entertainment career."[4] For two years she was featured in swimming shows at various amusement parks, including Cypress Gardens in Florida and Sea World. In 1985, Ruiz-Conforto married former Penn State linebacker Mike Conforto. The two met while Conforto was running a health club chain in Seattle along with former Seattle Seahawks lineman Ron Coder.

Ruiz-Conforto remained busy during her retirement by taking up body-building. She won the "Northwest Natural" title in November of 1986, but her experience made her realize that she missed synchronized swimming competition. After encouragement from her husband, Ruiz-Conforto decided to return to the pool and make another run at an Olympic medal. However, the second time around Ruiz-Conforto wanted to make sure that she took the time to really enjoy the sport and the Olympic journey. She was initially fearful of resuming her training since she was the first woman to attempt a return to the sport.

However, Ruiz-Conforto yearned for a strong comeback because she "never felt [like she] peaked individually."[5] She began training under her former coach, Charlotte Davis, and initially focused on body-building to shed the 15 pounds that she had gained during her layoff. She practiced seven hours a day in conditioning and endurance workouts, weightlifting and swimming, not just for a gold medal, but to achieve the "kind of performance [and] feeling that you nailed everything."[6]

After being out of the sport for many years, Ruiz-Conforto initially had a difficult time with her technical training, unfamiliar with many of the new routines and moves. She trained many intense hours with a swim coach to help refine her skills and to regain her competitive edge. In the summer of 1987, Ruiz-Conforto's hard work finally paid off when she won the gold medal at the Pan American Games over Canadian rival, Carolyn Waldo. In April she continued her promising comeback trail by scoring perfect marks for her routine and 9.8s and 9.9s on compulsory figures at the Olympic trials.

At the 1988 Seoul Olympics, Ruiz-Conforto only competed in the solo event, partly because Costie, her longtime partner, opted to remain retired. After winning the silver medal, Ruiz-Conforto retired once again, but her outstanding performance did not go unrecognized. During her 16-year career, she was a six-time U.S. national champion and was awarded 41 overall gold medals. She was inducted into the International U.S. Synchronized Swimming Hall of Fame, Class of 1992, and the International Women's Sports Hall of Fame. Ruiz-Conforto was also named "Synchronized Swimmer of the Century" in 2001 by the International Swimming Hall of Fame.

Following her retirement, Ruiz-Conforto served as a commentator for NBC Television, covering four Olympics games, including the Barcelona Olympics in 1992 and the 2000 Sydney Olympics. Recently, the United States Olympic Committee named Ruiz-Conforto a finalist for the U.S. Olympic Hall of Fame Class of 2009. The inductees will be revealed in early July and will be honored at a black-tie induction ceremony on August 12th at McCormick Place in

Chicago. Ruiz-Conforto and her husband have two children, Michael and Jacqueline, who are also outstanding athletes. Michael is a baseball and football star at Redmond High School, while Jacqueline is a standout soccer player and has been playing for the U.S. junior national team.

Notes

1. Sally Jenkins, "Ruiz and Retirement Weren't Synchronized; Sets Sights on Winning 1988 Olympic Gold: [FINALEdition]," *The Washington Post (pre-1997 Fulltext)*, August 15, 1987

2. "Tracie Ruiz-Conforto." *United States Olympic Committee.* 2009. http://www.team usa.org/halloffame/1/hof_answers/42

3. William Gildea, "In Barcelona, Everyone Gets Synchronized; Final Fine-Tunin for Games: [Final Edition]." *The Washington Post (pre-1997 Fulltext)*, July 23, 1992

4. Toni Ginnetti, "Time to Get Back in Sync // Ruiz-Conforto After 3rd Gold," *Chicago Sun Times.* September 18, 1988.

5. Ibid.

6. Ibid.

Pablo Morales

Summer Olympic Gold Medalist

by Cara-Lynn Lopresti

When Pablo Morales's mother, Blanca, was a child, she fell out of a raft and almost drowned. After that incident she promised to herself that if she had a child, that child would learn to swim, and so she taught Morales when he was five years old. Today, Morales is known as one of the greatest swimmers and coaches in United States history. He owns an NCAA record of 11 individual titles while swimming for Stanford University from 1983–1987. Morales held the U.S. Open and NCAA record in the 100-yard butterfly with a time of 46.26,

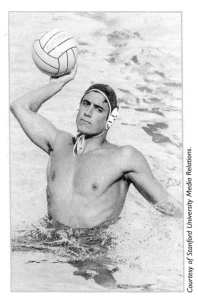

Courtesy of Stanford University Media Relations.

which stood for 13 years before being broken at the 1999 NCAA Championships. He also helped lead the Cardinal to three consecutive NCAA titles and four Pac-10 titles, earned two Pac-10 Swimmer-of-the-Year honors, and six individual Pac-10 titles. Morales is the all-time leading scorer at the NCAA Championships, tallying 235 points during his illustrious collegiate career. Morales holds the Stanford record in the 200-yard butterfly with a time of 1:42.60, and held the school record in the 100-yard fly until it was broken in 1998 by 00.07. One of Morales's greatest swimming accomplishments is holding the world record in the 100-meter butterfly with a time of 52.84 from 1986 until 1995.

Fans have described Morales as having "a personality St. Francis of Assisi would envy."[1] Since high school, Morales helped disabled elderly in his hometown of Santa Clara, California. While at Stanford, Morales was awarded the J.E. Sterling Award, which is presented to a student-athlete based on scholarship, leadership and community service. Morales was the recipient of the 1987 Al Masters Award, which is Stanford's highest award for athletic performance, leadership, and academic performance. He was the first male swimmer to win the award, and is one of two swimmers to have achieved the accomplishment. He was a CoSIDA Academic All-America selection in 1987, served as the director of Stanford's Volunteers for Youth Program, and worked on the campus newspaper as the beat writer for the women's basketball team.

As an Olympic swimmer, Morales won three gold and two silver medals in the 1984 and 1992 Games. The 1992 Olympics was especially meaningful to Morales as he captained the team after deciding to return to the pool at the age of 27. His decision to try a comeback had come upon him after a three-year layoff to go to law school. His mother was dying of cancer at the time, and then passed away in September. With his mother, himself, and the Olympics in mind, Morales "went off on his own little crusade. There were no shoe contracts or seven-figure deals being offered. He simply was giving a year of his life to see how well he could do."[2] When he started training, there were only seven months until the Olympic trials in Indianapolis and he was in terrible shape. He qualified for the team as a long shot, winning the trial race with a time of 54.05, more than a second slower than his world record. Then came the Olympics where he defied all odds by winning a gold medal in the 100m butterfly. Almost immediately following the race, Morales "started to cry" as "this was his Olympic story, as touching as any that ever had touched him."[3] Shortly after the Olympic Games, Morales was named the U.S. Olympic Committee's Sportsman of the Year.

Morales earned a law degree from Cornell in June of 1994, despite taking two years off from school to compete in the Olympics. After Morales retired from competition for good, he began a very successful career in coaching. Morales initially served as an assistant coach at his alma mater, Stanford, during the 1997–98 season, helping the team to the NCAA title. From 1998 to 2001, Morales held the reins as head women's swimming coach at San Jose State University. As head coach, Morales rebuilt a Spartan program that was near the bottom of the Western Athletic Conference. Under Morales' supervision the Spartans had six academic All-WAC swimmers and made it to the NCAA Championships after a 14-year absence. At the 2001 WAC Championships, five Spartans set school records, and three achieved NCAA qualification times. Seven others swimmers had times that placed among the top three in school history. Morales was named the 2000 WAC Coach of the Year for his role in rejuvenating the program.

In July 2001, Morales accepted his current position as the Head Swimming and Diving coach at Nebraska and is now entering his eighth season. In a similar fashion to his time at San Jose State University, Morales resurrected the Nebraska program. He led the Huskers to five consecutive winning seasons, owning an impressive .735 winning percentage over those five seasons. He finished the 2007–08 season with a 7-2 dual record, which was the fourth time in the last five seasons that he has led Nebraska to at least a 7-2 mark. Morales also plays a critical role in the academic achievement of his swimmers. Over the past three seasons, 78.6 percent of Morales' student-athletes have been named to the Big 12 Commissioner's Honor Roll each semester, including a school-record high 25 in the fall of 2007. Morales' former coach at Stanford, Skip Kenny, commented on Morales's accomplishments so far, stating that he may actually be "a better coach than he was a swimmer, and that is saying a lot since he was one of the best swimmers in the world. He has done things with kids that I thought I would never see."[4]

Aside from swimming, Morales is a devoted husband and father, a powerful public speaker and lecturer, and a contributing author to *The Swim Coaching Bible*. He is also very passionate about his ethnic background and supporting diversity initiatives. In April 2007, Morales was chosen as the U.S. Swimming Diversity Select Camp Head Coach. He also led motivational and educational sessions and team-building activities to boys and girls from all over the nation who are part of an ethnically under-represented population that is less than 20 percent of the current USA Swimming membership. However, even with all his accomplishments, Morales is not yet content. Morales demands excellence, and because of his sincere passion, drive, and dedication, he will experience success for many years to come.

Notes

1. Frank Litsky, "College Sports '87: Pablo Morales; A Gold Medal Winner Who is Never Satisfied," *New York Times*. April 5, 1987. http://www.nytimes.com/1987/04/05/sports/college-sports-87-pablo-morales-a-gold-medal-winner-who-is-never-satisfied.html

2. Leigh Montville, "Bravo, Pablo", *SI Vault*. August 3, 1992. http://vault.sportsillustrated.cnn.com/vault/article/magazine/MAG1004059/2/index.htm

3. Ibid.

4. "Pablo Morales." *Nebraska Huskers*. 2009. http://www.huskers.com/ViewArticle.dbml?DB_OEM_ID=100&ATCLID=3250&Q_SEASON=2006

Félix Savón

Summer Olympic Gold Medalist

by Charlie Harless

Following a legend can hardly be considered an enviable task. Cuban heavyweight champion Teófilo Stevenson had set the bar for excellence extremely high for future pugilists after becoming the first man to win three straight Olympic gold medals in the same weight division with his victories in 1972, 1976, and 1980. As a young boy, Félix Savón undoubtedly watched with pride along with the rest of the country as Stevenson became a national sporting icon, yet he did not harbor dreams of one day taking the mantle as Cuba's best heavyweight fighter. At the age of 13, Savón traveled away from his farming family and his home village near Guantanamo Bay to Havana to attend a sports academy in the hopes of becoming a rower. Savón would later reminisce and say that "I went to school to get on a rowing course but the professor told me it was full. I was unhappy and then another professor was calling out for people to join the boxing course and I agreed. That is how I became a boxer."[1]

Savón was not born to be a fighter, but after matching Stevenson's mark of three gold medals with victories at the 1992, 1996, and 2000 Olympic Games and winning 358 bouts with only 17 setbacks in his career, there was little doubt that Savón had joined Stevenson as one of Cuba's all-time greatest fighters. After his first Olympic win in 1992 at Barcelona, Stevenson himself boasted that "Three times I was the Olympic heavyweight champion. He [Savón] fought very well, and now he is the best."[2] When a member of the press asked Stevenson if Savón was "as good as you were?" Stevenson responded simply by saying, "Better."[3] The torch had been passed and Savón showed throughout his career that he had the athletic skill and pride for his country to not only admirably follow a legend, but become a legend himself.

While developing the skills that would allow him to dominate the sport of amateur boxing for the better part of a decade, Savón encountered one of his first major fights when trying to convince his family that he should participate in the sport at the academy in Havana. "My mother found out and wanted to take me out," Savón said. "One month later, my dad went to the school and told them he was taking me out of the school. But they [members of the sports academy] wouldn't listen to him. They came back to my mother and told her that I could win a gold medal. So, they thought it over and said it was OK to fight."[4] A teenage Savón would make good on that potential, growing into a towering six-foot, five-inch frame and an imposing build of just over 200 pounds while dominating opponents at the junior level. At fifteen, just two years after entering the academy, Savón won his first junior national title and a mere four years later claimed his first of an eventual six world championships. As he was rising in the sport, media and followers of boxing began to take notice of the young Cuban and predicted greatness in his future. In a 1986 *Wall Street Journal* feature, writer Frederick Klein wrote that "Savón is tall like Stevenson, resembles him facially and hits hard enough to more than offset his teenage clumsiness."[5] Savón was not the quickest of fighters, but what he lacked in mobility he made up for with a punishing assault of forceful and accurate punches. Some called the fighter one-dimensional for his attack style, but the formula proved tough to crack as he continued to rack up victories in his young career.

Fresh off of his first Pan American Championships in 1987, the year of 1988 should have been Savón's coming out party on the larger international stage in the Olympic Games, but a Cuban boycott of the Seoul Games delayed a 21-year-old Savón from marching toward history. In the wait between the 1988 and 1992 Olympic Games, Savón did not lose a single match and drove his career record to 137-9 just before leaving for Barcelona. Savón said in the midst of his dominance that he was "not invincible. Anybody with two hands and proper training could defeat me. But I always find some way to rise to the occasion."[6] Savón would rise to the occasion in Barcelona, winning the heavyweight division gold medal as expected by defeating Nigeria's David Izonritei by a score of 14-1. Four years later in Atlanta, Savón was even more dominant in his 20-1 victory over Canadian David Defiagbon that earned Savón his second gold medal. After the title bout, Defiagbon conceded that "Savón is very smart, the greatest. I was waiting for him to make a mistake, but he did not."[7]

While Savón spent the 1990s achieving at the highest amateur levels of boxing, there was great pressure from people outside of

Cuba telling him to leave his homeland and fight at the professional level in the United States. Reportedly offered around $10 million dollars to battle American heavyweight star Mike Tyson and millions more on several other occasions to defect from Cuba, Savón remained firm in his convictions and told everyone with deep pockets that he had no intentions of leaving Cuba. Savón has said that "A professional boxer is an item of merchandise and is exploited. I box for my ideals and the ideals of Cuba, but a professional boxer is boxing for somebody else and that takes the beauty away from the sport."[8] When asked about fellow Cuban boxers that had seized opportunities to defect while on travel at international tournaments, Savón responded by saying, "I would be the last to leave. My country has been good to me and I'm proud to serve it."[9]

Savón closed out his storied career carrying the Cuban flag at the 2000 Olympic Opening Ceremonies and making his country even prouder by matching Stevenson's three gold medals with a 21-13 victory over Sultan Ibragimov of Russia. Savón officially announced his retirement in 2001 at the age of 33, leaving behind a tremendous legacy in the sport. In addition to his three gold medals and six world junior championships, Savón racked up three gold medals at the Pan American games, and he managed to exit on his own terms before injury could force his hand. After announcing his retirement, Savón indicated that "all boxers miss the ring when they retire but it is better for a champion to withdraw at the top than to go into the ring and be shamefully beaten by a very young athlete. It was right for me to retire."[10] Although it has been said that he was not the speediest or most agile of fighters, in the end Savón proved that his impeccable timing and sense of his place in the sport were indeed his greatest strengths, ones that have made him a champion.

Notes

1. Steve Bunce, "Savon the Boxer Still Fights Noble Cause," *The Independent*, June 9, 2001.

2. William Nack, "Slight Heavies," *Sports Illustrated*, August 17, 1992.

3. Ibid.

4. Mark Riley, "The Rise and Rise of a Cuban Hero," *The Sydney Morning Herald*, September 12, 2000.

5. Ibid.

6. Steve Woodward, "Cuban Treasure Promotes his Country as Boxing Leader," *USAToday*, July 30, 1990.

7. Mike Wise, "Two Venerable Cubans Provide Day's Only Punch," *New York Times*, August 4, 1996.

8. Steve Bunce, "Savon the Boxer Still Fights Noble Cause," *The Independent*, June 9, 2001.

9. James Lawton, "Castro's Poster Boy; Boxer Shuns U.S. Temptations," *The Toronto Sun*, July 28, 1996.

10. Steve Bunce, "Savon the Boxer Still Fights Noble Cause," *The Independent*, June 9, 2001.

Trent Dimas

Summer Olympic Gold Medalist

by Charlie Harless

Courtesy of University of Nebraska Media Relations.

For Trent Dimas, Barcelona surely must have seemed more than just a day's flight away from his hometown of Albuquerque, New Mexico. The journey to the 1992 Olympic Games seemed improbable for Dimas, a gymnast who did not even make the cut for the United States World Championship team just a year before. Even when Dimas was able to refocus and earn a spot on the Olympic team, virtually nobody outside his immediate friends and family knew who he was or thought he would have a chance to get on the medal stand. Dimas's hometown paper, the *Albuquerque Journal*, only gave Dimas a fair chance of doing well at the Games, as they knew like everyone else that the Eastern European gymnasts dominated the sport. Yet by the time the hometown paper hit newsstands after the last gymnastics event, the cover story featured none other than a picture of local, or rather, "golden" boy Dimas in his first place moment of triumph with the a simple, yet telling headline of "YES!"[1] In his rise from an unknown to the only American to win an individual gold that year and the first gold medal performance by an American in a non-boycotted Olympics since 1932, Dimas showed that while the journey was tough, the ultimate reward made the struggle worthwhile.

Before Dimas ever practiced difficult flips or stuck his first landing, his family had a different vision for their son's future that did not include gymnastics. Dimas's father, Ted, was a former Golden Gloves boxer that wanted his son to follow in his footsteps, but his mother did not support this idea. Dimas recalled that "she said she wasn't going to come home every day and see her kids all beat up. She wanted us to do ballet. You never know; things can go either way. You just go through life hoping you made the right decision, and then you look back and say either it was the right one or it wasn't."[2] Even as Dimas took to the sport and showed a great talent for gymnastics, Dimas struggled with deciding whether gymnastics was the correct path for him in his life. Ted Dimas had been working long hours as a contractor to scrape together the money necessary to pay for his training and fees to travel to out-of-town meets. As the costs rose at the elite level, Ted could not find the necessary funds to pay for his son's expenses. Dimas' coaches made a deal with Ted that if he would build additions to their gym where Trent trained, such as a landing pit when Ted could not pay for a regional qualifying meet, then his services would be his payment and his coaches would cover the costs. Understanding what the resources his parents and coaches were putting into his success, Dimas undoubtedly felt pressure to perform well and make good on their investment. Dimas stated that "I owe a lot to my parents. My dad Ted, a 41-year-old contractor worked 16 hours a day to keep me at the top. He'd be so tired sometimes. I can remember mornings, we'd be leaving to go on a trip for some meet, and there would be my dad, paying in cash out of his pocket so I could go."[3]

Dimas had a great support system behind him, but mixed results in his teenage years often challenged the young gymnast. Kay Burch, one of the gym owners along with her husband and Dimas's coach Ed Burch, said that "there were times when Trent didn't know if he wanted to continue in gymnastics. He had some tough times trying to figure out what he wanted to do."[4] Upon missing the cut for the 1991 World Championship team, Dimas dropped out of the University of Nebraska and set forth on his mission to take all of his training and make the 1992 Olympic team. Dimas would later say that this decision was spurred by a change in mindset where "I'd reached the point where I decided, everything I've put into this, let me see how far I can go."[5] Burch and additional coaches, like John Curtin, worked to put Dimas in a position to rise above his disappointing result and achieve his dream of making the Olympics.

Curtin would later say "I told Trent in 1991 that he was as good as anyone around, especially on the high bar. From that day on we both had that dream of him making the Olympic team and the rest is history. It's a good feeling when you sit down and make some goals and you accomplish them after a lot of hard work."[6] Dimas qualified for the Olympic Team at the 1992 Nationals and reset his goals towards the seemingly impossible: winning a medal in Barcelona.

In an Olympic Games where all of the American focus going in was on the famed "Dream Team" of NBA Basketball stars and other famous stars in track, swimming, and women's gymnastics, Dimas flew well under the radar with the men's gymnastics team. In men's gymnastics, the Unified Team, led by phenom Vitaly Scherbo, rightfully took the entire spotlight. In addition to winning the gold in the team competition at Barcelona, Scherbo would go on to put on a show for the record books, winning not only gold in the all-around competition, but he took first place in the individual events of pommel horse, parallel bars, rings, and vault. This collection of six medals in one games demolished the previous individual record of four gold medals by Soviet gymnast Nikolai Andrianov at the 1976 Olympics. The horizontal bar was the last event of the competition, one that would ultimately allow another gymnast besides Scherbo to experience the thrill of Olympic glory. Dimas was the penultimate performer of the night. Going into his performance, other competitors had already put up medal-worthy performances with a pair of 9.837 scores from gymnasts of the German and Unified teams. As the world watched and the standard to win a medal was already set terrifically high, Dimas jumped on the bars and began his routine. The crowd roared with escalating delight at Dimas' routine of difficult twists and jumps, including a 1 1/2 backflip over the bar known as a Kovac. At the end of the routine, Dimas performed an extremely difficult dismount in the form of triple-back somersault. Upon sticking the landing and being rewarded with a near-perfect score of 9.875, Dimas recounted that "I was scared to move. I wanted to make sure the judges really saw I stuck."[7]

For a career that had to that point seen Dimas mostly unable to perform at his peak when the lights were on, Dimas seized the moment. Dimas's clutch routine would be his only such triumph at the Olympic level in his career, but the importance of that victory was never lost on Dimas. The gold medal performance was the first time an American had ever won a gold medal when gymnasts from the Soviet Union were competing at the same Games. Additionally, the win served as a validation for Dimas that he made the right decision to participate in gymnastics and that the support from his family was not for naught. Discussing the meaning of his gold medal, Dimas conceded that "maybe this can repay some of what he put into me."[8] For Ted Dimas to see his son rise from a young tumbler in a gym he helped build to sticking a perfect landing and inspiring millions of young gymnasts to pursue their own dreams of Olympic triumph, one would bet he must have felt that every penny was well spent. For in the end, Dimas showed that the achievement of Olympic glory is indeed truly priceless.

Notes

1. Erik Brady, "New Mexico Mines Gold with Dimas," *USAToday*, August 6, 1992.

2. Tony Green, "Dimas Still Flying High After Gold," *St. Petersburg Times*, October 7, 1992.

3. Kevin Paul Dupont, "Scherbo, Dimas Gems of Gym," *The Boston Globe*, August 3, 1992.

4. Erik Brady, "New Mexico Mines Gold with Dimas" *USAToday*, August 6, 1992.

5. Gerald Eskenazi, "On Sherbo's Night, Dimas Also Sparkles," *The New York Times*, August 3, 1992.

6. Fiona Chappell, "Olympic Champ is After Another Gold," *Sunday Mail*, May 14, 1995.

7. Steve Wieberg, "Thanks Dad: Gymnast Repays Father in Gold," *USAToday*, August 3, 1992.

8. Ibid.

Claudia Poll

First Central American Woman to Win an Olympic Gold Medal

by Jared Bovinet

In a soccer-obsessed country that heeds few other sports, one swimmer made huge waves. Claudia Poll, the swimmer who won Costa Rica its one and only Olympic gold medal, introduced swimming to many Costa Ricans and in the process became one of the best female swimmers ever.

Poll's parents are German but settled in Nicaragua to raise their family. She was born in Managua, Nicaragua on December 21, 1972 and that same year, an earthquake and increasingly hostile political tensions caused her parents to move to Costa Rica to raise their family in more stable surroundings. She became an official citizen of Costa Rica 21 years later.

At age seven, Poll started swimming lessons at the Cariari Country Club and began working with her lifelong coach, Francisco Rivas, soon after. At 17, she held seven swimming records at the Central American and Caribbean Championship and entered the world rankings in the 200 meter freestyle. Two years later, she competed in the Pan Pacific World Swimming Championships in Canada despite having fractured her hand a few weeks before. She placed sixth in the 400 meter freestyle and eighth in the 800 meter race of the same stroke.

At the 1993 Pan Pacific Championship in Japan, she placed first in the 200 freestyle, second in the 400 freestyle, and third in the 800 freestyle. In placing first in the 200 meter race, Poll became the first Latin American woman to win a gold medal in the history of the Championship.

In the two years leading up to the 1996 Olympics, Poll continued to swim well in freestyle competitions, breaking world records in the process. Her strong performances in several events at the World Swimming Championships in Rome foreshadowed her pioneering role as a Latina athlete at the Olympics. Hope for Poll to bring home an Olympic gold began to form in the hearts of Costa Ricans across the country.

At the 1996 Summer Olympics in Atlanta, Poll won the gold medal in the women's 200 meter freestyle, upsetting German Franziska Van Almsick and thrilling Costa Ricans, who had just seen their national hero win the country's first gold medal. Interestingly enough, Poll's sister, Silvia, also a swimmer, won the country's first medal by capturing a bronze at the 1988 Seoul Games.

The Olympics did not mark the end of Poll setting swimming records, however. She continued to set records and earn world championships at the Pan Pacific Championship, the Swimming World Cup, and the FINA World Cup. She performed well at the 2002 Summer Olympics in Sydney, Australia, where she won two bronze medals in the 200 and 400 meter freestyle events.

Poll's amazing success in the pool came under scrutiny in 2002, when she was accused of doping after testing positive for a performance-enhancing drug. The International Swimming Federation (FINA) banned her from the sport for four years, a sentencing she appealed. FINA reduced the ban to two years which allowed her to compete in the 2004 Summer Olympic Games in Athens. She finished ninth in the 200 meter freestyle at the Games.

Even if Claudia Poll's illustrious swimming career may not have been without controversy, Costa Ricans and fans worldwide continue to see her as a hero. She was declared an Honorary Citizen by the Costa Rican Congress in 1996, named *Swimming World Magazine*'s best swimmer in 1997, Costa Rican Sportswoman of the Year five times, and Costa Rica's Athlete of the Century in 1999.

Steven López

Summer Olympic Gold Medalist

by Cara-Lynn Lopresti

Steven López is an elite taekwondo athlete that grew up in a family of superstars. Jean, López's elder brother and the first to take up taekwondo in the family, was a member of the 1996 U.S. National team with López and now coaches his three siblings at the Elite Taekwondo Center in Houston, Texas. López, along with his younger brother, Mark and younger sister, Diana, "made history" at the 2005 World Taekwondo Championships, "for being the first three siblings to receive World Championship titles at the same event."[1] During the 2008 Beijing Olympics, "Team USA" was referred to as "Team López," as Steven, Diana, and Mark López, "earned three of the four spots on the U.S. taekwondo team,"[2] eventually taking home two bronze medals and a silver medal. The López's made history at the Beijing Olympics, as they were "the first trio from the same family to represent the United States at the Olympics since 1904" and "the first U.S. siblings to win medals at an Olympic Games."[3] Jean coached all three López siblings during the Beijing Olympics, the 2005 World Championships when Steven, Mark, and Diana each won their respective weight classes, and the 2004 Olympics when Steven took home the gold medal.

Steven López was born on November 9, 1978 to Ondina and Julio López, who are both from Nicaragua. His father was a great sports enthusiast and inspired Steven López to take up taekwondo as a five-year-old. Jean encouraged Steven during his childhood and played a crucial role in helping him master the tactics of martial arts. Soon all four of the López's, Jean, Steven, Mark, and Diana, were involved in taekwondo, and "turned the family's two-car garage into a makeshift gym."[4] Steven and his siblings woke up at 5 a.m. nearly everyday to "train before school, then practiced again after school and at night."[5] On cold days Steven's mother timed the washer and dryer cycle to coincide with practice to keep the children warm.

At the age of 15, López became a part of the U.S. National team and won his first silver medal in the Pan American Championships in 1994. He earned the bronze in his first World Cup Championships later that year. In 1996 López clinched two gold medals during the Pan Am Championships and the Junior World Championships. López graduated from Kempner High School in Sugar Land, TX., in 1997, where he was a member of the National Honor Society and was also voted "most likely to succeed." This superlative could not have been more fitting for this rising star. Over the next three years, López tallied three more gold medals winning the 1997 World Cup Taekwondo Championships, the 1998 Pan Am Championships, and the 1999 Pan American Games.

López won his first Olympic gold in the men's taekwondo event at the 2000 Sydney Olympics, a feat that was repeated with another first place finish at the 2004 Athens Olympics. He also won four gold medals and a bronze at the World Taekwondo Championships from 2001–2007. López lost his opportunity at a third gold medal in three Olympics after he was defeated in the 80kg quarterfinals at the Beijing Olympics. Entering the final round of the quarterfinals, López led the contest 2-0 against Italy's Mario Sarmiento. However, the match ended up going into overtime after Sarmiento scored a point and then López's score was deducted for a controversial penalty. With time running out, Sarmiento jumped kicked the 6'2"/175 lb López to win the match. The U.S. team protested the point deduction in the third round, arguing that it was a legal defensive move and not an illegal chop kick. However, the protest was denied. Despite the controversial ending to the match López still "flashed a big smile after bouncing back from his first loss since 2002 to win a bronze."[6]

The 31-year-old "Steven López has seemingly accomplished all there is in the sport of taekwondo."[7] So far he has captured 13 gold, two silver, and four bronze medals. López was also a three-time Sullivan Award Finalist from 2003–05, U.S. Olympic Committee Male Athlete of the Month, and was named 2005 USA Taekwondo Male Co-Athlete of the Year with his brother, Mark.

Aside from taekwondo, López has many other notable accomplishments and interests. He has appeared in *People* Magazine's 50 Most Beautiful People and participates in the USOC's Olympic Job Opportunities Program at the Home Depot in Houston, Texas. López's heroes are Muhammad Ali and his brother Jean. During his spare time, López enjoys reading self-help books, dancing, listening to Latin music and hip-hop, as well as playing other sports. Once he is finished competing, López aspires to coach taekwondo like his brother, but until then he plans to continue enjoying the journey of being one of the greatest taekwondo athletes in the world.

Notes

1. "Steven Lopez," 2009. http://www.stevenlopez.net/
2. "Lopez Siblings Make Olympics Family Affair," *Internet Broadcasting Systems, Inc*,. April 5, 2008, http://www.wdsu.com/sports/15804374/detail.html
3. Eddie Pells, "Seeking Changing in Judging, Lopez Appeals to CAS," *AP Worldstream*,. September 12, 2008, http://www.highbeam.com/doc/1A1-D935FQJ81.html
4. "Steven Lopez," *NBC Universal*. 2008. http://www.nbcolympics.com/athletesathlete=75/bio/
5. Ibid.
6. Gary Mihoces, "USA's Steven Lopez Adds Bronze to Family's Medal Hau," *USAToday* August 22, 2008.http://www.usatoday.com/sports/olympics/beijing/fight/20 08-08-22-taekwondo-medals_N.htm
7. "Steven Lopez," *NBC Universal*. 2008. http://www.nbcolympics.com/athletes/ athlete=75/bio/

Irving Saladino

First Central American Man
to Win Olympic Gold Medal

by Jared Bovinet

Irving Saladino arrived to a hero's welcome in his native Panama. Government offices and public schools closed to allow employees and students to attend the parade in his honor, and the country's president declared that a sports facility would soon be named after Saladino. There was good reason to celebrate; a few days earlier, the country earned its first Olympic gold medal because of Saladino's performance in the long jump at the 2008 Summer Olympic Games in Beijing.

Most people expected Saladino to win the gold medal, and rightly so. He had won the 2007 World Championship and was displaying remarkable consistency for a track and field athlete. At the FBK Games in the Netherlands a few months prior, he broke the event's long jump record that had stood for 14 years. He also won at the Pan American Games in Brazil and at the World Championships in Japan the year before. In anticipation of his winning the long jump gold, the government designated him as the flag bearer of the country's delegation at the Games. But the path to being the gold medal favorite was not as direct as one may think.

Saladino's journey from Panama to the pinnacle of many athletes' dreams started when he was born on January 23, 1983 in Colón. He was an outstanding athlete as a child and his parents nurtured his love of sports. Saladino enjoyed soccer but dreamed of one day following in the footsteps of fellow Panamanian Mariano Rivera and playing for the New York Yankees. He was good at baseball and showed great speed, but major league scouts cited his lack of hitting as a big liability.

Fortunately, Saladino's older brother took him out to a track one day and the projection of his athletic career changed forever. His speed on the baseball field naturally transferred to the track and he began winning national competitions. In his first international meets, he competed in El Salvador, Guatemala, and Jamaica and impressed fans and coaches alike with his ability to seemingly glide across fields and tracks. His natural abilities and practice soon helped him qualify for the 2004 Summer Games in Athens but was not able to compete because of an injury.

After this disappointment, he joined the São Paulo Regional Training Center in Brazil through the Olympic Solidarity Program. This program is designed to facilitate further training for Olympic hopefuls who may not have the means to afford the training on their own. In the next few years, Saladino continued to improve and prepare for the upcoming Games in China.

In August 2008, the premier sporting event in the world finally arrived. After years of dedication and discipline to become the best long jumper in the world, Saladino had his opportunity to prove that he indeed was the best. As it turns out, everyone was right in calling him the favorite—he won the long jump with a distance of 8.34 meters.

As he stood on the Olympic podium, Saladino made sure that the billions of people around the world watching him receive his gold medal knew that he was representing Panama, declaring to his compatriots, "As I have always said, this medal is yours."[1] He wore his national colors on his chest and toted one blue and one red shoe. Saladino was honored after winning his gold medal, and he pledged to continue training to create a bigger Panamanian presence at the Olympics. "It is worthwhile to keep up on the efforts because Panama deserves it,"[2] he said.

One year later, the world and Olympic long jump champion continues to train to give Panamanians another reason to celebrate. He is currently working to defend his gold medal at the 2012 Games in London and plans to retire thereafter.

Notes

1. "Saladino Hailed as Panama's Hero at Homecoming," *Xinhua News Agency*. 2008. *HighBeam Research*. 23 Aug. 2009 (http://www.highbeam.com).

2. China.org, "Saladino Hailed As Panama´s Hero At Homecoming," http://www.china.org.cn/olympic/2008-08/22/content_16302702.htm. August 22, 2008.

2004 Argentina Men's National Basketball Team

First Latin American Country to Win Olympic Gold Medal in Basketball

by Chris Kamke

The United States has dominated the game of basketball since its inauguration under Dr. James Naismith. The U.S. has been so commanding that they have captured 13 of the 17 gold medals awarded in the Olympic Games since 1936. In fact, there has been only one Olympic Games where the U.S. did not win a medal in basketball and that was the 1980 Moscow Games that were boycotted by the U.S. Historically, Argentina lies at the other end of the basketball spectrum. In a country with a rich soccer past, basketball, although popular, is a distance second in the minds of most Argentineans. That's a big reason why the accomplishment of the 2004 Argentina Men's Basketball team at the Athens Games was astonishing.

In 2004, Argentina was one of the 12-teams field competing for Olympic glory in Athens. The 12 man roster consisted of; Gabriel Fernández (#9), Fabricio Oberto (#7), Luis Scola (#11), Rubén Wolkowyski (#15), Carlos Delfino (#14), Leonardo Gutiérrez (#12), Wálter Herrmann (#8), Andrés Nocioni (#13), Emanuel Ginóbili (#5), Alejandro Montecchia (#6), Pepe Sánchez (#4), Hugo Sconochini (#10), with head coach Rubén Magnano. Entering the Games, Argentina had never medaled; their best Olympic finish had been fourth in the 1952 Olympics. This team, however, was considered to be one of the best the country had ever assembled and was fresh from a second place finish at the 2002 FIBA World Championship which included a win over Team USA.

Argentina made it through the group stage of the tournament, finishing behind Spain and Italy in Group A. Their third place standing set up a knockout round matchup with the host nation, Greece, the second place finisher from Group B. Playing in front of a predominately Greek crowd, Argentina held Greece without a field goal for almost six minutes until Nikolaos Chatzivrettas made a three point basket with just under 40 seconds remaining in the game to cut Argentina's lead to one. Those ended up being the last points for Greece. After Scola and Ginóbili each sunk a pair of free throws; Argentina earned a semifinal matchup against Team USA by defeating Greece 69-64.

The showdown against Team USA marked the first Olympic semifinal appearance by Argentina since 1952. Although Team USA had suffered a couple defeats earlier in the tournament, they had entered the Athens Games with a 109-2 Olympic record, bearing the reputation of being near unbeatable. Argentina was fearless and played with confidence generated from their 2002 victory over Team USA. Behind Ginóbili's 29 points, Argentina stunned Team USA in an 89-81 victory, humbling the nation who invented the game. The loss meant that for the first time since the Dream Team had recaptured the gold in 1992, Team USA would not be Olympic basketball champions.

With a roster composed mainly of the players that defeated Team USA in 2002, the first team to defeat a U.S. squad of NBA players, the Argentineans out-passed, shot, and defended throughout the game. "Our rival today was extremely tough, but in the few hours that passed between yesterday's game and today's, we realized that nothing was impossible," said Magnano, head coach of Argentina. "We had to go out there and attack them on an equal footing, go for them. That's what we did, and that's why we won."[1] A large factor in the game was three-point shooting. Argentina went 11 for 22 behind the arc while the Americans finished just 3 for 11.

Coming out of halftime with a five-point lead, Argentina turned the heat up and the five point margin quickly increased to 13. The gap would be closed to six points but behind Ginóbili, Argentina had an answer for everything the United States presented them with. "For us to get an Olympic gold would be amazing, and tomorrow our soccer team and us will be playing for gold," Ginóbili said. "That could be the happiest time ever for us."[2] Argentina's teamwork and creativity ultimately proved to be too much for the big-name NBA players and perhaps clarified the notion that basketball is a team game.

Argentina's victory put them in the gold medal game against Italy. Coming off the emotional high that came with defeating the United States, Argentina remained focused on their goal of Olympic gold. Playing without star forward Oberto who suffered a broken arm in their semifinal contest, Argentina continued to employ the same teamwork tactics that had gotten them into the finals. This time Scola led the way for Argentina, scoring 25 points and pulling down 11 rebounds. The game was close through the first three quarters. Then a 12-1 run by Argentina, highlighted by two three point baskets by Montecchia, started to put the game out of reach.

Argentina went on to handily defeat Italy, 84-69, to capture their first ever Olympic gold medal in basketball. "This is the most exciting moment ever," Magnano said. "I am so pleased and proud to lead these young men who have given so much joy to their country."[3] In the closing seconds of the game, Scola added the exclamation point to his country's quest for gold with a dunk followed by a chin-up on the rim. With the sound of the horn, complete jubilation overcame the Argentine squad. Some players greeted fans while others embraced on the court. Ginóbili remarked how special the medal was, "The most special thing you can do is win for your country," he said. "We win in soccer in the morning and then in basketball. Argentina is on top of the world because it is on top of the two biggest sports in the world today."[4]

Argentina was one of the eight founding countries of The International Basketball Federation, commonly known as FIBA, in 1932. FIBA has hosted a World Championship for men since 1950, with the first tournament being held in Buenos Aires where Argentina successfully defended their home court. It took another 54 years for Argentina to reach the top of the podium in international basketball competition, but on August 28, 2004 in Athens, 12 men from Argentina stood on top of the basketball world once more.

Notes

1. *Sports Illustrated*, "End of an Era. Gold Eludes Grasp of Team USA for First Time Since NBA Players Used",. http://sportsillustrated.cnn.com/2004/olympics/2004/basketball/08/27/usa.argentina.ap/index.html (accessed August 30, 2009).

2. Ibid.

3. Jim O'Connell, "Argentina Wins Men's Basketball Gold," *Associated Press*. August 29, 2004.

4. Ibid.

Alberto Salazar

American Marathon Star

by Charlie Harless

A successful athlete cannot win without heart. Sure, the human body can be strengthened, stretched, and pushed beyond its perceived limitations when putting in the hours in the gym or running miles while the rest of the world is sleeping. All elite marathon runners check their split times, build their endurance, and log the miles necessary to be successful. However, after more than two hours and twenty six miles behind them, heart undoubtedly separates the front of the pack from the rest. Alberto Salazar showed his heart when winning three consecutive New York Marathons, one in world record time, from 1980 to 1982. Salazar showed his heart when outpacing rival Dick Beardsley by two seconds and collapsing just past the finish line from dehydration at the infamous "Duel in the Sun" at the 1982 Boston Marathon. Salazar showed his heart when he came back from the brink of death following a grueling 1978 race in which his body temperature reached 107 degrees and he was prematurely read his last rites. Ultimately, Salazar gave his heart to racing and in turn, he won the hearts of the racing world who witnessed his magnificent feats and trying obstacles along his path.

Salazar demonstrated his resiliency early on in life, as when he was only two years old he was uprooted from Cuba to America as his family fled Fidel Castro's Cuba. Alberto's father, José, once a close friend of Castro, later recounted that "when it was evident that Castro was taking Cuba to communism, we had to get out. On October 1, 1960, I resigned from the government, left my home at 6:00 p.m. and went into hiding. At 8:00 p.m., my home was ransacked and they took two cars and all my papers . . . If Cuba had not gone Communist, we would still be there."[1] Spending the majority of his childhood in Wayland, Massachusetts, Salazar would soon take to running after watching several Boston Marathons and running on parts of its legendary course. Salazar would later recall that "when I was a junior and senior in high school, and during summer vacation from college, I trained with several of the top marathoners in Boston, including Bill Rodgers. I was confident I could do well."[2]

An eighteen-year-old Salazar arrived on the campus of the University of Oregon in 1976, following in the large footsteps of legendary Oregon distance runner Steve Prefontaine, who had his life cut tragically short in a car accident the previous year. At a school far from home and notoriously successful in developing top American runners, Salazar's confidence that he could do well was evident in his training regimen and early results. While at Oregon, he became part of the 1977 National Championship Cross Country team and achieved individual success the following year when he won the individual NCAA Cross Country Championship.

While Salazar was running well at the 5,000 and 10,000 kilometer distances, Salazar was logging an excessive number of miles with an eye on running in his first Olympic Games in 1980. In spite of having just suffered a death-defying post-race collapse from severe heat exhaustion at the 1978 Falmouth Road Race, Salazar continued to push his body to such an extreme limit that he developed severe tendinitis in his left knee and was ordered by doctors to halt all workouts in 1979. The timing for this injury was even worse considering the Olympic Trials in the 10,000 kilometers, his best event, were only a couple of months away. Time off the course would severely hinder his chances of making the team. After some time of enduring the torment of seeing his college teammates training without him, Salazar put pain and the risk of further injury aside and resumed training. Salazar, lacking the training he felt he needed, summoned the strength to place third at the 10,000 kilometer Olympic Trials, thus earning him a spot on the team that was to go to Moscow. The United States boycott of the games dashed his dreams of winning Olympic gold, but at those trials, Fred Brown, a close friend and coach, suggested he focus his efforts on running his first marathon at the famous New York City Marathon in 1980. Presented with a new challenge, Salazar would soon boldly and publicly state his prediction that he would run New York in a sub 2:10 time, the standard mark for an elite performance. While many scoffed at this notion of a rookie running such a race, Salazar proved prophetic, winning the 1980 New York City Marathon in a time of 2:09.33.

After announcing himself to the world as an elite marathoner, Salazar proved unbeatable for some time, winning the first four marathons he ever ran. Returning as defending champion, the 1981

New York City Marathon would prove to be one of his greatest performances, as he ran a then world-record time of 2:08.17 to retain his crown. Firmly entrenched as a great marathon runner, Salazar would claim the three-peat by winning in New York again in 1982 and also winning the Boston Marathon for the first time that same year. Salazar had the heart to pull out these grueling tests of the human body, a trait Salazar recognized in himself when stating "If I want to win it, it all comes down to 'can I take more pain than the next guy?' It's like both guys holding their hand over a flame saying, 'O.K., who's going to pull away first?'"[3]

Although Salazar had the mental fortitude to handle the pain and gut out wins in close races, his body would soon prove to not be as responsive. Salazar ran well enough to qualify and compete in the 10,000 km race at his first Olympic Games in 1984, yet chronic pain in his legs and respiratory and thyroid problems began to unfurl and could have played a large part in his disappointing 15th place finish. Speaking about his Olympic debut and injuries, Salazar said "when I finished 15th in that race, I felt like a total failure. At 23 I was the world-record holder, and by 27 it was all taken away from me."[4]

Salazar suffered from bouts of depression and did not reclaim a significant distance running victory until in 1993, when he began treating his depression and again found the drive within to win a 54 mile ultra-marathon in South Africa. As he aged into his 30s and 40s, Salazar was never able to fully scale back from running grueling distances or making running a fundamental part of his life. Beginning in 2001, Salazar began mentoring and coaching promising young American runners through Nike's Oregon Project in the hopes of returning the country to prominence in the sport of distance running and giving back to a sport that had given so much to him. Salazar had poured his heart into running, but this love for the sport took its ultimate toll on the marathon man when in 2007, he ignored months of telling signs and suffered a severe heart attack that nearly claimed his life. After once again eluding death, just as he had done in recovering from his post-race collapses and litany of physical injuries, Salazar concluded that, "I think [the heart attack] was the best thing that ever happened in my life. I'm a stubborn guy, and some days I need a real kick in the head. This was a life-changing thing. I don't worry about things like I used to. And I don't push too hard."[5]

Salazar is a man whose very character has been predicated on
pushing through the toughest of situations. At the height of his career, Salazar seemed nearly unbeatable, able to find the inner resolve
to pace himself just ahead of the pack nipping at his heals and waiting for a slip-up that would not come. Yet Salazar rejected this notion of unrivaled superiority, saying "not ever being beaten doesn't
mean that someone is invincible. It means he played his cards right
and was always ready at the right time."[6] Setbacks and sudden illnesses remind us all that time is precious and we can never truly
know what the future holds in store, but whatever the future holds
for Salazar, one can be certain that he will prepare himself to take on
life's winding roads and embrace the challenges with his incredible
heart.

Notes

1. Frank Litsky, "Salazar, in Pain at the Finish, Rates Run 'Almost Too Perfect,'" *The New York Times*, October 27, 1980.

2. Jim Hage, "First Finish," *The Washington Post*, October 23, 1998.

3. Neil Amdur, "Alberto Salazar is All Business," *The New York Times*, October 18, 1981.

4. John Brant, "The Marathoner Speaks to His God," *The New York Times*, October 28, 2007.

5. Steve Nearman, "Salazar Thankful for Heart Attack," *The Washington Times*, April 19, 2009.

6. Craig Neff, "They Grappled in the Big Apple," *Sports Illustrated*, November 1, 1982.

15

WINTER OLYMPICS

Jennifer Rodríguez

First Latina-American to Win Winter Olympics Medal

by Cara-Lynn Lopresti

The daughter of an American mother and Cuban father, Jennifer Rodríguez was born and raised in South Miami, "where residents define "freezing cold" as temperatures below 60 degrees."[1] Rodríguez began roller-skating at the age of four and won multiple national and world championship honors during her youth as an artistic roller-skater. After 16 years on roller-skates, 12 world championship, and 10 U.S. Festival medals, Rodríguez made another career move to speed skating at the urging of her longtime friend and recent boyfriend, KC Boutiette. Boutiette competed on the 1994 U.S. Olympic speed skating team less than a year after switching from in-line roller-skating to speed skating and was convinced that Rodriguez could do the same. Although Rodríguez had no prior "experience with winter, let alone winter sports"[2] she knew that speed skating was her only chance to compete in the Olympics, so she set out to achieve this lifelong long goal of hers.

Rodríguez's first two weeks on ice skates were frustrating, embarrassing, and cold to say the least. However, despite her early difficulties, Rodríguez made a remarkable transition and turned into one of the nation's best speed skaters. Less than two years after first trying the sport, the 21-year-old Rodríguez became the first Cuban-

American woman to participate in an Olympic Winter Game. The 1998 Olympics in Nagano, Japan, was highlighted by Rodríguez's fourth place finish in the 3000 meter race, a performance so unexpected even she called it "the biggest shock of my life."[3]

As one of the least-regarded competitors in her event, Rodríguez prayed that she would "have a top 16 placement," but "top four? [she] could never have expected that in [her] wildest dreams. It [was] something totally unbelievable for [her]."[4] Rodriguez's finish of 4 minutes, 11.64 seconds was more than four seconds better than her previous best and earned her the Olympic record, although all three medalists broke it approximately 20 minutes later.

By 2000, Rodríguez, also known as "Miami Ice" and "J-Rod," was "already considered the best distance skater in the U.S, so she shifted her focus to contending on the world level in the sprint distances."[5] In the fall of the following year, Rodríguez won a silver medal at the World Cup competition, her first ever World Cup Medal, followed by a gold medal in the 1000 meters event. At the 2002 U.S. Olympic Team Trials, Rodríguez became the first American woman in history to secure a spot on Team USA in all five speed skating events. In February 2002, Rodríguez competed in her second Winter Olympic Games in Salt Lake City and left yet another indelible mark when she became the first Cuban-American to win an Olympic medal. She skated her way to bronze medals in the 1000 meters and the 1500 meters races.

Over the next three years, Rodríguez tallied a remarkable 33 international medals, 15 of which were gold. During the 2003–2004 season, she was the World All-Around Champion in the 500 meters, World Cup Champion in the 1000 meters, and won silver and bronze medals at the World Single Distance Championships. Rodríguez maintained momentum during the 2004–2005 season, capturing 14 more international medals, and being named the World Sprint Champion. Although expected to perform very well in the 2006 Olympics, Rodríguez only placed fifth in the women's team pursuit, and finished no better than eighth in her three individual events. After a disappointing Olympics and feeling burned out and over trained, Rodríguez abruptly retired from the sport.

After two years of recovery and renewed love for skating, Rodríguez realized that she was not happy with how she finished her career. Under the guidance of her former U.S. coach, Ryan Shimabukuro, the five-foot, four-inch, 121-pound Rodríguez came out of retirement to vie for a spot on the 2010 U.S. Olympic Team and to make her fourth consecutive Olympic appearance. In October of 2008, Rodríguez proved that she was committed to her comeback when she won the 1,000 meter race at the Pettit National Ice Center and was once again selected to the U.S World Cup team. Rodríguez went on in December to win the 1,000 meter event at the World Cup in Nagano, Japan, clocking in at 1:16.34. Her victory marked the first time an American woman had won a World Cup event since [Rodríguez's] own win in 2005. Currently training with the National Long Track Training Team Program at the Utah Olympic Oval, Rodríguez is the favored American woman to win a medal at the 2010 Olympic Games in Vancouver.

Notes

1. Amy Shipley, "Out of Miami, Rodriguez is Warming to Ice; She Makes Speedskating Team," *The Washington Post,*. Feb 2. 1998. Pg. D.01.

2. Ibid.

3. Randy Harvey, "Winter Olympics 1998; Rodriguez Heating up Oval,". *Los Angeles Times*. Los Angeles,. Feb 12, 1998. Pg. 4.

4. Amy Shipley, "Miami's Rodriguez Brings Heat to Ice in Sprint," *The Washington Post*. Washington, D.C. Feb 12, 1998. Pg. C.08.

5. "Jennifer Rodriguez,"—http://speedskating.teamusa.org/athlete/athlete/2743.

Derek Parra

First Latino-American to Win Winter Olympics Gold Medal

by Jared Bovinet

The 14-year-old skated around the roller rink with an eye on the prize that he would win for finishing first in the race—a free Coke. Eighteen years later, as he skated around the Utah Olympic Oval in Salt Lake City, the prize was a little different—an Olympic gold medal. Derek Parra ended up winning both. Parra's achievement in the 1500 meter race marked the first time a Latino won gold at the Winter Olympics, a huge milestone in the history of the Games.

Parra was born in San Bernardino, California, on March 15, 1970. During high school, he and his brother began roller skating at the local rink. Parra quickly took to the sport and the rink's managers, who coached its speedskating team, took notice and invited Parra to join the team. He soon connected with George Cottone, who mentored and encouraged Parra as he developed his abilities. During one summer toward the end of high school, Parra had saved enough money to attend a training camp at the U.S. Olympic Training Center in Colorado Springs. There, he met Virgil Dooley, roller skating's preeminent coach at the time. Parra's natural abilities made a deep impression on Dooley, who encouraged him to finish school and stay in touch if Parra continued skating.

Parra's time spent with Dooley in Colorado Springs motivated him to return to finish high school quickly and pursue his passion. After graduating, he moved to Florida to train under Dooley, unbeknownst to Dooley, whom Parra called in the Tampa airport to say, "I'm here and I'm ready."[1] Dooley soon became aware of Parra's talent and immense potential.

Life presented more than its fair share of challenges when Parra was training in Florida. To make a few extra dollars and fit in a few more meals, he started working early-morning shifts at McDonald's before his training sessions later in the day. Egg McMuffins destined for the trash after sitting out too long soon became his go-to meal.

Lessons learned at McDonald's changed Parra's perspective on training and heartened his resolve to improve. I asked him the most important lesson he took from those days and what he would tell the thousands of present-day athletes who struggle to make ends meet, and he said, "The most important thing is that there is a way. You have to find a way. I wasn't going to go home and I wasn't going to give up."[2]

Parra's determination led him to follow his coach throughout the country, from Florida to Maryland to Delaware so that Parra could continue to train to become the best roller skater in the world. Long hours spent at rinks across the country eventually paid off as he won three national championships, two world championships, set two world records, and earned 18 gold medals.

The one problem: there was no Olympic competition for roller skating. He hoped that it would soon become an Olympic sport, but

to no avail. So at age 26, Parra retired from roller skating and took up ice speedskating with the goal of winning an Olympic medal. The decision was far from easy; Parra was making a comfortable living in roller skating but would have to start from scratch on the ice. "With roller skating, I was the big fish in a small pond, making a comfortable living. But I had an Olympic dream," he told me. "To hold your flag and represent your country at the Olympics is one of the greatest things you can do."[3]

Directly facing the challenge that lay ahead of him, Parra began training with the U.S. National Speedskating Team in Milwaukee, Wisconsin. The transition proved more successful than he could have ever imagined. After only a few weeks, he won two medals at the National Championships and in doing so rose to prominence among the sport's followers. He received an invitation to join the U.S. National Team and worked hard enough to earn a spot on the 1998 U.S. Olympic Team. This would lead him to compete in Nagano, Japan at his first Olympics, but a clerical error made during registration kept him from the competition.

This error "turned out to be a blessing in disguise,"[4] Parra reflected. He had qualified for the Games as the lowest-ranked skater, so his chances of medaling were small. Because he would have realized his dream of competing in an Olympics, there would have been no incentive for him to improve for future Olympic Games. In other words, without this error, Parra would most likely have not earned two medals four years later in Salt Lake City. "It was God's plan that I wasn't supposed to skate in Nagano,"[5] he said.

Although he felt cheated after learning of the error, Parra continued to train to reach his dream of winning an Olympic medal. To do this he followed a grueling schedule. His day consisted of a three-hour workout in the early morning, then an afternoon of working at the Home Depot with the Olympic Job Opportunities Program, a program in which Olympic hopefuls can work at a Home Depot store part-time but receive full-time pay so they have enough time to train. After work, Parra would return to the ice rink for another three-hour practice.

Parra moved to Salt Lake City with the U.S. Speedskating Team in 2000. There, his training intensified in an effort to ensure he would become the best male ice speedskater in the world. His preparation proved fruitful when he earned a silver medal in the 1500 meters at the World Championship. His years of moving around the country to win his Olympic medal were paying off and he had never been closer to realizing this dream.

Going into the 2002 Salt Lake City Olympic Games, expectations for Parra's performance in the 5000 meter race were not very high. His best previous finish in the event was ninth and very few people expected him to place much higher than that. At the race's onset, Parra was skating at world record pace. He maintained this amazing pace throughout the race and finished in second. Although it was not a gold medal, Parra was ecstatic about his performance. Newspaper headlines reflected his sentiment, writing "the little Mexican guy who thought he could . . . DID."[6]

The media buzz around his silver medal in the 5000 meter lead to great expectations for his strongest race, the 1500 meter. *Sports Illustrated* published an article about Parra's pursuit of the gold medal and he eventually had to distance himself from all the media trying to get an interview with him so that he had enough time to practice.

As Parra stepped onto the ice and looked around, he saw hundreds of people who supported him along his journey and became even more inspired to win. "After all the years it took me to get there, I was finally there, living my dream. I had to keep telling myself, 'Just believe, just believe, just believe,'" he recalled.[7]

Parra waited for the starting gun, the thousands of hours in rinks across the country leading to this moment. He started in a fury, setting a record for the fastest-ever 300 meter split at 23.5 seconds. He continued at record-setting pace through 700 meters and soon it was clear that Parra was the best competitor on the ice. He finished in 1:43:95, setting a world record and earning his beloved Olympic gold medal in the process.

Parra has enjoyed numerous awards and accolades from his ice skating career. On top of his two medals at the 2002 Olympic Winter Games, he won three medals at the Allround World Championships in 2002, the World Cup Gold Medal in 2001, and has earned the title of U.S. National Champion three times. For his inline skating career, he was the most decorated athlete at the 1995 Pan Am Games, winning a total of eight medals. Parra was inducted into the

464   *Part 3: International Sport*

Roller Skating Hall of Fame and currently serves as the coach of the U.S. Speedskating all-around team to prepare it for the 2010 Vancouver Games.

In 2002, Parra published *Reflections in the Ice: Inside the Heart and Mind of an Olympic Champion.* The book, which he wrote, describes his life from his childhood in California to the path he took to become one of the most successful skaters in Olympic history. It was a critical success, winning the 2004 Benjamin Franklin Book Award for best biography/memoir.

To conclude our interview, I asked Parra what steps can be taken to increase Latino participation in sports, and specifically in Winter Olympics. "The main step is exposure," he said. "I never imagined I would have been a speedskater. I would have never known I had the talent for it if I hadn't been exposed to skating." Parra continued, "We're so comfortable in our environments. Kids of all races need to get outside their homes and see what's out there."[8] The sporting world—and the Winter Olympic Games in particular—will benefit from having children who follow in Parra's footsteps by exposing themselves to the unfamiliar and becoming champions in the process.

Notes

1. Derek Parra, Q Sports http://www.qsports.net/derekparrastory.html
2. Derek Parra, telephone interview with Jared Bovinet, October 29th, 2009
3. Ibid.
4. Ibid.
5. Ibid.
6. Derek Parra, Q Sports http://www.qsports.net/derekparrastory.html
7. Derek Parra, telephone interview with Jared Bovinet, October 29th, 2009
8. Ibid.

LATINO INTERNATIONAL SUPERSTARS IN SPORTS

Edson Arantes do Nascimento (Pelé)

International Soccer Superstar

by Chris Kamke

Pelé's name is one that has become synonymous with his sport. Like Ruth with baseball, Jordan with basketball, and Ali with boxing, the words Pelé and futbol will be married for eternity. Although futbol was strongly supported in Brazil and throughout South America prior to Pelé's arrival to the pitch, he inspired creativity in the game and added potency to his nation's passion. Magical with the ball at his feet, Pelé provided astonishing trickery seemingly every time he possessed the ball which usually culminated with a stunning shot that found its way to the back of the net.

This legendary athlete almost never got his chance to shine. Pelé was born in Tres Coracoes, an impoverished district of Brazil in 1940. His father, Dondhino, was a futbol player who struggled to make a living at the sport. Pelé's mother was not eager to see her son face the same hardships. Luckily for the world, Pelé's persistence endured. Too poor to afford a proper ball, a barefooted Pelé honed his skills on a sock stuffed with rags.

Pelé was discovered by Waldemar de Brito, a former Brazilian player, at age 11. De Brito trained Pelé, placing him on a junior club team when he was 12. Receiving his first jersey, Pelé was thrilled to finally be a real futbol player like his father, "It may not seem such a big deal to some, but to me it was one of the thrills of my life."[1] From the moment he entered his first game it didn't take long for whisperings of Pelé's talents to spread across Brazilian junior soccer. Just before turning 16, he joined Santos, the professional club he would play for until 1974. In an exhibition in late 1956, Pelé entered the match in the second half for Santos and scored his first professional goal within minutes. By his second season with Santos, Pelé had secured a starting position. He would go on to finish his second year as the league's top scorer and in late 1957 at age 17, he joined the Brazilian National Team.

Pelé's first World Cup appearance came in 1958. Futbol's grand stage served as an appropriate entrance point for Pelé into the minds of the world. Arriving in Sweden with an injury, Pelé was held out of competition until Brazil's final group stage match against the Soviet Union. Pelé wasted no time entering the official scoring books by recording the assist on the second goal during Brazil's 2-0 victory. In the quarterfinal match against Wales, Pelé netted his first World Cup goal, the lone goal of the match as Brazil advanced to face France in the semifinals. It was in Brazil's match against France where Pelé had his true coming out party. In a 5-2 victory, Pelé earned a hat-trick, owning the second half of play by scoring goals in the 52nd, 64th, and 75th minute. His semifinal performance would be a tough act for anyone to follow, but Pelé would prove that he isn't just anybody. In the final against the host nation Sweden, Pelé scored two more goals, the second of which was truly mesmerizing. Standing just inside the penalty box, Pelé controlled a long pass with his chest and flipped the ball over an opponents' shoulder without letting the ball touch the ground, swiftly scooted past the defender and volleyed the ball out of the air and past the goalie. Brazil captured its first World Cup title with a 5-2 victory. Pelé's brilliant play in the finals received appreciation even from his opponents. Swedish defender Sigge Parling, assigned to mark Pelé, confessed after the game, "After the fifth goal, I felt like applauding him."[2]

After the World Cup, Pelé continued to build his futbol status; playing on both the Brazilian national team and Santos, he scored 127 goals in 1959. His play fostered interest from European teams, garnering offers of more than a million dollars, despite the fact that no team had ever paid more than $100,000 for a player. Santos refused to release Pelé's rights, President Janio Quadros declared Pelé "a national treasure."[3] Over the next four years, Brazil reigned over the futbol world and Pelé served as its king. Brazil entered the 1962 World Cup as the heavy favorite to win and big things were expected from Pelé. Pelé's star shone bright in the opening match against Mexico, scoring a brilliant goal in which he beat four defenders before putting the ball past the goalie. After that 2-0 win over Mexico, Pelé suffered a muscle injury in his next contest which ended his tournament. Brazil would go on to defend its title, giving Pelé his second World Cup championship.

Pelé's agility, tempo, and ball-handling skills revolutionized soccer. Serving as a critical part of Brazil's all-out attack style which was more exciting for casual fans than the traditional defensive-oriented game, Pelé's play increased interest for the game. A true scoring machine, Pelé scored five goals or more in a game on six occasions, scored four goals in 30 games, and had 92 hat trick games in his career.

The 1966 World Cup turned out much the same for Pelé as the one four years earlier. Pelé would again score a goal in the first match, this time off a free kick, a 2-0 win over Bulgaria. He was forced to sit out the second match due to injury before playing at less than 100 percent in the third and final game for Brazil, who would fail to advance from group play. Upon Brazil's exit from the tournament Pelé said it was his last.

By this point in his career, Pelé possessed global fame and had an interest in humanitarian causes. Pelé believed that part of his mission was to unite people. Pelé toured the world with his Santos club, cementing his reputation as the king of soccer and meeting with heads of state. In 1967, a cease-fire was declared in Nigeria's civil war so that both sides could watch Pelé play an exhibition game in Lagos.

Even though he declared he would not play in another World Cup, Pelé returned for the 1970 tournament in Mexico. Now a 29-year-old veteran, Pelé was surrounded by young talent that made up the powerful Brazilian squad. Pelé scored one goal in the opening game against Czechoslovakia and two more in the final match of group play against Romania. Brazil continued to advance and eventually made it to the final against Italy. Both teams had won the World Cup twice, meaning that the winner of this match would get to keep the Jules Rimet Trophy, a trophy that had exchanged hands between World Cup winners since 1930, permanently. In what would be Pelé's last World Cup match, the inspired Brazilian team took the pitch ready to stake claim to the Rimet Trophy. In front of over 100,000 fans in Mexico City, Pelé opened the scoring on Brazil's way to a 4-1 victory. After the match, Italian defender Tarcisio Burgnich, who had marked Pelé said, "I told myself before the game, 'he's made of skin and bones just like everyone else'—but I was wrong." Pelé and Brazil became the first nation to proudly win three World Cup tournaments.

Shortly after the 1970 World Cup, Pelé retired from international play but continued to play for Santos for several more years. He would finally call it quits from Santos at the age of 34. Santos honored Pelé by removing his number 10 kit from their starting lineup. Although it had appeared that Pelé's playing days were over, an extremely lucrative offer, $4.5 million, from the New York Cosmos of the North American Soccer League (NASL), drew Pelé back to competitive soccer in 1975.

Pelé's presence in the United States heightened the interest in futbol in the States. Players registered to play futbol increased four times and NASL attendance soared. One Cosmos playoff match in 1977 drew 77,000 fans. Pelé retired after that season, playing his final match in an exhibition against Santos. The game was attended by 75,000 people and broadcast to 38 nations. Pelé scored a goal in the first half while playing for the Cosmos. He then switched sides in the second half and played with Santos so that he could finish his career where he started.

Pelé was the first futbol player to become a millionaire. Throughout his career, Pelé was flooded with offers to make appearances and sign business deals. However, he maintained personal standards, refusing to endorse cigarettes or liquor, saying "I know that I have influence on youngsters and I don't feel that I want them to think if I should endorse these products I want them to use them."[4] In 1994, Pelé became Brazil's sports minister. He used his position to speak out against corrupt practices in his country's sports federations. He also continued to support children and impoverished regions.

Few athletes ascend to the level which Pelé achieved. One of the most electrifying draws in the history of sport, Pelé played with joy. He loved and respected the game of futbol and the power it carried worldwide. Owning complete capabilities in his sport, Pelé was simply a genius, uniting his brain and muscles into an art form.

Notes

1. Michael Betzold, 2004. "Pele," In *Notable Sports Figures*, The Gale Group, Inc.
2. K. L. Chan, 2002. "Pele! Pele!," *New Straits Times*, April 8.
3. Michael Betzold, 2004. "Pele," In *Notable Sports Figures*, The Gale Group, Inc.
4. Ibid.

Alfredo di Stéfano

International Soccer Superstar

by Charlie Harless

Long exalted as one of the sport's all-time greats, Alfredo di Stéfano stood at 81 years old, some four decades after his playing days had ended, to watch the ceremonial unveiling of a statue of his likeness honoring him as a soccer icon. In the time since his playing days ended in 1966, players had arrived on the global scene and were venerated with a greater deal of fanfare as the sport continued to boom in popularity. Yet time could not forget the amazing achievements of di Stéfano; from his 307 goals scored as a pioneering leader for Spanish soccer club Real Madrid to the European Player of the Year awards he won in 1957 and 1959.

UEFA Chief Michael Plantini indicated di Stéfano's place in history when at the statue dedication ceremony outside Real Madrid's practice facility, he stated that, "Your name is written in gold letters in the history of our sport, where there will always be a special place reserved for you."[1] Faced with this public recognition as one of the sport's original greats, di Stéfano remembered how long the road to become one of the greatest had been. Standing before his statue that was built in his honor, he acknowledged that "football brought me so many beautiful moments. It built my life."[2]

Born July 4, 1926 just outside Buenos Aries, Argentina in the town of Flores, di Stéfano quickly learned the value of hard work by working on his family's farm throughout his childhood. While farm labor could be grueling, di Stéfano still found time to cultivate his soccer skills so that by the age of 12 he was already playing and winning championships for local club teams. By his late teens, di Stéfano was playing for one of the top Argentinean club teams, River Plate. However, di Stéfano was primarily playing a back-up role with the team, prompting his family to ask him to be transferred on loan to another club team, Huracán (Hurricane), so that he could develop and display his natural goal-scoring skills. The 20-year-old di Stéfano quickly showed his brilliance when in a match against River Plate, he took the ball from midfield and scored the opening goal of the game in the first 15 seconds. Before long, River Plate began to fully appreciate this young talent and called him back from Huracán.

In 1947, his first full season back with River Plate, he led the team to the league title while leading the team in goals scored, with 27 in 30 games, and eventually being named the South American Player of the Year. Di Stéfano quickly found himself on the path to superstardom, based on his incredible skills and ability to play almost anywhere on the field. Yet when looking back upon his playing days, di Stéfano remained humble when recounting his good fortunes to play the sport and make a good living. "I was just incredibly lucky to become a footballer. I did not think that I would ever play in the top league . . . In my neighborhood, there were 40 better players than myself, but some opted to study, others had to work, and the rest could not afford to buy boots."[3]

By virtue of a player's strike in the Argentenian soccer leagues in 1949, di Stéfano seized the opportunity to play for higher profile international teams. The young Argentine was quickly picked up by Los Millionarios, a Columbian club team based out of Bogota. Just as he had done in River Plate, di Stéfano quickly became the team's leading goal scorer, scoring 267 goals and leading the team to three Columbian Championships in his four-year stint with the club. When Millionarios traveled to Spain to play in a friendly match against Real Madrid, spectators and officials from some of the top Spanish and European clubs got an up-close look at di Stéfano, by now commonly referred to as La Saeta Rubia, or the "Blonde Arrow." Both FC Barcelona and Real Madrid were impressed with di Stéfano. Soon both clubs became entwined in an intense dispute for the right to sign and utilize di Stéfano for their club. An arrangement was drafted to allow di Stéfano to play for both rival clubs for a four-year period, a move that Barcelona fans vocally disapproved of. Following the departure of the club's manager during this contract negotiation, Barcelona's in-house disagreement on how to proceed with di Stéfano allowed Real Madrid to step in and sign the South American star outright. Few could comprehend at the time the full impact of this signing, but soon it was clear that di Stéfano would help transform Real Madrid into one of the preeminent soccer franchises in the world.

Beginning his career with Real Madrid at 27 years old, di Stéfano would play for the team for 11 years. Along the way he rewrote all the record books and garnered accolades that would lead to stadiums being named after him and statues constructed in his likeness. Di Stéfano scored a total of 418 goals in 510 games, 307 of those goals coming in competitive club matches. This record of 307 goals was so prolific it stood for nearly half a century until Raúl González Blanco would break his record in 2009. As the leader of the team, di Stéfano guided Real Madrid to eight Spanish League titles, five European cup titles, and the inaugural World Club Cup championship in 1960.

Even after retiring from the sport for good in 1966, di Stéfano continued his legacy with Real Madrid by coaching the team for two separate stints in the 1980s and early 1990s and being named Honorary President of the club in 2001. Although the official goal tally for his career cannot be fully confirmed, most historians of the sport believe di Stéfano scored over 800 goals and perhaps as many as 893. Additionally, he coached several other teams, including his former team River Plate in 1981, to championships and received many accolades in his post-playing days, such as an induction to the International Football Hall of Fame in 1997, UEFA's Golden Player Award in 2004, the UEFA's President's Medal in 2008, and a nomination to FIFA's Hall of Champions, which recognizes the sport's ten greatest players of all-time.

While Alfredo di Stéfano holds that soccer built his life, he was in turn clearly influential in helping build soccer to its current level of worldwide popularity. A *Sports Illustrated* feature in 1961 discussed soccer's dominance of the national conversation in Spain, a country where bull fighting once reigned supreme, and attributed much of the sport's rise in popularity to the "Argentine boy who had been bought by Real in 1953 and was now the best player in Spain, with such speed, strength, and control that he was called the Manolete of Spanish soccer."[4] Di Stéfano was instrumental in laying the groundwork for future stars to gain international acclaim both for themselves and the sport in general. In 2009, when Real Madrid signed soccer superstar Cristiano Ronaldo to make him the highest paid superstar in the sport, Alfredo di Stéfano was on hand to present the young star the number nine Real Madrid jersey he once adorned and the one Ronaldo would now wear. Ronaldo paid tribute to the legacy of di Stéfano, stating that "someday I would like to have a winning record similar to Alfredo di Stéfano."[5] If Ronaldo or any star of tomorrow were to come close to matching the records of di Stéfano, then it is not implausible to think that they too would one day deserve a statue in their likeness.

Notes

1. Logothetis, Paul. "Real Madrid Unveils Statue to Honor di stefano," *APWorldstream*, February 17, 2008.

2. Ibid.

3. Ibid.

4. Ackerman, Gordon. "New Passion of a Proud People," *Sports Illustrated*, July 3, 1961

5. Harold Heckle, "Ronaldo aims to emulate di Stefano at Madrid," *Associated Press*, July 5, 2009.

Manuel "Garrincha" dos Santos

International Soccer Superstar

by Charlie Harless

"Like a poet touched by an angel, like a composer following a melody that fell from the sky, like a dancer hooked to a rhythm, Garrincha plays football by pure inspiration and magic; unsuffering, unreserved, and unplanned."[1] The poet Paulo Mendes Campos, who wrote these words of soccer star Manuel Francisco dos Santos, or "Garrincha" as he was affectionately known, encapsulated the beauty of the Brazilian's style of play. Garrincha dribbled the ball with such creativity and precision that his talents are virtually incomparable to any other player in the history of the sport. In a sport that celebrates inventiveness and a flair for the spectacular, Garrincha was one of soccer's greatest artists. Garrincha, translated to "little bird," was so named because although his play was so artful, his scrawny 5'6" frame and deformed legs brought forth the image of a bird. While Brazilian teammates like the famous Pelé had the classically athletic body of a Rodin statue, the sight of Garrincha's infamous legs would more likely recall Picasso.

Born with a left leg curved outward and a right leg that was two inches shorter and bowed inward, Garrincha would later use these legs to accelerate past defenders at a blistering speed and lead his native Brazil to back-to-back World Cup titles in 1958 and 1962. For all the glory Garrincha would achieve on the playing field, his life story was ultimately more akin to the narrative of a tragic artist than that of a revered athlete. Instead of spending his post-playing days as a celebrated ambassador for the sport, Garrincha spiraled into alcoholism that made his success fleeting and cut his life heart-rendingly short. Although gone too soon at the age of 49, Garrincha's art has not been forgotten and is still appreciated by those who knew his personal story or were witness to his spectacular play.

Born into poverty on October 28, 1933, Garrincha's family could not afford the medical and orthopedic treatment that would have easily straightened Garrincha's bowed legs. Add to the list of ailments a deformed spine, a dislocated hip due to his uneven legs, and the fact that he was cross-eyed, a condition that only exacerbated his inability to read, and there is little doubt that a young Garrincha was dealt a rough hand of cards that would require tremendous resiliency to overcome. However, Garrincha's malformed legs ultimately served to be his greatest asset, particularly on the soccer field. These legs led Garrincha to develop an unpredictable stride and extreme quickness with the ball as he dribbled past defenders on the streets and fields of Brazil. Dreams of soccer greatness were far from the mind of Garrincha when as a fourteen-year-old he left to work for the factories. Garrincha was a horrendous employee, not caring much for the responsibilities of the job, but managed to hold on to this position only because the president of the factory's soccer club wanted him to play on the team.

Playing on the factory's team once a week as part of the condition to keep his job, Garrincha did not show interest in taking the sport too seriously. While other teenage peers were scooped up early by amateur and professional clubs across the country, Garrincha did not possess the desire to play and it was not until he was 19 years old that he would sign with his first team, Botafogo. Garrincha had only gone to try-out for the club after an ex-Botafogo player pled for him to come, but Garrincha made his impact felt early on as he scored three goals in his first game, wowing crowds with his superior dribbling skills and blinding speed. The game was an excellent start to a 12-year career with the club in which he would become the face of Botafogo and score 232 goals in 581 career matches.

Garrincha's stellar play with Botafogo got the attention of the national team coaches and before long he was ready to make his debut for his home country at the 1958 World Cup. As a relative unknown to the international stage, the Brazilian team withheld Garrincha and their 17-year-old phenom, Pelé, from the first two games of the tournament to surprise their Soviet Union opponents with their young talents in the third match. The tactic worked as the first three minutes of the game saw Garrincha and Pelé blow by the defense and fire shots off the post. The onslaught resulted in a goal for teammate Vava in what would later be dubbed by many as "the greatest three minutes" in the history of Brazilian soccer. Brazil won the game and started an unprecedented streak of excellence, as the national team never lost a game in which both Pelé and Garrincha started together. After a 5-2 win over Sweden in the World Cup final, Garrincha had proven himself to be a key catalyst for the Brazilian attack and a star worthy of international acclaim.

Yet Garrincha did not seek out the endorsements or greater professional opportunities internationally as Pelé would, instead enjoying the thrill of the game and the night life of a Brazilian playboy. His second wife, a renowned Brazilian samba singer named Elza Flores, later recalled of her husband that "he was never interested in money. He was simple and for him, football was fun."[2] One of his national team coaches, Paolo Amaral, was more blunt in his assessment of the star player's lifestyle by saying that, "it would be hard to find a womanizer like him anywhere. He was unique."[3] Amaral's candid appraisal was likely rooted in the fact that Garrincha was believed to have had 14 children with five different women over his lifetime.

While his reputation as a lothario grew in his native Brazil, the legend of Garrincha the soccer superstar reached a fever pitch after his performance in the 1962 World Cup. Pelé suffered a hamstring injury in the second match against Czechoslovakia that ultimately would force him to sit out the rest of the tournament. With Brazilians fearing their chances of defending their title, Garrincha became the leading goal scorer for the entire tournament. Garrincha's play was superb in two of their toughest tests, a quarterfinal match against a tough English team and a semifinal versus the host nation of Chile. Against England, Garrincha scored two goals in a 3-1 victory and two goals and an assist in a 4-2 win against Chile. English player Jimmy Greaves witnessed firsthand the blazing speed, dribbling prowess and unique frame that made Garrincha such a lethal scorer and at that moment, the best player in the world. "He wobbles so much even when he comes at you to shake your hand," Greaves said of Garrincha. "You don't know which way he's going."[4] When the time came to face Czechoslovakia again in the final, the Garrincha-led Brazilian team was up to the challenge and repeated as World Cup champs after a 3-1 victory.

Unfortunately, Garrincha's fall from the top of the sporting world would happen faster than the time it took to reach the pinnacle. Garrincha's hard partying lifestyle and physical ailments caught up to the Brazilian star. His knees were in such bad shape in the year after the 1962 World Cup that Garrincha could barely play without intolerable swelling. Garrincha would never be the same player again and his career was over in a matter of years. In his last game with the national team in 1966, in which he was selected for the team more out of respect for his play in his previous 59 appearances with them, Garrincha experienced his one and only loss with Brazil in a 3-1 setback to Hungary. As the game passed him by, Garrincha had no money to fall back on as he had mismanaged or spent what he had earned throughout his career. Alcohol became his consolation for the end of his playing career as he hit the bottle hard, particularly after he was the driver in a car accident that killed his mother-in-law. After sinking into a deep depression, Garrincha drank himself to death, dying of liver cirrhosis on January 20, 1983.

While the fall of one of soccer's most beloved stars was tragic, time has not erased the legacy of Garrincha's profound effect on a sport and country. Alex Bellos, a biographer of Garrincha, summed up the appeal of this troubled star when opining that "Garrincha scored fewer goals than Pelé and won fewer medals, yet among Brazilians he is better loved. In contrast to Pelé's status as a footballing deity, Garrincha was a man of the people, his flaws all too human."[5] Garrincha, the little bird, flew to amazing heights in his career as a World Cup champion and prolific goal scorer. For fans of this seemingly unlikeliest of stars, they do not look past his downward spiral, but rather choose to celebrate Garrincha's memorable flight through life's ups and downs and his all-too-brief moment at the top of the game he loved.

Notes

1. Alex Bellos, "On a Glorious Bender," *The Guardian*, April 27, 2002.

2. Ben Lyttleton, "Brazil Looks to Spirit of 1962," *The Sunday Telegraph*, May 14, 2006.

3. Ibid.

4. Roy Terrell, "Viva Vava and Garrincha," *Sports Illustrated*, June 25, 1962.

5. Alex Bellos, "The Rise and Fall of Little Bird," *The Daily Telegraph*, August 7, 2004.

Hugo Sánchez

International Soccer Superstar

by Charlie Harless

It is a simple matter of fact that sport fans hold a special place in their hearts for champions. To be athletically gifted and perform at a high level is great, but most athletes will never be considered legendary unless they bring home a championship trophy. Soccer fans in Mexico have been trying to will their national team to become champions of the World Cup for generations on the sheer strength of their passionate devotion and faith that their talented young men will one day become the best. Try as they might, Mexican soccer fans have had little to cheer about, given that to-date, no Mexican squad has ever advanced beyond the World Cup quarterfinals. After reaching its first quarterfinals as the host nation of the 1970 World Cup, the Mexican team floundered over the next three World Cups, with a first round exit in 1978 sandwiched between two World Cups in which the Mexican team failed to qualify at all.

Without ever really coming close to conquering the soccer world, one had to wonder why over 100,000 Mexican fans, clad in green, white and red, would still find reason to pour into the Estadio Azteca to cheer for the home team. As the country prepared to host the World Cup in 1984, one man had the talent and emotion to pack a stadium and make Mexico a believer again. His name was Hugo Sánchez, a man whose goal scoring prowess and visible passion for the game captured the imagination of a nation during the 1980s. Although Sánchez would never be able to deliver his nation a championship, Mexican fans have paid him the ultimate honor by holding him in the same high regard as they would a champion.

Setting the stage for the 1986 World Cup, *New York Times* writer William Stockton wrote of Mexico that "this is a country filled with people whose optimism seems perennial, even in the face of economic crisis, collapsing world oil markets, and decades of disappointing soccer statistics. High expectations for the World Cup are rampant."[1] Aside from the fact that their team would have a decided home-field advantage, expectations were high since Sánchez, their biggest star, had proven over the previous few years that he had the ability and charisma to play at the sport's top level. One of the few Mexican players to play for a top international club, Sánchez had led the dynastic Real Madrid with 22 goals in the season prior to the World Cup. Sánchez had become quite the player since his World Cup debut in 1978.

Although he did not score in his first World Cup, Sánchez had begun to make a name for himself while playing for Club Universidad Nacional A.C, or Pumas as it is better known, where he led the team to two Mexican Football League Championship and one CONCACAF trophy as one of its top goal scorers. International offers for the young Mexican star came flying in, but Sánchez rejected these advances so that he could complete his college education in dentistry at Mexico's largest university. The degree would serve Sánchez well, as he would find time to put his education to good use while working twice a week for a dental clinic in Madrid even as he was playing at the elite club level of soccer. Sánchez later recalled that "my studies taught me to bide my time and football isn't the most important part of life."[2]

Atletico Madrid would become the beneficiary of Sánchez's decision to complete his education when in 1981, the Spanish club acquired the rights to the 22-year-old's talents for four outstanding seasons. Sánchez's play got better with each season with the team, as in his last season he scored 19 goals for Atletico Madrid and won his first of an eventual five "Pichichi" awards, which recognized the top goal scorer in the Spanish leagues. Sánchez had built an impressive resumé with Atletico, so there was little surprise when Real Madrid came calling and signed the 27-year-old in 1985 for a reported transfer fee of nearly $3 million. The move was rewarding for Real Madrid in the long run, as they secured a player in Sánchez that would score a remarkable 38 goals en route to winning the Golden Boot award in 1989 and would lead the team to five Spanish league titles and one UEFA cup during his seven-year stay.

The Mexican public also had been paying attention to the increasingly solid play of Sánchez overseas, so by the time he was back preparing to play for Mexico in the 1986 World Cup, he was a bona fide celebrity. Sánchez, by now known to many of his fans by the nickname "Hugol" for his scoring talents, first became a star to the Mexican fans not because of his ability to find the back of the net, but rather for what Sánchez did once the ball got past the goalie. Borrowing a move he learned from his gymnast sister, a young Sánchez performed a front somersault after a goal for Pumas, a feat that would became his trademark move. The front-flip became synonymous with Sánchez, even as others followed his lead and copied or created their own acrobatic celebrations. Sánchez recalled that "the fans and press loved it and it stuck. It gives me great satisfaction to see players around the world celebrating in the same way. It is important people express themselves."[3]

The Mexican people gave Sánchez a hero's welcome when he returned home from Spain in May 1986 to begin training with the national team for that summer's World Cup, as thousands flocked the Mexico City Airport to cheer for his plane's arrival. In Mexico's opening 1986 World Cup game against Belgium, with anticipation for the game at an all-time high among the Mexican fans, Sánchez unfurled a spectacular header for a first-half goal and performed his trademark celebration somersault on the way to a 2-1 victory over Belgium in a jam-packed Estadio Azteca. After the game, Sánchez expressed his love for both the game and his country when saying "my heart surged today. To be a Mexican player today was to have everything you could ever want from the game."[4] Although Sánchez was unable to score another goal in this tournament where the team was handed a quarterfinal exit by West Germany in an agonizing penalty-kick overtime loss, the Mexican faithful and international soccer community did not forget how terrific a player Sánchez was in his prime. In 1999, the International Federation of Football History and Statistics placed Sánchez as the 26th best soccer player of all-time and the greatest ever to come from the North America and Central America region.

Sánchez left the game for good in 1997, having crafted a vaunted career in which he scored a total of 239 goals in the Spanish leagues and competed in three World Cups for Mexico. Prior to his last World Cup in 1994, Sánchez acknowledged his impact on the country and the fact that he helped take Mexican soccer to the next level. Sánchez felt that he, along with the new crop of young talent, had "created a climate of ambition and confidence. Our inferiority complex is gone. We can play with anybody in the world."[5] For all his goal-scoring achievements and celebrated somersaults, Sánchez's lasting legacy has been the champion's mentality he has passed onto a new generation of Mexican youth, so that they too believe that they can deliver the faithful Mexican fans a championship at last.

Notes

1. William Stockton, "Hosts hope to Deserve the Invitation," *The New York Times*, May 28, 1986.

2. Rick Broadbent and Matthew Roberts, "Sanchez is Head Over Heals with Ambition," *The Times*, April 19, 2004.

3. Ibid.

4. Norman Chad, "Mexico Rises to Occasion, 2-1," *The Washington Post*, June 4, 1986.

5. Santiago O'Donnell, "Mexico Tries to Play a Hot Hand," *The Washington Post*, June 14, 1994.

Diego Maradona

International Soccer Superstar

by Charlie Harless

The feats of an athlete performing at the highest level can be so superlative, so seemingly extraordinary that those who are witness to such excellence often fail to find the words to describe what they just saw. Playing before a global audience at the 1986 World Cup, Diego Maradona transcended the sport of soccer to become a legend, leading his Argentinean national team to the title and scoring five goals in seven contests. Many who saw Maradona play made claims that no mortal, sans Pelé, was comparable in terms of skill and heart on the field. Maradona was seemingly blessed with such a raw ability that many began to deify the midfielder.

Years after his playing career ended, a "Church of Maradona" was formed in the Argentine city of Rosario for devoted members who celebrated the anniversaries of his notable athletic achievements as quasi-religious holidays and claimed on recruitment literature that "soccer has a god. That god is Argentine and his name is Diego Armando Maradona."[1] One of the holidays that the group observes falls on June 22, the day in which Argentina faced England in a quarterfinal match at the 1986 World Cup. In that game, Maradona would score both goals that led his team to a 2-1 victory and subsequently inspired a religious devotion to this man of great talent and faith.

While two scores alone are impressive, the fashion in which he found the back of the net that day have contributed to his legend more than any other game in his career. The second goal was recently cited by FIFA as the "Goal of the Century" for the magical way in which he single-handedly averted six English defenders in a ten second dash up the field, but the first goal secured Maradona's spot as an immortal legend of the sport. Dubbed the "Hand of God" goal, Maradona and English goalie both charged towards a ball flying off of an errant clear-out attempt by an English defender. Maradona leapt and reached the ball before the goalie, illegally hitting the ball with the outside of his left fist into the back of the net. Not seeing the infraction, the official allowed the goal to stand. After the match, Diego was asked about the controversial goal. Maradona asserted to the pool of reporters that the goal had been scored "a little with the head of Maradona and a little with the Hand of God."[2]

A childhood friend remembered that Maradona flashed an early glimpse of his special abilities despite a rough start to life. "He was shirtless and barefooted. He was just this street kid with a gift from God."[3] The first of eight children born to a factory worker and his wife in Villa Fiorito outside Buenos Aries, Maradona said of his childhood that "I never had many toys. If they gave me a choice between a car and a ball, I stayed with the ball."[4] In 1969 at the age of nine, Maradona began a five-year stint playing with Los Cebollitas, or the Little Onions. By the time he was 15 years old, Maradona was a rising star in the amateur ranks and began playing professionally for Argentinos Juniors. Clubs from across the world were trying to negotiate with the management of Argentinos Juniors to allow them to sign Maradona for large transfer fees and salaries. However, offer after offer was rebuked by the team president, Prosper Consoli, who said that "Dieguito (Maradona) is a little angel God has sent to bestow happiness on Argentinos Juniors and Argentine soccer."[5]

While the Argentine soccer club was blessed to have the services of Maradona, the young phenom experienced the first major setback of his playing career when the Argentinean national team cut him from the 1978 World Cup roster merely a month before the tournament began in his home country. Undoubtedly devastated from this slight, Maradona nonetheless continued to develop his skills with the Argentinos Juniors. In 1979, Maradona would be named South American Player of the Year as he was named to the Argentinean National Team, and thus started to capture the attention of international audiences, who by now were frequently hailing Maradona as "the new Pelé."

Predictably, it was not long before offers from wealthier European clubs became too lucrative for Maradona to pass up. Following Maradona's debut for Argentina in a disappointingly early exit for the defending champions at the 1982 World Cup, Maradona was transferred from Boca Juniors to FC Barcelona, where Maradona would score 22 goals in his 36 appearances for the club from 1982 to 1984. Between the transfer fees and payouts to his former club in

Argentina and to the player himself, Maradona's deal was believed to be worth around $12 million, then a record sum for the services of a soccer player.

FC Barcelona did not turn out to be the best fit for Maradona, as the star got into several arguments with management and was plagued with some of the worst injuries and illnesses of his career. Maradona asked to be transferred to SSC Napoli, a move that would prove fruitful for both the player and club. Maradona reached the peak of his professional career during the years of 1984–1991 and led Napoli to the greatest success in the club's history. Napoli won the Serie A Italia Championships for the first time ever in 1986 and the prestigious UEFA Cup in 1989 thanks in large part to Maradona's 115 goals in 188 games. The club president and owner, Corrado Ferlaino, addressed the impact Maradona had on the club and region by saying "Maradona brought a great spirit that drives his teammates. He always wants to win. A great actor is never afraid. That is what makes great theater."[6] In the middle of this successful run with Napoli, Maradona returned to the biggest stage to lead Argentina to another World Cup victory and firmly entrench himself as one of the all-time greats with his memorable goals against England and overall performance of 5 goals and 5 assists during the tournament run. Maradona returned to captain his national team again in 1990, this time coming up just short of repeat World Cup glory as a result of a 1-0 loss to West Germany in the final.

After Maradona's magical decade of excellence at the club and national level, the 1990s marked the beginning of a tragic detour in Maradona's life that for many would tarnish his illustrious career. A failed drug test for cocaine in 1991 led to Maradona being banned from the sport for 15 months. Maradona would struggle with addiction and obesity over the next several years, never fully regaining his once magical form before retiring in 1997 after several short stints with other club teams. Maradona's life of excess would catch up to him as he suffered his first heart attack in 2004, leading his fans across the world to pray for his survival. In recounting Maradona's legacy, sportswriter Daniel Grech wrote at the time of his heart attack that "as in a soccer game, there are two halves to the myth of Diego Maradona. The first half, filled with wonder and pride, is a devotion to the magical talent of Argentina's soccer god. The second half, dark and foreboding, speaks to the drug addiction that prematurely ended his career and today threatens his life."[7] While indeed there were dark moments for this soccer idol, today Maradona seems to have moved past these demons to find a new lease on life. Maradona recounts how in his darkest days following the heart attack, it was a faith in God that pulled him through and made him vow to live a cleaner life. In a 2006 interview, Maradona said, "I wanted to make my mother see that God doesn't want me up there yet and that there is someone who wants me down here."[8] Since his heart attack, Maradona underwent a surgical procedure to staple his stomach so that he could control his weight and began refraining from the alcohol and drug abuse that led to his decline.

With his health in check, Maradona became the host of a successful late night talk show in Argentina and saw his career with the national team come full circle when he was tapped to become the coach for the team in time for the 2010 World Cup in South Africa. This return to glory has sparked a deep pride for many of the country's faithful, who never lost hope that their idol would again find the road to greatness. As one member of the "Church of Maradona" so aptly stated, "It's in each and every one of us to believe in Maradona."[9] For those who saw him play and are witnessing him embark on a new chapter in his life, Maradona gives credence to the belief that the seemingly impossible is in fact possible when placed in the right hands, or rather, the Hand of God.

Notes

1. Dan Rosenheck, "An Earthly Realm for a Soccer God," *The New York Times*, November 4, 2008.

2. Jennifer Macey, "Maradona Says Sorry for 'Hand of God' Goal," *ABC News (Australia)*, February 1, 2008.

3. James Dart et al, "The Greatest Rags to Riches Story Ever," *The Guardian*, April 12, 2006.

4. George Vecsey, "Soccer's Little Big Man," *The New York Times*, May 27, 1990.

5. Clive Gammon, "Here's the New Pele," *Sports Illustrated*, June 9, 1980.

6. George Vecsey, "Soccer's Little Big Man," *The New York Times*, May 27, 1990.

7. Daniel Grech, "Argentina Ties Its Pride, Pain to Gravely Ill Diego Maradona," *The Miami Herald*, April 24, 2004.

8.Marcela Mora y Araujo, "That's One Hell of a Diet, Diego," *The Observer Sport Monthly*, January 8, 2006.

9. Jeannette Neumann, "Church of Maradona Celebrates Idol's Birthday," APWorldstream, October 30, 2008.

José Chilavert

International Soccer Superstar

by Charlie Harless

"I am the best in the world."[1] While on the surface this statement could seem quite audacious and even arrogant, very few would fault Paraguay's goalkeeper José Chilavert for expressing this sentiment at the start of the 1998 World Cup. The willingness to forgive such a statement is partly due to the fact that Chilavert walked the walk, stopping opponents left and right on the way to an improbable run to the World Cup quarterfinals. The other reason that people would be reluctant to criticize the keeper's bombast is that nobody wanted to mess with the man they called the "Bulldog." To amend a familiar idiom, Chilavert's bite was as big as his bark.

Over the course of his career, Chilavert has served suspensions for allegedly spitting in the face of a Brazilian competitor, attacking a reporter, hitting a ball boy, and publicly lashing out with pointed verbal criticisms of the sport's governing body and other players. Mention of these actions are not meant to celebrate nor condemn the temperamental keeper, but to illustrate the intense character and fighting attitude that defines the man in front of the net. When writing about his on-the-field performance, no bravado or unnecessary bark is necessary, as Chilavert's ability to both stop and score goals speaks volumes about his recognition as one of soccer's all-time greats.

Selected three times by the International Federation of Football History and Statistics as the world's best goalkeeper in 1995, 1997, and 1998, Chilavert was an impenetrable force in front of the net over the course of a career that saw him playing goalkeeper for not only the Paraguayan national team, but for clubs in Argentina, Spain, France, and his native Paraguay. In the 1998 World Cup, Paraguay's finest moment on the international stage, Chilavert relinquished just two goals in four games, displaying dominance by shutting out Spain and Bulgaria and pushing eventual champion France to the brink before they scored a golden goal in double overtime to eliminate the underdog Paraguayans.

Near the end of his career, Chilavert showed how special a talent he was with his play for the French club Racing Strasbourg. A team that had never achieved much over the course of its history, Chilavert's play throughout the season lifted Racing Strasbourg to its first French Cup in over three decades. The French Cup was just one of many titles Chilavert won in his career, including four Argentine national championships, the Intercontinental Cup, and the prestigious Copa Libertadores, South America's top club tournament, all as keeper for Velez Sarsfield over the course of a decade.

While Chilavert was a wall in goal, the skill set that made Chilavert truly remarkable was on full display in the French Cup championship game. After stopping a penalty kick shot in overtime by the opposing team, Chilavert walked down the field and scored the game winning, and championship clinching, penalty kick himself. Chilavert is virtually unchallenged as the most prolific goal-scoring goalie in the history of the sport. Asked about his desire to play both sides of the field, Chilavert has said "I am just a normal goalkeeper. But it isn't enough for me to stay in goal. I want to move up the field and score goals, too . . . The fans pay to see a match and I want to give them something special."[2]

Fans of Chilavert saw something special when witnessing the keeper's goal scoring in multiple games, and sometimes, multiple goals in one game. Striking three penalty kick goals past the Ferrocarril Oeste goalkeeper in Velez Sarsfield's 6-1 victory, Chilavert performed a feat that many believe to be a record for an organized club match. Chilavert had a goal of becoming the first keeper to score a goal in the World Cup, and he nearly made good on this ambition when he missed a shot on goal by just a few inches in the opening game of the 1998 World Cup. One of Chilavert's favorite goals of the 62 he wound up scoring in his career was in a club match against River Plate. Chilavert, channeling his inner Babe Ruth, told the opposing goal keeper that he would score against him and even indicated which side of the goal he would put the ball through. The Bulldog made good on his promise, scoring on a free kick from around 60 meters out and likely embarrassing River Plate's goalkeeper in the process. Able to both block the net and find the back of it, there is little wonder that Chilavert would win many accolades in his career, one of the best being his selection as the South American Player of the Year in 1996.

The unique nature of Chilavert's game made the goalkeeper one of the sport's most memorable figures, but Chilavert was special for being an athlete who openly embraced political activism and was willing to express bold opinions without worrying about potential recourse. At the height of his career, Chilavert made clear his intentions that after his playing days were through, he would seek to run for political office. Chilavert has said on multiple occasions that "I want to become president of Paraguay and put an end to corruption."[3] Chilavert proved that he vehemently opposed many of the policies of his home nation when he refused to play for host country Paraguay in the 1999 Copa America tournament. The nation's best player indicated that he felt the country was wasting money on hosting the tournament when it should be spending the funds on education and that he opposed the naming of a retired general, a man he and others suspected to have been corrupt, to the post of security chief for the tournament.

While his absence was felt in Paraguay's poor performance in the Copa America, Chilavert has shown that his political stances are done out of love for his home nation. Chilavert once said that "the economic and financial situation in our country is terrible, but at least the people have football to take their minds off things. What we do give our people, who are suffering terribly, is hope."[4] Chilavert gave his nation's fans hope time and again and showed that a Paraguayan could proudly represent and compete with the big dogs on the international stage. In the 39-year-old goalie's final game before retirement in 2004, Chilavert stopped all but one of the opposition's shots while fittingly scoring a penalty kick goal himself in a 2-1 victory for Velez Sarsfield, the Argeninte club team where the goalie enjoyed many of his best years.

Yet, no matter where in the world Chilavert's game took him, there is no doubt where Chilavert considered home. Before facing that vaunted French team in the 1998 World Cup, Chilavert spoke boldly of Paraguay's chances and rejecting the notion that they would not be able to compete. "We have brought many teams to their knees, why not France? We've got the best defense in the world."[5] Over the span of a 24-year career, Paraguay's best defense, and perhaps best offense, was found in the strength of a bulldog that was never shy to bark and never backed down from a fight.

Notes

1. Pedro Servin, "Chilavert Paraguay's Main Man," *The Gazette*, May 25, 2002.

2. Thomas Pruefer, "Jose Luis Chilavert, Goalkeeper and Goalscorer," *Deutsche Presse-Agentur*, January 8, 1997.

3. Ibid.

4. Norman Da Costa, "Soccer a Big Boost for Paraguayans," *The Toronto Star*, June 28, 1998.

5. Ibid.

Ana Fidelia Quirot

International Track Superstar

by Horacio Ruiz

It's as if Ana Quirot was born for Cuba. Quirot was born only a few years after the Cuban Revolution on March 23, 1963, in the Oriente province, the home province of Fidel Castro. Her parents named her Ana Fidelia, and she would grow to become one of the greatest athletic symbols for Cuba and its communist *comandante*. She mesmerized the track and field world with her grace, speed, and beauty. "She worked occasionally as a model, and many were the reporters who came away from interviews sure that Quirot had flirted with them. She liked to play. She liked the strength that being attractive gave her,"[1] wrote *Sports Illustrated*'s S.L Price. But beauty was only part of Quirot's appeal. Her fame was won on the track where she was a relentless competitor and representative of Cuba. "The nicest thing he ever did for me?" Quirot was once asked about Castro. "He made the revolution." In return she would glorify the revolution through her own tragedy, when she became a survivor—a phoenix rising from the ashes.

As a girl, Quirot was streamlined through Cuba's sports development program to run in the 400 meters and 800 meters. In 1986 she won her first major races in the 1986 Central American and Caribbean Games in both the 400 and 800 meters. The next year in 1987, she would again sweep both events in the Pan American Games in Indianapolis. Quirot's performance in the 800 meters in the 1989 World Cup Championship in Barcelona was historic. She became the fifth woman ever to break the 1:55 mark in the event, and to date there have only been six women to accomplish the feat.

Her winning time of 1:54.44 ranks as the fourth fastest time ever. It would not be until 2008 that a woman would run a faster time when Kenya's Pamela Jelimo ran a 1:54.04. As part of her wonderful year in 1989, Quirot was named the Women's Track & Field Athlete of the Year by *Track & Field News*. The award, given by a panel of international track and field experts organized by the magazine, has been given to women since 1974. Quirot is the only woman from Latin America to win the honor.

In preparation for the 1991 Pan Am Games in Havana, Castro had the entire nation working for him. Some of Cuba's best athletes were doing construction work on the athletic facilities. Outside the Pan American Village there was a sign that read: THE FIRST RECORD OF THE PAN AM GAMES WILL BE SET BY THE WORKERS—FIDEL.[2] Quirot, though one of the most distinguished runners in the world and the World Cup Champion in the 800, was also a fervent patriot. It was reported that she worked a week's worth moving rocks at a construction site. In Havana, Quirot was again sensational by winning two gold medals in the 400 and 800 meters. After one of her victories, Quirot took off her medal and put it around Castro's neck while the crowd chanted her name. At the 1992 Olympics in Barcelona, the same place as her stunning run in the 800, Quirot earned a bronze medal in a time of 1:56.80 in the 800. No one knew—not even Quriot—that she ran in the Olympics while a few weeks pregnant. No one could have seen what was coming next.

On the evening of January 22, 1993, Quirot was doing laundry, but without the luxuries of soap and bleach, even a track star like Quirot had to wash her clothes on the stove in a mixture of isopropyl alcohol and hot water. Thinking that her kerosene cooker was turned off, Quirot poured the alcohol into one of her pots. Some of the alcohol spilled out of the lip of the pot, down the cooker and into the fire when the flames shot up on the sweater she was wearing. Her chest, face, and arms were covered with third-degree burns. Doctors and nurses in the hospital were certain she would die. Quirot, then seven months pregnant, gave birth to a baby girl prematurely. The baby could not survive the burns Quirot had endured and died on Feb. 1, 1993.

Castro visited her in the hospital only a few hours after the accident. He asked her questions about the accident and told her to keep fighting. She says having Castro visit her was like having the entire Cuban state behind her. Then she told Castro, "I'm going to run again."[3] Castro smiled and left her in the hospital with 38 percent of her body covered in third-degree burns.

"Her will," said her coach, Leandro Civil, "that's what separates her from the rest."[4] Quirot underwent skin grafts and soon her condition improved dramatically, though the doctors were shocked with how quickly she was responding. Within two months, Quirot was riding an exercise bike and working out on a rowing machine. Doctors removed her bandages four months earlier than expected. At first, she could not close her hands or lift her arms to comb her hair. A few months later, Quirot was jogging up and down the hospital stairs to stretch her skin. Eleven months after the accident, Quirot participated in her first competition at the Central American and Caribbean Games in Ponce, Puerto Rico. She finished second in the 800 meters with a time of 2:05.22. It was a far cry from the 1989 World Championships, but Castro called her finish a victory for the Cuban people. "I couldn't tilt my head to the side or up; I looked like a robot!" Quirot said. "But a lot of people didn't expect me to run again, let alone win a medal. I showed the world that handicapped people can do things that seem impossible."5

Quirot continued to have surgeries so doctors could transplant skin grafts and stretch her skin. Despite her suffering, Quirot continued training for herself and for Cuba. In 1995, she made her comeback by winning the 800 meters in the 1995 World Championships in Sweden. At the 1996 Olympics in Atlanta she took home a silver medal in the 800 meters, before claiming yet another world title at the 1997 World Championships in Athens. Quirot had returned from her accident stronger than ever.

For her success, Quirot was given a house estimated to be worth $3,000 in a nice residential area of Cuba. She also has her medical expenses and those of her family covered by the Cuban government. Since retiring from competition, Quirot has been a representative on the Cuban Parliament and works with the medical and health commission and the health and sports department. She has since given birth to a daughter, Karla Fidelia, and a son, Alberto Alejandro. She is an icon to Cubans everywhere and a lifelong spokeswoman for the Cuban nation. "I could never leave my country," she said. "There are a lot of people who defect but they don't look at all the sacrifices the government has made to give them an opportunity for a sporting career. Like free education, for example. In other countries this would cost a lot of money. Here we get it for free."6

There's no doubt, though, that Quirot earned her keep.

Notes

1. S. L. Price, "Back In The Running," *Sports Illustrated*, May 22, 1995.

2. Ibid.

3. Ibid.

4. Ibid.

5. Ibid.

6. Spikes Website, "Cuba Where Athletics Legends Are Made Part 3," http://www.spikesmag.com/features/cubawhereathleticslegendsaremadepart3.aspx (accessed September 22, 2009).

Ana Guevara

International Track Superstar

by Horacio Ruiz

All of Mexico had pinned its hopes on their beloved athlete, 400-meter runner Ana Guevara, the "Mexican Gazelle." By the time of the 2004 Summer Olympics in Athens, Guevara was considered the fastest Mexican woman ever and one of the country's greatest athletes, if not the greatest. She was coming off a world championship in 2003 that made her a national hero in Mexico and the favorite to bring another gold medal in Athens. Leading up to the Olympics, there was a billboard advertisement in Mexico of a young man saying, "They tell me I run like a girl. Thanks, Ana."[1] The evidence of such a billboard in Latin America, which gave birth to the phrase "machismo," and for which its men have a reputation for a "machista," or sexist, view of women is further evidence of Guevara's status in her homeland.

As Guevara came off the blocks in Athens, the announcers extolled her virtues and her determination to be victorious. All of Mexico stopped to watch Guevara, anticipating a first-place finish that would have Guevara carrying the Mexican flag above her head in a victory lap for the whole world to see. But it didn't happen. With 30 meters left in the race Guevara and Tonique Williams-Darling of the Bahamas were in a dead heat when it seemed as if Guevara would make one last push, but it was Williams-Darling who made the push to take the gold medal with Guevara finishing with all her might a valiant second. Mexicans still loved their Ana, but the country was momentarily deflated by her second-place finish, almost defeated. Guevara still took a lap around Olympic Stadium draped in a Mexican flag and wearing a sombrero. "I couldn't have done any more," Guevara said. "Tonique was very good."[2] Guevara received a call from former Mexican President Vicente Fox who let her know that, "The whole of Mexico was moved by you."[3] While many Mexicans were disappointed, it was an inspiration for many others. Mexico would win three silver medals and a bronze in Athens, with three of the medals won by women.

"This Mexican society that is still conservative and macho will have to read these triumphs as an explanation for why there will be no turning back the pages, there will be no going back (in the pursuit of women's rights),"[4] said feminist leader Patricia Mercado. But perhaps more beautifully put was a sentiment by one of Mexico's common men. "For just a few seconds, we forgot our problems and our poverty," said Antonio Contreras, a shoeshine man who listened to the race on his radio. "The medal is not important. Her will won, and so did we."[5]

Guevara had been winning a long time before running in Athens. A former basketball player, Guevara took up running when her Cuban coach, Raúl Barreda, noticed her potential for the 800 meter race with her ability to take long strides. In due time, she would find that her specialty lay in the 400 meters.

Guevara's first major victory came in the 1999 Pan American Games when she won a gold medal in the 400m. A year later, in the 2000 Olympics, she qualified for the 400m finals and finished in fifth place in less than a second behind winner Cathy Freeman. In 2001, Guevara garnered a bronze in the World Championships in Edmonton. The biggest victory of her career came in the 2003 World Championships in Paris, where she won with a personal-best time of 48.89. As of September 2009, Guevara's 400-meter personal best ranks her as the ninth-fastest woman ever in the event. She continued her dominance in the Pan American Games with gold medals in 2003 and 2007, marking three consecutive gold medals she had claimed in the Pan American Games.

Following her silver medal finish in Athens, Guevara would again have a podium finish in the 2005 World Championships in Helsinki by winning a bronze medal. Two years later in the 2007 World Championships in Osaka, Guevara finished fourth. It seemed as if Guevara's best days were behind her. Guevara had been plagued by injuries since the months leading up to the Athens games. But her popularity, especially among Mexicans across the world did not diminish. In a 2005 race in the United States' Eugene, OR, Guevara attracted many of her devoted fans.

"You see her on television, hear her on the radio, and read about her in the newspaper," said Alexis Reyna, a Mexican national that lived in Eugene. "But you want to be there."[6] In a race in 2003 in Eugene, Reyna did not have a ticket but peaked through a fence to watch Guevara win the race. Another Eugene resident who attended the race, Eli Torres, said, "It was so emotional, and it was not just because of the quality performance, but because I also was Mexican."[7] Guevara was honored by the support she saw in Eugene both in 2003 and in 2005. "I never imagined," she said. "It was a great surprise. I can only say that all that I have been doing is for my people and all the people who like to see me run the 400. I've always dreamed of being an icon of the sport in my country. Apart from the walkers and the long-distance runners, Mexico has never had any heroes on the track. I am honored to be a role model for young people in the whole Latin region."[8]

But there was an undercurrent of tension between Guevara and the Mexican Athletics Federation that had been building for much of 2007. Guevara had grown tired of what she deemed was cronyism and corruption in Mexican sports. In the 2007 World Championships in Osaka, the Mexican team realized they did not have uniforms, and when they arrived, many did not fit the athletes. Some Mexican athletes were forced to compete without Mexican uniforms. Incidents such as those had become the norm for many Mexican athletes and Guevara had tolerated enough.

On January 16, 2008 she announced her retirement and in her press conference denounced the Mexican Athletics Federation, vowing to speak up so that future athletes would be better served by the governing body. Guevara sent a letter to Mexican President Felipe Calderón, detailing the athletes' grievances, which was signed by 25 of 27 athletes that were in Osaka. "I'm not going to change the world, but if I transform myself I'll transform my world," Guevara said in an interview with the Mexican sports journal *Record*. "I'm breaking the silence to make things better. I'd prefer to annoy with the truth rather than remain complacent with the lies."[9]

Despite her retirement, Guevara made it to the 2008 Beijing Olympics as an analyst for ESPNDeportes. She remains an iconic figure in Mexico and in Latin America. Her success and grace has inspired the youth, especially girls, to dream big and to believe that they can achieve their goals.

Notes

1. Hugh Dellios, "Bittersweet Time For Sprinter Guevara And Mexico After Olympics," *Chicago Tribune*, September 6, 2004.

2. Dick Patrick, "Roundup: Gold Dished Out in Hurdles and 1,500," *USAToday*, August 24, 2004.

3. Ibid.

4. Hugh Dellios, "Bittersweet Time For Sprinter Guevara And Mexico After Olympics," *Chicago Tribune*, September 6, 2004.

5. Ibid.

6. Bob Rodman, "Pride Of Her Homeland," *The Register Guardian*, May 31, 2005.

7. Ibid.

8. Ibid.

9. Kevin Baxter, "Mexican Track And Field In A State Of Uproar," *Los Angeles Times*, April 13, 2008.

Juan Manuel Fangio

International Formula One Superstar

by Horacio Ruiz

"El Maestro," the old man most observers thought could not with-stand the rigors of racing had just endured a disastrous pit stop that saw him go from holding a 30-second lead to falling behind the leader by nearly 50 seconds in the 1957 German Grand Prix. It seemed as if the race had been lost right there, but Fangio raced his car like never before. In a mad dash to catch up to the first and second-place drivers, Fangio would break the lap record at Nürbur-gring raceway ten times on his way to making up the 50-second deficit. With a lap to spare, Fangio caught drivers Peter Collins and Mike Hawthorn in what is considered one of the greatest feats in Formula One history. "I have never driven that quickly before in my life and I don't think I will ever be able to do it again,"[1] Fangio said after the race. At 46 years of age, it would be the last Grand Prix victory in Fangio's career. The race also sealed his fifth For-mula One world championship, a record that would stand for 45 years until 2003.

Fangio was born on June 24, 1911 in Balcarce, Argentina, about 220 miles south of Buenos Aires. By the age of 13, Fangio had fallen in love with cars and dropped out of school to become an as-sistant mechanic. Fangio came to know every working part of the car, learning what made the cars tick and go. One of his duties was to drive customer's cars from Balcarce to Buenos Aires where he would drive on treacherous, weather-beaten roads. This created a foundation for his driving success, especially in slippery and dan-gerous conditions.

In 1936, Fangio made his racing debut with a six-cylinder Ford engine. Fangio first attained success after finishing seventh in the 1938 Gran Premio Argentino de Carreteras, a 4,590 mile race. The locals in Balcarce were so proud of Fangio that they pooled their money together to buy him a better car, a six-cylinder Chevy Coupe. In 1940, Fangio won the Gran Premio Internacional del Norte after driving for 109 hours through 6,000 miles from Buenos Aires to

Lima, and back. In 1940 and 1941 he won the Argentine National Championship. Racing stopped because of a lack of resources due to World War II, but Fangio resumed racing in 1947. In 1948, Fangio made his first trip to Europe to compete and harness his skills. His previous experience in the endurance races gave Fangio an unrivalled amount of experience and an unmatched repertoire. The next year, Fangio returned to Europe where he won seven major races driving a Maserati. In 1950, at the age of 38, Fangio joined the Formula One racing circuit and finished in second place in the point standings. The following season, Fangio would claim his first world championship with three first-place finishes and two second-place finishes.

Fangio missed the 1952 season after nearly being killed during a race when he lost control of his car and was ejected as his car tumbled over and over. He spent most of 1952 in Argentina recovering from his injuries, which included a broken neck. In 1953, he made a successful return to Formula One racing when he finished second in the point standings. In 1954 Fangio moved to the Mercedes team and would begin a streak of four consecutive world championships that would culminate with his incredible triumph in 1957 in Germany. Fangio would find a way to drive in the best cars whether it was for Mercdes, Ferrari, or Maserati. "Because he was the best bloody driver!" said Stirling Moss, one of Fangio's teammates and rivals. "The cheapest method of becoming a successful Grand Prix team was to sign up Fangio."[2]

"He was humble, totally unassuming and a terror on the race track,"[3] said Fred Belair, a longtime friend of Fangio's. Throughout his career, Fangio gained a reputation for his maneuvering ability and a knack for getting the most out of inferior cars. Much of his success is credited to his strength, stamina, and incredible mental fortitude that had been galvanized early in his career. Fangio would sometimes lean in his car to help it maneuver around a corner. In an era much different from today's Formula One cars that appear to be more like jets, Fangio rode with a tucked in long-sleeve shirt, a tiny helmet, and flimsy goggles. His upper torso was also fully exposed, unlike today's drivers who are tucked into their cockpits. To see Fangio drive is to see a man mastering an ancient and powerful machine of his time, knowing that because of his ability to show what the machine is fully capable of, that it would be made much more powerful by those in charge of designing and building such machines. In the middle of the 1958 season Fangio retired after running in just two races. He feared that the cars had become too fast and was wary of having had more than 30 friends killed while racing.

In seven full Formula One seasons, Fangio won five championships, and finished in second place twice. He ran a career 51 Grand Prix races, 29 of which he started from the pole. His 23 victories give him the highest win percentage in the history of Formula One racing. In 1990, he was inducted into the International Motorsports Hall of Fame, the only Latino in the Hall of Fame and the first from Latin-America. After all the records Fangio had set, what most remembered about him was his gentlemanly demeanor and his willingness to be the consummate teammate. "Most of us who drove quickly were bastards," Moss said. "But I can't think of any facets of Juan's character which one wouldn't like to have in one's own."[4]

In 2003, when Michael Schumacher won his sixth of seven world championships to surpass Fangio in the number of career titles, he gave way to Fangio. "I am not trying to compare myself to Fangio. You cannot compare someone like Fangio with the present day," Schumacher said. "Fangio is on a level much higher than I see myself. There is absolutely no comparison. What he did stands alone and what we have achieved is also unique. I have such respect for what he achieved."[5]

In retirement, Fangio became an ambassador for car racing. He became a distributor for Mercedes-Benz in Argentina and at the time of his death in 1995, he was the honorary president of Mercedes in Argentina. There are six sculptures of Fangio around the world that were sculpted by Catalán sculptor Joaquim Ros Sabaté. The statues are located in Puerto Madero, Buenos Aires; Monte Carlo, Monaco; Montmeló, Spain; Nürburgring, Germany; Stuttgart—Untertürkheim, Germany, and Monza, Italy. Lucky to have walked away from the sport he loved so much, Fangio explained, "To race is to live. But those who have died while racing knew, perhaps, how to live more than all others. If there is one driver who has not waked in the middle of the night, fingers clutching a sweat-soaked pillow, eardrums bursting with shrieking tires, that man tumbled from another planet."[6]

Notes

1. Michael Rose. "Maserati And Fangio F1 World Champions In 1957," September 16, 2007. http://www.greatcarstv.com/history/maserati-and-fangio-f1-world-champions-in-1957.html

2. The Official Formula One Website, "Juan Manuel Fangio," http://www.formula1.com/teams_and_drivers/hall_of_fame/268/ (accessed September 14, 2009).

3. Joseph Siano, "Juan Manuel Fangio, 84, Racer Who Captured 5 World Titles," *The New York Times*, July 18, 1995, Obituary section.

4. The Official Formula One Website. "Juan Manuel Fangio," http://www.formula1.com/teams_and_drivers/hall_of_fame/268/ (accessed September 14, 2009).

5. Alastair Himmer, "Fangio Greater Than Me, Says Schumacher," *AAPSports News (Australia)*, October 13, 2003.

6. Norman Fox, "Fox's 20th Century: 1955–60: Juan Manuel Fangio," *The Independent (London, England)*, October 31, 1999.

Ayrton Senna

International Formula One Superstar

by Horacio Ruiz

Courtesy of Stuart Seeger.

They called him a genius for the way he drove a Formula One race car unlike anybody else. Like many of the supremely gifted sporting stars, Ayrton Senna was said to be egotistical, arrogant, and petulant. Even so, the characterizations of Senna were trumped by his greatness, his status as Brazil's most beloved sports hero since Pelé, and a desire for taking himself to the limits. "For me, this research is fascinating," Senna once said. "Every time I push, I find something more, again and again. But there is a contradiction. The same moment that you become the fastest, you are enormously fragile. Because in a split-second, it can be gone. All of it. These two extremes contribute to knowing yourself, deeper and deeper."[1]

On the night of April 30, 1994 the ultra-confident Senna wasn't feeling right. The next day he was to race in the San Marino Grand Prix in Imola, Italy. He called his girlfriend that night and told her he did not want to race the next day despite qualifying for the pole position. Earlier in the day, rookie driver Roland Ratzenberger of Australia died when his car spun out of control while turning a corner in qualifying. When qualifying was over, Senna stood at the turn where Ratzenberger crashed and cried. Senna was entering the 11th Formula One season of his career with what he termed a "new life,"[2] after switching from the McLaren Racing Team to the Williams-Renault team that had won the two previous Formula One championships. There was talk that Senna could very well win all 16 races of the season. What was supposed to be a dream season, however, did not begin memorably for Senna as he failed to finish the first two races before heading into the San Marino, the third race of the season.

Senna had come a long way from being the shy and awkward boy who grew up avoiding the attention of others. He had become a legend of the sport and captivated the imaginations of Brazilians by flying in a private jet to races from his ranch in São Paulo and for dating celebrities and supermodels. With his fame and globe-trotting lifestyle, Senna still kept his focus on racing so that he, in a way that only he could, would seemingly command and orchestrate each race's outcome in his favor. As a child, Senna was diagnosed with a motor coordination deficiency, but his father, a wealthy business-man and landowner in São Paulo noticed his son's love for race cars. When Senna was four years old he received a go-cart as a gift from his father. Behind the wheel, he seemed to become focused and con-fident and the family would spend many weekends in parks where Senna could enjoy his newfound sense of expression.

At 13, Senna began racing competitively and in 1977, as a 17-year-old, he won the South American Kart Championship. In 1981, Senna moved to England to compete in single-seater racing. "He was so quiet," said Denis Rushen, the owner of a Formula Ford team, "that he was always the guy you found standing shyly in the kitchen at parties."[3] In 1982, Senna won the British and European Formula Ford 2000 championship, and in 1983 he won the British Formula Three Championship, including a winning streak of nine consecutive races. By 1984, Senna was ready to make the jump to Formula One racing and joined the Toleman racing team. In his sec-ond start ever on the Formula One circuit, he scored his first-ever championship points with a sixth-place finish in South Africa. That year, Senna finished ninth in the point standings. The next year he would sign with the Lotus racing team where he would spend three seasons. In 1985, Senna finished in fourth place in the point stand-ings and earned the first two victories of his career. At the end of 1985, he had gained the reputation as one of the fastest drivers on the circuit by leading in the number of pole positions with seven.

For the next two years Senna continued to climb in the driver rankings with another fourth-place finish in 1986 and a third-place finish in 1987. But coveting the world championship and the oppor-tunity to join the best racing team, Senna left Lotus racing to join the

McLaren team. Senna joined the team when McLaren received permission from their other star driver, three-time world champion Alain Prost. The arrival of Senna would create an intense and often times bitter rivalry between the two drivers. The 1988 season, Senna's first with McLaren, would see him capture his first world championship with eight victories to Prost's seven. In 1989, the rivalry between Senna and Prost would be inflamed when in the Japanese Grand Prix in Suzuka, the second to last race of the season, Senna attempted to pass Prost who then turned into a corner and cut Senna off. The two drivers ended up with their cars stalled and their wheels interlocked. Senna was able to get a jump-start from race marshals, and after taking a pit stop to fix his car, finished in first. Following the race, Senna's first-place finish was nullified by the Fédération Internationale de l'Automobile (FIA), Formula One's sanctioning body. Prost would win the world title in 1989 and Senna finished second. After his championship season, Prost left McLaren to join rival Ferrari.

The 1990 season marked Senna's second world championship, but not without controversy that again involved Prost. In the same race as the previous season, the Japanese Grand Prix, Senna purposely crashed into Prost while making a move for the lead. Senna said he felt the FIA had unfairly ignored his protests about his starting position in 1989 and again in 1990. He protested that even though he had won the pole for the race, the right-handed starting spot for the pole was on the dirty side of the track, a disadvantage to the driver. Senna said he had received assurances from the FIA that the starting position would be changed to the left-hand side, where Prost, who qualified second for the race, was slated to start. After qualifying for the pole, Senna was informed that the starting positions would not be changed. Frustrated, Senna crashed into Prost when his rival attempted a pass at the very beginning of the race. Prost would say: "What he did was more than unsporting. It was disgusting. With him, racing isn't a sport, it's war. I appreciate honesty and Senna is not an honest man."[4] Senna had his own viewpoint:

"At Suzuka last year I asked the officials to change pole position from the right side of the track to the left. It was unfair, as it was, because the right side is always dirty, and there is less grip—you sweat to get pole position, and then you are penalized for it. And they said, 'Yes, no problem.' Then, what happened? [FIA President Jean-Marie] Balestre gave an order that it wasn't to be changed. I know how the system works . . . I said to myself, 'OK, whatever happens, I'm going to get into the first corner first—I'm not prepared to let the guy (Alain Prost) turn into that corner before me.' You should fight for what you think is right. If pole had been on the left, I'd have made it to the first corner in the lead, no problem. That was a bad decision to keep pole on the right, and it was influenced by Balestre."[5]

Senna, taking on the wrath of the FIA, Prost, and the British and French media, still finished the champion. He would claim his third world title in 1991, largely devoid of any controversy. In 1992, Senna mustered a 4th place finish and it became noticeable that the McLaren team was being displaced as the top racing team by the - Williams-Renault team. In 1993, Senna finished second in the world championship standings despite racing in a car widely considered to be running on an inferior engine. The following year, he made the jump to the Williams-Renault team where he was hoping to claim yet another world championship. By this time, Senna was one of the highest-paid athletes in the world, reportedly making more than $1 million per race in addition to his endorsement deals.

The 1994 season with Williams-Renault did not start as anticipated for Senna. He had fallen far behind the points standings to Michael Schumacher, who would become a Formula One legend unlike any other by capturing seven career world titles. Senna had qualified for the pole at the San Marino, but even so, there was something not in place. Perhaps Ratzenberger's death, the first in a Formula One race or qualifying run in nearly 12 years, had rattled Senna too much. After driving practice laps in the morning of the race, Senna only offered to tell reporters, "Today was not typical. My car is very difficult to drive."[6]

On the seventh lap of the race, after yet another accident had delayed the race for five laps, Senna was making a left turn when his car left the track at a speed of 195 miles per hour before hitting an unprotected concrete barrier. In the two seconds between leaving the track and crashing into the barrier, Senna was able to slow his car down to 135 mph. The impact of the crash tore off the right front wheel and the nosecone of Senna's car. It seemed as if Senna would be OK, that this was just another crash that the Superman of racing would walk away from, but the moments after the crash showed Senna motionless. The impact had loosened parts of Senna's cockpit that penetrated his helmet and caused several skull fractures that left him brain dead. In the cockpit, rescue workers found a bloody Australian flag that Senna intended to wave in victory in honor of Ratzenberger. Senna was kept alive for several more hours by an artificial respirator before being pronounced dead at the age of 34. A 25-year-old Schumacher, who was behind Senna during the accident and who would become one of the most influential athletes in the world, seriously considered retiring the day Senna died. In an ironic twist of fate, Senna had spent the morning of his last race leading his fellow drivers in a meeting to reform the Drivers' Safety group to make Formula One racing safer.

In the aftermath of his death, Brazil declared three days of mourning. When news of his death had spread, a crowd of 100,000 watching a soccer match between Flamengo and Vasco in Rio's Maracana Stadium began to chant, *"Ole-oleleo la, Sen-na, Sen-na."* The scene repeated itself across the nation's soccer stadiums. Three million Brazilians lined the streets of São Paulo on the day of Senna's funeral. After his death, it was discovered that Senna had donated millions of dollars from his personal fortune that was estimated to be $400 million. To this day, the Instituto Ayrton Senna has invested more than $80 million in Brazilian charities and non-governmental organizations. The 1994 Brazilian World Cup team dedicated its championship to the fallen race care driver, and more than 15 years later, Senna remains the last Formula One driver to be killed in an accident. After his death, several car and racetrack reforms were made to improve driver safety.

"To see Senna on a quick lap was to be awed by majesty,"[7] one writer wrote in his obituary for Senna. Michael Kranefuss, the head of Ford's international racing activities, compared the other drivers to Senna by saying, "It was like you were watching photographers, and then you were watching a painting done by Michelangelo." Martin Brundle, a former Formula One driver said, "Senna is a genius. I define genius as just the right side of imbalance. He is so highly developed to the point that he's almost over the edge. It's a close call."[8]

Senna finished his career with three Formula One world championships, 41 career victories, and 65 pole qualifiers. In 2000, he was posthumously inducted into the International Motorsports Hall of Fame. Senna was buried on a hillside overlooking São Paulo in the Cemiterio do Morumbi. His grave is marked by a simple bronze plaque, and it is estimated that his final resting place has more visitors every year than the graves of John F. Kennedy, Marilyn Monroe, and Elvis Presley combined. Almost prophetically in early 1994, Senna mulled his future by saying, "I want to live fully, very intensely. I would never want to live partially, suffering from illness or injury. If I ever happen to have an accident that eventually costs my life, I hope it happens in one instant."⁹

Notes

1. The Official Formula One Website, "Ayrton Senna," http://www.formula1.com/teams_and_drivers/hall_of_fame/45/ (accessed September 13, 2009).

2. Bruce Newman, "The Last Ride," *Sports Illustrated*, May 9, 1994.

3. David Tremayne, "Obituary: Ayrton Senna," *The Independent* (London), May 2, 1994.

4. Robert Philip, "Spirit Of Ayrton Senna Is Lewis Hamilton's Spur," *Telegraph*, October 17, 2007, Sports section.

5. Wikipedia.com, "Ayrton Senna," http://en.wikipedia.org/wiki/Ayrton_Senna (accessed September 13, 2009).

6. Bruce Newman, "The Last Ride," *Sports Illustrated*, May 9, 1994.

7. David Tremayne, "Obituary: Ayrton Senna," *The Independent* (London), May 2, 1994.

8. The Official Formula One Website, "Ayrton Senna," http://www.formula1.com/teams_and_drivers/hall_of_fame/45/ (accessed September 13, 2009).

9. Ibid.

17

CONCLUSION/EPILOGUE—
FUTURE OF LATINOS IN SPORT

by Richard Lapchick

In the course of researching a book on Hispanic athletes, I expected to find, and did, a strong Latino presence in baseball, soccer, and boxing. The area that surprised me most, though, was the Latino presence, success, and influence in the X Games, one of the most popular events among Generation X and Generation Y demographics. As we embark on the second decade of the 21st century, the sporting landscape will be shaped by the country's ever-evolving social landscape. It is possible that action sports, with the X Games as the premiere event, will be at the vanguard for Latino athletes. The U.S. Census Bureau predicts that Latinos will make up 30 percent of the U.S. population by 2050. There is no doubt that the Latino population is a burgeoning one. But Latino boys and girls still face barriers to participation in sport. In the midst of the greatest economic crisis the United States has faced since the Great Depression, median household income fell from $52,163 to $50,303 between 2007 and 2008. The median income of Latino households was $37,913— well below the national average. The national poverty rate was 13.2 percent in 2008. In comparison, Latinos were reported to have a 23.2 percent poverty rate and the rate for African-Americans was 24.7 percent.

Athletes featured in this book, including Rosemary Casals, Lee Treviño, and Joe Kapp, among others, fought back from poverty to reach superstardom. But the cost of playing sports goes beyond finances. The cost extends into life-altering decisions where boys and girls are forced to choose between competitively pursuing sport and finding a job to help boost their household's income. There also is a divide between second-, third-, and fourth-generation Latino-Americans and newly arrived Latino immigrants. The struggle and joy of sport, particularly for Mexican immigrants, was so beautifully portrayed by *Sports Illustrated* writer Gary Smith in his profile on Jim White's high school boy's cross country dynasty in McFarland, CA., in the story "Running For Their Lives."

At McFarland High, White won nine cross country state championships from 1980 through 2003, with Latino athletes coming from impoverished households and facing near-impossible obstacles. According to the 2000 Census, Latinos made up 85.7 percent of the population in McFarland and the median household income was $24,821, with 34.1 percent of families living below the poverty line. White's accomplishments in coaching and mentoring a "family" of athletes was nothing short of remarkable, but cross-country running, as Smith wrote, was as simple and as financially unrestrictive as laying "one sneaker in front of the other again and again."[1]

Perhaps there is something to participation in the X Games that parallels the requirements needed for cross country running. One of sport action's biggest Latino stars, Paul Rodríguez Jr., a second generation Mexican-American, knew he wanted to be a professional skateboarder when his father bought him a $30 skateboard for his 12th birthday. In a sport developed and revolutionized in empty swimming pools and urban landscapes, and expanding with the construction of skate parks, skateboarding and BMX riding has been remarkably accessible for young Latino athletes. The presence of skate parks and the ease of practicing in an empty parking lot or the steps of buildings are comparable to the accessibility of basketball courts both in inner-city and suburban settings.

Rodríguez became the first action sports athlete—and the first Mexican-American—to sign a signature shoe deal with Nike and was featured in a Nike commercial with rap star Ice Cube and basketball superstar Kobe Bryant. Rodríguez won gold in the 2004 and 2005 X Games. On June 21, 2009, the Paul Rodríguez Skate Park was unveiled in the Los Angeles district of Pacoima at the Ritchie Valens Public Park.

"This whole thing is a blessing. It took me by surprise," said Rodríguez of his success. "I knew I was going to skate, but I never thought I was going to be a leader for my people. Not that I didn't want to be, but I didn't realize what would happen. Latinos have embraced me and the sport of skateboarding—especially in L.A., where the Mexican-American population is growing so fast every day. It's a real blessing. I'm really grateful for what I can be to my community."[2]

Previously, I had wondered why Los Angeles has been the X Games host city for the past seven years, and will be again in 2010. I discovered that skating has its roots in Los Angeles and in the Latino community which, according to the U.S. Census Bureau, makes up 47.7 percent of the L.A. County population and 36.6 percent of the population of California. Tony Alva and Stacy Peralta, both Mexican-American, were two of the original members of the Z-Boys, a group of skateboarders from Venice, CA., who are credited with popularizing and introducing aerial tricks to the sport. The Z-Boys first got together as surfers and then expanded into skateboarding in 1975. Alva and Peralta were original founders, along with Chris Cahill, Nathan Pratt, Jay Adams, and Allen Sarlo.

The Z-Boys changed skateboarding by introducing a punk-rock aspect that is now tied to the skateboarding culture. Empty swimming pools in Southern California became the sites where new, high-risk aerials were practiced. The Z-Boys became famous for those aerial moves and became what is arguably the most influential skateboarding team ever.

Peralta wrote the script for the movie *Lords of Dogtown* about the Z-Boys. The 2005 film starred the late Heath Ledger. Alva is often credited with being the first to perform aerials on a skateboard, and in 1977, he became the first Professional Skateboarding World Champion. In addition to his athleticism, he has an entrepreneurial side. Instead of signing with a major skateboarding label, the 19-year-old Alva started his own skateboard company in 1977. Alva Skates was the first skateboard company owned and run by a skateboarder.

By the time Peralta was 19 years old he had created several new tricks and was at the top of the ranks of professional skateboarders. Peralta and manufacturer George Powell formed the Powell-Peralta skate gear company, which helped him create the Bones Brigade skate team. That group, composed of some of the best skateboarders in the sport—including Tony Hawk, Mike

McGill, Steve Caballero, Lance Mountain, and Tommy Guerrero—
further revolutionized skateboarding. Peralta helped spread the culture worldwide by directing and producing skating videos in addition to *Lords of Dogtown*. He has had a successful career in film and
TV as a director, producer, and writer.

For Generations X and Y, the X Games provide a new and exciting form of sporting entertainment. They lend an edginess and
sense of danger not often found in more traditional sports such as
basketball, baseball, and football. Action sport athletes continually
push their physical and creative abilities to what seems like un-
earthly limits. More than 111,000 fans turned out for X Games 15, a
four-day event in Los Angeles in August. Between the ESPN and
ABC broadcasts, the X Games reached a million households daily.

Sponsors are paying attention to the Los Angeles Latino community. According to an X Games on-site report conducted by
ESPN Research, 47 percent of all attendees at the 2008 X Games
were Latino. Last year, the X Games partnered with La Raza Radio
to air more than 120 spots promoting the Games, which were also
promoted on Latino Websites and LA TV, a Latino network in Los
Angeles that ran more than 50 20-second spots promoting the events.
With sponsorship, a promising crop of Latino action sport stars has
emerged.

Venezuelan-born Daniel Dhers became a serious athlete and
rider when he moved to Argentina at the age of 16. Dhers won gold
medals in the X Games as a BMX rider in both 2007 and 2008, and
also won the gold in the LG Action Sports World Championships in
2006 and 2008. In Venezuela, where BMX is not as developed as it
is in the United States, Dhers is viewed as a pioneer and is becoming an ambassador for the sport.

In 2003, the X Games featured skateboarding competitions for
women for the first time, and Latina Vanessa Torres won the first
gold medal by capturing the street course. She took the silver medal
in 2004.

The innovative Kyle Loza has become extremely popular in
the world of action sports. For three straight years, he won the Moto
X Best Trick at the X Games with stunts he calls "The Volt" and the
"Electric Doom." In the latter, Loza hops over his handlebars and
does a back flip in midair before landing back safely on his bike.

Mike Escamilla was voted one of the most influential BMX riders of the 1990s by *Ride* Magazine. In 2005, Escamilla broke and set two world records at X Games 11 for the longest backflip and the longest 360 on a BMX bike. He has his own action figure, signature model shoes, and is in several action sports video games.

Sandro Dias is a noted Brazilian skater who won the vert skateboarder world title from 2003 to 2007. He is best known for his mastery of the 540 and being in an exclusive club of competitors who can successfully pull off the 900. Dias took the gold medal for Skateboard Vert at X Games 12.

The future of Latinos in action sports is in capable hands. Chaz Ortiz, a third-generation Mexican-American born on May 4, 1994, is already one of the most distinguished skateboarders in the United States. He first made headlines as an amateur skater on the professional Dew Tour. In his first pro competition in June 2008, Ortiz, as an amateur, finished third behind Ryan Sheckler, the three-time defending Dew Tour champion, and Paul Rodríguez Jr. As a 14-year-old amateur on the professional tour, Ortiz won two events and had four total podium finishes on his way to claiming the 2008 Skate Park Dew Cup and unseating Sheckler for first place. Ortiz became the youngest champion ever on the Dew Tour. In 2009, he tied for second in the Skate Park Dew Cup standings with Rodríguez.

Following his 2008 Dew Cup championship, Ortiz traveled to Mexico City for the first time and captured a silver medal at the international X Games in Mexico. Ortiz caught the attention of sponsors and currently counts DC Shoes, Zoo York, and Gatorade among his biggest corporate endorsements. In his online biography for the Dew Tour he lists Rodríguez as the person he admires most in the sport.

As if the success of the now 15-year-old Ortiz were not startling enough, then the quick start of Johanny Velásquez merits attention. Velásquez, a nine-year-old, has a junior skate named after him, the JoJo Transformer, under the Universal Skate Design brand. Velásquez, an inline skater, is the son of Richie Velásquez, the 2003 gold medal winner of the Gravity Games' Inline Street Best Trick event. Skating has played a significant role in shaping the history of sport for Latinos. It was through speed skating that Derek Parra and Jennifer Rodríguez, the only athletes from the Winter Olympics featured in the book, were able to move on to ice skating to claim gold and bronze medals, respectively, in the Winter Olympic Games.

Like the great Latin American influence on Major League Baseball, the X Games and action sports can serve as perhaps a more viable platform for Latinos and Latino-Americans to pave the way in sport as the demographics of the United States continue to change. With its roots in the Latino community and its continued support by Latino spectators, action sports should continue to develop Latino athletes and draw a diverse crowd.

There is no doubt that Latino participation in all sports will grow in the 40 years leading up to 2050. The "Campeones" featured in this book shed light on the various inroads Latinos have made in the United States on and off the playing field. We can expect the number of players, coaches, and administrators to increase in the NFL, NBA, and NHL, as well as in college sports.

The 2009–10 NFL Playoffs featured two Latino quarterbacks in Mark Sánchez of the New York Jets and Tony Romo of the Dallas Cowboys. The NBA has continued its efforts to make basketball a global sport and the association's efforts in the Latino and Spanish markets have been most notable in the emergence of the Puerto Rican, Argentinean, and Spanish national basketball teams as serious rivals to the star-studded United States teams. In addition, the list of notable Latino players in the 2009–10 NBA season includes Carmelo Anthony, Charlie Villanueva, Luis Scola, Manu Ginóbili, Carlos Delfino, Al Horford, Trevor Ariza, and Eduardo Nájera. Puerto Ricans José Barea and Carlos Arroyo are enjoying considerable playing time for the Dallas Mavericks and Miami Heat, respectively, and Brazilians Leandro Barbosa, Anderson Varejao, and Nené Hilario have made an impact for their teams. The NHL had its first Latino goalie play in 2009 when Cuban-American Al Montoya made his NHL debut with the Phoenix Coyotes on his way to a shutout win versus the Colorado Avalanche. Montoya joined Bill Guerin, Scott Gómez, and Raffi Torres as the fourth Latino player in the NHL. Raymond Macías and Alec Martínez, both of Spanish descent, also made their NHL debuts in 2009.

Latino attendance and spectatorship will also surely increase, which means that teams and league offices that have developed communications and marketing strategies geared toward Latino audiences will reap the greatest benefits. Collectively, the athletes featured in this book represent a total of 20 countries (United States, Argentina, Cuba, Brazil, Panama, Ecuador, Nicaragua, Venezuela, the Dominican Republic, Puerto Rico, Mexico, Chile, El Salvador, Uruguay, Colombia, Costa Rica, Paraguay, Peru, Honduras, and Guatemala). Including Brazil, this collection of nations is evidence of the complex unity and diversity of Latino culture in sport that we should celebrate as the world comes closer together through the power of sport.

Notes

1. Gary Smith, "Running For Their Lives," *Sports Illustrated.* March 15, 2004.
2.Mary Buckheit, ESPN.com. "P-Rod and the Funny Man," September 29, 2009. http://sports.espn.go.com/espn/hispanicheritage2009/news/story?id=4516888

About the National Consortium for Academics and Sports

The National Consortium for Academics and Sports (NCAS) is an ever-growing organization of colleges, universities, and individuals. The mission of the NCAS is to create a better society by focusing on educational attainment and using the power and appeal of sport to positively affect social change.

The NCAS evolved in response to the need to "keep the student in the student-athlete." The NCAS was established by Dr. Richard E. Lapchick and since its inception in 1985, NCAS member institutions have proven to be effective advocates for balancing academics and athletics. By joining the NCAS, a college or university agrees to bring back, tuition free, their own former student-athletes who competed in revenue- and non-revenue-producing sports and were unable to complete their degree requirements. In exchange, these former student-athletes agree to participate in school outreach and community service programs addressing social issues that affect America's youth.

There have been hundreds of people who have worked in NCAS programs over the past 24 years to help us fulfill our mission. Each has helped because of his or her passion for combining academics, sport, and the way we use sport to bring about social change for our children.

The NCAS started with 11 universities in 1985 and now has more than 230 member institutions. Members of the NCAS have brought back 29,861 former student-athletes to complete their degrees through one of our biggest programs. The Degree Completion

Program was just a dream in 1985, but almost 30,000 now say that dream has become a reality.

Returning student-athletes participate in outreach and community service programs in exchange for the tuition and fees they receive when they come back to school. They have reached over 18.3 million young people in cities in America, rural America, and suburban America. Wherever there are college campuses, our student-athletes are in the community helping young people face the crises of the past 24 years. Member institutions have donated more than $322 million in tuition assistance to these former student-athletes. With no athletic participation in return this time around, the biggest return possible is to the student who leaves with the degree he or she was told would be there for them when first enrolling. The NCAS and its members have been able to work with children on issues like conflict resolution, improving race relations, reducing men's violence against women, stemming the spread of drug and alcohol abuse, and emphasizing the importance of education and the importance of balancing work in the classroom and on the playing field.

The NCAS has worked with organizations and schools to help them understand issues of diversity, not only as a moral imperative, but also as a business necessity. The NCAS utilizes the Teamwork Leadership Institute (TLI) to teach our colleges, professional athletes, and all of the people that sport touches, the importance and value of diversity which then, in turn, reflects back on society as a whole. The mission of TLI is to help senior administrators as well as team front office and athletic department staff, through the provision of diversity training services, to apply the principles of teamwork to all areas of athletic departments and professional sports organizations. Challenges that stem from cultural prejudice, intolerance, and poor communication can be aggressively addressed in intelligent, safe, and structured ways. TLI works with staff members to help them anticipate, recognize, and address the problems inherent to diverse teams and staff. Diversity training demonstrates that diverse people have a great deal in common. Rather than being divisive issues, racial, ethnic, and gender differences can serve as building blocks. Just as in sports, these differences can strengthen the group. TLI has provided workshops for over 150 athletic organizations, including college athletic departments, the National Basketball Association, Major League Soccer, Maloof Sports & Entertainment (Sacramento Kings), and the Orlando Magic.

The Mentors in Violence Prevention (MVP) National Program, founded in 1993 by Northeastern University's Center for the Study of Sport in Society, is a leadership program that motivates student-athletes and student leaders to play a central role in solving problems that historically have been considered "women's issues:" rape, battering, and sexual harassment. The mixed gender, racially diverse former professional and college athletes that facilitate the MVP National Program motivate men and women to work together in preventing gender violence. Utilizing a unique bystander approach to prevention, MVP National views student-athletes and student leaders not as potential perpetrators or victims, but as empowered bystanders who can confront abusive peers. The MVP National approach does not involve finger pointing, nor does it blame participants for the widespread problem of gender violence. Instead, it sounds a positive call for proactive, preventative behavior and leadership. MVP National has facilitated sessions with thousands of high school and college students and administrators at dozens of Massachusetts schools as well as with hundreds of student-athletes and administrators at over 120 colleges nationwide. MVP National has also conducted sessions with professional sports leagues including players and staff from the National Basketball Association (NBA), National Football League (NFL), and International Basketball League (IBL) as well as with personnel from the U.S. Marine Corps. MVP has also trained the rookie and free agents of the New England Patriots and New York Jets, minor league players of the Boston Red Sox, and Major League Lacrosse (MLL).

With the alarming rate of alcohol use and abuse among students, the NCAS, in collaboration with The BACCHUS and GAMMA Peer Education Network, sought a solution through education and developed the Alcohol Response-Ability: Foundations for Student Athletes™ course in 2004. It is a 90-minute, Internet-based alcohol education and life skills program designed specifically for student-athletes and those who work with them in the college and university setting. In this first program of its kind, student-athletes receive a customized educational experience that is interactive, interesting, and designed to help them reduce harm and recognize the consequences associated with alcohol abuse in their campus communities. In its first year on college campuses, results came back overwhelmingly positive. Ninety-three percent of the students who took the course said they learned something new, and 95 percent of them said they would try at least one of the strategies they learned to lower their risk. An impressive 83 percent said they would likely make safe decisions as a direct result of the course. These figures prove that much more needs to be done with alcohol abuse education.

After Hurricane Katrina devastated the Gulf Coast, the Hope for Stanley Alliance was formed. The mission of Hope for Stanley is to bring volunteers from all walks of life to the New Orleans area to perform community service. The type of community service includes, but is not limited to, rebuilding homes, creating and landscaping playgrounds, and delivering essential goods and materials to areas affected by Hurricane Katrina. The Hope for Stanley Alliance places a focus on student-athlete, athlete, and sport administrator involvement from across the world in the rebuilding of homes and playgrounds because of its belief in the power of sport for social change.

Created in 2008 by the National Consortium for Academics and Sports, Branded A Leader (BAL) is a leadership program that teaches critical decision-making skills to student-athletes while challenging them to be responsible for their decisions and those of their teammates. BAL is a highly interactive training that engages student-athletes in unusually effective ways. BAL utilizes the appeal of mainstream branding strategies as a foundation for student-athletes to discuss personal decisions and difficult social situations involving teammates. Student-athletes develop a success plan for enhancing their "personal brand" and share with their teammates. Branded A Leader trainers challenge the student-athletes to hold each other accountable for their espoused success goals and for making good decisions. Their role as their teammates "keeper" are reinforced through social scenarios where they decide the best options for intervening on a teammate's behalf.

In 2009, the newest NCAS program, Lights, Camera, Action! (LCA) was launched. LCA is designed to instruct student-athletes as well as university administration, staff and faculty on how to properly deal with all factions of media coverage with attention paid to insuring the University is always presented and judged in a fair and positive manner by the media and the general public.

Each of the 100 heroes whose lives you can read about in the first book of this series, *100 Heroes: People in Sports Who Make This a Better World*, was honored in celebration of another NCAS program, National STUDENT-Athlete Day (NSAD). NSAD is celebrated annually on April 6, providing an opportunity to recognize the outstanding accomplishments of student-athletes who have achieved excellence in academics and athletics, while making significant contributions to their communities. In addition to honoring student-athletes, the Annual National STUDENT-Athlete Day program selects recipients for Giant Steps Awards. These awards are given to individuals on a national level who exemplify the meaning of National STUDENT-Athlete Day. Each year nominations are received from across the country, and the Giant Steps Award winners are chosen by a national selection committee in categories ranging from civic leaders, coaches, parents, teachers, athletic administrators, and courageous student-athletes. *100 Heroes* was a compilation of the inspiring life stories of the first 100 to be chosen in honor of the "giant steps" they have taken in sports, in society, and in life itself.

The NCAS uses former athletes to deliver a message because so many can relate to sport. Many of today's young women as well as athletes of color do not realize how different their field looked 100, 50, or even 25 years ago. The history of race and gender in the United States may be studied by young Americans but too many cannot relate. But young people do relate to sport. By illustrating the history of America's racial and gender barriers through the vehicle of sport, the picture may become clearer. It can be the role of those who lived it to educate the next generation and there will be no better time to do so than now.

100 Campeones is the fourth book in a series devoted to shed light on the lives of people in sport whose life stories are important but are not well known enough. The series debuted with the courageous profiles found in *100 Heroes*. It is hoped that every profile in *100 Campeones* will shed more light on the history and influence of Latinos in international and American sport. As the United States continues becoming more of a melting pot, fusing cultures and nationalities from around the world, every profile in this book will lend a hand in explaining how these "Champions" have left their mark on the sporting landscape. *100 Heroes, 100 Pioneers, 100 Trailblazers*, and *100 Campeones* tell many courageous stories, our history, and how sport positively impacted race and gender relations in the United States and beyond.

About the Authors

Dr. Richard E. Lapchick

Human rights activist, pioneer for racial equality, internationally recognized expert on sports issues, scholar and author Richard E. Lapchick is often described as "the racial conscience of sport." He brought his commitment to equality and his belief that sport can be an effective instrument of positive social change to the University of Central Florida where he accepted an endowed chair in August 2001. Lapchick became the only person named as "One of the 100 Most Powerful People in Sport" to head up a sport management program. He remains President and CEO of the National Consortium for Academics and Sport and helped bring the NCAS national office to UCF.

The DeVos Sport Business Management Program at UCF is a landmark program that focuses on the business skills necessary for graduates to conduct a successful career in the rapidly changing and dynamic sports industry. In following with Lapchick's tradition of human rights activism, the curriculum includes courses with an emphasis on diversity, community service and philanthropy, sport and social issues and ethics in addition to UCF's strong business curriculum. The DeVos Program has been named one of the nation's top five programs by the *Wall Street Journal*, the *Sports Business Journal* and *ESPN The Magazine*.

In December of 2006, Lapchick, his wife, daughter, and a group of DeVos students formed the Hope for Stanley Foundation which is organizing groups of student-athletes and sports management students to go to New Orleans to work in the reconstruction efforts in the devastated Ninth Ward. As of the fall of 2007, Hope for Stanley members have spent 19 weeks in the city in a partnership with the NOLA City Council. Lapchick was named an honorary citizen by the New Orleans City Council in October 2007.

Lapchick helped found the Center for the Study of Sport in Society in 1984 at Northeastern University. He served as Director for 17 years and is now the Director Emeritus. The Center has attracted national attention to its pioneering efforts to ensure the education of athletes from junior high school through the professional ranks. The Center's Project TEAMWORK was called "America's most successful violence prevention program" by public opinion analyst Lou Harris. It won the Peter F. Drucker Foundation Award as the nation's most innovative non-profit program and was named by the Clinton Administration as a model for violence prevention. The Center and the National Consortium for Academics and Sports created the MVP gender violence prevention program that has been so successful with college and high school athletes that the United States Marine Corps adopted it in 1997.

Lapchick also helped form the NCAS in 1985. It is a group of over 230 colleges and universities that created the first of its kind degree completion and community service programs. To date, 29,856 athletes have returned to NCAS member schools. Over 13,700 have graduated. Nationally, the NCAS athletes have worked with more than 17.5 million students in the school outreach and community service program, which focuses on teaching youth how to improve race relations, develop conflict resolution skills, prevent gender violence and avoid drug and alcohol abuse. They have collectively donated more than 19 million hours of service while member colleges have donated more than $300 million in tuition assistance.

Lapchick was the American leader of the international campaign to boycott South Africa in sport for more than 20 years. In 1993, the Center launched TEAMWORK—South Africa, a program designed to use sports to help improve race relations and help with sports development in post-apartheid South Africa. He was among 200 guests specially invited to Nelson Mandela's inauguration.

Lapchick is a prolific writer. His 14th book was published in 2009. Lapchick is a regular columnist for ESPN.com and *The Sports Business Journal*. He has written more than 500 articles and has given more than 2,750 public speeches. Considered among the nation's experts on sport and social issues, Lapchick has appeared numerous times on *Good Morning America, Face The Nation, The Today Show, ABC World News, NBC Nightly News,* the *CBS Evening News,* CNN and ESPN.

Lapchick also consults with companies as an expert on both managing diversity and building community relations through service programs addressing the social needs of youth. He has a special expertise on Africa and South Africa. He has made 30 trips to Africa and African Studies was at the core of his Ph.D. work.

Before Northeastern, he was an Associate Professor of Political Science at Virginia Wesleyan College from 1970–1978 and a Senior Liaison Officer at the United Nations between 1978–1984.

In 2006, Lapchick was named both the Central Florida Public Citizen of the Year and the Florida Public Citizen of the Year by the National Association of Social Workers. Lapchick has been the recipient of numerous humanitarian awards. He was inducted into the Sports Hall of Fame of the Commonwealth Nations in 1999 in the category of Humanitarian along with Arthur Ashe, and Nelson Mandela and received the Ralph Bunche International Peace Award. He joined the Muhammad Ali, Jackie Robinson, Arthur Ashe and Wilma Rudolph in the Sport in Society Hall of Fame in 2004. In 2009, the Rainbow/ PUSH Coalition and Rev. Jesse Jackson honored him with "A Lifetime Achievement Award for Work in Civil Rights." Lapchick won Diversity Leadership Award at the 2003 Literacy Classic and the Jean Mayer Global Citizenship Award from Tufts University in 2000. He won the Wendell Scott Pioneer Award in 2004 and the NASCAR Diversity Award in 2008 for leadership in advancing people of color in the motor sports industry, education, employment, and life. He received the "Hero Among Us Award" from the Boston Celtics in 1999 and was named as the Martin Luther King, Rosa Parks, Cesar Chavez Fellow by the State of Michigan in 1998. Lapchick was the winner of the 1997 "Arthur Ashe Voice of Conscience Award." He also won the 1997 Women's Sports Foundation President's Award for work toward the development of women's sports and was named as the 1997 Boston Celtics "Man of the Year." In 1995, the National Association of Elementary School Principals gave him their first award as a "Distinguished American in Service of Our Children." He was a guest of President Clinton at the White House for National Student-Athlete Day in 1996, 1997, 1998, and again in 1999.

He is listed in Who's Who in America, Who's Who in American Education, Who's Who in Finance and Industry, and Who's Who in American Business. Lapchick was named as "one of the 100 most powerful people in sport" for six consecutive years and as "one of the 100 Most Influential Sports Educators in America." He was named one of the 20 most powerful people in college sport and one of the 20 most powerful people in sport in Florida. He is widely known for bringing different racial groups together to create positive work force environments. In 2003–04 he served as the national spokesperson for VERB, the Center for Disease Control's program to combat preteen obesity.

Lapchick has received eight honorary degrees. In 1993, he was named as the outstanding alumnus at the University of Denver where he got his Ph.D. in international race relations in 1973. Lapchick received a B.A. from St. John's University in 1967 and an honorary degree from St. John's in 2001.

Lapchick is a board member of the Open Doors Foundation and SchoolSports which created ESPN's *RISE* Magazine. He is on the advisory boards of the Women's Sports Foundation and the Giving Back Fund. He is a founder of the Hope for Stanley Foundation. He is a consultant to the Black Coaches and Administrators association.

Under Lapchick's leadership, the DeVos Program launched the Institute for Diversity and Ethics in Sport in December 2002. The Institute focuses on two broad areas. In the area of Diversity, the Institute publishes the critically acclaimed *Racial and Gender Report Card*, long-authored by Lapchick in his former role as director of the Center for the Study of Sport in Society at Northeastern University. *The Report Card*, an annual study of the racial and gender hiring practices of major professional sports, Olympic sport, and college sport in the United States, shows long-term trends over a decade and highlights organizations that are notable for diversity in coaching and management staffs.

In another diversity initiative, the Institute partners with the NCAS to provide diversity management training to sports organizations, including athletic departments and professional leagues and teams. The Consortium has already conducted such training for the NBA, Major League Soccer, NASCAR, and more than 80 university athletic departments.

In the area of ethics, the Institute monitors some of the critical ethical issues in college and professional sport, including the potential for the exploitation of student-athletes, gambling, performance-enhancing drugs and violence in sport. The Institute publishes annual studies on graduation rates for all teams in college football bowl games, comparing graduation rates for football players to rates for overall student-athletes and including a breakdown by race. The Institute also publishes the graduation rates of the women's and men's basketball teams in the NCAA Tournament as March Madness heats up.

Richard is the son of Joe Lapchick, the famous Original Celtic center who became a legendary coach for St. John's and the Knicks. He is married to Ann Pasnak and has three children and two grandchildren.

Jared Bovinet

Jared Bovinet is a graduate of the DeVos Sport Business Management Program at the University of Central Florida. He served as Dr. Richard Lapchick's graduate assistant in the program. Born and raised in Ohio, Jared earned his bachelor's degree in French and Spanish from The Ohio State University and enjoyed the opportunity to study in Québec City, Québec and Quito, Ecuador and during his time at OSU. After graduating in 2007, he volunteered with a homeless outreach non-profit in London, England. Bovinet received the Provost's Fellowship and the Joe Lapchick Scholarship for his studies at UCF and would like to work in community investment with a professional sports franchise.

Charlie Harless

Charlie Harless, a native Philadelphian who called Hollywood, Maryland his home for the majority of his childhood, has always had a keen interest in writing. At nine years old, Harless told his parents he was mad that the local paper never had movie reviews that were written with kids in mind. Filled with a sense of purpose, Harless hammered out passionate reviews to *Apollo 13* and the cinematic classic *Batman Forever* and sent them to the local newspaper editor. "Kids Flix Pix" soon became a weekly feature and earned Harless his first paycheck for writing at $5 a review, thus piquing his interest in further developing his writing skills. A 2004 graduate of

Leonardtown High School, Harless served for two years as editor-in-chief of his high school newspaper and was a contributing writer and editor for the yearbook as well. Harless started his college career at the University of Tennessee with aspirations of becoming a journalist, taking on assignments such as copy editing for the official campus newspaper, *The Daily Beacon*, and disc jockeying for WUTK 90.3 The Rock, an alternative college radio station.

In the spring of his freshman year on the Knoxville campus, Harless had an immediate change of heart and set his journalistic ambitions aside to work in the sport industry after walking into the offices of the Tennessee Lady Vols Basketball Program. Harless knew at that moment that the fast-paced and passionate environment of working in sports is where he wanted to be. After working legendary Coach Pat Summitt's summer basketball camps, he was selected to join the student managerial staff. Harless' duties ran the gamut from editing video, washing uniforms, and managing road game logistics, to learning the business of sport through all the behind-the-scenes efforts he shared with one of the best coaching and support staffs in the country. As the head manager for his junior and senior years, Harless was privileged to be a small part of two back-to-back NCAA Championship winning teams, Tennessee's seventh and eighth overall titles, respectively. Harless also broadened his experience in the sports industry by spending a summer as an intern for the United States Olympic Committee in Colorado Springs, Colorado. In May 2008, Harless graduated Summa Cum Laude from the University of Tennessee and its Chancellor's Honors Program with a bachelor's in Sport Management.

Continuing his education at the University of Central Florida, Harless earned a Masters in Business Administration and Masters in Sport Business Management from the highly regarded DeVos Sport Business Management Program led by Dr. Richard Lapchick. In his time at UCF, Harless worked as a graduate assistant in the Institute for Diversity and Ethics in Sport, researching and co-authoring several report cards examining the hiring practices and demographics of major sport leagues. A recipient of the Ralph Wiley and Joe Lapchick scholarships, Harless has aspirations of mixing his passions for writing, research and sport by working in the sport industry with a long-term goal of becoming a college professor or administrator.

Chris Kamke

Chris Kamke is a graduate of the DeVos Sport Business Management program at the University of Central Florida. At DeVos, he was a graduate assistant for Dr. Richard Lapchick in the Institute for Diversity and Ethics in Sport and a part-time employee for the Orlando Magic in game night operations.

Kamke was born in Corvallis, Oregon to parents Fred and Carol and is the oldest of three children. His younger sister, Kathryn was recently wed to Derek Larson and his younger brother is a student at Crescent Valley High School in Corvallis, Oregon. Kamke attended Blacksburg High School where he played varsity basketball and tennis. He was the captain of the basketball team his senior year. As a four-year member of the varsity tennis team Kamke competed in two state tennis tournaments. High school marked the end of Kamke's sports career as he decided to enroll at Virginia Tech as an engineering student rather than pursue basketball at the Division III level.

As a student at Virginia Tech he was a member of the professional business fraternity Alpha Kappa Psi. Kamke served one year as the President and one year as Vice President for Alpha Kappa Psi. He graduated with honors from Virginia Tech in May of 2006 with a B.S. degree in Industrial and Systems Engineering and a minor in Business. Before starting graduate school, he worked for two years as an estimator for Tindall Corporation, a pre-stress precast concrete manufacturer in Richmond, Virginia.

Realizing his desire to pursue a career in sports is what Kamke considers to be his greatest accomplishment to date. Upon enrolling at UCF, he received the UCF Provost's Graduate Fellowship. Kamke credits much of his success at UCF to the friendship he formed with his classmates. Currently, Kamke resides in Colorado and is employed by the Professional Bull Riders as the Research Database Manager.

Cara-Lynn Lopresti

Cara-Lynn Lopresti was originally born in Norristown, Pennsylvania on July 24, 1985, but grew up in San Diego, California. She was the youngest member of a large family of seven, consisting of two sisters, Angel and Cindy, two brothers, Jason and Anthony, and parents, Carolyn and Anthony.

Her sports background began with her playing roller hockey on the streets with the neighborhood boys. In seventh grade Lopresti took up field hockey and by her sophomore year in high school she made the U.S. U-16 junior national field hockey team. After high school Lopresti went to Stanford University on a full athletic scholarship and became the team's MVP and the Nor-Pac Conference Rookie of the Year. Although she absolutely loved the school, Lopresti decided to transfer to Duke University after her first year to pursue her athletic dreams.

She continued playing on the U.S. junior national field hockey teams throughout college, competing in several international tournaments, most notably the Junior Pan American Games in San Juan, Puerto Rico and the Junior World Cup in Santiago, Chile. Lopresti also excelled at the collegiate level. She was a Second-Team All-American, First-Team Regional All-American, First-Team All-ACC, and Academic All-American. She also helped lead the Blue Devils to NCAA runner-up finishes during her sophomore and junior years and the NCAA Final Four in her senior year.

In 2007 Lopresti graduated from Duke University Cum Laude and with honors in Sociology and Markets and Management. She then spent a year in Orlando, FL interning for FSN South/Sun Sports Network and working as an athletic academic mentor in the University of Central Florida's Academic Services for Student-Athletes (ASSA).

Lopresti earned her master's in Sport Business Management and Business Administration through the DeVos Sport Business Management Program at the University of Central Florida. While in graduate school she served as a graduate assistant in the Institute for Diversity and Ethics in Sport and volunteered in the athletic department and for the Y.M.C.A Black Achievers program. Lopresti is currently serving as a Student Services Program Coordinator and Club Field Hockey coach at Coastal Carolina University. Her ultimate career goal is to follow in Dr. Lapchick's footsteps by using the power of sports to positively impact society.

Horacio Ruiz

Horacio Ruiz is a contributing author to Dr. Richard Lapchick's 13th book, *100 Pioneers: African-Americans Who Broke Color Barriers in Sports*, and Lapchick's 14th book, *100 Trailblazers: Great Women*

Athletes Who Opened Doors for Future Generations. He is proud to be the editor and a contributing author for *100 Campeones*. Ruiz graduated in 2008 from the DeVos Sport Business Management Program at the University of Central Florida with master's degrees in Busines Administration and Sport Business Management. He earned his bachelor's of science degree from the University of Florida in 2005. He is currently a teacher in New York City taking master's courses in education at St. John's University. Ruiz was born in Managua, Nicaragua and raised in Miami, Fla. His mom, dad, and sister currently reside in Miami.

Alejandra Diaz-Calderon— Co-Editor and Researcher

Alejandra Diaz-Calderon was born and raised in Guadalajara, Mexico. She began her sports career at nearly six years of age, so her recruitment to play for the University of Notre Dame was no surprise. Diaz-Calderon played for the Fighting Irish for four years, and served as the Team Captain her junior and senior year. She graduated from the Mendoza College of Business with a 3.5 grade-point-average with a degree in Finance.

While at Notre Dame, Diaz-Calderon had a valuable presence on the team as a motivator and a leader, the athletic department and the community. She represented the golf team on the Student-Athlete Advisory Council (SAAC) and was selected as Notre Dame's SAAC Big East spokesperson. Diaz-Calderon received the team's Notre Dame Club of St. Joseph Valley Rockne Student-Athlete Award during her junior and senior seasons. Furthermore, Diaz-Calderon was asked to be the guest speaker at several Notre Dame benefaction dinners.

Diaz-Calderon's leadership extended beyond Notre Dame's athletic department and into the community. She participated in Habitat for Humanity where her team organized a golf tournament to raise money for Hurricane Katrina victims. She has volunteered as a mentor for Read to Succeed, ReadIT! and for Frontline Outreach. She has been involved in the D.A.R.E. program to educate elementary school children about the importance of goal setting.

Diaz-Calderon received one of the esteemed John McLendon Memorial Minority Postgraduate Scholarships to support her studies at the University of Central Florida's DeVos Master in Sports Business Management program. At UCF, Diaz-Calderon was a graduate assistant for The Institute for Diversity and Ethics in Sport (TIDES), where she co-authored *Major League Baseball's Race and Gender Report Card* as well as *The Black Coaches and Administrators Hiring Report Card* for NCAA Division I Women's Basketball Head Coaching Positions. Diaz-Calderon is serving as the advertising and branding intern at the Orlando Magic for the 2009–10 season.

Diaz-Calderon has a burning passion for sports and a desire to use that passion for something great.

Nathalie Reshard—Lead Researcher

Nathalie Reshard is a graduate of the University of Central Florida's DeVos Sport Business Management Program. As a Florida native, she grew up in Niceville, Florida the middle child with two brothers. She completed her undergraduate degree at the University of Alabama where she received her degree in business management. At Alabama she was a student athlete, serving as captain of the Crimson Tide Women's basketball team. She worked at The Institute for Diversity of Ethics in Sport as a graduate assistant and helped publish the NCAA Women's Basketball Graduation Rates Report along with the *WNBA Racial and Gender Report Card*. Reshard served as a basketball coach at Maynard Evans High School in Orlando, Florida.